Samuel Beckett's *How It Is*

# Samuel Beckett's *How It Is*

## Philosophy in Translation

Anthony Cordingley

EDINBURGH
University Press

Edinburgh University Press is one of the leading university presses in the UK. We publish academic books and journals in our selected subject areas across the humanities and social sciences, combining cutting-edge scholarship with high editorial and production values to produce academic works of lasting importance. For more information visit our website: edinburghuniversitypress.com

Edinburgh University Press Ltd
The Tun – Holyrood Road
12(2f) Jackson's Entry
Edinburgh EH8 8PJ

Typeset in 11/13 Adobe Sabon by
IDSUK (DataConnection) Ltd, and
printed and bound in Great Britain.

A CIP record for this book is available from the British Library

ISBN 978 1 4744 4060 8 (hardback)
ISBN 978 1 4744 4062 2 (webready PDF)
ISBN 978 1 4744 4063 9 (epub)

# Contents

# List of Illustrations

# Series Editor's Preface

In 1997 Apple computers launched an advertising campaign (in print and on television) that entreated us to 'Think Different', and Samuel Beckett was one of Apple's icons. Avoiding Apple's solecism, we might modify the appeal to say that *Other Becketts* is a call to think differently as well, in this case about Beckett's work, to question, that is, even the questions we ask about it. *Other Becketts*, then, is a series of monographs focused on alternative, unexplored or under-explored approaches to the work of Samuel Beckett, not a call for novelty *per se*, but a call to examine afresh those of Beckett's interests that were more arcane than mainstream, interests that might be deemed quirky or strange, and those of his works less thoroughly explored critically and theoretically, the late prose and drama, say, or even the poetry or criticism. Volumes might cover (but are not restricted to) any of the following: unusual illnesses or neurological disorders (the 'duck foot, goose foot' of *First Love*, akathisia or the invented duck's disease or panpygoptosis of Miss Dew in *Murphy*, proprioception, or its disturbance, in *Not I*, perhaps, or other unusual neurological lapses among Beckett's creatures, from Watt to the Listener of *That Time*); mathematical peculiarities (irrational numbers, factorials, Fibonacci numbers or sequences, or non-Euclidian approaches to geometry); linguistic failures (from Nominalism to Mauthner, say); citations of or allusions to contrarian aesthetic philosophers working in a more or less irrationalist tradition (Nietzsche, Bergson or Deleuze, among others); or in general 'the simple games that time plays with space'. Alternative approaches would be of interest as well, with foci on objects, animals, cognitive or memory issues, and the like.

S. E. Gontarski, Florida State University

# List of Abbreviations

CDW    Beckett, Samuel. *The Complete Dramatic Works.*
London: Faber, 1986.

HRC    Harry Ransom Center, The University of Texas at Austin

LSB    Beckett, Samuel. *The Letters of Samuel Beckett.*
*Volume 1: 1929–1940.* Ed. Martha Dow Fehsenfeld
and Lois More Overbeck. Cambridge: Cambridge
University Press, 2009. *Volume 2: 1941–1956.* Ed.
George Craig, Martha Dow Fehsenfeld, Dan Gunn
and Lois More Overbeck. Cambridge: Cambridge
University Press, 2011. *Volume 3: 1957–1965.* Ed.
George Craig, Martha Dow Fehsenfeld, Dan Gunn
and Lois More Overbeck. Cambridge: Cambridge
University Press, 2015.

TN    Beckett, Samuel. *Three Novels by Samuel Beckett*:
*Molloy, Malone Dies, The Unnamable.* New York:
Grove, 1959.

UoR    University of Reading

W    Windelband, Wilhelm. *A History of Philosophy.* Trans.
James H. Tufts. London: Macmillan, 1910.

les mots vous font voir du pays avec eux d'étranges voyages

*Comment c'est*

words my truant guides with you strange journeys

*How It Is*

# Introduction

When Samuel Beckett began his last 'novel', *Comment c'est*, the
task of writing proved almost insurmountable and its subject matter the darkest yet. The manuscript was finished in August 1960,
and appeared in bookstores by early 1961, followed by the English
translation *How It Is* in 1964. Given the extraordinary scholarly
attention Beckett has received since then, matching that of Shakespeare or Joyce, or, indeed, of the most revered canonical authors
in any language, it is remarkable that *How It Is* remains an enigma.
Beckett's most difficult and challenging text – arguably his master-
piece – was long ignored and is still only partially understood. This
incomprehension owes much to the poetic complexity of Beckett's
elliptical, allusive and fragmented prose, but also arises from the
lack of a sustained tradition of scholarly exegesis, commentary and
analysis. My book addresses this issue.

A critical commonplace maintains that *How It Is* almost exclusively reflects its procedures of articulation or composition, thereby
divorcing the narrative voice from a signifying narrative. My seven
chapters are devoted to specific areas within the history of philosophy that have shaped its subject matter. This text is not solely about
its process of composition because the act of poetically refiguring inherited narratives enters into a profound dialogue with the
very content of those narratives. *How It Is* remains unrelentingly
metatextual, but its writing about writing motivates its hero. Ostensibly an epic quest through a purgatorial underworld of mud, the
'I' seeks an answer to his most fundamental epistemological and
theological question: 'me sole elect' (11).[1] Itself inseparable from a
dialectic between author and character, this 'I' needs to know if he
is alone in the mud. Is his perception of any 'other', below or above,
illusory, or will he be one of God's chosen, finally reunited with his
'other above in the light' (3 passim)? The narrative presents itself
as the constantly interrupted repetition of this story, once dictated

by an 'ancient voice' above to the 'I' below, who hears this voice in the narrative present echoing imperfectly within his memory and assumes no agency over it. As narrator, he claims merely to 'quote' the already 'ill-heard' narrative of his past self, itself narrated (3 passim). The French appellation of this 'voix ancienne' is more clearly an old or former voice, although Beckett's provocative translation – *ancient voice* – accentuates an underlying discourse with the ancients that will be explored later. This troublesome dyad of voice, the past-I and its repetition, was termed by Beckett, in a letter to Hugh Kenner, the 'narrator/narrated' (Kenner, *Reader's* 94).[2] The record of ill-hearing between his various narrators results in a disarticulated prose characterised by ellipsis, aporia, paradox. The *Comment c'est* manuscripts attest to successive revisions during which Beckett fragmented the narrative and stripped it of information that might orient the discourse; this process reflects his aim, as expressed in numerous letters from this period, to forge a 'syntax of weakness' and so debilitate the ontological equation of a speaking subject with its language. This book is devoted to the hermeneutic activity of re-establishing the contexts that inform the content of this fragmented voice; the substantive content of the *ancient voice* is volatilised within the aesthetic and material processes of its (re) composition and translation within the bilingual oeuvre.

On the cover of the French edition, below the title, appears the word *roman*. Yet in 1961 the writing within was completely foreign to the French novelistic tradition; the cover could equally have borne the term *lyrique* or, even more ironically, *épique*. Modernist experimentation in the prose of Joyce and Stein set precendents in the Anglophone tradition, but with *Comment c'est/How It Is* Beckett resists modernist aesthetics. The text's three-part structure evokes a host of narrative archetypes and genres, each of which becomes an untenable structure as the narrative progresses, like its purported affirmation of Romance: 'the journey the couple the abandon' (167). The peculiar conditions of the story's telling, and its strophes of poetic prose, fashion a unique literary mode, whose dimensions are stated at the outset.

> here then part one how it was before Pim we follow I quote the natural order more or less my life last state last version what remains bits and scraps I hear it my life natural order more or less I learn it I quote a given moment long past vast stretch of time on from there that moment and following not all a *selection natural order* vast tracts of time. (3, my emphasis)

Faithful mimesis ('I quote') gives way to fabulation ('more or less') as the voice that claims to be a cypher for its past self produces variations on itself. Efforts to recover its autobiography – 'my life' – are undermined further by the voice of another, whom I term the *poet-in-text*. This voice subverts its own affirmations in a fashion that is sometimes openly comic or, as above, subtly ironic – the repeated claim to adhere to a 'natural order' affirms finally not a linear evolution but an inversion of Darwin's *natural selection*. Present devolves from the past, and *vast tracts* of geological *time* separate the 'other above in the light' and the 'I' below, who crawls through a subterranean plane of mud already 'half out of species' (141). Blind and dumb, this human lugworm journeys forth until he encounters Pim, a creature lying inert and deaf in the mud, whom the 'I' brutalises into learning his own language through blows and inscriptions in Pim's back and buttocks. The goal of the 'I' is to extract from Pim a song; his sadism and the suffering of Pim offers, fundamentally, an analogy for the tortures of artistic composition. Pim's song is the key to his departure; it allows him to leave the 'I', who will remain face down in the mud, anticipating the arrival of his own torturer from behind. The coupling of 'I' and Pim is imagined thus by the narrator/narrated as the archetypal event repeated eternally by beings stationed around a purgatorial circle, colliding and separating with each rotation of the mechanistic universe. The 'I' finally renounces this twisted amalgam of Dante, Sade, Newton and others, affirming his ultimate solitude and immobility, *how it is*. This too is provisional because the narrative wraps around itself, opening with the tale of *how it was*, told in the present tense, locking the 'I' into a hermeneutic circle within which his voice eternally reveals itself to itself in 'bits and scraps', as it 'quotes' itself awry.

Blanchot's appellation of the narrative voice in *Comment c'est* as 'le neutre' (the neuter) initiated its single most influential interpretation, with far-reaching effects in Francophone and Anglophone criticism. For Blanchot the radical open-endedness of *Comment c'est* undermines the reader's usual hermeneutic processes and precipitates a crisis in reading (Blanchot, *L'Entretien* 481–2). To read Beckett's text is rather to retrace its inscription, to follow *le neutre* that neither affirms nor negates its presence. This determines an experience beyond the sublime and the uncanny, within which the act of writing (*l'écrire*) and the writing itself (*l'écriture*) confront each other, exhausting and overwhelming the writer. In the grips of such *désœuvrement*, a creative dispossessing or unworking, writers in the space of writing lose all individuality, sacrificing themselves to the work. The loss of self-presence displaces the subject from the work, personal identity is lost, and, finally, the present itself dissipates. Here the voice of the 'I' is the indifferent and impersonal but incessant neuter. In 1973 with *Le Pas au-delà* (*The Step Not Beyond*) Blanchot returns to *le neutre*, redefining it as the *il* (he/it). This *il* does not inhabit a place, unlike the 'I' who is always connected to place; nor may the *il* be a speaking subject. Blanchot's *il* cannot replace the self-presence of an 'I' and it cannot become an 'I' (a self determined by its identity). There are several parallels between Blanchot's *il* and the narrative voice in *How It Is*. Beckett's 'I' is condemned to the mud, repeating his estranging other: 'scraps of an ancient voice in me not mine [. . .] ill-said ill-heard ill-recaptured ill-murmured' (3). Simultaneously, he asserts the presence of his *narrated*, his past-I, now infinitely differentiated and estranged within the circular narrative. Like the rupture between the *ancient voice* and Beckett's 'I', Blanchot's *il* draws itself into a dialectical opposition with identity (understood as wholeness), singularity or One (*Le Pas* 13–14). This plays out in the scene of writing, even as Beckett's text scrutinises the repetition of voices within its images of the voice-witness/scribe duality.

Confronted with this complicated and precarious narrative voice, which appears to undermine its own authority, and given the difficulty of making sense of *How It Is*, unlike their treatment of Beckett's earlier work scholars generally have lacked the confidence to decode the myriad allusions and intertexts to propose more sophisticated or theoretical interpretations. Blanchot's virtuoso argument that the text's meaning is its expression of the evacuation of meaning has dissuaded scholars from considering the content of its fragments, offering the perfect alibi for not attempting to make sense of Becket's complex intertextual patterning. *Comment c'est* has been contextualised, belatedly, within France's explosive political climate in the 1950–1960s, in which revelations of torture and dissent during the Algerian War of Independence led to widespread condemnation and protest (Cordingley, 'Pedagogy'; Morin, *Political* chapter 4; Overbeck, 'General Introduction'; Piette, 'Torture'; Verhulst, 'Howls' 149–51). The instrumentalising of Pim's body to extract voice has been read in terms of literary influence, as Sadean violence (Baroghel, 'Comment'; Stewart, *Sex* 117–32; Weller, 'Anethics') that dialogues with Kant (Lloyd, *Irish Culture* chapter 6), and as an outcome of Beckett's work with the medium of radio in the 1950s, which heightened his awareness of the materiality of voice (Albright, *Beckett* 120; Sinoimeri, 'Ill-Told'; Verhulst, 'Howls') and can even provoke 'the spoken word' in *Comment c'est* 'to lose its semantic aspect' (Baroghel, 'My' 197). Yet the text's words are always mediated through print and they are never completely abstracted from their semantics. The incessant return of the 'voix ancienne'/*ancient voice* introduces ideas from the Ancient world as well as France's *Ancien Régime*, the social and political system which, from the late medieval period up to the Revolution, was organised upon principles of hereditary monarchy and absolute rule. Laden with Enlightenment ideas and disciplinary knowledge, the 'voix ancienne' articulates this period's ideal of reason. Yet like the *Régime*, as much as France's post-Revolution governments, it propagates its narrative of progress by masking a darker history of slavery, torture and subjugation. Beckett passes judgement upon the French Republic's disintegrating moral authority at the time of his writing by inscribing his 'I' within the long Western tradition that conducts *ratio*, Enlightenment and liberation under the guise of terror. The fragmentation of the 'voix ancienne' generates a unique and highly aural discourse that disrupts the authority and inherited norms of the written word (Cordingley, 'The Reading Eye'). These political and aesthetic contexts expand the significance of the text's central narrative of atrophying 'humanities' (35 passim), the fragmenting of Western philosophy's grand narrative, which inhibits the 'I' from transmitting a fiction of Enlightenment but frees him to arrange its fragments anew. The network of ideas that subtends his fragments has, however, never been mapped.

Many insightful articles,[3] book chapters and reference works[4] have discussed *How It Is*, yet each typically focuses on the dynamics of voice and textuality from a limited philosophical perspective. Ziarek's (*Rhetoric* chapter 5) seminal reading of the text through Derrida and Levinas as an encounter with alterity has been consolidated by Fifield (*Late* chapter 4) and Houston Jones (*Testimony* chapter 2). This line of criticism effectively secularises the theological concerns or transcendentalist trajectories emphasised by others (see R. Smith, 'Bearing'). Early incursions into the novel's philosophical frame of reference were made by Abbott, Ackerley, Duffy, the Hamiltons and Pilling, yet scholars have only begun to explore in depth its philosophical content. Three recent monographs contain substantial segments devoted to *How It Is*, detailing connections with Dante (Caselli, *Beckett's* chapter 7*)*, Leibniz (Dowd, *Abstract* chapter 4) and Geulincx (Tucker, *Beckett* chapter 6). Yet none has considered how these separate influences relate to each other or to other allusions within the text. Increasing interest in *How It Is* can be gauged in recent studies by authors whose work in the past century helped shape a post-structuralist interpretation of Beckett (Katz '*How It Is*'; Rabaté *Think, Pig!* 52–5; Sheehan 'Scenes'; Weller 'Anethics'). However, the vast majority of such monographs have passed over *How It Is*, even though the text performs the problematising of textuality, language, archive and signification at the heart of post-structuralist theory. Such studies often privilege the so-called 'trilogy' (a term Beckett rejected) of *Molloy*, *Malone meurt* and *L'Innomable*, advancing their canonisation yet circumscribing the critical appreciation of how Beckett's intensive exploration of the novel form evolved through his writing in French following World War II.[5]

One influential post-structuralist monograph, Leslie Hill's *Beckett's Fiction: In Different Words* (1990) was exceptional, for it devoted a dozen pages to *How It Is*, synthesising two dominant critical themes – Dante and Blanchot – into a theory of 'purgatorial' aesthetics. For Hill, in the intermediate zone of mud of *How It Is* the dynamics of Belacqua's purgatory find their literary exposition in the Blanchotian 'neuter'. Beckett aligns the orbits of Belacqua and the 'neuter' around a metaphysical centre, stymying any chance for the 'I' to advance towards a teleological end, yet allowing him to signify the exhaustion of humanistic beliefs. Blanchot wrote of *Comment c'est*: 'Oui, et ainsi se trouve justifiée, dans le cas de Beckett, la disparition de tout signe qui ne serait signe que pour l'œil' (*L'Entretien* 481; 'Yes, and thus one finds justified, in Beckett, the disappearance of all signs that would be signs only for the eye'). For Blanchot, the text's only signs are those recreated by the reader, whose hermeneutic act becomes one of authorship, and who brings a referential system to bear upon the signs of writing.[6] Hill likewise finds little meaning in Beckett's signs: 'The novel is a far from easy text to interpret and contains relatively little of the allusive density so important for making sense of *Molloy*, *Malone meurt* and *L'Innommable*' (*Beckett's Fiction* 134–5). This relegates *How It Is* to the status of a text essentially about the 'theatrical event' (135) of the hermeneutic demands it places upon the reader. Focusing on aspects of the text's rhetoric allows Hill to argue that the text of *Comment c'est* is, 'as a result, more performative than descriptive or representational' (137). His intuition of Dante's purgatorial dynamics contributes, perversely, to diminishing the presence of other literary or philosophical intertexts. He acknowledges the allegorical potential, the novel's invitation to be construed as a 'cosmological fiction' (138), yet he accepts the narrator/narrated's declaration that his entire narrative is a fabrication, without questioning the authority of this assertion. Hill does not, therefore, consider that the 'narrator's' refusal to signify is a highly symbolic act that has meaning in the context of his previous compulsion to concoct the 'cosmological fiction' itself. This leads him into the trap of concluding that 'the fiction as a whole remains radically and disturbingly *empty of apparent symbolic purpose*' (138, my emphasis). Doubtless, the fragmented and aporetic nature of the narrative requires the reader to project personal readings into its gaps, reconnecting its disparate fragments and thus participating in the writing process. Yet those fragments contain a wealth of philosophical material which, in this study, will be analysed holistically, to reconnect traces of an interrelated dialogue with different philosophical schools.

In 1992, two years after Hill's monograph, Bersani and Dutoit offered a reading of *How It Is* that effectively restates Blanchot's paradigm, but from which they draw psychoanalytic conclusions. This influenced Caselli's ground-breaking study of Beckett's poetic use of Dante in *How It Is*, allowing her to argue for Belacqua as the figure of 'unlocatable source' therein (*Beckett's* 152). Her affirmation that Dante is not actually present in the text while remaining of central importance follows Bersani and Dutoit's denial of the referential possibility:

> The invention of the narrator helps the witness to determine the message. There is, that is to say, *no real message*, only an interminable, indeterminate, unbounded verbal flow that carries *no messages or information* prior to the transmitting stations which in fact constitute them. (Bersani and Dutoit, 'Beckett's Sociability' 6, my emphasis)

Perceiving impenetrabilities within Beckett's elliptical prose and complex narrative structure, Bersani and Dutoit express in the conditional their theory that '[t]he fable of *How It Is* may be the form of the witness's listening' (6). The text is esteemed as a work that is *about* the accommodation of a discourse that asserts 'no messages or information'. Yet when Bersani and Dutoit arrive at their destination Beckett's text allows them to ascribe its deeper moral: 'To be tortured is a precondition for being humanized' (7), because listening involves an injunction to speak. Here the authors identify certain psychoanalytic procedures: 'ego-constitution is inseparable from the birth of the superego'; and '[t]o be tortured out of monadic self-containment into a self-identifying speech is to *become* the brutally authoritative voice that summons others to speak' (8). Yet closer listening to the *content* of the narrator/narrated's *messages* allows one to 'witness' the text's contemplation of these procedures within the domain of the history of Western philosophy, if not with explicit reference to Freudian psychology (Cordingley, 'Psychoanalytic'). By giving this content its requisite attention, one comes to appreciate Beckett's contemplation of psychoanalytic procedures as richer and more complex than Bersani and Dutoit's valuable first steps might indicate.

Alain Badiou, in the same year, argued in 'L'écriture du générique' that Beckett's oeuvre hinges around *How It Is*, which although 'ultimately a little known book' constitutes 'a major transformation in the way that Beckett fictionalises his thinking' (*On Beckett* 15). Like Ziarek before him, Badiou believes that with this text Beckett transcends the monadic subjectivity of his earlier work, typified by *The Unnamable*, instead moving from the One to the Two, opening to alterity, to the Other, 'which fissures and displaces the solipsistic internment of the *cogito*' (16). In *Becket and Badiou* Gibson offers a sympathetic account of Badiou's redefinition of Beckett as an ethical writer, yet Dowd (*Abstract* 192–200) and Weller ('Anethics' 113–14) demonstrate convincingly that to do so Badiou must distort fundamental relationships within the text and pass over many of its complexities in silence, a problem symptomatic of his tendency to enlist Beckett in the service of his own philosophy (see Rabaté, 'Entre'). Nonetheless, Badiou intuits presences crucial to understanding the text when he affirms that in *How It Is* 'ascesis – metaphorically enacted as loss, destitution, poverty, a relentlessness based on almost nothing – leads to a conceptual economy of an ancient or Platonic type' (*On Beckett* 47). While my reading does not endorse this causality – in which a Platonic economy arises from ascesis – Badiou nonetheless appreciates how the text's fragments marshal ancient philosophical dialectics. My seven chapters will establish more precisely the way *How It Is* engages with the philosophical and theological issues defining the schools of Ancient Greek philosophy, the birth of the Christian Church, and neo-Platonism, as well as various mystical traditions and problematics manifest in the seventeenth-century philosophers with whom the text engages. Beckett's reading of Wilhelm Windelband's *A History of Philosophy* (W) was crucial in shaping this encounter, and his notes from this and other sources establish the many contexts from which I orient the fiction. Writing *How It Is* shifted Beckett's relationship to his European intellectual heritage and led him towards a pronounced late modernist aesthetics.

The prevailing Blanchot line of criticism reads *How It Is* within contemporary philosophy to maintain Beckett's text as a quasi-philosophical narrative *about* the impossibility of reconciling writing with self-presence. Willis ('*How It Is*' 579–93), for instance, reads the problematic nature of 'limits' to the voice in *How It Is* as evocative of Blanchot and the issue of speechlessness. Such readings are theoretically inflected (perhaps derivative) accounts of what earlier critics identified as a concern with 'creating process' (Hamilton and Hamilton, 'Process' 1–12; Smith, 'Fiction' 107–21). P. J. Murphy offers an original reading which departs from the Blanchot 'neuter' by viewing the text as a positive trajectory of linguistic discovery until, finally, 'the rituals of syntax have succeeded in their invocation of being' (*Reconstructing* 75). This approach of the rhetorician advances the familiar notion that the text's subject is little more than language and its production. Adelman made a critical departure by arguing that the text is about neither Dante nor philosophical issues, while upholding the argument for narrative process:

> It is invented out of nothing, mud and darkness – which is to say, the cycle of [the I's] torment is no less his fiction than the fiction which he creates by its process; he must create the method as well as its product. ('Torturer' 82)

This asserts God's judgement, for which 'Dante is the supreme model', though this is promptly dismissed: 'correspondences between *How It Is* and *The Inferno* do not play out, but are details of minor significance in a larger design' (84). Other philosophical concerns are merely 'how Beckett garnishes the entrée' (89).

In various guises, the *ex nihilo* theory of creation perversely confers divine status on the author, diminishing the importance for *How It Is* of the mechanics of memory and habit, which are inextricable from the repetition of past learning and experience. Yet attention to the muck at hand must recognise Beckett's all-too-human labour. While language cannot be separated from this, the omission implies that the text becomes *about* only its own processes (including its opening to the Other), fostering an easy glossing over its *content*. While very much about creative process, *How It Is* offers a particular vision of authorship whereby Beckett's poetics of refusal and recycling enters into a dialogue with the quantum of its education (philosophy, ethics, Christianity, science . . .). In focusing on the elements of the history of philosophy that have had the profoundest influence on the voice of Beckett's 'I', this book moves from the Ancient Greeks into the seventeenth century. The interpretation offered draws from Beckett's use of philosophy across his oeuvre, and from recently accessible archival materials, especially his 'Philosophy Notes'.

If this book aims to revitalise its subject by opening it up to new trajectories of enquiry, it equally resists foreclosing discussion of the significance of the source material it presents. It repudiates the assertion that this material has primacy over knowledge that is not empirically verifiable because chance did not spare its evidence from loss or destruction. I make extensive use of archival sources but resist the role of archon, or guardian of the archive and arbiter of its law. I acknowledge, rather, Jacques Derrida's identification in *Mal d'archive* (Archive Fever) of the nomological function of the archive as the house of power and command. For Derrida, the archive is situated at the beginning of structural breakdown; at the antagonism between the domiciliation of power, its need for a technique of repetition and a relationship with the outside. Respect is therefore accorded to Beckett's presentation in *How It Is* of the distance between the absent rule of *ancient voice*, 'ill-heard' in the present, and its fracturing within a series of narrative repetitions and bearers of voice. Indeed, I consistently reinstate orders of 'archival' law to observe their corruption within Beckett's poetics. This runs the same risks as the 'visitors' who pay their respects to the novel's 'I' and, in his words, 'ne sach[e]nt rien de mes débuts hormis ce qu'ils avaient pu glaner par ouï-dire et dans les archives' ('kno[w] nothing of my beginnings save what they could glean by hearsay or in public records') (10–11). Beckett's conscious deployment of Freudian tropes of narcissism and the death drive is complemented by his shaping *How It Is* into a circular narrative, generating, in Freudian jargon, a repetition compulsion, one that infinitely re-enacts its formal estrangement from the unknowable unity of *ancient voice*. Beckett thus fashions a scene of writing which concurs with Derrida's belief that forgetting and distortion is necessary to the logic of the archive, which is equipped with its own anarchy drive, the archive destroying 'archiviolithic' violence.

On 14 April 1962 Beckett admitted that when reading Lawrence Harvey's treatment of his poem *Whoroscope*, he enjoyed being reminded of all that he had forgotten from Adrien Baillet's biography of Descartes (Pilling, *Chronology* 159). Yet there is little evidence of any reading from Baillet, unlike the wealth of connections with Mahaffy's 1904 intellectual biography *Descartes* (Doherty, 'Mahaffy's'). Facts from Descartes' life which had appealed to the young Beckett for their potential transformation into his poem have now become, during their revisitation some thirty years later, signs of an aporia within his memory. His observation testifies to the danger of assuming that allusions drawn from past learning continue to signify what they did when initially experienced; firstly, because the meaning of any new use of Descartes is inextricable from Beckett's sense that he is recovering details that were lost; and, secondly, because Beckett's memory of that process appears unreliable (his source was Mahaffy). Yet to suggest that a rupture and complete effacement exists in Beckett's biography between the point at which he had forgotten those details of Descartes' life and their revisitation in 1962 underestimates the silent presence of the archive of the unconscious, as he presents it in *How It Is*. The 'I' of the text is incubated within the excreta of his past, the inchoate 'voice quaqua' (3 passim). The signifying *boue* (mud) in which he is surrounded is unequivocally identified as his discharged *ancient voice*, the ancestral residue of his past selves now dissolved into mess. Like his 'I', Beckett is not the author who creates *ex nihilo* but rather one who journeys out with his 'I' into that which is not consciously before him. He experiences anew the content of what was unobserved or previously forgotten, he discovers what might have formerly been present but not perceived, and he generates new poetic relations from inherited sense, thereby delivering himself into new fictions of the present.

Yet the 'I' of *How It Is* comically travels in the hope of recovering some order, *nomos*, or what he haplessly imagines to be the 'justice' (77 passim) of his *ancient voice* authorised from on high.

Through engagement with the physicality of his mud, he is revisited by past sensations. This book attempts that which can never be achieved: to restore the substantive content of *ancient voice* so as to offer contexts to orient its poetic transformation. From these most serious of intentions, it keeps step with the farcical episodes that befall Beckett's 'I', his bouts of ludicrous rationalism and overzealous piety. It connects these events with other texts and celebrates, above all, Beckett's hilarious satire upon pretensions to recover first and divine causes, the content of one's education, uncorrupted knowledge and 'original' voice.

I benefit enormously from the editorial work of Édouard Magessa O'Reilly, whose majestic critical-genetic edition, *Comment c'est, How It Is* and/et *L'Image: A Critical-Genetic Edition*, allows readers to follow the many allusions and details within Beckett's pre-publication manuscripts and self-translation. I refer to this frequently and encourage the reader to read it in consultation with my digital-genetic edition of *Comment c'est/How It Is*, which is part of the Beckett Digital Manuscripts Project (www.beckettarchive.org), where the manuscripts to which I refer may be viewed along with transcriptions of Beckett's often inscrutable handwriting.[7]

My investigation opens with a new understanding of Beckett's use of what has been assumed to be his primary intertext: Dante's *Inferno*. It offers a hypothesis for when the *Inferno* entered the textual genesis, and accounts for degrees of cultural translation that arise when Beckett's transposition of phrases from Dante's *Divina commedia* into French and English multiplies their allusive potential within those literary traditions. Here, the study of 'allusion' does not assume unproblematic diachronic relations between a source and text; it responds to Machacek's notion of 'phraseological adaptation', in which verbal echoes are 'culturally mediated and therefore do not automatically occur in a transhistorically stable and predictable fashion' ('Allusion' 524). Indeed, within *How It Is* Beckett exercises a hyperactive awareness of how inherited discourse becomes dislocated within its repetition in altered contexts to the extent that this becomes a central source of creative irony within his poetics. Mapping Beckett's creative transformation of ideas as he appropriates the words or thoughts of others, I eschew the imposition of a hierarchy of transfer within intertextual relations. My first chapter moves therefore into a broader consideration of Beckett's self-writing by attending to his aesthetics of refusal and the abdication of authority. His discourse with Gœthe and the German tradition of intellectual and moral formation, *Bildung*, and its quintessential genre, the *Bildungsro-man*, establishes a central concern within both *How It Is* and this book: education.

In attempting to quell his metaphysical anxiety, the narrator/narrated becomes especially concerned with *ancient voices* of philosophy and religion. Chapter 2 begins the extensive investigation into the philosophical contexts of what he calls, 'the humanities I had' (35). The narrator/narrated is revisited by images and problems from pre-Socratic philosophers. To account for his life in the mud he develops a thesis that owes much to his recovery of Pythagorean geometry, which he cobbles into a Platonic cosmology. Yet he consistently intuits images of a materialist counter-thesis: Democritean and Heraclitean fragments trouble his fanatical assembly of the teleological ladder that will raise him above life in the mud. In Chapter 3 he emerges as the engineer of a confused scientific debate about time, space and bodies, which pits an Aristotelian world view against an alternative vision. The opposition of Ancient Stoicism to Aristotle's physics is considered as a potential source of this creative dialectic. In Chapter 4 his 'I' attempts to harmonise these accounts of the physical cosmos with their respective ethical philosophies. At times, he files in behind an Aristotelian ethics of reason and work, a striving that is otherwise checked by a position resembling the Ancient Stoics' *apatheia*, or renunciation of will to cosmic reason, his oft-repeated intuition of a 'natural order' (3 passim). Indeed, Chapter 4 builds upon these ancient debates to establish Beckett's comedy of ethics in *How It Is*. It establishes the central concept from which the reception of *ancient voice* will hereafter be measured: the ideal of Platonic education, *paideia*, or the shaping of young minds towards their autonomous appreciation of the Good. Beckett's satire exploits the foundational role Socratic method plays in the *paideia* and the way it was assimilated into Christian theology by early Church theologians. The conflicting outcomes that arose from this process – the transformation of the Good life of the philosopher into that of the Christian or its *total* renunciation by the ascetic – becomes the principle source of the narrator/narrated's philosophical equivocation. This conflict propels him out into the mud, motoring both his 'Thebaïd' (183) and the meiotic 'training' of the creature he encounters, Pim, to see it blossom upon the 'moral plane bud and bloom of relations proper' (71). This fourth chapter retraces, furthermore, how the narrator/narrated constellates philosophical motifs within Biblical images from the visual arts, drawing from Rembrandt and Elsheimer.

The earnest hope of Beckett's 'I' for a sign of his divine election moves, in Chapter 5, beyond the sphere of his rational mind. His revisitation by Augustinian voices coincides with the hope for an experience of God's ineffable discourse of the heart, the *verbum cordis*. He invests his repetition of voice with the spiritual values of recitation, in particular the virtue of psalmody accorded by Augustine and Saint Gregory of Nyssa. His use of the tropes of mysticism and negative theology is then compared with the text's evocation of various 'geometric methods' deployed by seventeenth-century rationalists. As the 'I' takes a route to God that now passes through the geometric discourse of his 'Cartesian' mind, his attention turns to the philosophies of Nicolas Malebranche and Arnold Geulincx. Chapter 6 delves deeper into these seventeeth-century contexts when it discovers traces, via *The Unnamable*, of networked allusions to the more colourful events in the biography of Blaise Pascal, and Pascal's record of his visitation by God's voice, the poem 'Mémorial'. Through his allegiance to a programme of Pascalian miracles, the narrator/narrated emerges in the full splendour of his absurd asceticism. Chapter 7 concludes this investigation by detailing the way that the narrator/narrated weighs up a philosophy of immanence (Spinoza) against a philosophy of transcendence (Leibniz). Spinoza's pantheism and Leibniz's gallery of fantastical images in the *Monadology* figure prominently in Beckett's translation of philosophical dialectics into polyvalent tropes. The dialectic that he maintains between these two figures synthesizes the wide range of philosophical concerns of the preceding chapters. He is inspired particularly by the way Leibniz leverages his discovery of infinitesimal calculus within a narrative of pre-established harmony. This book, like Beckett's novel, closes with an exposition of the attempts by the 'I' to recover from the fragments of his *humanities* sufficient knowledge to emulate a Leibnizian system in the hope that it will resolve not only the ancient paradoxes that have plagued his understanding of the physical cosmos but his deepest existential and theological anxieties.

## Notes

1. All references to French and English versions and their manuscript drafts are to the critical-genetic edition of *Comment c'est/How It Is* compiled by Magessa O'Reilly (2001). Except when specifically identifying the French or English version, or when stressing the bilingual nature of the oeuvre, I prefer the English title, with the understanding that neither text exists in isolation from the other.

2. The letter is dated 8 April 1960. I respect Beckett's terminology except when I distinguish different aspects of this voice – past narrated or present narrator – or emphasise the textual 'I' as a character.
3. Articles on *How It Is* typically focus on the dynamics of voice and textuality or approach the work through one philosophical theme or perspective. See, for example, Abbott ('Farewell', 'Beginning'), Bersani and Dutoit ('Beckett's Sociability'), Dearlove ('Voice'), Duffy ('Prisoners'), Grossman ('Beckett'), Hamilton and Hamilton ('Process'), Heise ('Erzahlzeit'), Hutchings ('Shat'), Krance ('Alienation'), Locatelli ('"my life"'), O'Reilly ('Ni prose'), R. Smith ('Bearing'). These and other studies are discussed later.
4. Ackerley and Gontarski (*Faber Companion*), Blanchot (*L'Entretien*), Boulter (*Interpreting*), Fifield (*Late*), Knowlson and Pilling (*Frescoes*), Murphy (*Reconstructing*), Shaw (*Impotence*), Stewart (*Sex*).
5. Post-structuralist philosophy is habitually evoked in critical discussion of Beckett's work, though *How It Is* does not receive extended discussion in books by Clément (*L'Œuvre*), Connor (*Repetition*), Katz (*Saying*), Trezise (*Into*), Uhlmann (*Beckett, Philosophical*) and Weller (*A Taste*). Abbott's *The Author in the Autograph* contains an insightful chapter on *How It Is*, though his approach is narratological and historical, rather than post-structuralist.
6. *Le mot entendre, pour cet acte d'approche, conviendrait mieux que le mot lire. Derrière les mots qui se lisent, comme avant les mots qui s'écrivent, il y a une voix déjà inscrite, non entendue et non parlante, et l'auteur est, auprès de cette voix, à égalité avec le lecteur: tous deux, presque confondus, cherchant à la reconnaître* (Blanchot, *L'Entretien* 481).
7. At the time of submission of this manuscript this digital edition is edging towards completion.

# A Poetics of Translation: Dante, Gœthe and the *Paideia*

To analyse *How It Is* once seemed impossible without considering Dante's *Inferno*. Beckett's notes to *Comment c'est* in the 'Été 56' notebook (reproduced in the critical-genetic edition) contain the unambiguous entry: 'Enf., Purg. Paradis' (199), but if Part 1 of the novel might be a descent into the *Inferno*, there is no ascent to heaven in Part 3. Rather, the book is structured around an unresolved dialectic between the one and the many, between the solitary 'I' whose narrative may or may not be how it is, and his sense that he is part of a purgatorial cycle of bodies that rotate and collide beneath a realm of light, suspended in a plane of mud that threatens to consume them. The encounter with Pim offers the measure by which the narrator/narrated gauges events: 'the journey the couple the abandon' (21). This banal expression of Romance barely accommodates the complex narrative relationships of voice, memory and recitation, and the structure of the *Commedia* is not particularly useful as reference. *Comment c'est* might have begun with the intent of engaging with the *Commedia*, yet its journey into the underworld became no brief sojourn but rather the enduring record of how it is. Fragments of the *Commedia* circulate amongst other residua; and digested voices become matter, the mud itself, to be chewed over, excreted, retasted, reborn. Even when they lose their Dantean bearings, elements of the *Commedia* persist in the narrator/narrated's discourse within a poetics that shapes new images out of past fragments, for Beckett uses the *Commedia* as a painter might colour, allowing selective features of representation to assume new symbolic meaning within a personal vision.

Yet Dante's *Inferno* effectively illuminates the murky universe of *How It Is*. Commentators were quick to notice the resemblance of Beckett's creatures crawling through the *boue* (mud) to the Sullen and Slothful punished in Canto 7 and the Wrathful of the fifth circle of hell. A lasting scholarly perception that this is Beckett's most Dantean text is often coupled with Beckett's epigraph from Leopardi to the 1931 edition of Proust: 'e fango è il mondo' (and mud is the world). Dante's sullen and slothful were damned for the medieval sin of *acedie* or *accidie*, slackness in good works and spiritual gloom. In hell they smite and mangle one another, tearing each other apart with their teeth. This pure violence differs from the institutionalised torture which the 'I' administers to Pim; his is a systematic, pedagogical inscription in the flesh.

This chapter accentuates the figures and uses of education in *How It Is* to argue that Beckett used translation and self-translation to undermine allusion to recognisable sources. This is a late modernist strategy to escape perceived fallacies in traditional forms of artistic representation in a poetics which relies upon a stable edifice of tradition, as typical of earlier modernists. I challenge two dominant criticical assumptions about *How It Is*: firstly, the commonplace that the *Commedia* is *the* ur-text underwriting the novel; and, secondly, that *How It Is* nevertheless denies the possibility of referring to anything but its own procedures of witnessing and inscription. Beckett's bilingual text generates a complex echoing between his 'Dante' and other sources in the French and English traditions. This destabilises the transmission of culture from *ancient voice* to 'I', and from 'I' to Pim, confronting the tradition of the *Bildungsroman*. The conceptual framework and reading practice that this discloses underpins my methodology, in which archival knowledge offers purchase on the philosophical images, ideas and dialectics that are translated and transmogrified therein.

### 'Another Dante Season'?

In the spring of 1958 Beckett reread Dante's *Paradiso* (*LSB* 3, 130; cf. 126, 139). Later that year he composed *Pochade radiophonique*,[1] translated as *Rough for Radio II*, in which Animator asks Stenographer, 'Have you read the Purgatory, miss, of the divine Florentine?' She admits to having only 'flipped through the Inferno' (*CDW* 279). *Comment c'est* is generally assumed to have been written under the shadow of Dante's *Inferno*, yet it is not clear from where that shadow is cast. Knowlson affirms that Beckett reread the whole *Commedia* in spring 1958 out of 'sheer boredom' (453); he appears to translate Beckett's more modest confession to

Jacoba van Velde: 'Je m'emmerde tellement que je relis le Paradis de Dante' (*LSB* 3, 130). Beckett mentioned his rereading *Paradiso* to many correspondents, but I find no such claim for the *Inferno*. An isolated phrase from its cantos that may surface within his discourse does not confirm a recent reading, but there is evidence to suggest that he may have returned to the *Inferno* during the difficult parturition of his 'new moan' (*LSB* 3, 210). On 5 November 1959, he wrote to Jacob Schwartz: 'the hole I have got myself into now is as "dumb of all light" as the 5th canto of HELL and by God no love' (*LSB* 3, 252–3). Nearly eight months earlier, on 17 March 1959, Beckett 'mentions' the *Inferno* in an unpublished letter to Ethna MacCarthy while 'struggling with the 6th version of the opening of the new work' (Pilling, *Chronology* 145). Suggestive also is his comment in an unpublished letter of 15 April 1959 to Barbara Bray, 'I finished first draft of first part of book', adding that he will revise it before moving on to the next part and is looking forward to 'another Dante season' when back to his country house (TCD MS 10948). Either Beckett had reread *Paradiso*, and perhaps *Purgatorio*, and is looking forward to another 'season' of the *Commedia* (with the *Inferno*), or, having recently read all or part of the *Commedia* before or while writing the first draft of Part 1, he is looking forward to another 'Dante season', a return to his own purgatorial narrative.

Crucially, the pattern of allusions to the *Inferno* is present in the first manuscript proper of *Comment c'est*. In the critical-genetic edition, O'Reilly describes this manuscript ('ms') as comprising six notebooks, numbered 'Pim I (*Comment c'est*)' to 'Pim VI (*Comment c'est*)' (xvii–viii). The second notebook is dated 'Ussy 11.3.59'; at Part 1, paragraph 95, Beckett wrote: 'NEW WRITING/EDWARD'S BIRTHDAY/59' (xv–viii).[2] As his nephew, Edward, was born on 13 March 1959, the following material was written after this date. The beginning of Part 2 is dated 27 May 1959 (xviii).[3] Apart from the wider allusion to the underworld of mud from *Inferno* 7, the passage of Beckett's text most obviously provoked by the *Inferno* begins 200 paragraphs into Part 1. Whatever the March 1959 comment to MacCarthy implies, evidence suggests that Beckett engaged more intensively with the *Inferno* soon after 15 April 1959, which accounts for the density of allusion to it in the latter half of Part 1.

This argument, while justifiable, has some catches. Firstly, the 'boue originelle' (234; primeval mud) is present very early in the genesis of Part 1, along with a specific allusion to the 'cuisses de Lucifer' (219; Lucifer's thighs) from *Inferno* 34 (discussed below); secondly, all the echoes of the *Inferno* in Part 1 could be drawn from Beckett's memory and lifelong interest in Dante. Nevertheless, the most specific allusions to the *Inferno* date from the period in which Beckett indicates to Bray that he will reread, or refocus his imagination on, Dante. His writing did not begin with this frame exclusively, for in the early manuscript drafts the 'I' is alone in a wilderness, where he is visited by those who have known him, or by others who 's'enfuient dans un endroit désert' (247; flee into a desert place). He attempts to clear his mind of thoughts, but unsuccessfully; the *ancient voice* and the device of its quoting is not yet present and the 'I' is preoccupied with his sack and its rations. He emerges as an authorial figure, composing an autofiction that recalls *L'Innomable* and *Textes pour rien*, inflected with the topoi and topology of desert asceticism. The *Inferno* is not foregrounded, but when his mind takes a Dantean turn Beckett scores his words with polyphonic intertextuality.

## Abdicating Authority: Dante, or *The Great Refusal*

Lo buon maestro disse: 'Figlio, or vedi
l'anime di color cui vinse l'ira;
e anche vo' che tu per certo credi
   che sotto l'acqua è gente che sospira,
e fanno pullular quest' acqua al summo,
come l'occhio ti dice, u' che s'aggira.
   Fitti nel limo dicon: "Tristi fummo
ne l'aere dolce che dal sol s'allegra,
portando dentro accidïoso fummo:
   or ci attristiam ne la belletta negra."
Quest' inno si gorgoglian ne la strozza,
ché dir nol posson con parola integra.' (*Inferno* 7.115–26)

The good master said: 'Son, now you see
the souls of those whom anger overcame.
And I would have you know for certain
that plunged beneath these waters,
as your eyes will tell you, are souls whose sighs
with bubbles make the water's surface seethe.
Fixed in the slime they say: "We were sullen
in the sweet air that in the sun rejoices,

filled as we were with slothful fumes.
Now we are sullen in black mire."
This hymn they gurgle in their gullets,
for they cannot get a word out whole.'
                    (*Inferno*, trans. Robert Hollander and Jean Hollander)

Beckett's 'I' claws through this slime: 'the mud never cold never dry it doesn't dry on me the air laden with warm vapour' (29). A traveller like Dante, he yet joins the sullen and slothful in their punishment; at other times he imitates the cruelty of the *Inferno*'s torturers. With his tongue in the mud, gurgling his discourse, he imbibes and mixes it with the ooze: 'my life as nothing man a vapour' (103). Dante meets the sullen and slothful on the banks of the Styx, and Beckett's 'I' trawls through his mud without memory. Like Dante, who is led by Virgil, he follows his guiding 'ancient' voice. Virgil has the authority to translate the gurgled 'hymn' of the Wrathful. Like Dante, who has transformed the *content* of Virgil's translation into his own song, the discourse of the narrator/narrated is born from the already-translated, fragmented voice which forms his consciousness, and therefore his external world (the *voice quaqua* as caca/mud). Caselli (*Beckett's* chapter 7) affirms that Virgil's authority is as fragile as that of his own translator, Dante, and his ear for the incomprehensible hymn of the Wrathful mirrors Dante's failure to disclose the content of that hymn. Thus, the unknowing experienced by the reader with respect to this source (Virgil) reflects Dante's position with the hymn of the Wrathful. Beckett's reader remains equally ignorant of Pim's song. If the text implies a poetic translation of the incoherent hymn bubbling up from the mud, its source, Beckett suggests, is unidentifiable.

The narrator/narrated occupies the Virgil-Dante nexus; he hears the gurgling 'voice once without quaqua on all sides then in me' (3). This voice is constantly imbibed and excreted: 'je pissais et chiais autre image dans mon moïse', 'I pissed and shat another image in my crib' (4–5). This *moïse* or *crib* was, in earlier *Comment c'est* manuscripts, a 'barcelonnette', like the rocking cradle in the philosophy of Arnold Geulincx.[4] The powerlessness to affect change in the world becomes for the English reader a comic image of infantile regression layered with Freudian associations of scatological fixations and narcissism;[5] but the lower-case 'moïse' trips a Francophone reader, who might hear the word as Moïse (Moses), the baby Moïse in his cradle among the bulrushes. And when Moses read God's inscription of the Commandments upon the tablets, and then transcribed them (smashing the originals), did that transformation of God's word into Hebrew corrupt its essence? Beckett's 'I' reflects on these metatextual complications, for an original voice, at times perhaps his own, is dictated from 'above in the light' but perpetually ill-heard below. The dialogue between his French and English texts generates thus an ironical parallel between the narrator/narrated and his M/moïse, the eternal infant trapped in his crib of neuroses, unable to alter his destiny or ascend to any spiritual heights, for he will never climb his mountain, be it Pisgah, Purgatory, Sinai or Calvary, behold his promised land, or be united with 'the other above in the light'.[6]

This thorny passage deflates the tropism of the 'I' and his philosophical speculations. From paragraph 202 of Part 1, images from Dante's *Commedia* are like a canvas over which Beckett layers a multitude of allusions, yet these fail to offer a scaffolding on which the narrative might 'depend'; on the contrary, they exacerbate the text's hermeneutic intractability:

[. . .] close the eyes at last and wait for my pain that with it I may last a little more and while waiting

prayer in vain to sleep I have no right to it yet I haven't yet deserved it prayer for prayer's sake when all fails when I think of the souls in torment true torment true souls who have no right to it no right ever to sleep we're talking of sleep I prayed for them once if I may believe an old view it has faded. (43)

The 'I' prays for sleep to release him from the pain of waiting, then charitably for 'the great damned' who cannot sleep. In *Purgatorio* 4 Belacqua puts off his own prayers, his sighs of penance, waiting indolently while the heavens wheel around him:

se orazïone in prima non m'aita
*che surga sù di cuor che in grazia viva;*
l'altra che val, che 'n ciel non è udita? (4.133–5, my emphasis)

unless I'm helped by prayers that rise
*from a heart that lives in grace*
What good are those that go unheard in Heaven?

In *How It Is* the narrator/narrated's self-identification with Belacqua recalls this moment and suggests an inevitable consequence of his/their waiting: 'asleep I see me asleep on my side or on my face

[. . .] Belacqua fallen on his side, tired of waiting *forgotten of the hearts where grace abides* asleep' (27, my emphasis). Denied God's grace, he allows the narrator/narrated to express, momentarily, a negative response to the philosophico-theological question motivating his quest: 'me sole elect [?]'.

Traditional representation secured through allusive discourse is complicated by the religious overtones of Beckett's translation of Dante's Italian. Belacqua is 'oublié des cœurs où vit la grâce endormi' (26). Beckett's French construction uses a poetic, indeed, Pascalian turn of phrase. For a French reader, ignorant of a minor character from *Purgatorio*, the rhetoric of *le cœur* and *la grâce* is more likely to resonate with that of Pascal than Dante, to suggest that this enigmatic Belacqua has been excluded from Pascal's blessed *ordre du cœur* or *ordre de la charité* (order of the heart, order of charity) who enjoy God's grace at the pinnacle of His hierarchy in the *Pensées*. This is the more poignant given the other Pascalian themes, allusions and echoes in the manuscript genesis and published text of this section of Part 1. In Chapter 6, retracing these, I will show Beckett's attraction to Pascal's life and extreme asceticism, and to a series of supposed miracles within which Pascal felt himself implicated. His poem of visionary fragments, '*Mémorial*', attests to the night of fire, his ecstatic communion with the divine. Beckett's unconventional French formulation in his translation of Dante, 'oublié de[s] cœurs', invokes this call to asceticism: 'Oubli du monde et de tout, hormis DIEU' (*Pensées* 4).

Such echoing is more difficult to quantify than transparent allusions that stand out and may be linked to their particularity within the source text. Yet the exploitation of literary echoes is a key technique which Beckett uses in *How It Is* to generate moments of gravity, significance, irony and humour. Questions of style impact upon the study of allusion, as becomes evident when comparing Beckett's translation of Dante with Pascal's syntactic positioning of his substantive 'oubli' (above), which has posed problems for his English translators:

> 'The world forgotten, and everything except God' (*Pensées* 309, trans. A. J. Krailsheimer).

> 'The world forgot and all save God' (*Pensées* 363, trans. H. F. Stewart).

> 'Oblivion of the world and of everything, except God' (*Pensées* 333, trans. Martin Turnell).

Krailsheimer uses the passive participle of the verb *forget* ('The world forgotten'), while Stewart poetically refigures its simple past form into an adjective ('The world forgot'). This echoes Pope's famous lines from 'Eloisa to Abelard' – 'How happy is the blameless vestal's lot! / The world forgetting, by the world forgot' (*Selected* 60–1). It casts Pascal in an ironic light, given that Pope's Eloisa equates, heretically, Abelard's identity with God. Both translations dissipate the force of the substantive forgetting in Pascal's formulation, for which Turnell risks a *contre-sens* signifying the world's oblivion/forgetting/annihilation ('Oblivion of the world'). Yet Beckett's phrase offers an adjectival modification in the present tense of a state of being whose elision of subject and verb mirrors the poetic *shape* of Pascal's phrase: Belacqua is 'forgotten of the hearts'. Pascal famously opposed the philosophical reasoning of the mind to find faith in the grace of God, who speaks a language of truth through the human heart rather than the mind: 'Le cœur a ses raisons, que la raison ne connaît point' (*Pensées* #277; The heart has its reasons, which reason does not know). The Aristotelian striving of one who attempts rationally to perfect himself and thus become closer to God is the motivation for Dante's journey in the *Commedia* and ostensibly that of the 'I' in Beckett's text; by allowing this grand narrative to be assailed by Pascalian echoes, Beckett's 'translation' of Dante undermines the very authority of Dante's voice.

The prophetic tone Beckett achieves through his unusual French construction may owe its origins to sources that also influenced Pascal. Ackerley ('Bible' 53–125) has discovered several allusions to the Psalms in *How It Is*; Beckett was familiar with Psalm 31 in the David Martin edition of *La Sainte Bible* – a copy of which remained in his library at his death – where the outcast David laments that he is spurned by society:

> J'ai été mis en *oubli dans le cœur* [des hommes], comme un mort: j'ai été [estimé] comme un vaisseau de nul usage. (31:13–14, my emphasis)

Louis Segond's well-known Protestant Bible of 1887, in Beckett's possession at his death, reveals a direct correspondence with the Psalms:

> Je suis
> comme un mort *oublié des cœurs,*
> comme un objet de rebut. (31:14–17, my emphasis)

Similarly, the celebrated *La Bible de Jérusalem*, published to critical acclaim in 1955, uses the same construction as Beckett: '*Je suis
oublié des coeurs* comme un mort, Je suis comme un vase brisé'
(my emphasis). The subversive import of putting the prayer of
David, who was saved by the Lord, into the mouth of Belacqua,
who ignores God, registers in the English translation of *Comment
c'est* in the bathos with which Beckett undoes the high Biblical
mode: Belacqua is 'forgotten of the hearts where grace abides',
rather than '*be*gotten of the heart where grace abides'. Beckett's
subversion of the Biblical register converts the King James rhetoric
of begetting into his own rhetoric of forgetting. Such resonances
open up the possibility that his transportation of a phrase from
Dante's Italian into French involved no conscious allusion to
Pascal nor to any French Bible but was implicitly shaped by his
English tongue; his unusual French construction is thus born from
a circuitous series of bilingual translations. The absence of an
authorising speech is a productive trope; for the bird's-eye view
of the Belacqua-I images the rupture between the transcendent
authorial 'Je'/'I' and its 'il'/'he' in mud/text. No prayer will
descend from the realm of 'grace', 'above in the light', to the
mud below: rather, the text generates its own order of forgetting/
meaning within its 'novel' poetics.

Further, Beckett mixes from the *Commedia* various details that
are irreconcilable with their representation in Dante's text, but
which through their poetic associations with the *Inferno* enter into
a discourse with his Dantean vocabulary developed since *Dream
of Fair to Middling Women*.

> me again always everywhere in the light age unknown seen from
> behind on my knees arse bare on the summit of a muckheap clad in
> a sack bottom burst to let the head through holding in my mouth the
> horizontal staff of a vast banner on which I read

> in thy clemency now and then let the great damned sleep here some-
> thing illegible in the folds then dream perhaps of the good time their
> naughtiness procured them what time the demons may rest ten seconds
> fifteen seconds

> sleep sole good brief movements of the lower face no sound sole good
> come quench these two old coals that have nothing more to see and
> this old kiln destroyed by fire and in all this tenement

all this tenement of naught from top to bottom from hair to toe and finger-nails what little sensation it still has of what it still is in all its parts and dream

dream come of a sky an earth an under-earth where I am inconceivable aah no sound in the rectum a redhot spike that day we prayed no further. (45)

Belacqua is cast with the 'great damned' of the *Inferno*, yet his prayer begins, 'in thy clemency', which echoes the standard English translation of the intercessory prayer to the Virgin, 'Memorare', as popularised by St Bernard of Clairvaux, protector of the poor, of prisoners and the condemned: 'Noli, Mater Verbi, verba mea despicere; sed audi propitia et exaudi. Amen' (O Mother of the Word Incarnate, despise not my petitions, but in thy clemency hear and answer me. Amen).[7] Beckett's 'original' French, 'en ta clémence' (44) 'quotes' no standard French version of the Latin poem; rather, his French anticipates the English translation, and his search for a French religious rhetoric passes by way of his English as he self-translates *avant la lettre*. Yet the original displays its characteristic awareness of its already-translatedness: it presents this prayer as issuing from an inscrutable, absent original: 'ici des mots illisibles dans les plis', 'here something illegible in the folds'.

Hutchings traces the final composite allusion in the above passage to Marlowe's *Edward II* and to the Paolo-Francesca episode in Canto 5 of the *Inferno*: 'quel giorno più non vi leggemmo avante' (5.138; that day we read no further) (68; cf Caselli, *Beckett's* 162, 'The Promise' 248). Francesca answers Dante's question about the 'dubious desires' which led to her damnation: she and Paolo had been seduced by their reading of Galahaut's account of Lancelot and Guinevere. In his review of Papini's *Dante Vivo*, Beckett referred to this episode and 'the incompatibility of the two operations [reading and love]' (*Disjecta* 81).[8] The narrator/narrated's plea to let 'the great damned' sleep recalls Dante's naïve pity for Francesca, to let them dream of 'the good time their naughtiness procured them'. That God might suffer his damned the pleasure of returning to their transgression is farcical – the comic effect generated in the drop in register from 'thy' to 'naughtiness' – and would, Francesca suggests, reinforce the melancholy pain of their situation: 'Nessun maggior dolore / che ricordarsi del tempo felice / ne la miseria' (*Inferno* 5.121–3;

There is no greater sorrow/than to recall our time of joy/in wretchedness). Yet 'naughtiness' suggests punishment, evoking the word's archaic meaning of a defect, be it of argument, theology or reason. The red-hot spike therefore anticipates their divinely sanctioned punishment: for Paolo and Francesca, either to love or not to love is damnable.

Dante's voices intermingle with his narrator/narrated's, who freely inverts the import of Francesca's line – the aporia which signals sexual intercourse – when it becomes the ironic refrain to Edward II's murder ('that day we prayed no further'). Marlowe's homosexual king, Edward II, was murdered for being an effeminate, 'unnatural' leader who failed to achieve military success or conduct himself with the *dignitas* requisite of the king's office. He was assassinated when Lightborn (the Anglicised Lucifer) fatally inserted a red-hot poker into the source of his sin and failure.

Scenes at Erebus endure when the narrator/narrated refers to his own eyes as 'two old coals that have nothing more to see', imagining himself as Charon, the transporter of souls between earth and Erebus in *Inferno* 3: 'Caron dimonio, con occhi di bragia' (3.109; Charon the demon, the son of Erubus with eyes of glowing coals). This 'dimonio' appears to have suggested to Beckett the 'demons' in the previous paragraph, who are nevertheless distinct from the Charon-I. Enacting a mythico-psychoanalytic poetics of identity the 'I' reconstitutes itself anew, bursting out of his penitents' sackcloth and telegraphing from his mouth 'the horizontal staff of a vast banner'. In place of his tongue he finds this metonym of 'una 'nsegna che girando', the whirling, recirculating banner from *Inferno* 3 (52–3).[9] This banner heralds the unheroic and indifferent who lived 'sanza "nfamia e sanza lodo"' (3.36; without praise and blame), worthy of neither heaven nor hell. Dante approaches ante-Inferno, the vestibule of hell sanctioned for the indifferent who never took sides.[10] He recognises a familiar shadow, one he identifies only as he *'Che fece per viltate* il gran rifiuto' (*Inferno* 3.60, my emphasis; who made, through cowardice, *the great refusal*). This shadow is commonly assumed to be that of Pope Celestine V, a Benedictine monk of extreme asceticism who became a religious hermit, living in a cave and later sanctified for the severity of his penitential rituals.[11]

Celestine V was called by the Council of Cardinals in 1292 to become Pope. He reluctantly assented but finding himself a mere puppet without real power he abdicated five months later. He was then imprisoned by his successor Boniface VIII in a castle, where he perished after ten months, allegedly at the cruel hand of Boniface himself. Francesca Del Moro (86) links the 'great damned' in *How It Is* to Celestine, noticing the evocation of the 'gran refus' (great refusal) of *Eleuthéria* (29–30) and its appearance in 'What a Misfortune' (*More Pricks Than Kicks* 136). In *How It Is* Beckett exploits Dante's symmetry between his resistant figures: Celestine V, discovered as a shadow; and Belacqua, who is first encountered, indolent and 'a l'ombra dietro al sasso' (4.104; in the shade behind the boulder).

In a letter to George Duthuit of 3 March 1949, five weeks after finishing *En attendant Godot*, Beckett aligned his aesthetic position (in terms reminiscent of Blanchot) with that of Dante's figure of the 'gran rifiuto' and the indifference of those without praise or blame in *Inferno* 3, as an expression of sympathy in the painting of Bram van Velde for the refusal to relate inner subjectivity with the forms of the outside world:

> Je ne dis pas qu'il ne cherche pas à renouer. Ce qui importe, c'est qu'il n'y arrive pas. Sa peinture est, si tu veux, l'impossibilité de renouer. Il y a, si tu veux, refus et refus d'accepter son refus. C'est peut-être ce qui rend cette peinture possible. Pour ma part, c'est le <u>gran rifiuto</u> qui m'intéresse, non pas les héroïques tortillements auxquels nous devons une chose si belle. J'en suis navré. Ce qui m'intéresse c'est l'au-delà du dehors-dedans où il fait son effort, non pas la portée de l'effort même. (*LSB* 2, 136)[12]

This statement raises crucial issues that will be addressed over my next six chapters: the denial of simple representation in Beckett's artistic practice; the non-relation between elements of representation which arise out of this practice, *the state of being in front of*; their resistance to a reader's 'intuition'[13] or immediate apprehension; the importance of the effort to represent when knowing that representation is never achievable, or even desirable; and, now, most importantly for Beckett, the private (and agnostic) but religious character of an artistic submission to this very activity. In *How It Is* the image of the self in melancholy communion with itself masks its author's engagement with the refusal of high office, *le gran rifiuto*, his necessary failing, becoming ridiculous and unworthy.

Early in the evolution of *Comment c'est*, in the first manuscript 'ms/a', at paragraph 22b of Part 1, Beckett's hero was again trapped, unable to escape his present state or inch up or down like 'd'autres plus heureux' (219; others with more luck) who climb 'le long des cuisses de Lucifer' (219; the length of Lucifer's thighs).This refers to Virgil and Dante descending Lucifer's thighs to escape through the centre of earth and the ninth circle of the *Inferno* when they 'appigliò sé a le vellute coste [. . . e] giù discese poscia tra'l folto pelo e le gelate croste' (34; took a handhold on those hairy flanks [. . . and] clambered down between the thick pelt and the crusted ice). Escaping hell, they descend through the earth's centre and begin their ascent towards the light of purgatory, in Beckett's word 'being shat into open air the light of day the regimen of grace' (161). Beckett is playing on the idea of being expelled into the air above within a digestive economy governed by a Pascalian 'régime de la grace' (160). Dantean tropes in *How It Is* equally accommodate a climbing and descending the rungs of Pascalian *grace* (Laporte, *La Doctrine*), as thematised subsequently in Beckett's *Le Dépeupleur/ The Lost Ones* but also present in his first play, *Eleutheria*: 'Pitié, pitié pour ceux qui rampent dans les ténèbres! Silence, on dirait l'espace de Pascal' (137).

The grappling at thighs is re-enacted at the first clawing into Pim's backside when he is first encountered, as if Pim too might offer a path into the light. The sadism of Pim's education arises from the frustrated longings of the pedagogue to transcend the hopeless repetitions and eternal return of his platitudinous rituals. Indeed, Beckett reiterated the allusion to Lucifer's thighs in an autograph revision of paragraph 37a from the later typescript 'UoR MS 1661' – a paragraph he would later erase – when the narrator envisions himself climbing up towards earth and heaven 'par les cuisses de Lucifer' (233; by the thighs of Lucifer). In the next revision ('Tx1') of this paragraph, Beckett adds a remarkable interlinear clarification: 'par les <les prières aux> cuisses de Lucifer' (234; by <the prayers to> Lucifer's thighs). In the ninth circle of hell 'Belacqua's' dreaming-praying is twisted into the composite Dante-I praying to Lucifer's thighs to be allowed to pass.

Beckett fashions in *How It Is* a raw image of his artistic refusal: the subject excretes itself into the 'outside' as itself from within itself. Innumerable declarations in *Molloy*, *Malone Dies* and *The Unnamable*, seemingly exhausted, suggest that for Beckett 'what lies beyond the outside-inside' (above) is a realm of being prior to epistemological categories and language that in turn give birth to hilarious tropes that mock the very attempt to represent. In the

*Commedia*, the banner that heralds Celestine V and those 'without praise and blame' is simply a banner; but Beckett's banner issues from the mouth, becoming the tongue, as he (narrator) becomes character (narrated). The French reader is more likely to recognise not the obscured Dantean analogy but Beckett's ironic inversion of the opening to Diderot's comic novel, *Jacques le fataliste et son maître*. Like Beckett's narrator/narrated reciting the *voice above in the light*, Diderot's raconteur parrots the beliefs of his 'Captain', insisting throughout the novel 'que tout ce qui nous arrive de bien et de mal ici bas était écrit là-haut' (475; and 'that everything which happens to us in this world, good or bad, is written up above' (25)). Jacques imagines his life as the unfolding of a great scroll written above, 'comme un grand rouleau qu'on déploie petit à petit' (480; like a great scroll which is unrolled little by little (25)).

Beckett's election of a literal translation of the 'voix ancienne' of *Comment c'est* as the *ancient voice* eschews the more obvious meaning of the French voice as 'former' or 'old', drawing attention to the heraldry of his English 'ancient', a standard-bearer, or 'ensign'. Mocking the logocentric discourse of the Ancient of Days as much as his own authorial transcendence, Beckett's multilingual poetics is interlaced with intertextual literary images that undo the singular authority of any one textual element. With 'arse bare on the summit of a muckheap' the 'I' projects its Dantean tongue inscribed with an illegible appeal for religious salvation (from Clairvaux), but this heralds the arrival of Beckett's figure of the authorial abdicator. The image is part of a scatological economy of *voice quaqua*, the material residues of once-ingested voice circulating between mouth and anus in a poetics of translation that generates 'a fart fraught with meaning issuing through the mouth' (29), and other digressions: 'I fart and piss in the same breath' (47). This process involves both a diachronic transformation of philosophical and literary discourse, and its synchronic transposition between languages. Therefore, a Dantean or Pascalian 'allusion' acknowledges less the content of that source than a formative influence that continues to inflect the discourse and thinking. Like the art of Van Velde 'refusing and refusal to accept refusal', Beckett's text rejects the explanatory relation between its interior voice and a purported outside: when Dantean fragments are translated and rearranged into an image of the self as Dante-Francesca-Charon-Edward II-Celestine V-Jacques there is ultimately no coherence on the level of representation between Dante's text and Beckett's. This writing represents the act of refusing, and like Van Velde's images 'it does not manage to'. It continues to signify a correspondence in Beckett's text with Dante without being explanatory in its representation but rather through its poetics of memory, language and image.

Beckett's Dantean images *represent* a consciousness reconstituting itself as a poetics; that is, they collectively offer the image of a self listening to its *ancient voice[s]* of memory, composing them anew as a method of continuing to represent the act of not representing, while the masked and occluded allusions guarantee this failure. The narrator/narrated's 'I quote' extracts the *ancient voice* from its 'natural order' and grafts it onto his own, giving rise to original voice. This is hardly giving form to the mess but is, rather, a poet's stirring of the chaos. This notion of Beckett's Dantean 'tongue' contrasts with Daniella Caselli's undoing of the assumption of Dante's authority in Beckett's texts, designating Belacqua as both 'a humorous figure of unlocatable source' (*Beckett's* 152) and the likely origin of the mysterious voice which the 'I' recites. This voice is not just a composite of Beckett's biography and Belacqua's textual existence (in both Dante and Beckett) but the composite voice:

> The voice is 'in me' but 'not mine', it is 'with/out', thus articulating that the notion of within and togetherness can be observed only from outside. Belacqua, the voice speaking Italian, mediates the idea of the self; in order to hear his voice, he splits into self and non-self. To be heard as 'in him' the voice has to be no longer 'his'. (152)

The voice, 'speaking Italian', which the 'I' hears inside him is first 'mediate[d]' by Belacqua and the Italian language, then this voice becomes 'his'. Equally, the text offers Pim's education as an image of this internal voice passing into the extended world, becoming *quaqua* ready to be imbibed anew. When Pim is conducted into the language of the 'I', his song externalises the voice of the 'I', transformed into its other, even artistic, form (Pim's song). Caselli points to an anxiety with respect to language, for when Pim sings (in French) the narrator/narrated declares, 'we use the same idiom what a blessing' (81). The narrator/narrated's comment that should Pim speak Italian then 'obviously it will be less amusing' (71) refers to the perverse potential for his pedagogical activity to be undermined, but not necessarily from the Italian in his own *ancient voice*, for he has just taught Pim his own *idiom*.

Caselli's intimation of a split within the self mediated by the experience of language is astute, yet if one searches for Derridean grounds for the text's questioning of the suppositions upon which Western ontology rests – where 'the voice cannot signal the "originary presence" of "the being which is human" because voice and humanity are demonstrated to be mutually dependent' (Caselli, *Beckett's* 152) – one might also consider the text's self-interpenetrating French and English versions when the rituals of language learning and self-translation foreground Beckett's rhetorical strategies (Cordingley, 'Beckett's "Masters"'). Beckett consistently performs the undoing of his French or English tongue by its immanent other,[14] confounding such terms as 'original', 'copy' and even 'translation'. Moreover, the author paradoxically writes himself into this discourse while presenting the very impossibility of his being as self-presence in language. Indeed, the striking proximity between Beckett's intertextual and bilingual poetics and post-structuralist readings of *How It Is* remains problematic but, as I have argued in the Introduction, the solution is not, as Blanchot would have it, to neutralise Beckett's 'I'. A return to Erebus should clarify these relations.

### Abraham's Bosom

In 1961 and 1962, after Beckett had finished *Comment c'est*, he offered the American scholar Lawrence Harvey some rare interviews. In *Samuel Beckett: Poet and Critic* Harvey holds that Beckett's perception of the world and art 'divides the world of consciousness into an upper zone of light where forms correspond to those in the physical world outside and a lower zone of darkness without such correspondence (*Murphy*, chapter 6)', and that Beckett 'links the new art to this zone of darkness' (Harvey, *Samuel Beckett* 436). This descent from inherited knowledge accords with what occurs in *How It Is* when Beckett submits the material of past learning to a poetics that refuses inherited connections, taking that refusal for its subject.

Limbo, Dante's ante-chamber to hell, offers an appropriate psychic topography for this operation. The *Limbus Patrum* or *Sinus Abrahæ* ('Bosom of Abraham') is the place where the saints of the Old Testament abided before Christ's descent into hell set them free. Under its entry for 'Limbus', Beckett's 11th edition of the *Encyclopaedia Britannica* defines the *Limbus Patrum* as 'the mere *caput mortuum* of the old Catholic doctrine of Hades, which was gradually superseded in the West by that of purgatory' (16: 693).[15] After Thomas Aquinas and Bonaventura, theologians maintained that the soul in purgatory is tormented by fire; but like Dante's voyagers climbing Lucifer's thighs at the end of the *Inferno* to be delivered into the light, Beckett's 'I' returns to the fantasy of escape from his Limbo:

> blessed day last of the journey all goes without a hitch the joke dies too old the convulsions die I come back to the open air to serious things had I only the little finger to raise to be wafted straight to Abraham's bosom I'd tell him to stick it up. (47)

This *little finger* is that of the beggar Lazarus, who was carried by angels into Abraham's bosom (Luke 16:19–31), whence he might offer relief to the rich man, Dives, tormented in the underworld, from whose table he used to collect fallen crumbs. Now, punished with fire, Dives pleads to Abraham: 'Father Abraham, have mercy on me, and send Lazarus, that he may dip the tip of his finger in water, and cool my tongue; for I am tormented in this flame.' Denying compassion, Abraham appeals to divine justice:

> But Abraham said, Son, remember that thou in thy lifetime receivedst thy good things, and likewise Lazarus evil things: but now he is comforted, and thou art tormented.
> And beside all this, between us and you there is a great gulf fixed: so that they which would pass from hence to you cannot; neither can they pass to us, that would come from thence. (Luke 16:25–6)

Beckett's narrator/narrated ascending from the underworld triumphs over Abraham's justice, suggesting that he will stick his finger 'up' (that is, Abraham's rear). This is both an amusing insolence before returning to 'serious things' in the light, and a poetical revenge of Edward II, reversing the sadistic justice administered with the 'red hot spike'. This irreverent gesture, which flips its *little finger* to righteous moralising, mocks the finger God used to inscribe his Ten Commandments and that of Christ, who refused to judge the adulteress of John 8:6, but rather 'stooped down, and with his finger wrote on the ground, as though he heard them not'.[16] For the 'I' below, more generally inclined to 'scrabble about in the mud' (61) pastiching narratives of the *voice quaqua*, the 'blessed day last of journey' is but a fleeting delusion, for he is condemned to the justice Abraham articulates in Luke, which governs the series ... Bom-I-Pim ..., where tormentor and victim alternate and compassion cannot bridge Abraham's 'great gulf' or reach the Ancient of Days. The finger that, applied to the self's psyche, might repair its torment now condemns it to Limbo; the escape from the *Inferno* is closed, hell's sphincter has contracted, and the sadistic outcome is the psychological frustration that stabs Pim's rear end and tears it open with fingernails.

In Part 3 the narrator/narrated redirects his energies towards figuring out the cosmological model for God's harmonious distribution of justice, attempting to reconcile physical, moral and spiritual laws into one 'formulation'. In so doing he will extend his engagement with justice in Plato, Aristotle and perhaps the Stoics into the great natural and metaphysical systems of the seventeenth century, notably Spinoza's *Ethics* and Leibniz's *Metaphysics* and *Monadology*. The narrator/narrated's self-image within Limbo is instructive: here Dante encountered the virtuous pagans (Homer, Horace, Ovid and Lucan) and philosophers (Euclid, Democritus, Diogenes, Anaxagoras, Thales, Empedocles, Heraclitus, Zeno, Socrates, Plato, Cicero, Seneca and Averroes) (*Inferno* 5.135–44). These were condemned for having insufficient faith to believe in a heaven beyond their own reason, just as the philosophers who emerge in Beckett's Erebus confront arational doctrines from theology and asceticism. Attempting to reconcile himself with his 'other above in the light', the narrator/narrated avails himself of the *paideia*, his Greek education in reason. In so doing he activates the dialectic which animates the entire novel, and from which Beckett's poetics departs: the tension between reason and the absence of reason; and a corresponding coherence of representation or its wilful, indeed playful, neglect. The legacy of the *paideia* is manifest in satisfying one's acquired need for a rational portrait of the cosmos that accounts for its pre-established harmony, and the acceptance with humility of one's insignificance in the face of either a materialist eternity (as in Democritus and the Ancient Stoics), or God the almighty. Yet the dialectic emits from Erebus as much as Dante, and this inferno represents in *Ill Seen Ill Said* the academic hell of pre-formatted minds from which the writer enjoys only the rarest of sabbaticals: 'The eye will return to the scenes of its betrayals. On centennial leave from where tears freeze' (*Company/Ill Seen Ill Said* 57).

## Wallowing in Gœthe: Unwinding the *Bildungsroman*

Beckett's resistance to Dante recalls the objections of John Donne, whose Reformed Christian attitudes cut the poet no slack for condemning Celestine V to the ante-chamber of hell. In 1600, Donne complained to Sir Henry Wotton:

> Alas! what would Dant have him do? Thus wee find the story related: he that thought himself next in succession, by a trunke thorough a wall whispered in Celestines eare counsell to remove the papacy: why would not Dant be content to thinke that Celestine tooke this for as imediate a salutacion and discourse of the holy ghost as Abrahim did the commandment of killing his sonn? If he will needs punish retyrednes thus, what *hell can his witt devise for ambition.* (*Complete* 442, my emphasis)

For Donne, Celestine V's abdication proves the absence of a corrosive 'ambition' in his spirit. Donne does not share Dante's respect for the sanctity of ecclesiastical rule, esteeming ascetic devotion as a calling fit to turn one's back on the Holy See.[17] He thus criticises Dante for failing to make the connection between Abraham giving up his son, God His, and, therefore, Celestine V denying himself the power and riches of the office bestowed unto him. *How It Is* casts the shadow of Celestine V without profit of blasphemy or judgement, as Beckett's self-caricature: he denies himself the gravity bestowed by religious allusions while yet evoking them. He thus mocks his own authority, at once denigrating himself for aspiring to practise the virtue exalted by Arnold Geulincx, the *despectio sui*, or 'disregard of oneself'. Yet this is inextricably bound to the practice of the 'inspectio sui', for within Geulincx's ethic of *humilitas* only after one has scrutinised the self can one dismiss it as worthless. A coded textuality therefore suggests Beckett's identification with a praxis that is neither an ethics of heroism nor that of anti-heroism, for he had learnt from Pascal that anti-heroism must not succumb to an inverted heroism, just as humility should ultimately reject the deceptive *virtus* of Ancient Stoicism and what is arguably its twentieth-century manifestation: existentialism. In neglecting to authorise itself through transparent analogy to canonical authors his writing had to accept an abject self-emasculation, the undoing of its *Bildung*.

Beckett's post-World War II novels reverse the aesthetics of the quest, swerving away from this positivist streak in the English novelistic tradition, and the narrative mode that came to define the French *nouveau roman*. *How It Is* rejects Dante's trajectory in the *Commedia* to engage with Gœthe's dramatisation of such a journey in *Faust*, translating his aheroic concern into an erratic dynamic between movement and rest, as visible in the fits and starts of *How It Is*. A January 1937 entry in the 'German Diaries' associates Faust's journeying and a repulsive heroism; and after reading Walter Bauer's *Die Notwendige Reise* Beckett demurred from the 'heroic, the nosce te ipsum, that these Germans see as a journey':

> Das notwendige Bleiben [the necessary staying-put] is more like it. That is also in the figure of Murphy in the chair, surrender to the thongs of self, a simple materialisation of self-bondage, acceptance of which is the fundamental unheroic. ('German Diaries' 4, 18/1/37; cited in Nixon, *German Diaries* 73)

Beckett here reveals his knowledge of how the Socratic ideal of the 'nosce te ipsum' or 'know thyself' underlies and was appropriated by the German tradition of intellectual formation, the *Bildung* and its artistic form, the journey within the *Bildungsroman*.

A major strand of humanistic German thought, the ideal of the *Bildung* increased its potency during the Enlightenment. Designating physical beauty, intellectual formation, the impregnation of the divine in the human soul, or the integration of the individual into society, the notion of the *Bildung* translates the Greek *paideia* rather than the Latin *cultura* as the actualisation of human perfectibility: the capacity for culture rather than culture's accumulation.[18] Of all philosophers of the *Bildung*, Wilhelm von Humboldt most influentially reclaimed for German culture what he identified as the Greek paradigm of self-determination and self-regulation, whereby the moral progress of humanity is realised in the autonomous individual, who expresses and brings into being the holistic dimension of German culture (Humboldt, *Über* 14–17). Language has a determining role in this expression, facilitating not only the individual's symbolic rapport with the world, but his or her very aspiration towards the universal and, importantly, the exploration of the interior self.

The narrative of *Bildung* – of the adolescent's progressive development into an ethical, rational and well-integrated adult – is most naturally reflected in the logic of the *Bildungsroman*.

Introduced in 1870 by Wilhelm Dilthey in his *Leben Schleiermachers* (*Life of Schleiermacher*), this term describes the classical novel of the young man who discovers himself and his position within the social fabric through his education and the refinement of his passions. Fusing many threads of Western morality and aesthetics, the *Bildungsroman* emerges out of the German reception of Rousseau's thought, in particular *Émile ou De l'éducation*[19] of 1762, and Christian piety, such as *Anton Reiser* by Philipp Moritz of 1785 (Cassin, *Vocabulaire* 195–204). And for Beckett, of course, there was the more immediate example of James Joyce's *A Portrait of the Artist as a Young Man*.

For Beckett, German classicism succeeded French eighteenth-century enlightenment, with the consequence that 'Beckett produces not so much antinarratives as anti-*Bildungsromans*' (Sheehan, *Modernism* 161), a proposition explored in greater depth by Bixby (*Postcolonial* 21–63). Yet with their circuitous syntax and narrative structures, as much as their over-educated but wandering and forgetful narrators and heroes, Beckett's novels relentlessly subvert a longer Western narrative of the *formation* of the *ratio* – from Plato to Freud – than a single focus on the German *Bildung* provides. This dimension to Beckett's novels remains under-appreciated, although by giving the schoolmaster centre stage in *How It Is* Beckett not only invites this exploration but allows his superlative artistic response to the traditions of *paideia* and *Bildung* to cast its retrospective gaze across his earlier writing. Close readings of his intertextual material indicate that Beckett strove to transform this narrative principle into a poetic practice.

Once animated by the *ancient voice* of his *paideia* the 'I' of *How It Is* becomes occasionally prone to bouts of resistance which in the absence of ambition manifest as indifference and laziness. He links these with self-examination, narrative and his own production of voice:

> stay forever in the same place *never had any other ambition* with my little dead weight in the warm mire scoop my wallow and stir from it no more *than that* old dream back again I live it now at this creeping hour know what it's worth was worth. (49; 1.221, my emphasis)

The narrator/narrated will stir from his life its stirring, at once 'that old dream', Beckett's *Dream* as much as Belacqua's lethargy, and the most recent episode in the text ('last state last version'). Where neither inside nor outside is collapsed the world *is* the hermeneutic continuity of self-exploration. This involves constant listening to the voices in one's head and their re-articulation, where they are heard once more in the present, becoming memory, are said again, and so on. Beckett's art moves beyond what he termed to Tom MacGreevy Gœthe's 'autological darkness' (*LSB 1*, 368) and the gratuity of Murphy's 'vicarious autology' (*Murphy* 107), even when gratuity becomes its subject. This figures once more as a private poetics of renewal born out of refuse where the 'wallow', the depressive or melancholy state of mind, is externalised as fertiliser for the scooper. Its genealogy stretches back to at least November 1932, when, having swerved off the programmed track through academia, Beckett claimed to be 'wallowing in [. . .] German' (TCD MS 10402, 11/11/[1932]), as he established the foundations of his next intellectual journey, albeit one that lacked clear direction, his formative but solitary six-month voyage through Germany from the beginning of October 1936 to the end of March 1937. In preparation for this trip he continued to learn German, reading Gœthe's *Faust* in August 1936. Unsurprisingly, in Beckett's thinking this 'wallow' is associated with Gœthe, for the paragraph quoted above in its early manuscript version ('ms') of *Comment c'est* concluded: 'pour une fois je suis d'accord avec Gœthe' (362; for once I agree with Gœthe). In version 'Tx1' the phrase is replaced with the anonymous 'et sais à l'égal du poète ce qu'il vaut et ce qu'il valait' (362; and I know just like the poet what it's worth and what it was worth). The published text offers no trace of this knowing poetics of the *poète*, nor any intertextual context for the comment 'know what it's worth was worth'.

Beckett's turning to Dante when finding the writing of *Comment c'est* almost insurmountable suggests that he might have sought out Gœthe for similar reasons. He wrote to Avigdor Arika on 31 March 1960 of his 'Pim' manuscript, 'It doesn't interest me at all, and I don't believe in it any more', then quoted two lines from Gœthe's 'Annonce': 'Die Welt geht auseinander / Wie ein fauler Fisch / Wir woollen sie nicht / balsamieren' (*LSB 3*, 320; The world is disintegrating like rotten fish. Let's not embalm it). This could be Gœthe's sentiment with which the narrator/narrated said he was *d'accord*, and the previous manuscript paragraph refers to the 'boîtes pouantes mal vidées' (361; stinking tins ill emptied), where *pouantes* was added during a manuscript revision. This connection is questionable because Beckett wrote to Bray on 25 May 1959, some ten months before the letter to Arika, to tell her that he had finished this part of his manuscript (the end of Part 1 of 'ms'). Indeed, by March 1960 he had retyped this section in the UoR MS 1661 typescript.

Gœthe nonetheless figured intermittently if not persistently in Beckett's thinking during the composition of *Comment c'est*, and the *poète* stirring his *wallow* should recall Gœthe's autobiographical project, *Aus meinem Leben: Dichtung und Wahrheit* (*Autobiography: Truth and Fiction Relating to My Life*). Beckett took forty pages of notes on this work, outdone in the 'German Notes' only by his notes on *Faust* (Nixon, *German Diaries* 68). What he would have remembered from *Dichtung* is Gœthe's early artistic resolution, and the guidelines for self-writing:

> Und so begann diejenige Richtung[,] von der ich mein ganzes Leben über nicht abweichen konnte, nämlich dasjenige was mich erfreute oder quälte, oder sonst beschäftigte, in ein Bild, ein Gedicht zu verwandeln und darüber mit mir selbst abzuschliessen, um sowohl meine Begriffe von den äussern Dingen zu berichtigen, als mich im Innern desshalb zu beruhigen.
>
> (And thus began that tendency from which I could not deviate my whole life through; namely, the tendency to turn into an image, into a poem, everything that delighted or troubled me, or otherwise occupied me, and to come to some certain understanding with myself upon it, that I might both rectify my conceptions of external things, and set my mind at rest about them.) (Nixon, *German Diaries* 68; TCD MS 10971/1, 54v–55r; *Dichtung* 311–12; *Autobiography* 1.240)

In his famous letter to Axel Kaun, Beckett cites approvingly Gœthe's 'Lieber NICHTS zu schreiben, als nicht zu schreiben' (*LSB* 1, 513; 'better to write NOTHING than not to write' 517). He followed Gœthe into a self-exploratory mode of writing out of the everyday, while rejecting his model of the quintessential *Bildungsroman*, *Wilhelm Meisters Lehrjahre* (*Wilhelm Meister's Apprenticeship*). For the narrator/narrated of *How It Is* turning life into art necessitates a parallel divestiture of his *ancient voices*, the unwinding of the *Bildung* until he refuses to speak within its voice, merely quoting it within his novel syntax: 'my life last state last version' (3 passim).

### 'words my truant guides'

The narrator/narrated's self-image as a scattered archive of deceptive voices invites and complicates genetic approaches to *How It Is*. Dirk Van Hulle opens his discussion of 'Samuel Beckett's *Faust*

Notes' by laying bare the genetic critic's anxiety: 'The danger is in backshadowing. Since it is often enticing to retrospectively read too much of an author's later poetics into his early reading notes, the case at issue is a diabolical temptation' (283). Van Hulle's conclusions with respect to Beckett's 'literary Mephistopheles' (291) explore the paradigm of Beckett's 'poetics of ignorance' (291), whereby purging oneself of learning is a means for producing art: 'Beckett's paradoxical way of going on was by writing towards the ineffable while trying to find an end to this effing' (293). In *Beckett's Dantes* and 'The Promise of Dante in Beckett's Manuscripts' Caselli sustains a poignant critique of the failure to question the epistemology of the archive and its ability to 'explain' literary phenomena; she identifies its insufficiencies and the hermeneutic problems that arise if one takes Beckett's early notes on Dante at face value, rather than interrogating the contexts of their production. To whatever degree *Comment c'est* was conceived with the purpose of unwinding the narrative of personal quest within Dante's *Commedia*, at its inception the creative process appears to have been contingent upon the associative power of words, a troubled witnessing-reciting, and the lack of memory and forgetting, which the text takes for its central subject.

Beckett's return to Dante's *Inferno* and its precipitation of allusions in the *Comment c'est* manuscript shows why any description of his poetics of ignorance/residua/unknowing should not assume a stable edifice able to be systematically, or poetically, dismantled. Rather, his return to sources reflects an active grappling with his own fallible archive and his desire to return to foreign bodies – Italian, French, German . . . – to dispense with them anew. For this purpose, a poetics of translation is a powerful tool: it allowed him at once to appropriate, subvert and transform a voice which might have overpowered his own, and to which he might have otherwise deferred through conventional practices of translation/representation. The example of Dante is *Comment c'est* and *How It Is* is emblematic of this artistic practice.

As his letters indicate, Beckett returned to Dante for relief or inspiration at an extremely difficult moment during the composition of *Comment c'est*. Rereading the *Inferno* sparked his imagination and offered him a rich tapestry of images not only to visualise a fictional world, but also to problematise his use of mystical and Quietist tropes as emblems of the search for an original voice, a productive dialectical opposition to dramatise a positivist and rational striving. While the scenes of desert mysticism from the early drafts of *Comment c'est* assume a Quietist retreat, their concerns and earliest justifications never subside. Motion towards the *Inferno*'s mud and terror are regularly countered by alternative images of isolation, of waiting; an individual communion with Pim by the hope of 'the other above in the light'.

Beckett's translation of Dante into *Comment c'est*, and of *Comment c'est* into *How It Is*, demonstrates the futility of pinning his allusive discourse to a single source: given that his transposition of Dante's Italian involved indirect translation into (and out of) other French and English 'sources', such as his experience of religion or his reading of Pascal or Diderot, it becomes impossible to define the 'real subject' of his allusion. The baroque layering of images in *How It Is* obscures any singular 'origin' of the text's allusiveness, and their sparse expression in a 'syntax of extreme weakness'[20] further magnifies their resonance; the danger of neat identification is dispersed.[21] Despite the feeling of linguistic precariousness and imperilled representation that pervades *How It Is*, the text affirms the need for an artistic resistance to inculcated pedantry: 'words my truant guides with you strange journeys' (121). The following chapters define the reshaping of this philosophical dialectic, and attest to Beckett's consummate skill in manipulating the plasticity of words and ideas, of his artist's intuition of synthetic connections and his truant's dissenting from their schooled representation. Indeed, his so-called poetics of ignorance or unknowing always involved feigning an attitude or posture, while the appellation of 'poetics of indifference' misdiagnoses an ethical commitment to *go on*, underplaying Beckett's deep investment in the outcome of this action. Taking leave of his education – but carrying it with him beyond the jurisdiction of its pedagogy – Beckett relies on no Virgil or Dante to guide his poetics, but rather trusts in the signifying plasticity of his words, his *truant guides*. But the truant is indeed the idle one, like Belacqua, who steps outside pedagogy's tropism and its apparatus for enforming students according to its predetermined path. Etymologically linked to the sturdy beggar, vagabond, idle rogue or knave, the *truant* absents himself from the teleology and discipline of a reasoned pedagogy delivered from on high. Nor does he bow to the coercive praxes of devote religiosity. His presence can be felt in *How It Is* slipping in between *ancient voice* and 'I', when this impudent *poet-in-text* orchestrates unexpected ironies and felicitous 'ill-hearing'.

## Notes

1. See Verhulst's ('Howls') dating.
2. The first extant manuscript version is known as 'ms/a' and is followed by what Magessa O'Reilly, following various catalogue references, terms, '55/1', 'ms/b', '55/2', 'ms/c', '55/3', 'ms/d', '55/4', until 'ms' ('the manuscript proper' xvii).
3. This is consistent with Beckett's comments to Bray on 25 May 1959: 'Finish version 1 of Part I today or tomorrow and wonder what Pim is going to say now stimulated by tin-opener' (TCD MS 10948). Two days later, on 27 May, Beckett confirms: 'I have laid aside Part I and wrote first paragraph of Part II this morning. Part I is less than alright' (*LSB* 3, 232).
4. The 'moïse' is an old-fashioned word for a wicker basket lined with fabric and used as a basinet. This image recalls Murphy strapped to his rocking chair or the woman in *Rockaby*, in her rocking chair, and other permutations of this image. Ackerley in *Obscure Locks* (#131.4) annotates the image of Galileo's cradle in *Watt* with reference to Geulincx's philosophy; and Uhlmann gives further images of the mother rocking the cradle, which for Geulincx illustrates the fundamental axiom of God's unique causality. 'The baby cries because it wants the cradle in which it lies to be rocked. And the cradle is rocked, but not by the baby; rather, it is rocked by the hand of the mother or the nurse, who in turn rocks the cradle because she thinks the baby wants the cradle to be rocked. To the baby it might seem that there is a direct relation between the desire and the action, but the action is in fact brought about by another. Geulincx likens this to our situation in relation to God. We want something and God might bring it about, not because we want it but because God wants it' (Ulhmann, *Philosophical* 80).
5. I explore these Freudian dimensions in 'Psychoanalytic refuse in Beckett's *Comment c'est*/*How It Is*', linking specific textual details, such as anal obsession, masochism, neurotic fantasies and the holding back of stools, to Beckett's studies of Freudian psychology, as recorded in his notes held in the Trinity College Dublin Library (MS 10971/7–8).
6. When Moses had climbed Pisgah (Mount Nebo) God said to him, 'This is the land which I sware unto Abraham, unto Isaac, and unto Jacob, saying, I will give it unto thy seed: I have caused thee to see it with thine eyes, but thou shalt not go over thither' (*Deuteronomy* 34:4).
7. Note the coincidence between the prayer's title and Pascal's 'Mémorial'; the common motif of 'miracles' associated with both texts (divine inspiration for Pascal and, for Bernard, the Virgin's intervention which cured him of a life-threatening illness); and

the way that both men practised an ascetic devotion, mistrusted human philosophy and subordinated reasoned theology to faith. When Charles Juliet mentioned St Bernard in a discussion with Beckett in 1975, Beckett laughed and said that he had a grievance with the saint (Juliet, *Conversations* 38–9). Mary Bryden suggests that this is probably Berhard's association with the Second Crusade (*Beckett*, 190).

8. Paolo and Francesca were witnessed by Giovanni who subsequently murdered them. Beckett's point is that Dante should not be loved as the human Dante of Papini's book, but rather that he should be read.

9. Oxenhandler ('Seeing' 222) holds that the banner alludes to the Easter banner of *Inferno* 34, noting the affinity between Beckett's French 'vexille' and Dante's 'vexilla'. Caselli (*Beckett's* 161) suggests that both banners enter *How It Is* to mix with Beckett's translation of 'Ni traverser l'orgueil des drapeaux des flammes' from Rimbaud's *Le Bateau ivre*: 'Nor breast the arrogant oriflammes and banners'.

10. Mazzoni's Dante scholarship gives a clear account of this space (*Saggio* 355–67) and Silverstein discusses the existence of this vestibule in the *Visio Pauli*. Paul's apocryphal vision contains a river of fire separating sinners from 'those who were neither hot nor cold' (Revelations 3.15–16).

11. There has been some controversy in Dante scholarship about this figure, yet Beckett's 'Dante Notebook' identifies 'Celestine V' (TCD MS 10966/3) in its references to *Inferno* 3.

12. I am not saying that he makes no effort to reconnect. What matters is that he does not succeed. His painting is, if you will, the impossibility of reconnecting. There is, if you like, refusal and refusal to accept refusal. That perhaps is what makes this painting possible. For my part, it is the *gran rifiuto* which interests me, not the heroic wrigglings to which we owe this splendid thing. It is awful to have to say so. What interests me is what lies beyond the outside-inside where he does his striving, not the scale of the striving itself (*LSB* 2, 140).

13. Beckett uses this term within a philosophical vocabulary as the immediate grasping of the object, without need of proof or deduction. Uhlmann considers the possible influence of Bergson on Beckett's concept of intuition (*Philosophical* 21–3, 114–18).

14. Beckett offered a metaphor for bilingualism in the radio play *Rough for Radio II*, a work contemporaneous with *Comment c'est*, through Fox, an allegorical figure of the emerging artistic voice (*vox*). During his torture, Fox reveals that he is haunted by an unborn sibling inside him: 'my brother inside me, my old twin' (*CDW* 279).

15. The narrator of *Texts for Nothing* '11' issues his 'prayer got by rote' from the 'caput mortuum [skull/residue] of a studious youth' (*Complete Short* 145); this allusion to *Inferno* XX is directly implicated, like all the Dantean allusions in *How It Is*, to the text's self-conscious Freudianism.

16. In his annotations to *Texts for Nothing* (#6.29), Ackerley retraces Beckett's earlier uses of Christ's 'little finger' from John 8:6 one of the most memorable being when the narrator of 'First Love' traces the letters of his companion 'Lulu' (after the fallen woman of Berg's opera), into an old cow-pat.

17. Beckett wrote to Barbara Bray on 17 October 1959 and mentioned that he was reading Donne, but gives no precise details (*LSB* 3, 247).

18. In *L'Effet sophistique* (470–3) Barbara Cassin offers the illuminating account of how the Greek *Logos* became the depository of the *paideia*, explaining how in Hellenic schools, culture presented itself under the form of *mimêsis rhêtorikê* and 'literary cultivation' was the imitation of the creativity of great authors, of their culture, no longer nature itself.

19. Beckett alludes to *Émile* to Tom MacGreevy in a letter of September 1934, in which he also refers to Rousseau's *Rêveries*.

20. Beckett wrote to Barbara Bray on 11 March 1959, early in the genesis of *Comment c'est*: 'I'm struggling with the new moan, trying to find the rhythm and syntax of extreme weakness, penury perhaps I should say. Sometimes I think I'm getting on, then realise how far I am from it still. This is the fifth or sixth version of the opening' (*LSB* 3, 211).

21. Beckett warned against the 'neatness of identifications' is early 1929 essay, 'Dante . . . Bruno. Vico . . . Joyce': 'Must we wring the neck of a certain system in order to stuff it into a contemporary pigeon-hole, or modify the dimensions of that pigeon-hole for the satisfaction of the analogymongers? Literary criticism is not book-keeping' (*Disjecta* 19).

2

# Pythagorean Mysticism/Democritean Wisdom

This chapter explores how education is thematised within the fragmented philosophical dialogue of *How It Is*. The inherent contradictions of Western thought between pre-Socratic and Platonic philosophy have an inestimable effect upon Beckett's narrator/narrated, shaping his sense of his cosmos and the horizon of his poetics. Beckett's pre-Socratic and Platonic images pays less respect to the strict doctrines of ancient philosophy than to his poet's *élan*. They emerge from the grand narrative of the history of philosophy and constellate within the narrator/narrated's discourse in an eccentric representation of dialectic oppositions. They settle into patterns with pretensions to philosophical dialogue; shaped into thesis and counter-thesis they testify to the slow death of a mind trained in the discursive habits of the *paideia*. Philosophical images are integral to the text's form and field of interdependent meaning, the fabric of narrative itself. Yet the bizarre, often contradictory nature of the pattern in which they are found renders their potential for philosophical truth somewhat ludicrous. Beckett's use of ancient philosophy in *How It Is* complicates conventional intertextual hermeneutics by depriving his allusions of the power to affirm past meanings and their traditions, a strategy that defines him as a late modernist.

Beckett's extensive 'Philosophy Notes' are housed in the archives of the Trinity College Dublin Library. Those devoted to the Ancient Greek period were drawn largely from Archibald Alexander's 1907 *A Short History of Philosophy*, John Burnet's 1914 *Greek Philosophy* and the 1902 English translation of Wilhelm Windelband's *A History of Philosophy* (Frost and Maxwell, 'Catalogue' 67–73), an original German edition of which remained in Beckett's library at the end of his life.[1] Windelband was also Beckett's principal source for his 'Philosophy Notes' on texts written after the ancient period. Feldman shows how the Notes emerge, albeit fleetingly, in Beckett's 1964 prose piece 'All Strange Away', whose narrator abruptly recalls that 'ancient philosophers ejaculated with place of origin when possible suggesting pursuit of knowledge at some period' (Beckett, *Complete Short* 175; Feldman, *Beckett's* 33). Here, Beckett fictionalises his writing process by making his narrator evoke an erstwhile 'pursuit of knowledge', an apparent allusion to a map he drew in his 'Philosophy Notes' that located ancient philosophers within the Mediterranean (Frost and Maxwell, 'Catalogue' 76). 'All Strange Away' was published in the same year as *How It Is*, and the quotation represents more than just a memory of an earlier desire to acquire an encyclopaedic, Joycean erudition: when Beckett wrote *How It Is* he was still engaging with the philosophical doctrines, or, rather, with his memory of engaging with those doctrines.

Beckett constructs in *How It Is* an ingenious dialectic between pre-Socratic (particularly Democritean) and Platonic (including neo-Pythagorean) ideas. Archives and intertextuality, memories and the status of their contents in recitation/repetition, are explicit concerns. Indeed, the text purports to be both a recitation and a 'quotation' (193) channelled through the narrative dyad of the narrator/narrated. The *ancient voice* speaks in the first person present tense to an 'I' who attempts a verbatim recitation of that voice (Kenner, *Reader's* 94). This *ancient voice* opens an archive in 'pursuit of knowledge', of what is referred to as 'the humanities I had' (35). Yet the 'I' speaking in the present hears only 'bits and scraps' (5 *et alibi*) of his past-I, and the voice is 'ill-said ill-heard ill-captured ill-murmured in the mud' (3). The archive is thus scattered into fragments, which challenges intertextual reading to a far greater extent than in the prose of Beckett's earlier, less experimental writing.

This chapter reconstitutes some of this contextual information to reveal an archive of the *ancient voice*. Its genetic strategy does not 'explain' episodes and images through the discovery of allusive discourse, because Beckett had moved beyond his earlier more conventional practice of drawing upon a source principally to enrich his own text. In *Comment c'est*, the meaning of a reference is more often its functional value as, for instance, a metonym of objects in the memory, the residue of past learning, or the past learning-self. This does not entirely neutralise the content of the allusion, as Beckett exploits the conjunction between the residua of an allusion and its present function. His 'I' seems often 'ignorant' of the ancient doctrines he divulges, and the archive to which he has access is always deficient, like Dante's unfurling scroll with its partially illegible script or the manuscript of *Watt* riven with hiatuses, to which the published text gestures.

Beckett did not read philosophy formally before his intense private study in 1932. Although he had made notes on Descartes at the École Normale in 1925–6, his diligent note-taking from Windelband's *A History of Philosophy* impressed on him a sense of the history of philosophy as a grand narrative of the progress of reason. Windelband's enthusiasm for the virtues of a Greek education (*paideia*) and the assimilation of Aristotelian ethics into Christianity exemplifies the teleological current of intellectual and artistic history against which Beckett stands. In his concluding remarks Windelband, a prominent nineteenth-century Kantian, rails against relativism and Nietzsche, while relentlessly defending philosophy against the dilution of its eternal truths and the encroachment of other disciplines: 'Philosophy can live only as the science of values which are universally valid [. . .] *the organising principle for all the functions of culture and civilisation and for all the particular values of life.*' It must not shy away from the '*giving of laws* – not laws of arbitrary caprice which it dictates, but rather laws of *reason*, which it discovers and comprehends [. . .] to win back the important conquests of the great period of German philosophy' (680–1, my emphases).

In *How It Is* the philosophical 'formulations' of Beckett's 'I' are sabotaged not by relativism but by a Nietzschean laughter unbeholden to the strictures and aspirations of the *ratio*. Like Nietzsche, who was trained in theories of atomism, Beckett's exposure to pre-Socratic thought (filtered through Windelband) shapes his sense of possible alternatives to both Platonic idealism and Aristotelian teleology. His anti-Platonic saboteur is the *poet-in-text*, described in my previous chapter as passing through the manifold layers of the narrator/narrated's *ancient voice* and the 'I'. Excluded from the Republic, *paideia* and regenerative dialectics, he orchestrates 'ill-hearing' into a parody of ratiocination, a process best charted by examining the discourse between the 'Philosophy Notes' and the present 'I', whom Beckett frees from the institutional constraints of the discipline of philosophy, allowing him to edit, cut, and hear anew tradition's *ancient voice*. This 'I' makes creative, formal decisions that shape or arrange the past discourse and its inherited dialectics into a novel poetics. The fragmenting and undermining of those dialectics exemplifies Beckett's late modernist aesthetic strategy. Although he undermines the modernist 'mythic method', the philosophical tradition is not 'neutralized' within the narrative discourse, as might be expected in a post-modern text, but neither is the status of the metanarrative affirmed. Indeed, Beckett's use of ancient philosophy in *How It Is* offers an exemplary demonstration of a crucial 'limit' of modernist aesthetics.

## Thesis: Pythagorean Mysticism in the Platonic Cosmos

The very nature of philosophical method, indeed of reason itself, is at stake in *How It Is*, as Beckett's 'I' struggles to find a satisfactory 'solution' (189; 3.296) that will allow him to mount the cosmological ladder towards 'the other above in the light'. This figure, which he calls the *ancient voice*, often appears to be an estranged self, a voice which speaks to him of his own life. His goal is to become one with his past-I and, by performing its perfect repetition, lift himself out of his muddy/textual morass. The metafictive elements of this situation are not hidden, for the 'I' often alludes to the writing and reciting of his narrative. The scene is thus set for the cosmological comedy that unfolds during a mock-existential journey when the nameless 'I' crawls through an underworld of mud in what appears to be a purgatorial afterlife: he must meet a being named Pim, torture him until he can speak and sing, and then discover the physical and theological 'order' of his mud-bound predicament. His 'solution', referred to as his 'formulation' or 'calculation', involves accounting for his universe with an elaborate, if confused, philosophical model. He takes pains to prove a logically incontrovertible ratio of 'sacks' (material/spiritual provisions) to 'souls' (individuals), thus echoing such rationalist cosmologies as Leibniz's *Monadology* and its 'exquisitely organized' (189) pre-established (dis)harmony. The scaffolding of seventeenth-century rationalism is obvious, yet the text looks back to the 'rationalism' within Pythagorean and Platonic philosophy. This is complicated by the way that one singular relationship, rather than a monadic *cogito*, dominates all interactions in the invented cosmos: the meeting of a sadistic master and a tortured student. Plato is pertinent here, for the master's punitive mode of questioning Pim is a dark inversion of Socratic method, the ethical dimensions of which I return to in Chapter 6. The narrative structure echoes this: the 'I' is in a situation analogous to that of the subjugated Pim, for rather than interpret the world and the *ancient voice*, he claims to 'quote' obediently the voice that speaks to him. Crucially, as I have noted, the French 'voix ancienne' evokes an old or former voice while the English appellation inflects its discourse with that of the 'ancients'; this transferral of voice and learning finds its allegory in principles of Pythagorean and Platonic education.

Beckett's notes from chapter 12 of Burnet's *Greek Philosophy* acknowledge that Pythagoreanism is deeply implicated in this corruption of Platonic pedagogy:

### PROGRAMME OF STUDIES

Based on principal (Pythagorean) that the function of education is the conversion of the soul from contemplation of Becoming to that of Being. Hence course to consist of 4 Pythagorean sciences (arithmetic, geometry, astronomy, harmonics). (TCD MS10967/89v; Burnet *Greek Philosophy* 223–8)

The 'I' of *How It Is* employs these four Pythagorean sciences as he ploughs through the mud, seeking evidence of a cosmos as rational as that of Plato's *Timæus*: 'Pythagorean mysticism plus idealism of Socrates' (TCD MS 10967/80r).

The 'I' calculates his path as a perpetual 'zigzag', advancing four yards, turning 90 degrees, advancing four yards, turning back 90 degrees. There is thus a hypothetical straight line, cut at 45 degrees, creating right-angled triangles at either side of the line, each with two sides of two yards and a base that is twice the square root of two. Their hypothetical hypotenuses form his 'old line of march' (59), but because this line is a consequence of surds or irrational numbers, Beckett undermines the proposition of the 'I' by insinuating that his trajectory is 'irrational', a literary corruption of mathematics rather than a geometric truth.[2] Nevertheless, from his *ancient voice* the 'I' receives intimations of meaning in the blind spots along his connected hypotenuses: 'between two vertices one yard and a half a little less dear figures golden age' (61). The 'little less' eventuates for the square root of two generates an infinitesimal, and its irrational 1.414241 . . . is less than a yard and a half. The 'golden age' of rational integers has passed, and more is at stake than simple calculation.

Although the surd undermines the Pythagorean equation of
the mathematical truths within the physical world, the narrator/
narrated affirms his own Pythagorean mysticism, indifferent to
the absurdity that his fractions cannot express.[3] Further, in perceiving triangles within the mud and aligning his path over them,
the 'I' evokes Plato's infamous idea, in the *Philebus*, that triangular forms inform the essential structure of all matter. Beckett's
'Philosophy Notes' echo from Windelband Plato's rationale in the
*Timæus* that our cosmos is the most perfect and the most beautiful since, formed in reason, all phenomena act towards reasonable ends. The Platonic universe *as a whole* moves according to
the organising principle of the World-Soul, unlike Democritus'
material universe, where matter circulates as a consequence of
its earlier being. However, Windelband stresses the momentary
dualism in Plato's doctrine when the world comes into being from
Not-being, when matter emerges out of form: 'Not-being is char-
acterized as infinite plasticity, which takes up all corporeal forms
into itself [. . .], and yet at the same time forms the ground for
the fact that the Ideas find no pure representation in it' (130). He
calls this a 'mechanical necessity' which cannot be understood
teleologically. Matter emerges out of Not-being into form:

> Divine activity according to ends and natural necessity are set over
> against each other as explaining principles. On the one hand for the
> perfect, and on the other hand for the imperfect in the world of phe-
> nomena. Ethical dualism passes over from metaphysics into physical
> theory. (130)

Windelband questions Plato's unusual theory that triangular
forms inhere in matter: 'These triangular surfaces, which were,
moreover, conceived of being indivisible, have a suspicious simi-
larity with the atomic forms of Democritus' (131). He likewise
dismisses Plato's reliance on Pythagorean number theory as a
'deplorable construction' (123) that he would rather pass over
but for its influence on the likes of Speusippus, Xenocrates,
Philippus and Archytas, not to mention the neo-Pythagoreans
and neo-Platonists, 'even to the threshold of modern philosophy'
(123). Unlike other historians of philosophy who typically stress
the opposing inheritances of Platonic idealism and Aristotelian
materialism, Windelband emphasises the influence of Democritus
on Plato and hence (2,000 years later) the Enlightenment.

Beckett's triangles in the mud usher in Windelband's 'mechanical necessity' by generating a point of dialectical contention with the narrator/narrated's assertions of the Democritean atomism of his world. This is both typical of Beckett's use of philosophical contradiction (in *Murphy* he exploits Descartes' uncomfortable reliance upon the 'conarium' or pineal gland) and characteristic of what Anthony Uhlmann describes as his use of the 'occluded' philosophical image, an allusion that points not to a referent but to an aporia or irresolution in the philosophical discourse, thereby complicating the process of representation between text and source (*Philosophical* 68–9). The narrator/narrated's zigzag forms a 'series of sawteeth or chevrons' (59), which for the reader of *Comment c'est* generates the image of French *guillemets* – « » – the journey through the mud on hands and knees cutting a path of open-ended quotations. These reflect the piecemeal survival of an archive of *ancient voice* in the memory of the 'I', but also the pre-Socratic texts themselves: surviving voices assembled into incomplete collections of textual fragments and second-hand testimony, often with unquantifiable influences (such as the debated presence of Democritus in Plato's thought).

Beckett's doodling on the grid or quadrille pages of the six notebooks of the first complete manuscript of *Comment c'est* highlights how the material conditions of his writing became inseparable from the narrative content. More than twenty times in the first five notebooks Beckett traced over the grid squares of his notebook pages triangles or sequences of triangles forming paths or trajectories. For instance, early in Notebook II (page 3 verso, bottom left), the zigzag connecting the hypotenuses of connecting triangles is merely suggested by a doodle, with this nascent imperfect trope (verso, two-thirds down the page) but one among numerous forms. Thirty-seven verso pages later the precise zigzagging triangulator materialises in both the narrative (recto) and in its accompanying doodle/sketch and geometric equation.[4] Given that in the earlier versions the narrator claims more explicitly than in the published edition to be an author composing a narrative, the scattering of these triangles throughout the manuscript must reinforce the link between the effort to produce the script on the facing recto, where slanting letters cut their path through lines of grid paper, and the churning, zigzagging of the novel's 'I' through the mud. The writing and editing process mirrors, furthermore, the journey of the 'I' recursing his past mud as he revisits his

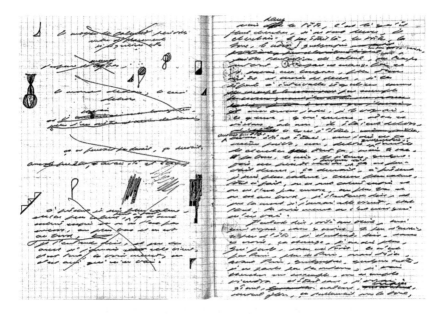

Figure 1 Samuel Beckett, *Comment c'est*, Notebook II (MS HRC SB/1/ 10/2/3v–4r), Harry Ransom Center, The University of Texas at Austin

Figure 2 Samuel Beckett, *Comment c'est*, Notebook II (MS HRC SB/I/ 10/2/40v–41r), Harry Ransom Center, The University of Texas at Austin

formation in philosophical discourse, a zigzag which generates eye
movements not unlike the scanning of pages, as if he were poring
over a patchy archive of past learning, voices and experience, parts
of which, perhaps the 'Philosophy Notes', may have played a less
distant role in the actual writing of *Comment c'est*.

In the cosmological calculation that dominates Part 3, the
straight line that the 'I' plots by connecting the hypotenuses of his
triangles subtends the great circle of interacting beings in a subterranean realm, something that had previously occupied him, and
itself indicative of the incommensurability between the linear and
circular modes:

> whether four then revolving or a million four strangers a million
> strangers to themselves to one another but here I quote on we do not
> revolve
>
> that is above in the light where their space is measured here the
> straight line eastward strange and death in the west as a rule. (159)

With this pomander of ideas the narrator/narrated rejects his
hypothesis of circling bodies to affirm a metaphysical principle
recovered from the Platonic philosophy of movement recorded in
the 'Philosophy Notes'. In the margin of the following entry, Beckett
wrote '<u>God</u> proof of':

> Motion of heavenly bodies must be caused by good souls or soul indeed
> by the best, since they are the most circular by all measures. That is
> due to their circular character, which must have been given them by a
> good soul, since things, if left to themselves, do not move in a circle,
> but in a straight line. (Divine Gravity!) (TCD MS 10967/96v–97r;
> Burnet, *Greek Philosophy* 335)

In spite of his best Pythagoreanism, the 'I' moves without the measure apportioned 'above in the light' in the realm of the circle.
Beckett's exclamation '(Divine Gravity!)' is a sardonic jab at the
deity, which invokes the predicament of being. It draws on Burnet's
footnote, that Aristotle tied circular motion to the heavens while
Plato saw that it must have a cause, which we call gravity: 'Plato
knew there was a problem here; Aristotle denied that there was
any' (fn. 1, 355). Beckett's comment may also intimate knowledge of the geometry of hyperbolic space pioneered by Riemann
and Gauss and developed by Einstein: the critique of Euclidean
geometry, whereby the theory of general relativity proved that

gravitational force bends lines in space-time so that, as Einstein showed, under gravitational force the interior angles of a triangle do not add up to 180 degrees. In any case, estranged from the good souls of the revolving heavens, the 'I' is forced instead to calculate his advance by his neo-Euclidean, Platonic-Pythagorean triangles. Beckett's father was a surveyor, and the young Sam doubtless understood the triangulation of distance mapped over the ground, and he would have known that the earth's curvature gives traditional Euclidean figures an ideal rather than a pragmatic validity. But even if the 'I' is following the contour of the planet, all the while divulging the spatio-temporal relations and coordinates that preside above, his experiential sense is that he is, wormlike, charting his own linear course through the mud.

Finding himself in the unformed chaos of mud, the 'I' imputes an ethical purpose to his own form, inscribing it within a teleological hierarchy that gives his life purpose. Like Plato in the *Timæus*, he introduces 'mechanical necessity' into his cosmology, calculating his advance in dyads: 'clung on to the species we're talking of the species the human saying to myself [. . .] two and two twice two and so on' (59; 1.274). Plato's *eidos* or soul-as-Form is translated as Species (a word adapted by Aristotle), and the process of perfecting of the individual soul (the Species) brings it closer to the One. The narrator/narrated discerns the universal from two or more particulars, and eventually laments his 'loss of species' (31). Noting this Platonic dimension, Ackerley describes it as 'his loss of what makes one One with others; hence the unnamed narrator's tragic conclusion (a final Nominalist irony) that he is "sole elect"' ('Science' 152). Now, clinging to his species, the 'I' aligns himself with the imperceptible ideal triangles inhering in matter. His zigzag charts a straight line while he hangs on desperately to his Form, the Platonic *eidos*: 'the eternal straight line effect of the pious wish not to die before my time in the dark the mud' (59; 1.272). Schooled in Pythagorean mysticism, he attempts now to stave off submersion in the chaos of Platonic non-Being by advancing along a course unambiguously divulged in the manuscript 'ms' of *Comment c'est* (but erased from the final version) as 'la vieille ligne de marche une série <un nombre impressionnant> des triangles isocè [sic] isocèles' (392; the old path a series <an impressive number> of isos isosceles triangles).

The 'Philosophy Notes' attest to Pythagorean principles of harmony, universal order and the music of the spheres as supported by the discovery of the mathematical ratios of the musical octave

(TCD MS 10967/20v). The analogue with the visual arts returns in Beckett's 'Three Dialogues', when 'B' advocates the painting of Van Velde, differentiating it from the 'spiritual Kandinsky' and Mondrian ('no painting is more replete') (144–5; cf. his letter to Georges Duthuit, 9 March 1949, *LSB* 2 134–43). In *Concerning the Spiritual in Art* Kandinsky argues that the artist inhabits the tip of an upward-moving triangle, whereas Mondrian's neo-Plasticism emerges from the neo-Platonic revival and geometric mysticism of the De Stijl movement. In B's dialogue both are aligned with 'a kind of tropism towards the light [. . .] a kind of Pythagorean terror, as though the irrationality of *Pi* were an offence against the deity, not to mention his creature' (*Disjecta* 125). The narrator/narrated of *How It Is* has bouts of Pythagorean/Platonic zealotry: all fictive names in his underworld end in m; thus Pim's singularity is *Pi*. As a surd, the irrational *Pi* cannot be expressed as a fraction of two rational numbers, and *Pi*-m's emergence out of unformed chaos is an affront to the Pythagoreanism of the 'I', provoking his violent effort to inscribe Pim within the *Logos*. Commenting on the irrational in Beckett's work, David Hesla observes that Latin translations of Euclid used the term *surdus* (deaf) for *alogos*, an irrational or 'deaf' root (*Shape* 7). Pim is deaf, and his ab*surd*ity must be hammered into order until his 'song ascends in the present' (81). In the ear of the narrator/narrated, Pim's song is stripped of the pure absurdity of its primary being, for Pim has been coerced into a 'tropism' towards the mysterious 'deity' of the 'I', his 'other above in the light'.

The narrator/narrated claims that the differing size of his buttocks conforms to an unusual ratio 'one buttock twice too big the other twice too small', whereas 'Pim's though undersized were iso' (45). This satirises Pythagorean-Platonism harmony:

> health was '<u>isonomy</u>' of opposites in the body, disease undue predominance of one or other.
>
> Health was 'attunement' (Apmonia) and blend (temperament). (TCD MS 10967/21r; Burnet, *Greek Philosophy* 50; see Ackerley, *Demented* #3.8)

Like Watt's discordant piano, Pim's body needs 'attunement', for the Pythagoreans 'held the body to be strung like an instrument to a certain pitch' (TCD MS 10967/21r). But music offers no encouragement to the rationalist obsessive: when Watt hears the mixed choir on his way to Mr. Knott's house, the subject of its song is the number produced by division of a leap-year year into weeks – though an error (probably intentional) creeps in when 51 is used for the weeks of the regular year (Ackerley, *Obscure Locks* #70.3). To Heath Lees, Mr Knott's piano demonstrates the 'Pythagorean comma', a gap in Western music between acoustic reality and the musical octave ('*Watt*' 14). Pythagorean ratios are not exact, and harmonics arise in the tuning: 'In Wattian terms, Art is Con; tuner, piano and pianist are all doomed' ('*Watt*' 15). In like manner, the rejection of Pythagorean geometry in *How It Is* at the beginning of Part 2 (with Pim) – 'no more figures' (62) – acknowledges the irrational numbers that added together form the line at the end of Part 1: 'all measures vague yes vague impressions of length length of space length of time vague impressions of brevity between the two and hence no more reckoning save possibly algebraic yes I hear yes then no' (63).[5] The final 'no' intimates the doubtful abandonment of a Pythagorean geometry for algebra.

The narrator/narrated apparently *needs* to express his universe with Pythagorean consistency to feel confident that it will supply him with a mathematical 'solution' to his material and spiritual questions (one or 'not alone', the balance of sacks and souls). In Part 3, a third option of the infinite line is declared 'possible' (161), though within its infinitude are 'two kinds of solitude two kinds of company [. . .] being regulated thus are of equal duration' (163); and the now familiar machinery of calculation begins again. The measure of 'stages' is introduced (with its theatrical echo): 'one stage per month this word these words months years I murmur them' (163); but the proceeding calculation and proof is not compelling, for he soon reverts to the familiar measures of 'yards' and 'hours'. Whether these terms hold the same value they once did is uncertain, but the universe retains its equation of theoretical bodies with numbers: 'last reasonings last figures number 777777 leaves number 777776 on his way unwitting towards number 777778 finds the sack without which he would not go far' (179). The 'figures' *prove* the nature of the encounters with Pim and Bom as the narrator/narrated attempts to harmonise his universe by reducing distance, time, hearing and recitation to a single recurring ratio (mathematic reason restoring his unity of mind, a philosophical rather than a poetic mimesis).

The prevailing 'movement' of the 'I' is his reiterated 'ten yards fifteen yards push pull'. This proportion orders the recitation of the 'one above in the light': 'when the panting stops ten seconds fifteen seconds [. . .] the breath we're talking of a breath token of life when it abates [. . .] then resumes a hundred and ten fifteen to the minute when it abates ten seconds fifteen seconds' (173). The *ancient voice* has from the outset a puzzling relationship to the 'I', who states, 'voice once without then quaqua on all sides then in me when the panting stops' (3); that is, when the voice is without there is only 'quaqua', caca, the material universe of shit/mud, and unknowing, like the French language's suite of 'qu' interrogatives. The narrator/narrated's 'I hear it my life' (3; 1.7) is literal: he receives his life as breath. Yet his breath will never enter into *Logos* or catch the breath of Christ, the Christian *Logos*, for it is fundamentally 'ill-heard ill-recaptured ill-murmured' and thus 'ill-said' (3). This divine voice of unity is said to be heard at a rate of 'a hundred and ten fifteen to the minute', closer to verbatim than its recitation, then filtered through the ratio that governs the narrator/narrated's movement: 'ten seconds fifteen seconds' (13); 'this voice ten words fifteen words long silence ten words fifteen words' (165). Between this 'silence', this listening, 'the mud gibbers ten seconds fifteen seconds of sun clouds earth sea patches of blue' (173). Words find their harmonious concert in physical movement through the mud, the hearing of the ancient voice, their recitation and the temporal measure of their annunciation. This hypothesis is possible only if the words are enfolded consistently into this ratio of performance; such discourse negates the intonation patterns of habitual speech rhythms. There is a 'Pythagorean gap', analogous to that of Mr Knott's piano, between the musical necessity of a consistently measured octave and the acoustic reality of its fine tuning.

If the narrated's words are repeated verbatim by the narrator, there is the unity of one divine *Logos*; if not, 'losses everywhere'. As a species of imperfect recitation, the 'I' differs from his narrated or supreme monad: 'so many words so many lost one every three two every five first the sound then the sense same ratio or else not one' (123). The 'ratio' 1:3, 2:5 initiates a series, asymptotic to 0.5 and $n/(2n+1)$, hence 3:7, 4:9, 5:11. His 'tampering' ratiocination further estranges his own listening to and discourse with the *ancient voice* by generating a progression by halves. This logic of Zeno's paradox of the heap undermines the attempt to prove that he is not alone but part of a 'procession' (161). The conditions may be represented as such: the totality of the procession (P) will be represented at its limit, say Z, yet $P_{z-1}$ is still a procession, and each coupling, say $P_{z-1}$ and $P_{z-2}$ (or Y and X), appears equally true in respect to Z. The sorites series is inscribed into a 'life above', a constant shuffling: 'A to B B to C [. . .] B to C C to D from hell to home hell to home to hell always at night Z to A divine forgetting' (101). Just as the order 'to hell to home' is stuttered and confused, in terms of the series that this logic suggests, home is hell: the sorites paradox is often represented as A=B B=C C=D therefore A=D, which manifests linguistically as vagueness; a 'heap' or a 'hell' is both A and D.[6] The circularity of Z to A is a linguistic, not a geometric limit, historically linked with the Euclidean geometry that Pythagoras inherited. Similarly, the narrator/narrated flirts with attributing his own ratio to the 'other above in the light', who is imagined 'bending over me noting down one word every three two words every five', even if this is 'impossible [. . .] folly [. . .] folly folly' (113). The balance of Part 2 is calculated: 'it still can end it must end it's preferable only a third to go two fifths then part three leaving only part three' (113; 2.217). That is (. . . 1:3, 2:5 . . .) can end only when artificial or generic divisions are imposed.

The sorites paradox is written *into* the mathematical 'harmony' of the universe and exemplified in the Pythagorean series of triangular numbers, $n(n+1)/2$:

> Universe a harmonious disposition of numbers, based on the perfect number 10 [. . .] [T]he sum of first four natural integers (1+2+3+4 = 10) [. . .] Extended indefinitely it takes the place of a formula for the sums of series of successive natural integers – 3,6,10,15,21, etc., which were therefore called "<u>triangular numbers</u>"'. (TCD MS 10967/16r, 10967/21v; cf. Ackerley, *Demented* 5.4)

An unwitting Hippasos, the narrator/narrated conceives his universe through a wilful blindness to the irrational, proceeding on a logic that subverts any possibility of progression. Like the clown unaware that his trousers have fallen to his ankles, he trips ahead with a burlesque measure. Yet Beckett does not promulgate a rationalist art; on the contrary, the strategy begins to resemble that of the artist described in his 1938 essay 'Les deux besoins' ('Two Needs'):

> Deux besoins, dont le produit fait l'art [. . .] la route réflète [sic] mieux que le miroir [. . .] Pythagore, divine figure dont la construction dépend d'un irrationnel [. . .] Côté et diagonale, les deux besoins, les deux

essences, l'être qui est besoin et la nécessité où il est de l'être, enfer d'irraison d'où s'élève le cri à blanc, la série de questions pures, l'œuvre. (*Disjecta* 55–6; essay unpublished until 1983)

Two needs, whose product is art [. . .] the road reflects better than the mirror [. . .] Pythagoras, divine figure where the construction depends upon an irrational [. . .] Side and diagonal, the two needs, the two essences, the being which is need and the need for being, hell of irrationality raising the stuck cry exhausted, the series of pure questions, the *œuvre*.

The narrator/narrated's art straddles diagonal and side, his indifference to the irrational dimensions of his 'old line of march' (diagonal) existing alongside his need to commit to his reasonable zigzag (side). In the 'hell of irrationality' the mute 'I' attempts to surpass his own 'stuck cry' by making Pim sing. Yet Pim's art is born out of the perverted 'reason' into which it is inscribed, and these absurd travails are very funny. The dark irony is compounded when Democritean fragments resurface in the discourse, intimating the existence of a materialist reality that subverts the idealist tropism of the 'I' towards 'the other above in the light', and thereby conducting the axes of side and diagonal into a more perilous and conflicted end.

### Antithesis: Keeping it Real, Democritus (via Heraclitus)

Pythagoras son of Mnesarchus pursued inquiry further than all other men and, choosing what he liked from these compositions, made a wisdom of his own: much learning, artful knavery.

Pythagoras was the prince of imposters. (Heraclitus, fragments 25, 26; Kahn, *Art* 39, 41)

At the end of Part 1 the narrator/narrated's Pythagorean and Platonic speculations are momentarily checked when an image of his earlier identity ('one blessed day') is qualified, 'saving the grace of Heraclitus the Obscure' (41). This imperils a confident Pythagoreanism and the continuous identity between 'I' and *ancient voice*, for not only did Heraclitus reject Pythagoras' 'knavery' and consider him an 'imposter', but their cosmologies are mutually exclusive. Beckett's 'Philosophy Notes' cite Heraclitean ethereal fire, in which the world is periodically dissolved and recreated. The Deity is motion itself, Becoming, which produces no Being, just as the Being of Parmenides produces no Becoming. The law of order in Heraclitus' universe is the primacy of strife: 'The 'flux of things' is a ceaseless strife of opposites and this strife the father of all things . . . Becoming is unity of opposites' (TCD MS 10967/25r; W 50). The cosmological alternation of tormentors and victims in *How It Is* suggests a Heraclitean presence, anticipating Empedocles' universe of warring 'love and hate'. The mythical structure of Beckett's narrative evokes in the split between the voices 'above in the light' and 'quaqua' (in the mud) Anaxagoras' foundational myth of the mind-body dualism and hence the 'link between the physical and moral periods' in his doctrine of the *Nous*: 'Intelligence (Nous) acts as originating principle, formative principle, essentially different from homoiomeriae, self-moved, reason, superessential, a manner of cosmic Deus ex machina' (TCD MS 10967/35r).

In *How It Is* the 'strife of opposites' is imagined as the solution to the problem of singular identity: 'these two aspirations warring in each heart' (187), though Beckett recognised that for Heraclitus there was no fixed identity: 'For him it is not possible to step down twice into the same stream' (TCD MS 10967/24r). Like the undermining of a consistent ratio by the paradox of the sorites logic, the Heraclitean law impels the 'divine forgetting' or discontinuity of being. For Heraclitus, cosmic change unfurls within oppositional relations: 'This rhythm of events [. . .] is the only permanent, the destiny, the order, the <u>Logos</u> of the world' (TCD MS 10967/25v; W 36). His theory of fire as the breath of life is renewed in the constant becoming and fading of the 'I' of *How It Is*, but while the clockwork regularity of alternating opposites evokes his cosmos and *Logos*, the come and go of universal Becoming is retarded through the persistence of life in the 'I' below. The vertical ascent and descent of material transformation in the Heraclitean cosmos thus gives way to what was for Beckett a more compelling antithesis to Platonic cosmology: the atomism of Democritus.

Allusions to Democritean materialism permeate *How It Is*, though their specificity and concentration is greatest in Parts 1 and 2, with the ending of Part 2 echoing the tropes introduced in Part 1. Such figures include atomism, post-mortem consciousness, the world as infinite and recycled waste, and fire atoms as the primary indivisible substance of consciousness, perception and being. Democritean materialism traced human life to its beginning in sludge (mixed earth and water). Alice and Kenneth Hamilton

('Guffaw' 8) suggest this as the source in *How It Is* for 'slime' (19, 61, 103), the 'warmth of primeval mud' (9). Although Feldman finds no support for this theory because of its absence from the 'Philosophy Notes' (59–60), Beckett's exposure to the Democritean world can be traced to Robert Burton's 'Democritus Junior to the Reader', his introduction to *The Anatomy of Melancholy*, where Burton summarises Democritus' 'Paradox of the Earths motion, of infinite Worlds, *in infinito vacuo, ex fortuitâ atomorum collisione*, in an infinit[e] wast[e]' (*Anatomy* 1). The first entry from Burton's *Anatomy* in Beckett's *Dream Notebook* is a description of Democritus as a 'little wearish old man' (104), a phrase used in the poem 'Enueg I' and in *Krapp's Last Tape*.[7]

Beckett layers his images with such dense philosophical substrata that his burlesque take on the Dantean inferno is the comic mask of a philosophical satire:

> sleep sole good brief movements of the lower face no sound sole good come quench these two old coals that have nothing more to see and this old kiln destroyed by fire and in all this tenement

> all this tenement of naught from top to bottom from hair to toe and finger-nails what little sensation it still has of what it still is in all its parts and dream. (45)

As life wastes away from the 'old kiln', fire passes out of the body, which is transformed into a material shell. Beckett writes of Democritus: 'He uses "tabernacle" for body, which is also probably Pythagorean. Our bodies "booths" at the "fair" of human life' (TCD MS 10967/79v). Democritus' *skenos* has evidently been Christianised, though in *Comment c'est* Beckett used the French 'guenille' (44; 1.205), which recalls the abode of the soul, while the English 'tenement' suggests the decomposition of the body into the 'under-earth' (45). The 'tenement of naught' echoes Democritus' 'Naught is more real than nothing'.[8] An acceptance of the material reality of the void is complemented by the fact that for Democritus the world is 'composed of atoms that fill entirely the space they occupy, i.e. that are incapable of further compression' (TCD MS 10967/75r). When the body deteriorates, its atoms separate, retaining the material reality of their non-Being.

For Democritus, consciousness is enacted by fire atoms: 'Consciousness of self implies a certain minimal activity of fire-atoms' (TCD MS 10967/76r). When they occupy the tenement of the body (the 'old kiln'), fire atoms animate the coagulation of other atoms with mind, for they are the principal agents of perception:

Doctrine of Perception: We perceive through our high class fire-atoms. The emanations from things set in motion the fire-atoms of the soul of man. These emanations are the images (infinitely small copies) of the things whence they proceed and their effect on fire-atoms constitutes perception. (TCD MS 10967/75r)

The narrator/narrated imagines that his Democritean body once perceived sensations of the world above through its 'fire atoms': 'the eyes raised to the blue [. . .] the little clouds you could see the blue through the hot stones' (57). In *A Defence of Poetry* Shelley likens the 'mind in creation' to 'a fading coal' (*Shelley's* 504). Beckett's 'I' echoes this Romantic trope for the epiphantic nature of poetic inspiration: 'these sudden blazes in the head [. . .] like a handful of shavings aflame' (43). Joyce had exploited Shelley's conceit in *A Portrait of the Artist*, and the narrator/narrated expresses a late modernist despair when he claims that his 'hot stones' have already fizzled. They are 'two old coals that have nothing more to see' but there is nothing clichéd in the way Beckett fans the coals of atomism with his narrator/narrated's post-Romantic panting.

The body of 'I' is buried, and its consciousness is dissipating, suspended in its subterranean 'Erebus' (41) between life ('above in the light') and death (Hades). 'Erebus' is in *Comment c'est* a 'four' (40), the word that designated the 'old kiln': 'ce vieux four'. Beckett's French plays on the uncommon theatrical 'four' (a flop), while his English seeks a more specific reference. Erebus is the mythological son of Chaos, the name designating the place of darkness encountered immediately after death by souls on their way to Hades. Here, via Beckett's pun ('oven'), it becomes the 'old kiln'. Suspended before the ultimate resting place of the soul (Hades), the body as Erebus translates Democritus' blurring of the division between life and death. J. I. Warren ('Democritus' 193–206) reads this as following from Democritus' desire to avoid a concept of the soul incompatible with his atomism: fire atoms gradually disperse from the corpse; they are not extinguished at a finite moment with the soul passing to another realm. Democritus employed this distinction to avoid any notion of a transmigrating soul.

The 'I' in the mud of *How It Is* is similarly suspended as he continues to suffer in his 'old kiln'. He prays for release, for dreams to come and to pass into another state. The English 'old coals' long to be 'quenched', a more emphatic slaking than that called for by the French 'éteindre' (44; to put out). The denial of water and the invocation to sleep and dream suggests a Heraclitean impasse:

> Sleep and death are due to increase of moisture. 'It is death to souls to become water'. Waking and life are due to increase of warmth and fire: 'The dry soul is the wisest and the best'. As sleep alternates with waking and life with death, so fire is fed by exhalations of water and these are in turn produced by warmth of fire. (TCD MS 10967/26r)

Final sleep is denied; the dream of release is punished: 'inconceivable aah no sound in the rectum a redhot spike' (45). The punishment of life is mercilessly renewed with each return of the infernal 'little voice', the breath of *Logos* that fans images to the eyes: 'not the blue the others at the back [. . .] that's all is left breath in a head nothing left in it almost nothing only breath' (133).

The poker returns eight paragraphs later: 'fire in the rectum' (46–7). Manuscript drafts confirm the more explicit Democritean heritage when two paragraphs later in manuscript 'ms' the narrator/narrated utters, 'c'est un fou rire que j'ai dans le cul comme dans toutes mes parties d'ailleurs' (360; it's a mad laugh that I've got in my arse like in all my parts moreover). The laugh of Democritus pervades the *parties*, Beckett's French echoing *partir*, which he translated in accordance with the Aristotelian ethics of progress as 'goings on'. In *Happy Days* (written in 1961, the year Beckett finished *Comment c'est*), Winnie's 'old joke' is similarly obscure; when questioned about this by Alan Schneider, Beckett clarified its source: '"Old joke" not Winnie, rather the joke of being that is said to have caused Democritus to die of laughter. To be related also if you like to Nell's "nothing is funnier than unhappiness etc." Same idea in Watt (the 3 smiles)' (*No Author* 103). In *Watt*, Arsene decries the three laughs as the:

> successive excoriations of the understanding, and the passage from the one to the other is the passage from the lesser to the greater, from the lower to the higher, from the outer to the inner, from the gross to the fine, from the matter to the form. (46)

The three laughs intensify in anguish: the bitter 'laughs at that which is not good, it is the ethical laugh'; the hollow 'laughs at that which is not true, it is the intellectual laugh'; the mirthless laugh is the dianoetic laugh: 'It is the laugh of laughs, the *risus purus*, the laugh laughing at the laugh, the beholding, the saluting of the highest joke, in a word the laugh that laughs – silence please – at that which is unhappy' (47).

Ackerley shows how this 'reflects classical doctrines of the tripartite soul (rather than Murphy's description of his mind), rising from the mundane to the divine' (*Obscure Locks* #48.3; cf. Ackerley, *Demented* 110.5). He cites Brett's *History of Psychology* as an excellent exposition of the idea, without claiming that it was Beckett's source:

and as the soul is itself intermediary between Pure Forms and the Formless, so the process of development through which it goes is threefold: for there is first the process of moulding the material, irrational nature; then the intermediary stage in which concrete embodiments of law are studied; and finally the highest stage in which the laws of nature are made the subject of thought and the mind thinks over the last great law of all things, the Good in which they live and move and have their being. (Brett 1.93; Ackerley, *Obscure Locks* #48.3)[9]

Arsene's three laughs move from the irrational (ethical) to the intellectual (truth) to the dianoetic (thought and mind). This stratification weighs upon how the 'I' perceives his own situation: 'to that it all comes in the end a panting in the dark the mud not unlike certain laughs but not one' (167).

Beckett's identification, by way of Horace's designation of Democritus as the 'laughing philosopher' (TCD MS 10967/78r) and Heraclitus as the weeping philosopher, is therefore mapped over an Aristotelian 'becoming'. Text '12' of *Texts for Nothing* refers to 'the long silent guffaw of the knowing non-exister' (*Complete Short* 120), the *risus purus* that prefigures the narrator/narrated's fuller dianoetic self-image in *How It Is*: 'man continues standing laughing weeping and speaking his mind *nothing physical*' (31, my emphasis). This singular 'man' is a composition of his 'generations' in which both the past-I and Pim played a part, yet in their coupling the 'I' is endowed with the 'ever mute laugh' (39). In Part 1, it is not the 'I' who deals out the fire of torture/being but the *ancient voice*. While this voice is embroiled within the problematics and aspirations of the Pythagorean-Platonic ratio, it administers its Democritean antithesis within the rational dialogue of the history of philosophy. Democritus was anti-theistic, and his philosophical mode of exposition was challenged by Christian asceticism, mysticism and piety, all aspects of which are present in *How It Is*. The body that receives its life through the spirit of a cruel God is not foreign to Christian theology, and the *poet-in-text* entangles the 'I' in contradiction, denying this self/ character either transcendence or textual reconciliation with himself.

With its sadistic but knowing indifference, the Abderite's 'comic equivalent of apperception' (Ackerley, *Obscure Locks* #48.3) reanimates a foolish tormented being in the mud who must forage in a 'providential' sack: 'the head in the sack where saving your reverence I have all the suffering of all the ages' (47). A Eucharistic deliverance in the form of hermetically sealed tins of fish dropped from the heavens is sidelined: 'I don't give a curse for it' (47), for the lesson of the 'red-hot poker' two paragraphs earlier is fresh in the mind. The material world is permeated with its dianoetic *Logos*, and here its laughter is accompanied by a vision of its profane concert of matter and body, as the celestial tins are devilishly transformed into macaronic claws, and misused like the can-opener twisted into the pedagogue's ploughshare to express a comic af/flatus: 'howls of laughter in every cell the tins rattle like castanets and under me convulsed the mud goes guggle-guggle I fart and piss in the same breath' (47; cf. 167: 'to that it all comes in the end a panting in the dark the mud not unlike certain laughs but not one').

The 'tenement of naught' incites the comment that 'from top to bottom from hair to toe and finger-nails what little sensation it still has of what it still is in all its parts'. Beckett has in mind the observation of Democritus that hair and nails continue to grow after 'death', which led him to believe that consciousness dissipated gradually (Taylor, *Atomists* 107). Beckett further articulates the more contentious belief that Democritus' post-mortem body continues to perceive: 'what little sensation it still has of what it still is'. In the beginning of Part 2, the narrator/narrated pauses: 'quick my nails a word on them' (65); 'quick' meaning at once to enliven and to be alive, to be vigorous and burning, and the sensitive material out of which nails grow. Beckett deals the nails a sadistic twist: 'quick a supposition if this so-called mud were nothing more than all our shit' (65) – where 'supposition' introduces the quasi-philosophical reasoning at play. An apparent diversion into the anecdote of the 'eastern sage' (65) indicates instead a transformation of the factual material of life into art. Philosophical images are integrated once more into a poetics of invention when Gautama Buddha is no

longer the one who sits beneath his 'bo' (65), awaiting enlightenment and clenching his fists until just before his death, when his
nails come out the other side of his hands.[10] With his last breath
Gautama then said to himself 'that they'd grow on' (65). By the
end of *How It Is*, the 'monstrous nails' (133) of the 'I' point not
only to their occupation in Pim's flesh but also to the Democritean
circulation that outlives the flaring of imagination and memory:
'few old images always the same no more blue the blue is done
never was the sack the arms the body the mud the dark *living hair
and nails all that*' (135, my emphasis). The post-mortem growth
of hair and nails (a myth disproven by science) persists even in its
denial; these images are sensations in the mind of a corpse-like
narrator; when the eyes ('the blue') are eclipsed they 'go on', like
Gautama's nails and the *ancient voice* itself.

At the end of Part 2, the inexplicable persistence of the voice
invokes 'the nails that can go on the hand dead a fraction of an
inch life a little slow to leave them the hair the head dead' (111).
Life expires 'a fraction of an inch', as in a paradox of Zeno,
that life will never meet its end. As immortal fire atoms disperse
from the body they move further from each other, so loss of consciousness becomes a 'matter' of apperceptive degree.[11] Yet the
Heraclitean fire of the materialist universe punishes both transcendental fantasies of post-mortem existence and the celestial
hopes of the Christian heart, should the fire atoms return: 'ah
these sudden blazes in the head as empty and dark as the heart
can desire then suddenly like a handful of shavings aflame the
spectacle then' (43).

In one version of the opening of *Comment c'est* (UoR typescript 1655/1) the narrator/narrated reflects upon figures and voices
perceived suddenly from afar: 'il y avait quelque chose *et* soudain
*il n'y a rien, pas de peu à peu qui tienne*, c'est toute la différence
entre le mourant et le cadavre. *Oh ratio acervi ruentis!*' (250; there
was something and suddenly there's nothing, not stuck in the little by little, it makes all the difference between the dying and the
corpse. *Oh ratio acervi ruentis!*). This comment was first made
by a narrator, not 'I', a distinction erased in the text's evolution.
The heritage of that onetime narrator is felt in the *ancient voice*,
who laces the English of the 'I' with the logic of the sorites paradox as expressed by Horace in the 'Epistle to Augustus' – 'ratione
ruentis acervi' (2.1.47; 'after the fashion of the falling heap') – to
subvert the Pythagorean-Platonic thesis: 'that hypothesis such an

*acervation* of sacks [. . .] such an *acervation* of sacks at the very outset that all progress impossible' (179, my emphasis). Beckett used Horace's phrase in the 'Riverside Notebook', as reprinted in the *Theatrical Notebooks* to *Endgame*: 'C perplexed. All seemingly in order, yet a change. Fatal grain added to form impossible heap. *Ratio ruentis acervi.* Last straw' (195). The time taken for a poet to become 'ancient' is determined by the sorites logic, because 'ancient' is a term as vague as Zeno's 'heap'. The series subverts any reconciliation of object and subject, *ancient voice* and 'I', let alone 'I' and his habitual speech, memory and recitation, or 'I' and his *Logos* 'above in the light'. Beckett's use of Zeno's paradox of the heap has been noted, but its use in the early manuscript is remarkably novel, lending support to Democritus' materialist concern with the shift in perception and apperception between the dying and the dead.

Indeed, *le mourant et le cadavre* offers a typically Beckettian twist on the counsel to sinners in the 'Apostles' Creed' of *Acts* 10:42 or in the *Anglican Book of Prayer*, that Christ will 'come to judge the quick and the dead'. Its echo suggests another heap, in *Hamlet* when Laertes leaps into Ophelia's grave and declares, 'Now pile your dust upon the quick and the dead' (5.1.255). These tropes converge imaginatively with Beckett's subterranean sinner, observed from above but speaking from under his muddy heap, now focused on the *quick* of his nails: a metonym of a buried life that expires asymptotically: 'another little difference perhaps compared to what precedes but quick my nails a word on them they will have their part to play' (65).[12]

Towards the end of Part 1 Democritean ideas and Zeno's paradoxes frequently cohabit within a single image, undoing teleological and neo-Platonic delusions. One comic emblem inscribed into Dante's tripartite universe immediately precedes the 'old kiln' and a discourse that further estranges itself from the *Inferno*:

> seen from behind on my knees arse bare on the summit of a muckheap clad in a sack bottom burst to let the head through holding in my mouth the horizontal staff of a vast banner on which I read

> in thy clemency now and then let the great damned sleep here something illegible in the folds then dream perhaps of the good time their naughtiness procured them what time the demons may rest ten seconds fifteen seconds. (45)

Obscene and hilarious, the 'I' sees himself atop a sorites muckheap of perhaps his own excrement, dressed as a Christian penitent 'clad in a sack'. His burlesque prayer begins with its intercessional plea for atonement (renewed life above), or an end to suffering in one last long sleep. Yet the Heraclitean subject persists, for the narrator/narrated cannot read the message of his former tongue, and when sleep arrives as the 'sole good' the pun (soul/sole) offers no blessed release from this perpetual near-death experience. The prayer will fall onto the 'muckheap', the residuum of a life of received orthodoxies amounting to nothing, be they Christian, philosophical, scientific or literary. They will be ingested by another 'slime-worm' (145), thus allowing the narratives to per-petuate themselves. They are a material but not a spiritual reality; they do not advance the 'soul' towards a destination, for they are finally undifferentiated from the 'muckheap'.

The infinite suspension that marks the sorites paradox envel-ops subjectivity and transforms all matter into the same 'mud', circulating like Pantagruel's watery efflux: 'little heap in the stern it's me all those I see are me all ages the current carries me out the awaited ebb I am looking for an isle home at last drop never move again' (111). The 'I' longs to go on if only 'to finish to be finished' (113) and gathers himself to muster an end: 'stop your drivel draw the mud about your face' (113). Ironically, he here mimics Heraclitus' attempt to cure himself of dropsy by burying himself in dung. Heraclitus' earthly solution to his watery prob-lem failed to alleviate his ailment (he died of the cure), but the involuntary muttering of past voices in his consciousness brings about for the narrator/narrated an extraordinary temporal vision:

> all about pressed tight as a child you would have done it in the sandpits even you the mud above the temples and nothing more be seen but three grey hairs old wig rotting on a muckheap false skull foul with mould and rest you can say nothing when time ends you may end. (113)

The Heraclitean who covers himself in mud to *will* his degeneration within the cosmos is as futile as he who hopes for transcendence.[13] The realisation sprouts an image of 'three grey hairs', three sin-gular hairs, a 'wig', as in Zeno's logic of 'the Heap (which kernel of grain by being added makes the heap?) & the Baldhead (which hair falling out makes the head bald?)' (TCD MS 10967/42r). With rococo brush strokes this 'wig' is cast on top of a 'muckheap', the 'false skull' of the 'I', and in the English left to rot: 'foul with mould' the skull illustrates the Heraclitean transmission through water to earthly matter: 'When fire in man is quenched by damp, reason is lost' (TCD MS 10967/24r). But just as the 'old coals' earlier could not be 'quenched', one cannot escape the return of the *Logos* as fire, nor the internalised pedagogical voices of the past intruding upon the present.

The import of 'when time ends you may end' is stronger in the French version, with its plosive 'peut-être'. The constant factor in the image is neither Zeno's nor Heraclitus' critiques of motion, but the way that both undermine the Pythagorean ratiocination of the narrator/narrated. The evocation of an end to suffering leads into Plato's cave, the archetypal Western image of the flight from ignorance:

> E then good and deep sick of light quick now the end above last thing last sky that fly perhaps gliding on the pane the counterpane all summer before it or noonday glory of colours behind the pane in the mouth of the cave and the approaching veils. (113)

The fly aches to be born into the glorious colors of 'all summer before it'. Its life cycle, long understood to be regulated by the sun and light, is assimilated into a series of rebirths, which in turn alludes to Plato's adoption of the Pythagorean doctrine of the transmigration of the souls:

### Transmigration of Souls (Pythagoras).

> Souls garaged in a place of reward or punishment. After 1000 years the soul can choose a new lot of life. To choose, thrice, a higher life is to gain access, after 3000 years, to the Home of the Gods in the *Kingdom of Thought*. Some souls wander indefinitely, falling lower & lower. (TCD MS 10967/83r, my emphasis)

Beckett's fly is condemned to a wandering, falling fate that undermines the possibility of any 'recollection' of its innate ideas. The second-century satirist, Lucian of Samosata, criticised Plato's theory of the immortal soul for overlooking the fly's power of resurrection, which confounded the belief in transmigration:

> When ashes are sprinkled on a dead fly, she revives and has a second birth and a new life from the beginning. This should absolutely convince everyone that the fly's soul is immortal like ours, since after leaving the body if comes back again, recognises and reanimates it, and makes the

fly take wing. It also confirms the story that the soul of Hermotimus of Clazomenae would often leave him and go away by itself, and then, returning, would occupy his body again and restore him to life. (1:89)

Beckett's reborn fly ascends to the light, yet as the curtains are drawn across the cave/skull/window pane it is returned to darkness and must renew itself within the body below. As one of Plato's forlorn voyagers, having once set his eyes upon the eternal truth in the light of the outside world, the fly and, by extension, the human soul finds itself condemned to the ignorance of those below. Unlike the 'serotines abroad already' (115), the 'I' will never leave his cave, for the fly is an image of his soul, locked in a Democritean body, trapped in Erebus, half-dead, not quite alive, 'dead as mutton warm and rosy' (123).

This Platonic imagery also informs the fly's precursor in Part 1, where it is offered in defiance of the Democritean *four*/Erebus and a Heraclitean vision of ceaseless change:

[. . .] in Erebus in the end I'd succeed in seeing my navel the breath is there it wouldn't stir a mayfly's wing I feel the mouth opening

on the muddy belly I saw one blessed day saving the grace of Heraclitus the Obscure at the pitch of heaven's azure towering between its great black still spread wings the snowy body of I know not what frigate-bird the screaming albatross of the southern seas the history I knew my God the natural the good moments I had (41)

The soaring frigate-bird or albatross issues out of involuntary memory, an unexpected and fugitive release from the life in the mud, an image of hope for respite from the tedium of the mayfly's grounding and one's own navel gazing. The stillness of *its* wings is no impediment to motion as it glides above the sublime expanse of the sea. Albatross traditionally represent the souls of lost sailors, as in Coleridge's 'The Rime of the Ancient Mariner'. Beckett's poetic prose lifts his albatross, in *Comment c'est* 'au plus haut de l'azur' (40), like the rising soul of Baudelaire's *poète maudit*, 'rois de l'azur' ('L'Albatros', *Les Fleurs* 11), and as testimony to a brief flaring of the imagination, animating a memory that, despite the cautionary touch of Heraclitean cynicism retains its splendour.

The poetic epiphany defies the image of the trapped fly that recurs as a metaphor for the poet's impotence and alienation in 'Serena I' and 'La Mouche' (The Fly) (*Poems* 16, 95), in *Watt*

(236–7) and in 'Text 6' (*Complete Short* 123–4; Ackerley and Gontarski, *Faber Companion* 199). Such moments, however rare and fleeting for one 'on the muddy belly', encourage a return to the Pythagorean strategy of geometric mysticism, perhaps to find a similar release from the cave of shadows:

> a first pair then others on top as many times as necessary or a first one two three or four a second two three four or one a third three four one or two a fourth four one two or three as many times as necessary

Pairs of bodies can pile up 'as necessary', or they may form a figure, reminiscent of a magic square, that Beckett may have connected with Dürer's *Melancholia*:

$$
\begin{array}{cccc}
4 & 1 & 2 & 3 \\
3 & 4 & 1 & 2 \\
2 & 3 & 4 & 1 \\
1 & 2 & 3 & 4
\end{array}
$$

Combined 'as many times as necessary', these four integers whose sum is 10 represent Pythagorean harmony:

> Every physical body has a numerical equivalent.
> Universe a harmonious disposition of numbers, based on the perfect number 10.

| Every | solid | an expression of | 4 |
|---|---|---|---|
| -- | surface | -- -- -- -- | -- 3 |
| -- | line | -- -- -- -- | -- 2 |
| -- | point | -- -- -- -- | -- 1 (TCD MS 10967/16r) |

Similarly:

> Early Pythagoreans represented numbers and explained their properties by means of 'figures' (as on dice). Most celebrated of these was the *tetraktys*, by which they used to swear, which showed at a glance what they regarded as most important property of number 10, namely that it is the sum of first four natural integers (1+2+3+4 = 10):

$$
\begin{array}{c}
\cdot \\
\cdot \ \cdot \\
\cdot \ \cdot \ \cdot \\
\cdot \ \cdot \ \cdot \ \cdot
\end{array}
$$

> (TCD MS 10967/21v)

In *Murphy*, Neary has a Pythagorean academy in Cork, and Miss Hounihan ('My tetrakyt [sic]!') is his 'perfect ten' (5; cf. Ackerley, *Demented* 5.4). A Newtonian whose discourse is a comic parody of philosophical and literary pretension, Neary eventually concludes that 'Life is all rather irregular' (152). To the irreverent, unimpressed by such symmetry, the tetraktys looks rather like a heap. In its sequence, 15 is the next number after 10, and right until the end of *How It Is* the narrator/narrated persists doggedly with his own tetraktys logic ('ten yards fifteen yards') in an effort to replicate the perfection imagined to exist above.

## Beckett's Late Modernism (Resisting Synthesis)

Beckett's philosophical imagination uses Zeno's distinction between sense and thought – the 'two worlds thesis' (TCD MS 10967/23r) of the difference between thinking and perceiving – to undermine the absurdities of reason propagated by the narrator/narrated's Pythagorean-Platonic intrigue, as Beckett harnesses the paradox to affirm the materialist reality in Democritus' doctrine. This delightfully ironic use of philosophical imagery generates the irrational or, perhaps, the unscientific and poetic dimension of his art. Mining this vein of philosophical dialectic indicates how Beckett manages to bring an 'ignorant' or truant perspective to philosophical discourse: his articulating 'I' is a conduit for philosophical images of which he may have traces of understanding but which he unwittingly confuses. Beckett has no interest in offering a philosophical synthesis, yet the internal dynamics of philosophical thesis-antithesis within and between the images of *How It Is* mark a defining moment in his oeuvre, and indeed in modernist literature *tout court*. Not only does he present the history of philosophy as that of a discipline whose internal contradictions stymie any synthetic knowledge arising from ratiocination but, with a logic reminiscent of Gödel's, his narrator/narrated also deprives his allusions of clear links to the affirmation they would derive from the Tradition (the monolithic interpretation of intellectual history typified in Windelband's primer in philosophy). Paradoxically, his voice can allude to an allusion and affirm it, while systematically freeing itself from the limitations that the content of that allusion might impose upon its literary use.

Textual allusions, therefore, no longer confirm the meaning of their sources, but rather register the breakdown of that possibility. This situation recalls Jacques Derrida's identification in *Mal d'archive* (*Archive Fever*) of the nomological function of the archive (Beckett's *ancient voice*) as the house of power and command. Yet for Derrida the archive is located at the beginning of structural breakdown, at the antagonism between domiciliation of power (its need for a technique of repetition) and a relationship with the outside. The representation of the voice in *How It Is* as an eternally diminishing archive enacts a similar deferring of authority and draws attention to the distance between the absent rule of *ancient voice* (a philosophical tradition coherently articulated) 'ill-heard' in the present, and to its fracturing within a series of narrative repetitions and voices. Orders of 'archival' law (the 'Philosophy Notes', in particular) observe their corruption within Beckett's poetics, which represents itself as fragmented, like many surviving pre-Socratic texts. Indeed, when the final words of *How It Is* return the reader to the opening, the circular narrative generates a repetition compulsion that infinitely re-enacts its formal estrangement from the unknowable unity of the *ancient voice*. Beckett thus fashions a scene of writing that parallels Derrida's observation that a priori and central to the death drive is the forgetting ('archiviolithic') of the archive-destroying anarchy drive.

Beckett therefore refashions his experience of a philosophical education into a narrative mechanism designed to render that experience 'ignorant' of its sources. Refusing to relate inherited philosophical orthodoxies within the boundaries of their established coherence, he revels in a novel and unique set of relations whose meaning arises in the stirring of this residual 'mud' of learning. More than offering just isolated images that point to 'occluded' philosophical aporias (Uhlmann, *Philosophical* 68–9), *How It Is* presents the entire history of Western philosophy as an unremitting series of unresolved questions ripe for satire. Although any single philosophical image may be inscribed with whole episodes of coherent philosophical dialectic, the bizarre and often contradictory pattern in which these images now find themselves renders their potential for truth ludicrous, and hence the entire history of reasonable discourse within philosophy emerges as one long extended self-contradicting aporia.

Because this late modernist innovation offers no 'solution' in reaction to the Tradition, it cannot contribute to that Tradition's edification in the manner of Eliot or Pound, and it cannot see itself as advancing human progress. The way in which Beckett in *How It Is* abstracts and then deforms philosophy's grand narrative defines his relationship to modernism, which is aptly expressed in Jean-Michel Rabaté's comment about his relationship to artistic modernism: 'Beckett refuses the teleology that presents modernism as a step forward in the historical evolution from representation to abstraction' (*Think, Pig!* 85). Yet the incessant return of the *ancient voice* that frustrates the desire of the 'I' in *How It Is* to free itself entirely from inherited ideas and forms of thought also typifies the pedagogical trope running through Beckett's post-World War II novels, in which his narrators become increasingly obsessed with past voices that usurp their agency over their narratives and contaminate their speech. Here, Beckett's central concern is the authenticity and originality of his artistic voice. Indeed, the hilarious episodes that arise from grappling with this problem exemplify his ability to deploy that dianoetic laughter within his own art, a laughter that revels in the knowledge that he will never employ its idealised 'pure' voice of authentic creation, freed of all taint of Tradition.

Beckett's parable of an 'I' composing in the residua of its *humanities* is the testimony of a writer who once harboured encyclopaedic Joycean pretensions, and for whom the act of writing has now arrived at its *telos*. *How It Is* comes to terms with the anxiety of wanting to suppress those haunting past voices. Images from philosophy and all the stuff of learning can now be received and exploited for their plastic qualities, apprehended as the inevitable stuff with which one reworks form, depth and texture into the shapes (or as *Worstward Ho* would have it, the *shades*) evolving before the mind's eye. This residual, allusive substance, the impure 'mud' of Beckett's pen, has, like colour, no necessary relation to the image of the objective world or its source in the mind that it might be supposed to represent. In the manner of his admired Cézanne, Beckett uses his creative substances entirely subjectively, and the certainties afforded by a philosophical synthesis are entirely superfluous.

## Notes

1. Beckett's Library, archived at www.beckettarchive.org, lists a 1935 edition of Windelband's *Lehrbuch der Geschichte der Philosophie*.
2. Just as Beckett described the 'dark zone' of Murphy's mind as a 'matrix of surds' (*Murphy* 66).

3. Ackerley first explored Beckett's use of Pythagoreanism when annotating *Murphy*, tracing Beckett's reading to Burnet's *Greek Philosophy*, which Feldman later cross-referenced to Beckett's 'Philosophy Notes': 'Tradition represents Hippasos as divulger of Pythagorean secrets, and he is said to have been drowned at sea for revealing the incommensurability of side and diagonal' (Ackerley, *Demented* 47.7–9; Feldman, *Beckett's* 68–9; TCD MS 10967/22v).

4. Beckett's encircled equation clearly invokes the Pythagorean theorem: '[Pythagoras'] proofs of Euclid 1.47 arithmetic rather than geometric $(3^2 + 4^2 = 5^2)$, which broke down in case of most perfect triangle, isosceles right-angled, since the side of a square is incommensurable with the diagonal, just as tone or octave cannot be bisected. P. referred such incommensurability to the nature of the Unlimited' (TCD MS 10967/22r).

5. Beckett's 'Philosophy Notes' discuss how Plato's geometry superseded the Pythagorean opposition of the One and the many with its One (limited) and the Indeterminate Dyad (unlimited), the latter not the number 2 but an increase and decrease caused by the motion of the un-moved mover: 'The new idea here expressed is the <u>infinitesimal, infiniment petit</u>. This "destroys" [. . .] hypothesis of natural integers, & extends conceptions of number to include the irrationals. The series now begins, not at 1, but at 0, & the [. . .] surds are numbers [. . .] The one combines with I.D. [Indeterminate Dyad] to permeate the numbers, just as the forms with the finite & small to permeate sensible things' (TCD MS 10967/95v).

   Thus, from Burnet's *Greek Philosophy* Beckett learnt how the Pythagorean hierarchy of begetting descends from monad to dyad to numbers to point to lines (two dimensions) to entities (three dimensions) to bodies and finally to the four elements.

6. Chapter 5 argues that Beckett's knowledge of such formal logical structures came from T. K. Abbott's *The Elements of Logic*, a 108-page course in Aristotelian logic and the required text during the two-year course in logic that he took at Trinity College Dublin.

7. In *Demented Particulars* Chris Ackerley contends that in preparation for writing *Murphy* Beckett acquainted himself with Burnet's two books on early Greek philosophy, Bailey's *The Greek Atomists and Epicurus* (50.5), and various studies of Heraclitus, Pythagoras and Democritus.

8. 'All qualitative differences in the universe are merely apparent & a delusion of the senses (pro-Eleatics). Unlike the Eleatics he [Democritus] accepts reality of vacuum separating atomic plena. "Naught is more real than nothing." Non-Being is as real as Being' (TCD MS 10967/75r). This appears in *Murphy* (246), and in *Malone Dies*: 'one of those phrases that seem so innocuous and,

once you let them in, pollute the whole of speech. *Nothing is more real than nothing*. They rise up out of the pit and know no rest until they drag you down into its dark' (192, my emphasis).

9.  Ackerley cites Beckett's notes from Windelband's discussion of Aristotle's dianoetic: 'The highest perfection of its development is achieved by the rational nature of man in knowledge. The dianoetic virtues are the highest' (TCD MS 10967/109r; W 154).

10. For a different reading of Eastern influences on the text see Wimbush ('Biology'). Also, according to some legends, Pythagoras let his hair and nails grow. If Beckett had this in mind, he delivers an ironic blow to the narrator/narrated's Pythagoreanism.

11. This suggests an imaginative engagement with the Democritean procedure: 'On the departure of a certain number, sleep. On the departure of the main body, death. Death does not destroy the atoms, but only the individual corporation formed by their temporary association' (TCD MS 10967/76r).

12. The *Comment c'est* manuscripts show that 'vite', from which 'quick' derives, was introduced late in the genesis, as an addition inscribed on the penultimate typescript 'Tx2'. Given that Beckett had already made a translation of a small section of *Comment c'est* he may have introduced this term in anticipation of exploiting the possibilities of *quick* in English, while benefiting from the fact that *vite* shares its etymology with *vif*, *vita* and other such things appropriate and lively.

13. The eternally combustive universe of Heraclitus is described in the 'Philosophy Notes': 'We "are and are not" at any given moment. The "way up" (earth – water – fire) and "way down" (fire – water – earth) are one and the same, forever being traversed in opposite directions at once so that everything consists of two parts, one travelling up, the other down' (TCD MS 10967/26v).

# 3

# The Physical Cosmos: Aristotelian Dialectics

– ah yes, I nearly forgot, speak of time, without flinching, and what is more, it just occurs to me, by a natural association of ideas, treat of space with the same easy grace[.] (*TN* 390)

The Unnamable's gentle rhyme mocks the presumed 'natural association' between time and space. He continues: 'as if it [space] were not bunged up on all sides, a few inches away, after all that's something, a few inches to be thankful for, it gives one air, room for the tongue to loll, to have lolled, to loll on' (*TN* 390). Restricted space gives way to time; from an infinite form, to its present perfect, to the continuity of the phrasal verb, each 'loll' of the tongue complicating a simple correspondence between space, time and language. Yet the image of one inches before a wall imagining the nature of space beyond triggers the familiar paradox of Zeno's progression by halves, or the sorites problem of *Endgame*, where an infinity of space plunges into an infinite regress between the subject and a limit, as the Unnamable speculates:

[. . .] the question may be asked, off the record, why time doesn't pass, doesn't pass, from you, why it piles up all about you, instant on instant, on all sides, deeper and deeper, thicker and thicker, your time, other's time, the time of the ancient dead and the yet unborn, why it buries you grain by grain neither dead nor alive, with no memory of anything [. . .] saying any old thing, your mouth full of sand, oh I know it's *immaterial*, time is not one thing, I another, but the question may be asked, why time doesn't pass just like that (*TN* 389, my emphasis)

The 'natural association' of linear time with linear space is, in Beckett's texts, constantly stymied by paradoxical intuitions of correlative infinites of space and time. And if time is 'immaterial', lacking substance, it is not 'immaterial', of no concern, for time may be accordingly material (substantial, of concern): 'time is not one thing, I another'.

Beckett's characters often display an anxiety with a purported 'natural association' of time with space. Belacqua is a 'cubic unknown' (*Dream* 124), while Murphy is likened to a point in a matrix of surds (*Murphy* 66), evoking the Ancient Greek debate about whether a point is limited or unlimited. In *Watt*, Mr Hackett refers to 'the frigid machinery of a time-space relation' (21), and Watt, before a painting, contemplates different planes of point and circle 'in boundless space, in endless time'; despite knowing 'nothing about physics' (126), he senses the possibility of 'time without number' (128) yet also the 'absurdity of these constructions' (131). Such 'absurdity' has material consequences for Moran, who considers the problem of nourishing his body with a finite quantity of food by dividing its calories and vitamins into 'a series of menus asymptotically approaching nutritional zero' (*TN* 149–50). I have explored Beckett's comic use of Zeno's paradoxes, including the progression by halves, to undermine Platonic and rationalist fabulations of the narrator/narrated in *How It Is*. Beckett saw their comic potential, but these paradoxes were deadly serious in the Ancient world; their intractable nature could not be ignored by the Ancient Stoics, who structured their cosmology to accommodate vexatious relations in space, time, corpora and language.

This chapter explores the impact of the dialectics of the Ancient world after Plato upon Beckett's French novels and the peculiar set of relations between characters and their physical environment in *How It Is*. Continuing the cosmological comedy, I consider Aristotle as Beckett's source for the 'natural association' between space and time, a world view that is challenged by a set of relations resembling those of the Ancient Greek Stoics, which find their equivalent or analogy in the new physics of his own age. I interrogate the materiality of spatio-temporal relations in *How It Is* and the metaphysical coordinates between the 'I', its cosmos and any transcendent other. Beckett's 'Philosophy Notes' again offer a prism through which to read the novel; his knowledge of the Ancient world informed his rhetoric and images by harnessing and subverting philosophical dialectic, even as he pared it into simple forms of great originality and suggestive power. Aristotelian and Stoic physics and metaphysics are not the only potential sources of the curious cosmology of *How It Is*, but this dialectic offers a conceptual framework for discussing many of the contradictions within Beckett's text, as well as the many confusions and digressions of its narrator/narrated.

Hugh Kenner first suggested a Stoic dimension to Beckett's art:

> The Stoic is one who considers, with neither panic nor indifference, that the field of possibilities available to him is large perhaps, or small perhaps, but closed. Whether because of the invariable habits of the gods, the invariable properties of matter, or the invariable limits within which logic and mathematics deploy their forms, he can hope for nothing that adequate method could not foresee. (Kenner, *Stoic* xiii)

To Kenner, Beckett is a 'stoic comedian': a writer who imposes limits in order to flaunt them. 'Stoic' for Kenner is a trope, a way of bringing Beckett's texts into conversation with other clowns of order, such as Flaubert and Joyce. Kenner's account is witty and insightful, though 'Stoic' is simply a rhetorical term, advancing a whimsical connection between Stoic philosophy and Beckett's writing. The only extended treatment of Beckett's work to suggest the influence or exploitation of Stoic philosophy is Anthony Uhlmann's *Samuel Beckett and the Philosophical Image* (114–46), further echoed in his contribution on Ancient Stoic ethics of assent to the *Beckett and Ethics* collection.[1] Uhlmann observes that Stoic ontology and metaphysics informs the comprehensive representation and image, which, he argues, Beckett exploits in his writing after *Play* (1963), foremost in the drama and late television plays: in these works 'dysfunctional relationships are seen, through habit, to harden into circuits which repeat themselves' (*Philosophical* 130). Beckett's 'ontological image' discloses itself as 'the cause which it is', as understood within the Stoic cosmology of corporeal bodies, where each is a cause of the other. Here, Beckett is less the clown than the ringmaster of psychic violence. In his second publication, Uhlmann finds in Beckett's work from the late 1950s parallels between Ancient Stoic moral psychology, within which individual dispositions assent to the logical outcomes of the social body, and Beckett's characters who withhold their assent to oppressive mechanical structures that subjugate the individual.

Freudian tropes in *How It Is* point to the narrator/narrated's masochistic rather than stoic psychology (Cordingley, 'The Passion'). A 'stoic' in the familiar Roman tradition is one resilient in face of hardship; Kenner's Beckett is more 'comedian' than 'stoic', and his masochism is ultimately performance and ventriloquism, a *masocriticism* (Cordingley, 'Psychoanalytic'). However, the Ancient Greek Stoics should not be discounted, for elements of their physical cosmos infiltrate the discourse of Beckett's narrators from *Molloy* to *How It Is*. Beckett inherited from Windelband the dialectic between Plato and Democritus (see my Chapter 2), and a comparable poetical manipulation of ideas underlies his reading of Aristotle and Stoicism. Aristotelian ideas of cosmic order, syllogism, space and time are countered by a set of relations within Stoic cosmology. Beckett is neither an Aristotelian nor a Stoic, and beyond the very few authors for whom he felt an affinity (Schopenhauer, Geulincx) his interest in philosophy was fixed on its contradictions and paradoxes – not philosophy *per se* but his experience of philosophical narrative, its recurrent motifs and images, and their literary potential. In this chapter, I examine Beckett's study of formal logic as a student at Trinity College Dublin, his private study of philosophy in 1932, and his contact with Ancient Stoicism, to demonstrate how the creative transformation of Aristotelian and 'Stoic' ideas in *How It Is* influenced its formal and literary innovations in that novel, but also in the earlier trilogy.

## The Syllogistic Cosmos

In Part 3 of *How It Is*, the 'I' obsessively tries to account for how each 'soul' in his underworld is supplied with its sack(s) of material provisions. Seeking a consistent cosmological 'formulation' (185), with everything assuming its place within the 'natural order' (3), he becomes fixated with testing his quasi-formal, logical exposition:

> at the instant I reach Pim another reaches Bom we are regulated thus our justice wills it thus fifty thousand couples again at the same instant the same everywhere with the same space between them it's mathematical it's our justice in this muck where all is identical [. . .]

> at the instant Pim leaves me and goes towards the other Bem leaves the other and comes towards me [. . .]

> at the instant Pim reaches the other to form again with him the only couple he forms apart from the one with me Bem reaches me to form with me the only couple he forms apart from the one with the other

illumination here Bem is therefore Bom or Bom Bem and the voice
quaqua from which I get my life these scraps of life in me when the
panting stops of three things one.

(143–5)

The 'I' imagines all couples in the universe (whether one or 50,000)
as involved in the same alternation of domination and subordination that characterises his encounter with Pim. Tormentor and
victim alone constitute the links 'all along the chain in both directions' (185). The intimation in Part 1 of a serial grammar governing this great chain of being – 'series subject object subject object
quick succession' (9) – expands into a universal syllogism with
alternating subject and predicate. Like major and minor propositions in the syllogism, each coupling of tormentor and victim
issues forth a consequent being, predicated in the language and
behaviour of his teacher (or major proposition). The once empty
vessel or 'victim' now journeys forward, moulded in the ways of
the 'master', to encounter its own 'victim'.

This bizarre hyper-determined vision of universal interaction
is the more profoundly comic for its dark inversion of Aristotle's
syllogistic reasoning. The 'Philosophy Notes' sketch the Aristotelian system across ten folios. Beckett identifies the three classes of
Aristotle's syllogism: the apodictic, dialectic and sophistic, and the
corresponding distinction between certain truth, disputable truth
and fallacy (TCD MS 10967/100r). He was well versed in syllogistic reasoning from his compulsory studies of logic in his modern
languages degree at Trinity, which drew on T. K. Abbott's *The
Elements of Logic*, a 108-page course in Aristotelian logic and the
set text during the two-year course; the *Term and Examination
Returns 1925* in the College archives attest to Beckett's fine result
of 8/10 (TCD MS Mun V/30/82-85; cf. Luce, 'Samuel' 33–45).

From Abbott's *Elements* Beckett learnt to demonstrate different
kinds of syllogisms with the notation of formal logic. For example,
the descending rules for the 'four figures' of syllogistic reasoning –
with subject (S), predicate (P) and middle/mediate term (M) – are
tabled in chapter two of Part 3, 'Of Inferences':

| First. | Second. | Third. | Fourth. |
|--------|---------|--------|---------|
| MP | PM | MP | PM |
| SM | SM | MS | MS |
| SP | SP | SP | SP |

(Abbott, *Elements* 47)

The 'I' of *How It Is* names his interacting couples and their offspring (Bom, Bem, Pim . . .) in comparable order. He denominates his former dog, Skom Skum, and wife, Pam Prim, as if they were issued from a union of premises, a pseudo-couple, like Krim and Kram. Such naming evokes the medieval technique of mnemonics to help students of syllogisms remember the different moods. Propositions were classed as either A, E, I or O (A and I as positive [from *affirmo*], universal and individual respectively; E and O [from *nego*] their negative equivalents), and learnt by the position of vowels, as Abbott outlines in his *Elements*: '*Barbara, Celarent, Darii, Ferio*que prioris / *Cesare, Camestres, Festino, Baroko* secundæ [. . .]' (53).[2] The vowels and certain consonants represent the different combinations of propositions that produce different moods.

Such coherence detracts from the narrator/narrated's naming. Estranged from his 'voix ancienne', his old, former or *ancient voice*, he tries to articulate his key to memory, chanting imperfectly in his head: 'm at the end and one syllable the rest indifferent' (75). His scholastic autism is revealed in a comment in the manuscripts 'ms' of *Comment c'est/How It Is*, reproduced in the critical-genetic edition: '<j'ai toujours aimé l'arithmétique <*et spécialement par* [sic] *règle de trois*> *et* elle me l'a bien rendu, *c'est arabe comme le ousia*,> (356; <I always loved arithmetic <and especially [with/by] [the] rule of threes> and it's repaid me handsomely, it's Arabic like the ousia,>). The origin of the Pythagorean 'règle de trois' in Babylonian science is equated with the 'Arabe' arithmetical heritage, in turn linked to the Greek philosophical vocabulary of Being, *le ousia*.[3] The first of Aristotle's ten categories, *ousia* is defined in Abbott's *Elements*: 'Οὐσία 'The "whatness" of a thing, or what it is named, called in Latin logicians "substantia," "substance," as man, horse' (27). Stephen Dedalus echoes Abbott's curious phrasing when he unsheaves one of Aristotle's 'dagger definitions' (presumably honed by St Thomas Aquinas, the *Wake*'s *tumass equinous* [93.8–9]), and declares, 'Horseness is the whatness of allhorse' (*Ulysses* 9.84–5),

In the *Comment c'est* manuscript the narrator/narrated conflates the 'rule of three' with his triadic syllogistic archetype. The Arab connection with *ousia* acknowledges the Arabic philosophy that influenced Scholastic logic when it brought 'Aristotelian' thought to the West around the twelfth century. Ackerley identifies a similar strain in *Watt*, with its reference to Alexander of Hales (1175–1245) whose '*Summa Universae Theologiae* correlated the Augustinianism of his day with Aristotle and the Arabs; Beckett noted that this work introduces scholastic method "far more cogently" than the earlier summists (TCD 10967/161r)' (*Obscure Locks* 45; cf. W 313). In his 'Philosophy Notes' Beckett followed Windelband by charting the evolution of the concept from Platonic 'becoming' to Aristotle's primary being: in the *Phædo*, Plato distinguished 'between the higher realm of οὐσία and lower world of γένεσις, between what *is* and what is in process of Becoming' (W 120), Plato having observed how mathematical Pythagoreanism assumes a correspondence between archetypes and their tokens. Aristotle remodelled Plato's Being (*ousia*) into *essence*, as he attempted to mend Plato's schism between forms or ideas (Being) and phenomena (Becoming) (TCD 10967/103v; W 132–4). Aristotle's Being as *ousia*, or essence, resides and unfolds within phenomena: matter is a corporeal substratum, standing in a relation of potentiality to its realised or actual *form*. The essential nature (*ousia*) in matter exists only in *potentiality*, like the x value immanent within an equation of the rule of threes, or the x carved into Pim's backside – the action that provokes the 'I' to represent being through mathematics.

### 'I For Him Animate': Aristotle's Analogy of the Plastic Artist

The continuous gradations in Aristotle's teleology, from lower to higher, towards the final and supreme cause, bear directly on the universe of mud which incubates the 'I' in *How It Is*. Its substance is the inchoate matter of the *voice quaqua*, a material substrata of discharged *ancient voice*. The 'I' claims to quote the voice he hears of his former self speaking to him from 'above in the light', and once this voice is spent it enters the excreta – the *caca* of the *voice quaqua* – of this messy archive, the viscous landscape through which 'I' advances, taking mouthful after mouthful. The narrative is curled into an infinite recursive loop (the end of Part 3 returning the reader to the beginning of Part 1), and the reader cannot distinguish the voice above dictating to the voice below from dictation recovered from the mud as it is ingested anew. When he commences his journey the 'I' attempts to recover some form from the mess by probing it with his tongue and chewing it. Through this new experience of this fragmented archive, the 'I' attempts to piece together a hypothesis of cosmological relations, hoping that if he hits on the correct 'formulation' he may ascend (back) into the light 'above' (for all is dark in the mud). His integration of syllogistic configurations into his cosmic model of couples engaging in cause and effect finds a parallel in Aristotle's metaphor, as recorded by Beckett. Windelband notes: 'Thus the cosmic processes are regarded by Aristotle ultimately under the *analogy of the plastic artist*' (144, author's emphasis; cf. TCD 10967/107r).[4] Critics of *Comment c'est/How It Is* largely agree on one point: that the text is *about* its creation, and its narrative – the 'education' of Pim by the 'I', and the effort to make him sing – is a gruesome allegory of the creative process. The analogy of the plastic artist becomes the archetype of interaction for all beings in its universe. Pim is first discovered lying in the mud, a 'dead soul' (125). Apparently a formless being, he is present to the 'I' or artist as raw material imbued with potentiality: 'I for him animate' (127). Their interaction, then, accords with an Aristotelian process: inert matter is not only animated by contact with the actual, but that contact is necessary to release the potentiality within matter so that when Pim's 'song *ascends* in the *present*' (81, my emphasis) it also lifts the 'I' from his *eternity* below.

By implicating the 'I' in such grandiose aspirations for metaphysical coherence, Beckett satirises rationalist philosophers (and anyone disposed to credulity) who affirm the intellect's power to transcend fundamental human ignorance. While his play with *ousia* disappeared in revisions of the French text, in *How It Is* the 'I' often refers to his fall from 'species', which Beckett's notes record as the translation of *eidos* – Plato's Form, appropriated by Aristotle as 'essence' (or species-in-general) (TCD 10967/101r; cf. Abbott, *Elements* 7–8). Like *Watt* (82), the 'I' experiences 'loss of species' (31; cf. 29, 141, 165) as in Aristotelian terms he devolves from his Form/essence. Falling from purity and virtue, he is suspended between the rational and animal soul (cf. TCD MS10967/108v-109r). Indeed, *contra* Aristotle's ascending entelechies in the *Organon* (cf. TCD MS 10967/99r), the 'I' declares in Part 1: 'when the great needs fail the need to move on the need to shit and vomit and the other great needs *all my great categories of being*'[5] (13, my emphasis). His higher *species* failing, he strains to hear his *ancient voice*, hoping for a clear channel to his transcendent Author 'above in the light', the '*ideal* observer' (125, my emphasis), *Logos*, his being of perfect language and reason.

Aristotle held that in Plato's system every Idea would need to be subsumed beneath a higher one: Beckett adds that a *third man* is needed to integrate the *ideal man* and *Belacqua* (TCD MS10967/100v, my emphasis). This form is needed to reify ideal man, just as the ideal is necessary to reify material man, a theme hinted at in the early drafts of *Watt*, where the ratification of Mr Knott depends on his having a father (and so part of a series); but it is better known from Flann O'Brien's *The Third Policeman*. Belacqua derives from the indolent figure of Dante's *Purgatorio* 4. Indifferent to the teleological universe (like matter devoid of form), in *Dream* he calculates his identity as 'trine': 'the three values, Apollo, Narcissus and the anonymous third person' (124). *Dream*'s narrator uses logic to deny his characters the hermetic, generic representation of realist literature: 'We can state them as a succession of terms, but we cannot sum them and we can't define them' (124). This echoes the traditional logical distinction between generic character (*species*) and individual, which Beckett encountered in Abbott's *Elements*. Abbott defines 'Terms', 'Genus', 'Species' and 'Definition' to conclude: 'Description is an enumeration of the attributes of the thing described sufficient to distinguish it from other things', adding, like the narrator of *Dream*, that 'Individual things can only be described, not defined' (12).

Early in *How It Is*, the 'I' compares himself to Belacqua as one excluded from grace: 'asleep I see me asleep on my side or on my face [. . .] Belacqua fallen over on his side tired of waiting forgotten of the hearts where grace abides' (27). The 'waiting' of this Belacqua-'I' involves, in his fabricated cosmology, the return of his anticipated 'tormentor', Bom; but his syllogistic model of cause and effect – 'before Pim with Pim after Pim' – fails to produce a lasting modification of form that might lift him to a higher realm. Beckett regularly subverts his syllogisms by implying that they unwittingly generate a kind of universal stagnation or paralysis. The paradoxes of logic detailed in the previous chapter, especially Zeno's sorites paradox, again undermine the dogged effort of the 'I' to exercise his *ratio* as he attempts to harmonise his golden braid (. . . 10, 15 . . .) of space, time and recitation. Beckett probably first encountered the sorites paradox in Abbott's *Elements*. Like the Enthymeme (a series in which one premise is suppressed), the sorites is 'a chain of reasoning consisting of a series of syllogisms in which each intermediate conclusion is not expressed, but is assumed as a premiss of the succeeding syllogism' (63). Equally, to his series of torturers and victims Beckett adds the fatal condition of 'divine forgetting'; this entails that after leaving its 'tormentor', the consequent being (the syllogistic 'conclusion' of the 'I' predicated with Pim) must forget his 'education' and so the series necessarily tends A = Z. While the

integrity of both propositions remains intact, and torturers and victims are matched, any logical or substantial progression is stymied
because further predication in the world of mud does not follow.
Similarly, in *Dream*, the 'succession of terms' to Belacqua's 'trine'
'*tail off vaguely* at both ends and the *intervals* of their series are
demented' (124, my emphasis). This fading into vagueness evokes
the progression by halves of the sorites paradox, a 'demented' measure that exists only in the 'intervals' between terms of the series.
No Author, let alone an *ancient voice*, can impose its order within
what was, for Beckett, the irrational, involuntary and necessarily
vague space of fiction.

Beckett's imagination expresses itself in systematic philosophical opposition to Aristotle's doctrines (the evolution of form, its
progression through space and time). Indeed, when Aristotelian
positivism is identifiable in his texts it is often checked by events,
situations or comments that resemble the critique of Aristotle by
the Ancient Stoics, whose place in philosophy, and especially in the
first half of the twentieth century when Beckett encountered the
school, must be considered next.

### Beyond Vagueness: Beckett and the Stoics?

When Beckett began *Comment c'est* at Ussy-sur-Marne in late
1958, the relationship between Ancient Stoic[6] physics and ontology
had been disseminated through two works of the eminent French
historian of philosophy, Émile Bréhier: *La Théorie des incorporels
dans l'ancien stoïcisme* (1908) and *Chrysippe et l'ancien
stoïcisme* (1910). Sensing a Stoic presence in Beckett's late work,
Uhlmann contends that these two books, and Bréhier's *Histoire
de la philosophie*, are his likely sources of Stoic doctrine, but in
a footnote he also suggests another in Jean Beaufret (Uhlmann,
*Philosophical* 177, fn. 8). During 1928–30, when Bréhier was
lecturing at the Sorbonne, Beckett was a visiting *lecteur d'anglais*
at the École Normale Supérieure, where he was befriended by
Beaufret, a lively young student of philosophy. Knowlson relays
Beckett's comments that Beaufret was 'particularly interested in
Greek thought' (*Damned* 97) and that he sought Beaufret's help
with 'some of the major classical and more modern European
philosophers' (*Damned* 96). Writing to Tom MacGreevy, Beckett
reported that Beaufret 'comes and talks abstractions every second
day and déniche [unearths] books for me in the library' (*Damned*

97; TCD MS 10402, July 1930). Whatever the later relationship between the two, the greatest impediment to establishing a Beckett-Beaufret-Bréhier/Stoics connection is the absence of interest in Bréhier or Stoic philosophy in Beaufret's published seminars, *Leçons de philosophie*, I. *Philosophie grecque, Le Rationalisme classique*,[7] reconstructed by his students from their course notes in *première supérieure* at Lycée Condorcet over a twenty-two-year period (1950–72).[8] Nor did the Stoics leave any trace in Beaufret's first volume of four, *Dialogue avec Heidegger*, entitled, *Philosophie grecque*, which examines Heidegger's thought in a dialogue stretching from the birth of Greek philosophy to Heraclitus, Permenides and Zeno, then continuing into Plato and Aristotle, and passing to Augustine and Aquinas.

Beckett's first demonstrable encounter with Ancient Stoic thought can be traced in the 'Philosophy Notes' to his private study in 1932 of Archibald Alexander's *A Short History of Philosophy* (118–33) and Wilhelm Windelband's *History* (TCD MS10967/114r-128v). He read them, later, for his 'Whoroscope' notebook records: 'The Stoics aspired to apathia, the repression of all emotion, and the Epicureans to ataraxia, freedom from all disturbance' (UoR 3000/82r). Alexander (118–33) is a richer source, contributing eight pages among the five folios on the Stoics of the 'Philosophy Notes' (slotted between Aristotle and the Gnostics). They are typed, which suggests that they were probably made at his London lodgings, whereas the handwritten notes from Windelband's first chapter of Part 2, 'The Ethical Period' (159–63) were made at the British Museum reading room over the summer of 1932.[9] Beckett gathered together his notes on this subject by beginning those from Windelband on the verso of those from Alexander.[10] These notes did not inspire any mention in the introduction to Beckett's 'Philosophy Notes' in the *Notes Diverse Holo* catalogue, and beyond Uhlmann's brief comments, scholars have not drawn any direct connection between them and Beckett's oeuvre.[11]

Uhlmann posits a shift in Beckett's 'beings of violence' (*Philosophical* 138), from individuals who perform arbitrary violent acts which typify (non)-relations (Mercier and Camier's killing of the policeman, Lemuel's murders, Molloy's attack on the charcoal burner) to works after *How It Is*, such as *Play, Come and Go, The Lost Ones, What Where* and *Quad*, in which the interaction between beings no longer represents either relations or non-relations between individual bodies but rather the idea that these 'bodies become bodies themselves'

(138). *How It Is* invokes not so much Stoic moral psychology as the Stoic theory of the physical universe, with which the narrator/narrated haplessly attempts to accord his ethical practice (see my next chapter). *How It Is* generates its stoic farce by setting up a dialectic between the two elements Uhlmann has identified: the simultaneous existence of, firstly, the non-/relational dimension of Pim's violent encounter (in its event rather than its retelling); and, secondly, the absence of 'relations' between bodies, that is their implacably determined nature.

### Cutting Both Ways: From Aristotle's Interval to the Stoics' Incorporeal Time

In *Purgatorio* 4, Belacqua mocks Dante: 'Hai ben veduto come 'l sole da l'omero sinistro il carro mena?' (119–20; 'Have you marked how the sun drives past your left shoulder?'). Temporal relations in *How It Is* are anything but obvious, and perception of the earth's revolution is thrown into doubt:

> [. . .] here I quote on we do not revolve
>
> that is above in the light where their space is measured here the straight line the straight line eastward strange and death in the west as a rule. (159)

This distinction has been traced to the observation in Beckett's notes of the Pythagorean-Platonic notion of the circular motion of souls above against the rectilinear motion of those below. Beckett learned from Windelband how this distinction was developed by Aristotle (W 147) and in his 'Philosophy Notes' he registers the consequences of Aristotle's failure to solve Platonic dualism: the problem of how the thought of thoughts, or unmoved mover, can affect motion in the universe:

> How can that which is unmoved, changeless, self-identical & self-contained be the occasion of movement, change & variety?

| | |
|---|---|
| Motion: | Transition of potential into actual. |
| Space: | Possibility of motion. |
| *Time:* | *Measure of motion.* |
| Soul: | Form & Final Cause of the body. |
| Intelligence: | Locus of ideas. (TCD MS 10967/102r, my emphasis) |

Divorced from a revolving sky the narrator/narrated doggedly attempts to harmonise his perceptions of movement through time and space: 'ten seconds fifteen seconds', 'ten yards fifteen yards' (that Pythagorean harmonising of his 'ratio'). His spatio-temporal 'straight line' ('before Pim with Pim after Pim') echoes, as I have argued, Aristotle's influential formulation of the number or measure separating bodies and the necessary 'interval' (*diastêma*) between them. While Aristotle's definition of time as 'interval' was adopted by the early Stoic, Zeno of Citium (Arnim 1.26.14–15), in *La Théorie des incorporels dans l'ancien stoïcisme* Bréhier demonstrates how Chryssipus, leader of the second generation of Ancient Stoics, responded to Aristotle's exploration of definite time. The infinite, single and continuous rotation of the spherical heavens was the only uniform definable movement against which one could measure an undetermined, rectilinear time (*La Théorie* 55).

Alternatives to Aristotelian relations often mystify Beckett's characters. Molloy awakens in Lousse's room to find the moon occupying the centre of his window: 'two bars divided it in three segments, of which the middle remained constant' (39). As the moon charts its way across the pane, the fixed instant dissolves into the measured time of past, present and future. Molloy calculates the course of the moon, wondering if its eastward progress is its motion, or if his room rather moves left and right, if indeed left and right are valid terms. He ponders this motion but concedes, 'That movements of an extreme complexity were taking place' (39). The Unnamable considers measuring the 'orbit[s]' of Malone and the unnamed menacing figure apparently circling about him, but he cannot: 'For I am incapable not only of measuring time, which in itself is sufficient to vitiate all calculation in this connexion, but also of comparing their respective velocities' (298). Unable to know their speed or measure their positions, he speculates on the likelihood of the two meeting. He digresses on what separates them, concluding that given their orbits, which appear predetermined, and their 'erratic interval', it is likely they will 'collide and perhaps even knock each other down' (298). The narrator/narrated of *How It Is* states that his space does not 'revolve' and he is divorced from any possibility of knowing a defined time. In the 'ms/a' manuscript his contemplation of certain 'vérités premières' (first truths) includes a reflection on spacio-temporal periods; he compares animals that live above the earth's surface and pinpoint their location 'à l'aide du ciel' (instructed by the heavens), with the *taupe* (mole), with its 'tout autant de méthode' (just as much method) of 'une ponctualité extreme' (233–4). Incubated in Erebus, denied a view of the rotating heavens, the 'I' relies upon his Pythagorean definition of harmony to recover form from chaos, obsessively submitting space, time, discourse, listening and speaking to his fatal ratio … 10,15 … He is nonetheless aware of an alternative, non-Aristotelian *method* to determine his spatio-temporal coordinates. His reflection on the distinction between sublunary animals and the blind *taupe* was prefaced by an acknowledgement that the question 'Avoir tant changé et être encore au même endroit?' may be answered: 'Puisque l'espace est imaginaire' (233–4; To have changed so much and still be in the same place? Since space is imaginary.)

The measured time of the revolving sky is considered time's unity, and Chryssipus transformed this into an *effect* of the only real being, the world (Bréhier, *La Théorie* 55). Bréhier reiterates how this principle required the Stoics to divorce the world from what was for Plato and Aristotle its essential element, the infinite or undetermined. For Plato and Aristotle, the world contained at once the limited and the unlimited, the mathematically stable and the undetermined. In changing the meaning of these two elements the Stoics wanted to separate them out, not like Plato and Aristotle by considering them as distinct elements of one totality but by giving them a nature which *obstructs* the action of one upon the other (*La Théorie* 51) (consider Neary's tractrate, 'The Doctrine of the Limit'). Contrary to Aristotle, movement was not the passage from a force to an act, but the act which repeats itself forever anew.

Language too is incorporeal, the divine breath (*Logos*) expiring as it enters linear (incorporeal) time: like space, nothingness and time (the other categories of incorporeals), language is merely a logical attribute of events without real qualities. Beckett sketched this distinction in his 'Philosophy Notes', following Windelband's comments on the Stoic's separation of the objective and subjective and its epistemological problems (TCD MS10967/126r; W 199–200). Bréhier references Chryssipus' expressibles with his well-known proposition: 'If there is a scar, there was a wound' (*La Théorie* 32). The scar implies the existence of the past wound, but what the scar really signifies is the fact of having had a wound, and this, therefore, is the new present of which the scar is the sign. The relation between the sign and the signified exists between two incorporeal terms. Bréhier stresses that, for the Stoics, this relation is between two expressibles and not between two realities. While wound and scar do not cease to be real (reflected in their substantive grammatical form), they simultaneously exist incorporeally.[12]

Tearing into the flesh of Pim's back marks the separation of the past body with that of the present. In Stoic terms, Pim's back exists upon a plane of incorporeal effects; within the reality of his corporeal being, he must forever be the *tabula rasa* defining that 'instant'. Though Pim is always the future body who has already been met countless times – his back having been turned into a bloody pulp, he journeys forwards, only to stop, be found again and bloodied – remarkably, he never bears the scar tissue of his past:

> from the next mortal to the next leading nowhere and saving correction no other goal than the next mortal cleave to him give him a name train him up bloody him all over with Roman capitals gorge on his fables *unite for life in stoic love* to the last shrimp and a little longer

> till the fine day when flip he vanishes *leaving me his effects and the sooth comes true* the new life no more journeys. (79, my emphases)

The colliding of mortals is ironically dubbed their 'stoic love', the union of active 'I' and the passive blank slate. Modification of the body of the 'I' generated through the 'effects' of its contact with Pim tantalise him with a possible escape from this meaningless series, of delivering him into his 'new life'. Aristotle uses the analogy of the plastic artist moulding clay, but in *How It Is* positive effects which rise towards the '*ousia*' find a Stoic leveller. While 'sooth' undermines Stoic doctrine with an insinuation of hearsay, the next paragraph reasserts the grim irony of the doctrine of fate generic to the Roman capitals of Stoicism, not only its Ancient Greek fragments. Destiny asserts its law that the 'I' is condemned to:

> lie there *same as before Pim after Pim the same as before* [. . .] the old road towards my next mortal ten yards fifteen yards push pull season after season *my only season towards my first mortal*. (79, my emphasis)

The implacable destiny for the body as cause is its stoic corporeality, immune to events: when mortals meet, one leaves its 'effects' with another, yet this does not penetrate the latter's being. One is essentially 'the same as before', eternally in one's 'only season' (cf. Beckett's poem of 1955 'Vive morte ma seule saison').

Pim's being does not exist within the reality of a traditional understanding of cause and effect: he exists not just *in* futurity but *as* futurity; without his virgin back there would be no 'atrocious spectacle on into the black night of boundless futurity' (179). He is 'boundless' or unlimited only in a continuous present, for if encountered in a state 'less than the future' he would be bloodied by the 'instant' or scarred by the 'past'. The asserted logic of 'before Pim with Pim after Pim' is generated *by* the universal principle of linearity, 'the natural order', solipsistically *as* that natural order. Defined by the linear relations it expresses, it corresponds to the incorporeal time of the Stoics. Beckett's use of 'mortals' to stake out past, present and future projects the body as event into a universal solipsism that is a parody of ontological relations, linearly devised. The *ancient voice* of 'memory' has thrown up an image of corporeal interaction which has departed from any habitual, even Aristotelian, sense of cause and effect, and which strongly resembles that of Stoic logicians, perhaps as mediated by Émile Bréhier.

### Stoic *Pneuma*, Beckett's '*Flammèche*'

The Ancient Stoics advocated a world composed entirely of bodies, each participating in the one cosmic body, and in which the possible existence of inert matter was untenable. Bréhier intuits the Cartesian dilemma in Stoic materialism: the only possibility of a soul's action on the body is by contact, yet if the soul is immaterial this is impossible. Chryssipus' solution was to deny the soul's immateriality, admitting its corporeal properties (*La Théorie* 9). Beckett's notes on the Stoics reflect Windelband's focus on the ethical implications which they drew from their physics. He also follows Windelband's sketch of the Stoics' elaboration of the Heraclitean *Logos* doctrine as their *pneuma*, or divine reason, which animates each material soul and unites it with the one World-Reason: 'Their logos (world mind, vital principle) is, as per Heraclitus, not only law, but necessity. They assert an unbroken chain of causal determination, which makes the world a purposeful, connected whole' (TCD 10967/117r; W 181–2). By transforming the Heraclitean *Logos* into their notion of the *pneuma*, the divine breath of fire, the Stoics sought an intellectual synthesis between active and passive matter within a pantheistic materialism:

> The <u>pneuma</u> is the active part of the world-God – force: the passive is moisture; fire is the soul, 'moist' is the body of world-god.[13] This pneuma doctrine is an extraordinarily condensed conception, full of relations – from Heraclites [. . .], Anaxagoras [. . .], Diogenes of Apollonia [. . .], Democritus (fire atoms), & the peripatetic natural philosophy & physiology. (TCD 10967/117r-v – 'PNEUMA' written in the margin; W 186–7)

Beckett drew this summary from a paragraph of Windelband who elaborates: 'As force, the deity is fire or warm, vital breath, *pneuma*; as matter, it changes itself out of *moist vapour (air)* partly into water partly into earth' (W 186, second emphasis mine). Earlier references to Anaxagoras, Heraclitus and the fire-atoms of Democritus in the body of the 'I' may thus be assimilated into the enveloping 'moist' body of the World-god: 'the mud never cold never dry it doesn't dry on me the air laden with warm vapour' (29). In its entry on the 'Stoics', the 11th edition of the *Encyclopaedia Britannica*, to which Beckett regularly turned, offers a clear outline of Stoic theory of corporeality, which emphasises the gaseousness of *pneuma* and its influence upon the notion of the 'esprits animaux' of Descartes, Leibniz and Locke:

> A certain warmth, akin to the vital heat of organic being, seems to be found in inorganic nature: vapours from the earth, hot springs, sparks from the flint, were claimed as the last remnant of Pneuma not yet utterly slackened and cold. (25)

Beckett's narrator/narrated offers a comparable self-diagnosis: 'my life as nothing man a vapour' (103). He considers himself one of the *esprits animaux*, following Stoics-Descartes-Leibniz-Locke, an Aristotelian 'animal soul', with the 'rational soul' above. His vapours do not rise to feed an ascendant purer body, as in Raphael's idyllic portrait where 'corporeal to incorporeal turn[s]' (*Paradise Lost* 9.15–22). Nor does he attribute to his exhalations the moral condemnation pervading Milton's notion of putrefying man. Beckett's figure inhabits a materialist universe where corporeal to corporeal turns; vapours are exhaled, become incorporeal, then are imbided as cosmic excrement: 'voice once

without quaqua then in me'. As incorpora they pass through the
system without affecting the body. Oscillating between Stoic and
Aristotelian notions of time and space, an implacable materialist
reality imposes itself on the text, muddying the transcendence of
*ancient voice*.

Before it is transformed into vapour the pneumatic breath of
fire delivers life, and in manuscript 'ms' the narrator/narrated
contemplates his *'petite langue de feu vite morte'* (309). This
phrase was subsequently revised to refer more elegantly to the
tongues of fire in typescript '1661': *'languette de feu <flammèche>
vite morte'* (309, Beckett's underlining; little tongue of fire <little
flame> quick dead). These phrases quickly expired, not surviving
into the published text, yet they suggest how the 'I' may be
weighing how Stoic *pneuma* contrasts with the fire permeating his
Democritean materialism. Such a discourse with Atomism would
parallel the Stoics' positing their *pneuma* doctrine against that
of the Epicureans. The narrator/narrated's 'flammèche' carries
the implications of the *pneuma* as fire, divine breath and soul; a
notion Beckett also gleaned from Windelband: 'The individual soul
is also pneuma, *fiery breath*, in forming the blood & circulation,
separating at death from the lower elements which it animates,
consubstantial with divine Pneuma & dependent on it' (TCD
10967/117v, my emphasis; W 187). Beckett doubtless recognised
this idea as predating the Christian doctrine of Christ as *Logos* and
the Holy Spirit of the Trinity. In Dante's *Inferno* sins are punished
by tongues of fire; and when in Canto XXVI Ulysses' speech is
likened to a 'tongue of flame' Dante is clearly parodying the descent
of Pentecostal fire in Acts 2:1–11 (Logan, 'Characterization' 42).
As in the early 'ms' draft, eight paragraphs after the *'petite langue
de feu'* (308), the narrator in the typescript 'Tx2' (313) refers to his
speech as 'ma glossolalie', or the Pentecostal speaking in tongues.
The *flammèche* expires into 'un petit bout de temps', that *bout*
which is a fraction or 'bit' cancelling any *but* or 'goal' within its
evocation of Zeno's conundrum.[14] It conducts the *boue* (mud) into
its temporal line of past, present and future. The opposition of an
undefined versus a relative time informs Beckett's translation when
two paragraphs earlier he revised the former 'd'un seul instant' in
'ms' into *'d'une seule éternité'* (307), for an eternity may replace an
instant only when both exist beyond linear time.

Circular time is announced in the final line of the novel: 'good
good end at last of part three and last that's how it was end of

quotation after Pim how it is' (193). The words 'after Pim how it is' are the 'beginning' of emancipation from the 'other above'. Yet the narrative just retold was consistently asserted to be an uncorrupted 'quotation'. The narrator/narrated may cut and edit the *ancient voice*, yet comments and editorial interpolations *already* permeate that voice. This is witnessed above when discontinuity itself seems to be 'an image too of this voice'. The number of pre-existing repetitions is potentially anything between one and infinity, though 'preexisting repetition' is misleading because pre-existence in this hermetic, temporal instant is meaningless.[15]

Given the novel's circularity, Part 3 might logically precede Part 1, except that once the circle has been closed precedence disappears. Part 3 does 'precede' Part 1 in that the purported liberation of the narrative voice occurs at the end of the novel so that it can recount the story that 'begins' at the 'beginning', but which has 'already' occurred. This situation replicates those relations imagined to exist between bodies: the eternally returning Bem/Bom and Pim. While his conception of time is stated 'before Pim with Pim after Pim', the 'I' reasons that he must have left behind a tormentor, a Bem/Bom, before moving towards his Pim. His 'beginning' is the ever coexistent 'future' of another body and the past of another. The ill-hearing ill-saying of the narrator/narrated expresses time as defined by corpora in relation to a defined instant ('with Pim'), but the linear 'natural order' of the event is necessarily disrupted when the cosmos consistently repeats the originary occasion: 'as I depart', 'time to forget all lose all be ignorant of all whence I come whither I go' (141). Here 'no one knows himself it's the place without knowledge whence no doubt its peerlessness' (159). There are no peers in this world because, as in the sorites paradox which undermines the *ratio* of the 'I', all couples repeat that one couple I-Pim, and after each union the voyager loses his memory. This forgetting annihilates the new depository of *ancient voice*; like Derrida's archive-destroying 'archiviolithic' dimension to the death drive in *Mal d'archive*, Beckett's corpora are assimilated into a repetition compulsion which erases the corpus' repetition. This rule echoes the logical argument against metempsychosis: if one cannot remember the identity of a previous soul and if identity is a function of memory, then no past identity exists. The necessary loss of memory impels the event – 'with Pim' – to be repeated eternally anew. Once Pim crawls away the 'I' is tormented by Bom, then the 'I' then crawls from Bom to meet Pim once more; he remembers nothing yet reaffirms what he intuits to be the universal law of archive and *ancient voice*, reasserting measured instants of his linear time.

When the 'I' sees a 'Stoic' explanation to his ontological predicament and his epistemological parameters, he appears less haplessly blinded by his dogged commitment to this law, but rather conscious of his temporal quandary when forced to translate his experience into language: 'how it was before Pim first say that natural order the same things the same things say them as I hear them murmur them to the mud divide into three a single eternity for the sake of clarity' (27). In shaping the novel into a circle, Beckett delivers an image of undefined time within its hermetic covers. Like the rotating heavens, lacking any external point of reference, the novel is its own material universe: its three parts revolve eternally, at once undefined in their temporal moment and yet potentially determing how any moment may be orientated, as past, present or future. This structural circularity generates a narrative present which dissolves the structure of the defined 'instant'. In terms of the 'Cartesian centaur' of Kenner's imagination (a mind atop its mechanical chariot/universe), the corporeal vehicle may well roll to a stoic life force, carried on the breath of its *pneumatiques*.

## The 'Orgy of False Being': Beckett's Stoic Humour

The Stoics believed that, from his position in eternity, only Zeus was privileged with a complete view of what they termed the 'natural order' of the event. Beckett's 'other above in the light' presides over the oft-repeated 'natural order' of the discourse of his 'I'. In harmonising his movement in space-time with a moral theory derived from the reason inherent in nature, the one below attempts to mirror the fate his monotheistic deity inscribes in all life from above. The need to express this belief in *language* offers Beckett abundant opportunities to satirise the earnest aspirations of his hero, who attempts to cast a sceptical glance towards his *ancient voice*, dismissing its imposed order of the event 'with Pim':

> orgie de faux être vie commune courtes hontes je ne suis pas perdu à l'inexistence pas sans retour l'avenir le dira il est en train mais une telle souille bah même pas même pas bah

> orgy of false being life in common brief shames I am not dead to inexistence not irretrievably time will tell it's telling but what a hog's wallow pah not even not even pah. (86–9)

The philosophical register is remarkable, and underlying its evocation of 'being' and 'inexistence' in the early manuscript 'ms' is a Stoic-Deleuzian evocation of difference: '*Ah vie commune vie commune quelle différence d'avec avant d'avec après quelle différence et quelle orgie de faux être ?? et les moments perdus où le visage dans la boue je sens y monter l'incarnat de la honte*' (442–3). Wedged between bodies before and after is Pim, whose 'ageless body' (119) resists change like Deleuze's Stoic, Alice. Within the mechanics of repetition ('vie commune vie commune', 'quelle différence [. . .] quelle différence') 'false being' is the illusion of temporally differentiated relations 'd'avec avant' and 'd'avec après'. Against the notion of (corporeal) time, the final version of this paragraph introduces another: 'time will tell'. Indeed, when 'time will tell it's telling', only an apostrophe recovers the syntactic ambiguity between time's possession (its telling) and the continuous present *en train* (it's telling), though both are offered to the ear, and then derided. Such effects trivialise the philosophical register of the narrator/narrated's discourse of 'being' and 'inexistence'. His voice issues through a prism of contemporary jargon (*vide* the Sartrean catch-cries in *Being and Nothingness*), typical of Beckett's lack of enthusiasm for the existentialist fashions of his day. Beckett typically mocks that register, destabilising its claims with poetic effects, and diverting attention from the more private uses of philosophy in his own work.

In the context of bodies passing away and being reanimated the narrator/narrated's 'I am not yet dead to inexistence' is provocative. As in the French version, 'dead to' has its straightforward meaning: I am not lost to inexistence (I have not ceased to exist), or perhaps, I am dead but not (yet?) inexistent. Beckett's English is duplicitous, suggesting also: I am not unresponsive to inexistence (inexistence exists and my being may be in it), in which case this 'inexistence' is a possible alternative to 'existence', defined as 'false being'. A prevailing Democritean sentiment (the reality of the void and the infinite cycle of life in atoms) thus mixes the possibility of an alternative series of relations within an ontology not dependent upon bodies colliding in series of past, present and future. When Beckett refers to Pim as the 'causeur émérite' (443, emeritus postulator), he plays on the the fact that a 'causeur' is also a raconteur, or a pontificator, perhaps a legal witness or one who causes things (in the intransitive sense of *causer*: to effect something) (*Le Trésor*). Pim may be enlivened as the cause of the next coupling, in which sense he is like the Stoic corporeal, or permanent cause. For the Stoics, bodies resist the effects inscribed in them, while incorporeals, such as the words provoked in Pim by the tearing of his skin, have a role to play between causes. These do not, however, alter the pre-existent fact that each body is a cause and bodies are causes of each other. Against the 'orgy of false being', the eternal present of this alternative being resembles that of Stoic incorporeal time, its intermixing of bodies coalescing with other allusions to *pneuma* doctrine, continuous present and austere ethics. Here, the obsessions of the 'I' with respect to the space-time interval, the limits between bodies and the sorites paradox indicate that he feels, sometimes, that his material cosmos resembles that of Stoic pantheism.

## The Cosmic 'Slime-Worm': Stoic Pantheism

The 'I' of *How It Is* ingests voices that are both heavenly and abject: the 'rations' dropped from his monotheistic deity feed his piecemeal reason, a blurring of the material and spiritual realms drawn from the Christian Eucharist:

> this anonymous voice self-styled quaqua the voice of us all that was without on all sides then in us [. . .] certainly distorted there it is at last the voice of him who before listening to us murmur what we are tells us what we are [. . .]

> him to whom we are further indebted for our unfailing rations which enable us to advance without pause or rest. (183)

As the 'I' worms through the mud, he ingests not only the excreted voices of his 'past selves' but this voice of 'him', the source of all 'rations'. Beckett blends these voices within his metafiction so that his character's 'memory'/speech ironically blurs the celestial and sublunar realms. Such Spinozist tendencies, detailed in Chapters 5 and 7, conflate a monotheistic idea of God with an original pneumatic voice of reason, and the result is often confusing as the source of the narrator's discourse ('other above' or 'quaqua') is often unclear. This destabilising of allusions and referential contexts allows Beckett to inscribe himself, ironically, into the author/God and uncorrupted archive, the divine orchestrator 'above'.

Curiously, Beckett states these relations by making apparently explicit references to the Stoic theory of eternity and penetrable bodies. The above passage continues:

> of him who God knows who could blame him must sometimes wonder if to these perpetual revictuallings narrations and auditions he might not *put an end without ceasing to maintain us in some kind of being without end* and some kind of *justice without flaw* who could blame him

> and if finally he might not with profit revise us by means for example of a pronouncement to the effect that *this diversity is not our portion* nor these refreshing transitions from solitary travellers to tormentors [. . .]

> but that *in reality we are one* and from the unthinkable first to the no less unthinkable last *glued together in a vast imbrication of flesh without breach or fissure*

> for as we have seen part two how it was with Pim the coming into contact of mouth and ear leads to *a slight overlapping of flesh in the region* of the shoulders

> and that linked thus bodily together each of us is at the same time Bom and Pim tormentor and tormented pedant and dunce wooer and wooed speechless and reafflicted with speech in the dark the mud nothing to emend there. (183–5, my emphases)

This interconnected body is incompatible with the hylomorphic advance of Aristotelian bodies, whose colliding cause and effect seemed to define the machinic world of *How It Is*. Mechanical action dominates the whole Aristotelian universe: the unmoved mover touches the outer sphere of the heavens generating the circularity of its motion, essences unfurl in the series of effects which determine the genre and species of the sublunary bodies. As containers, bodies are modified by their contact with the external world. Yet here the narrator/narrated contemplates an alternative body: 'that in reality we are one and from the unthinkable first to the no less unthinkable last glued together in a vast imbrication of flesh without breach or fissure'. Within this one cosmic body individual bodies share the same space with 'a slight overlapping of flesh'. Aristotle's notion of space and time as the interval between two bodies rests upon his presumption that two bodies cannot occupy the same space at the same time. Aristotelian bodies are containers and contents of each other, the flow of effects occurring through the contact of one with the other. For the Stoics, the infinite divisibility of space meant that contact became radically impossible: *they took seriously Zeno's logical paradox of space, believing that since the edges of bodies split into infinity bodies cannot have limits.* Apperceived or not, the limits of bodies become infinitely dispersed within the extent of matter in the cosmos. The narrator/narrated's obsession with his sorites ratio, and his intuition of the infinite divisibility of his own limits, thus enters into a new realm of understanding.

Bréhier argues that the Stoics' quarrel with Aristotle allowed them to counter Epicurean atomism explicitly. To Plutarch's astonishment, the Stoics argued that without a precise point at which they come into contact bodies interpenetrate one another. If a place has the dimensions of an interval of space occupied by a full body, for instance a vase filled with different liquids, then that place may be divided into infinity. The aporia within the Aristotelian theory of bodies of contents and containers dissolves if one does not maintain that bodies are impenetrable. Bréhier draws this Stoic notion into Leibniz's 'tout est dans le tout' represented by his 'mélange total' (*La Théorie* 41; cf. *Monadology*, App. F §61). Beckett's edition of the *Monadology* cites the letter to Arnauld of 1686 in which Leibniz writes of deficiencies in the definition of the continuous, which must admit that 'bodies have no definite and precise shape, because of the actual sub-division of their parts [ie. their sub-division ad infinitum]' (108). Without actual matter and its modifications bodies would be, Leibniz asserts, 'merely imaginary' (108). I will return, in Chapter 7, to Beckett's interest in this crucial disjunction between the reality of matter and its mathematical description,[16] as part of the 'calculation' to prove a logically incontrovertible ratio of sacks to souls, this directly echoing Leibniz's *Monadology* in its 'exquisitely organized' (189) pre-established (dis)harmony. When the 'I' ponders that 'in reality we are one', this *reality* is the alternative to a series of bodies of containment and contents, as per Aristotle. It expresses a 'Stoic' 'reality', of the one material and cosmic body: 'a vast imbrication of flesh without breach or fissure' (185).

The corporeal equation of tormentor with victim is likewise a Stoic relation, the germination of which in Beckett's thinking may have been Windelband's discussion of Stoic opposition to the dualism of Plato and Aristotle:

> Their doctrine became in its fundamental principle <u>pantheism</u>, & (in opposition to Aristotle) conscious pantheism. Its immediate consequence is the effort to overcome the Platonic-Aristotelian dualism, & remove the opposition between sensuous & supersensuous, between natural necessity & reason acting according to ends, between matter and form. This the Stoic attempts by a simple identification of those opposing conceptions. (TCD 10967/117r; W 180)

Windelband shows how Stoic and Epicurean materialism is directed against Plato's sense that the properties of bodies are incorporeal: 'they regarded the presence and charge of properties in things as a kind of intermixture of these bodies with others, a view from which resulted the theory of the universal mingling and reciprocal interpenetration of all bodies' (W 186).

Before citing the familiar Stoic example of cutting the flesh, Bréhier refers to Stoic metaphor for the action of *pneuma* on bodies, and bodies on bodies: when fire heats the 'iron red-hot' one does not say that the fire has given it its qualities, or that the fire has given the iron new qualities, but that the fire '*a pénétré dans le fer pour coexister avec lui* dans toutes ses parties' (*La Théorie* 11, my emphasis). Just as the 'red-hot poker' (previously discussed) evokes the laughing philosopher, Democritus and elemental fire – '*c'est un fou rire que j'ai dans le cul* comme dans toutes mes parties' (360, my emphasis); it's a mad laugh that I've got in my arse *like in all my parts*) – it is now linked to the fire atoms (and thus consciousness) as a metaphor for the returning breath of the *Logos*. The breath as *pneuma* is the *philosophical* precedent for this idea; the Stoics may enter Beckett's polyvalent metaphor of penetration, given that the narrator/narrated typically accommodates contradictory philosophical doctrines within his images. The Stoic interpenetrated cosmic body entertains the Atomists' conglomeration, which in the Stoical age was Epicurean, and against which the Stoics defined their physics and *pneuma*.

Such paradoxes also inform Beckett's earlier fiction. Mercier and Camier's journey, for instance, crossed no 'seas or frontiers', yet they did not 'remove from home' (7). Molloy cannot escape his 'region' as, he says, '*the limits of my region were unknown to me*', for he imagines to be a borneless expanse: '*For regions do not suddenly* end, *as far as I know, but gradually merge into one another'* (*TN* 65, original emphasis). His 'region' is coextensive with his body, which he perceives to have no denied limit and which merges into those beyond it. His sense of time accords with this 'Stoic' spatial dimension: if he could have breached the limits of his 'region' then he would have 'left it changing slowly' (65). Yet the infinite limits of his region stretch time accordingly: 'And wheresoever you wander, within its distant limits, things will always be the same, precisely' (*TN* 65). The narrator/narrated of *How It Is* declares, 'it's the same kingdom as before a moment before the same it always was I have never left it it is boundless' (55; 1.249).

Unlike Aristotle, the Stoics believed the location of the body to extend from its centre of seminal reason, to a limit in space *not determined or delimited by an outside circumstance or its position with respect to another body*, but by its own nature. With an inverse movement, this vital reason returns to the centre from the outside. The place of the body is the result of such internal activity rather than its orientation with other bodies (Bréhier, *La Théorie* 41). Its nature is predetermined, though its extension is the result of its unique qualities: an individual body is but part of the cosmic tension holding together the cosmic body (*La Théorie* 42). Space is nevertheless predicated upon this action of bodies, and is thus, like language and time, incorporeal.[17] Windelband mentions such a notion in his discussion of the pneumatic force active in each individual, as Beckett noted:

> As the universal Pneuma animates all things, so the individual Pneuma, in which dwell ideas, judgments & impulses, in which dwell ideas, & whose seat is the heart, extends its ramifications, 'like the arms of a polyp', shoulder to the body. (10967/117v; W 187–8; cf. Bréhier, *La Théorie* 42)

In *How It Is* bodies overlap 'in the region of the shoulders' (185). In *Malone Dies* Macmann's universe dilates; his body follows:

> But this sensation of dilation is hard to resist. All strains towards the nearest deeps and notably my feet, which *even in the ordinary way* are so much further from me than all the rest, from my head I mean, for that is where I am fed, my feet are leagues away. And to call them in, to be cleaned for example, would I think take me over a month, exclusive of the time required to locate them . . . I feel they are beyond the range of the most powerful telescope. (234, my emphasis)[18]

The 'ordinary way' reveals that Macmann is thinking about an inordinate explanation for the dilating universe and his radically stretched body.[19] The Unnamable explodes the Aristotelian 'natural association' of the space-time interval, as in his refrain, 'the space of an instant' (316 passim); his lurching forward on crutches inscribes 'a kind of inverted spiral' (316), or a winding and unwinding pendular motion that militates against linear time:

> I don't seem to have gained much time, if by dint of winding myself up I must inevitably find myself stuck in the end, once launched in the opposite direction should I not normally unfold ad infinitum, with no possibility of ever stopping, the space in which I was marooned being globular, or is it the earth (316)

This may replicate Yeats' gyres and winding stair (the Unnamable refers to his 'gyrations' [316]), or Dante's spiralling ascent from hell (Ackerley and Gontarski, *Faber Companion* 657);[20] but being 'stuck in the end', as much as unfolding 'ad infinitum', engages Zeno's paradoxes of impossible motion even as the expanding and contracting body in space-time iterates the Stoic body.

## Pastiche and Dialectic

The ludic saboteur of the Pythagorean *ratio* laces the advancing calculations of the mind with paradox and irrationality. Similarly, within the grand cosmological 'calculation' of *How It Is*, the dialectic between Aristotelian and 'Stoic' positions is assimilated into one rhetoric of paradoxical progress – mocking the narrator/narrated's claims to *represent* a reasonable 'justice' above. At times he advances his Aristotelian or Stoic logics separately, but at other times historical dialectic is present as mere pastiche (from *pasticcio*, the Italian word for a pie containing both meat and pasta). Fredric Jameson's definition of twentieth-century pastiche as 'blank parody' neatly describes the philosophising of the 'I' in *How It Is*:

> Pastiche is, like parody, the imitation of a peculiar or unique, idiosyncratic style, the wearing of a linguistic mask, speech in a dead language. But it is a neutral practice of such mimicry, without any of parody's ulterior motives, amputated of the satiric impulse, devoid of laughter and of any conviction that alongside the abnormal tongue you have momentarily borrowed, some healthy linguistic normality still exists (*Postmodernism* 79)

The next chapter explores how the earnest ('blank') formulations of the narrator/narrated of *How It Is* are undone by the parodic impulse of the overarching organiser of his discourse, the spectral *poet-in-text* who stirs into one textual 'poss' (a word used in *Watt*, but not unlike the 'mess' that Beckett described to Tom Driver)[21] apparently incompatible Aristotelian-Stoic positions. One ample serving suffices: the Stoic logic italicised, the Aristotelian underlined, and their overlap in a sans serif font:

no sun no earth *nothing turning the same instant always everywhere*

<u>at the instant I reach Pim another reaches Bom</u> we are regulated thus our justice wills it thus fifty thousand couples again at *the same instant the same everywhere* with <u>the same space between them</u> it's mathematical it's our justice *in this muck where all is identical* our ways and way of faring right leg right arm push pull

as long as I with Pim the other with Bem *a hundred thousand prone glued two by two together vast stretch of time* nothing stirring save the tormentors those whose turn it is on and off right arm claw the armpit for the song carve the scriptions plunge the opener pestle the kidney all the needful

<u>at the instant</u> Pim leaves me and goes towards the other Bem leaves the other and comes towards me *I place myself at my point of view migration of slime-worms then or tailed latrinal scissiparous frenzy days of great gaiety*

<u>at the instant</u> Pim reaches the other to form again with him *the only couple he forms* apart from the one with me Bem reaches me to form with me *the only couple he forms* apart from the one with the other

illumination here Bem is therefore Bom or Bom Bem and the voice quaqua from which I get my life these scraps of life in me when the panting stops *of three things one.* (143–5)

In this theoretical calculation the 'instant' is divorced from the revolving sun or earth: 'nothing turning'. There is no measure against which to define space and time, yet the rhetoric of the Aristotelian 'instant' is assimilated into 'Stoic' relations. The 'I' locates himself within the procession of bodies: 'I place myself at my point of view migration of slime-worms then or tailed latrinal scissiparous frenzy days of great gaiety'. The image is reminiscent of how Aristotle's notion that the present is the limit between the beginning of the future and the end of the past is countered by Chryssipus, who places himself inside continuity itself. By denying that time can be measured by the beginning and ending of movement he rejected the possibility of taking any defined portion of time, thus placing himself *within the perspective* of time's infinity (Bréhier, *La Théorie* 57–8). Scissiparity is reproduction by division; the image of the cosmic body as a giant worm, segmented as a migrating whole, has a Stoic import: the scissiparous parts partake of the one while existing as individual causal bodies, each with its unique centre. The cosmic worm may be divided infinitely but its innumerable parts remain within the genus of the one corporeal substance. Within the 'latrinal' universe, these individual bodies are the only reality and all else is undifferentiated excrement (effects). The image generates its Aristotelian contradiction: if one does not believe that Zeno's logical paradox applies to phenomena, the segments then become discrete measures of the intervals of space, their movement measurable in time.

The phrase 'days of great gaiety' is later repeated in an allusion to the cosmic body, when the future infinity of Christian eschatology, so foreign to Stoic materialism, offers a release from the harsh reality of 'a slowness difficult to conceive' (161). A 'slowness' like that of Stoicism is almost impossible to conceive, and the narrator/narrated dreams himself as spat out of the continuous present of the intestinal universe:

> a procession advancing in jerks or spasms like shit in the guts till one wonders *days of great gaiety* if we shall not end one after another or *two by two* by being shat into the open air the light of day the regimen of grace (161, my emphases)

Again, the only way to sustain hope in the teleological universe is if one remains blind to the *two by two*, the fatal measure of the 'irrational' zigzag traced through the mud.

When embarking upon his rational proof for the 'ideal observer', in the passage above, the narrator/narrated claims 'it's mathematical', that is, it's logical, and in a Stoic context, incorporeal. Understood as such, he simply acknowledges as a condition of entering into that sphere the 'rations' fed to him during his own enforming. The logical operation is the antithesis of his quietism/mysticism and his agnostic abandonment of reason at the end of the novel. The 'scriptions' mark the Aristotelian transferral and for the Stoics, the aporia of predication.[22] *Our* 'justice' is an invented justice; that attributed to 'the other above in the light', as in the logical proof of a Leibnizian pre-established harmony. From this perspective, one of many that the narrative sustains, the trinitarian voice 'of three things one' is not that of God, Christ and the Holy Spirit, but rather the hermeneutic circle generated by epistemological excreta articulating through 'I', the *voice quaqua* and the transcendent *ancient voice*.

The narrator/narrated asserts the pedagogical relationship at the core of his universe in terms of the Aristotelian transferral, by trying to release the essence of Pim's species. Bouts of 'Stoic' consciousness suggest that he acknowledges the possibility that the logical operation merely overlays the materialist reality of Stoic doctrine, and thus all transferral is immaterial, without bearing upon the reality of bodies. His attribution of multifarious importance and number to the bodies 'all along the chain in both directions' is the relentless 'formulation to be adjusted assuredly in the light of our limits and possibilities' (185). Yet crawling through the mud, the 'I' does not accommodate the mess, but rather stirs up its chaos, mixing contradictory philosophical doctrines within his 'distorted' ratiocination. The *voice quaqua* offers him only distant and confused sensations of its more perfect archive (*ancient voice*). Presented with another being in his universe, he is affronted with a challenge to his hope (or fear) of being 'sole elect'. The Stoics advocated the moral obligation of all men to enter into social life: 'The Ideal State of the Stoics is a rational society of all men – an ideal universal Empire, cosmopolis, world-citizenship' (TCD MS10967/116r-v; W 176). The farcical encounter of 'I' and Pim thus acts as a parody of what might happen if the Stoics are taken literally, or flagrantly misread – when the cutting of flesh, corporeal pantheism and the ideal society 'unite for life in stoic love'.

This chapter has dis-covered the Aristotelian and anti-Aristotelian dimensions of the physical universe of *How It Is*, by following the mapping of its Platonic-Democritean tensions in the previous one. The Ancient Stoics offer a cogent counterpoint to Aristotle's teleology, but they are not the only source of the axis that cuts across its vertical teleology, located in the Dantean Inferno-like underworld. In what follows, I remark the presence of the early Church Fathers, Christian ascetics, Spinoza and other mystics, each of whom refutes in a different way the guiding anthropomorphism of a rationalist cosmic vision unfurling towards its final ends. The question abides: why is Beckett's 'I' so concerned with these historical dialectics, and what role do they play in his dystopia of pedagogical transfer? To answer this, I delve into the ethics of these various philosophical schools and examine their implications for one listening to or searching for his original voice, attempting to be reunited with his 'other above in the light'.

## Notes

1. Steven Rosen comments in *Samuel Beckett and the Pessimistic Tradition* (26–9, 86–90) on the Roman Stoics, but does not consider any connection with the Ancient Greek Stoics.
2. Ackerley notes that Murphy charms Celia with witty perversions of Aristotelian mnemonics, corrupting, for instance, 'Bokardo' into 'Baccardi' (the rum) (*Demented* 24–5). For 'Bokardo' see Abbott (*Elements* 53–5).
3. The rule of three allows for a fourth term (x) to be calculated from the proportional axiom $a : b = c : d => a : c = b : d$. Thus in $a/b = c/x$. The product of $a$ and $x$ is equal to that of $b$ and $c$, thus $x = (b.c)/a$.
4. Beckett was familiar with this section of notes for it is the same folio from which he drew his parody of Aristotle's *actus purus* informing the *risus purus* of *Watt*.
5. 'et défaut les grands besoins le besoin d'aller plus loin le besoin de manger et vomir et les autre grands besoins toutes me grandes catégories d'existence' (12). These categories augment the frugal 'two needs' of Beckett's essay, 'Les deux besoins'.
6. One must be careful to avoid anachronisms and not attribute to Beckett knowledge of the Stoics that was unlikely or impossible at the time of his writing (as with Democritus). The Ancient Stoics are not Roman Stoics, such as Seneca, Marcus Aurelius and Cicero who promulgated the doctrine of austerity and self-denial that has found its way into our vocabulary.
7. Only in one footnote, following a quotation from Pyrrho, does Beaufret indicate a 'Cf.' to Diogenes Laërtius' *Vie, Doctrines et Sentences* (IX, t. II) (Beaufret, *Leçons* 172).
8. Lycée Condorcet is a prestigious Paris high school whose programmes challenge some of France's most gifted students. The introduction to *Leçons* (13–16) testifies to the mesmerising and sometimes bewildering brilliance of Beaufret's discourse. Students' notes from Beaufret's 1946 lectures at Ashburne Hall (Manchester), repeated at Lycée Condorcet in 1956–7, are published in *Notes sur la Philosophie en France au XIXe siècle: De Maine de Biran à Bergson*, but the Stoics do not feature in these either.

9. On 4 August 1932 Beckett wrote to Thomas MacGreevy, 'I couldn't stand the British Museum any more. Plato & Aristotle & the Gnostics finished me.' This was eight days after Beckett received his first reader's ticket from the British Museum; the 'Philosophy Notes' probably date from this burst of study (Feldman, *Beckett's* 35).

10. Curiously, the second page of notes from Alexander begins mid-sentence, 'integrity. Resistance against, not conquest of, the world' (TCD MS 10967/115r), which does not follow the first page, nor did Beckett use the verso of this second page when summarising Windelband. This suggests that one or more pages of notes on the Stoics from Alexander were misplaced at the time Beckett turned to Windelband. He presumably found this second page from what was once a greater number of pages taken from Alexander, then slotted it into his other notes on the Stoics. There is no reason to believe that Beckett subsequently turned to the missing notes from Alexander's *A Short History of Philosophy* while creating any literary texts.

11. Commentators have noted the intractable problems of temporality in *How It Is* (Ackerley, 'Uncertainty' 39–51; Clément, *L'Œuvre* 113, 285–6; Grossman, 'Beckett' 39–52; Heise, 'Erzahlzeit' 245–69; Murphy, *Reconstructing* 71; Ratcliffe, 'Savage' 147–72; Smith, 'Beckett' 139–46; Thomas, 'Traduire' 139–46). The text's Aristotelian-Stoic negotiation of time has never been noticed, although Eric Levy comes near with a reading of the text in the terms of Hegelian dialectic ('Metaphysics' 27–38).

12. The example is well known; Uhlmann cites the 'famous Stoic example [. . .] a body cuts another body' (*Philosophical* 135), though it is not in Windelband's *History*.

13. Cf. Diogenes Laërtius: 'They hold that there are two principles in the universe, the active and the passive. The passive principle, then, is a substance without quality, i.e. matter, whereas the active is the reason inherent in this substance, i.e. god' (*Lives* 7.151).

14. The singular 'flammèche' is retained through subsequent drafts, 'ms/r' and 'Tx2', but this entire paragraph was then revised. In this paragraph of 'ms/r' the term 'élan' appeared – '*d'abord repartir élan vite calmé et première tentative de savoir je le dis comme je l'entends*' – its modifiers, 'vite calmé', bringing the 'élan' into dialogue with the '<flammèche> vite morte'. The 'élan' is that which generates movement and the spirit of something, its discourse with the *pneuma* evoking Bergson's 'élan vital' of *L'Évolution créatrice* (254). Gontarski (*Creative Involution*, 'Creative') and Addyman ('Different', 'Speak') have connected Beckett with Bergson's notions of finite and infinite time, which suggests a promising line of research within the triangulation of Aristotle, the Stoics and Bergson. Beckett's use of Zeno's paradoxes in the context of defined and undefined time recalls Bergson's point when detailing his

theory of durational continuity in his 1903 essay 'Introduction à la métaphysique', reproduced in the 1934 *La Pensée et le mouvant* (*The Creative Mind: An Introduction to Metaphysics*): 'As a result of an illusion deeply rooted in our mind, and because we cannot prevent ourselves from considering analysis as the equivalent of intuition, we begin by distinguishing along the whole extent of the movement a certain number of possible stoppages or points, which we make [. . .] parts of the movement. Faced with our impotence to reconstruct the movement with these points, we insert other points, believing that we can in this way get nearer to the essential mobility in the movement. Then, as this mobility still escapes us, we substitute for a fixed and finite number of points an "indefinitely increasing" number [. . .] Finally, we say that movement is composed of points [. . .] [Yet] [i]t is movement that we must accustom ourselves to look upon as simplest and clearest, immobility being only the extreme limit of the slowing down of movement, a limit reached only, perhaps, in thought and never realized in nature. What we have done is to seek for the meaning of the poem in the form of the letters of which it is composed' (*Introduction* 43).

15. The radically open-ended 'conclusion' means that indefinite, circular time is not the necessary end but a probable one, the inevitable conclusion from the way that repetition is enacted in the text. Despite claiming to cast off the overarching demiurge, the 'I' is still trapped in his *ancient voice*, returning to the beginning of the narrative to repeat anew that which apparently he was just made to recite.

16. This is not where one body fills the empty space between, where 'containing' and 'contained' bodies may persist, but rather an intimate fusion in all points of two bodies.

17. For Bréhier, the incorporeality of place plays an analogous role to the ideality of space for Kant – place does not affect the nature of beings (*La Théorie* 43).

18. I explore Beckett's use of the telescope as a Leibnizian trope in Chapter 7. The implication here is that Macmann cannot perceive the extremity of his body through his senses, nor perceive its *petites perceptions* with the use of his telescope (a proxy for the infinitesimal calculus that would resolve the infinite series between his point of reference and the limit).

19. Macmann refers to the Maia in this passage, yet Beckett often harnesses the whatness of more than one philosophical horse in a single image.

20. Ackerley reports that in *Dream* (129) a butterfly on 'the eternal toilet-roll' is said to 'pern' [sic] in a gyre, as in 'Sailing to Byzantium' (Ackerley and Gontarski, *Fabber Companion* 657).

21. '[T]he world that Beckett sees is already shattered. His talk turns to what he calls "the mess," or somethings "this buzzing confusion" . . . The only chance of renovation is to open our eyes and see the mess. It is not a mess you can make sense of . . . One cannot speak anymore of being, one must speak only of the mess. When Heidegger and Sartre speak of a contrast between being and existence, they may be right, I don't know, but their language is too philosophical for me. I am not a philosopher. One can only speak of what is in front of him, and that now is simply the mess' (Driver, 'Beckett' 218).

    'What I am saying does not mean that there will henceforth be no form in art. It only means that there will be new form, and that this form will be of such a type that it admits the chaos and does not try to say that the chaos is really something else. The form and the chaos remain separate. The latter is not reduced to the former. That is why the form itself becomes a preoccupation, because it exists as a problem separate from the material it accommodates. To find a form that accommodates the mess, that is the task of the artist now' (Driver, 'Beckett' 220–1).

22. As species of reason, rather than the Stoics' image of 'comprehensive representation'.

4

# From the Cradle to the Cave:
# A Comedy of Ethics from Plato to
# Christian Asceticism (via Rembrandt)

No god indulges in philosophy[.] (Plato, *Symposium* 204a)

In the *Phaedo* Plato forewarns that after death 'the tutelary genius of each person [. . .] leads him to a place where the dead are gathered together; then they are judged and depart to the other world' (107d). One is conducted through the afterlife by one's education, or *paideia*, and the immortal soul can escape a dire end only if it has learned how to become good and wise. Plato unifies the *phronesis* or philosophical thinking within what he terms in the *Phaedo* the 'practice of death' (81a), of learning how to die, and in the *Theaetetus*, as turning from the world 'to become like God, so far as this is possible' (176b). To experience this supreme Good involves treading the path to self-perfection. Formed in reason, one learns to appreciate the goodness in things. In the *Laws*, Plato terms 'the goodness that first comes to children "education"' (2.653b). Education must be given to children 'in respect of pleasures and pains, so as to hate what ought to be hated [. . .] and to love what ought to be loved' (2.653b–c). The 'goodness' of education is not the accumulation of laws but rather giving to children the ability to 'consent thereunto that they have been rightly trained in fitting practices' (2.653b). The 'goodness' of the 'fitting practice', its reason (*Logos*), is its potential to train the mind to reflect upon the goodness in all things. For Plato, the attainment of the 'Idea of the Good' is not only the task of philosophy but the apprehension of divine unity as the goal of the truly philosophical life. Yet while the 'Idea of the Good' is a transcendent order the form of its Idea was conceived as akin to mathematical logic.

    *How It Is* inverts this Platonic archetype into a gothic allegory, the quest of the 'I' through the underworld seeking to know if he is 'sole elect' (11). The idealised (pre-fragmented) pedagogical voice and a monotheistic deity are conflated, and a philosophical history of a teleologically structured universe shapes the journey. His two principal resources are his reasonable faculty (*ratio*) and the voice of his past life, the very abandonment of the need for the *ratio*. He exercises ascetic humility, journeying alone through his wasteland in the hope of a sign from the *other* above, or God, and attempting to recover the knowledge of *ancient voice* by quoting it, hoping to rise from his morass to be reunited with the transcendent *other above in the light*. Dante absorbed an Aristotelian teleology into his neo-Platonism in the *Commedia*; and Beckett's 'I' likewise longs to follow his Virgil in the hope of ascending towards perfect unity, the divine One. Beckett's 'I' avails himself of various options within Christian praxes (as discussed in the next chapter), but here I follow the motivating dialectic which first draws him out of the circuitous entanglements of his *ratio*, then into the essential tussle animating his journey: whether to engage the *ratio* in a comprehension of the cosmos, or reject the very attempt to do so as an 'anthropomorphic insolence' (*Watt* 202).[1]

The question is quintessentially ethical, involving nothing less than the wholesale rejection of the *paideia*. The opposition between Aristotelian and anti-Aristotelian or Stoic interpretations of the physical world conditions the narrator/narrated's interpretation of his journey. He considers both the measured advance of progress and, like the Stoics, suspension from judgement itself. His 'Stoic' tuning in to the 'natural order' of universal Reason rejects the striving that holds the Christian *theoria* as its *telos*, but needs no rational categories to account for its ascent. Like Moses and the Holy Family, Christian ascetics took their faith into the deserts of Egypt in a hope of solitude and/or of being blessed with a vision of God. Images of their journeys – many derived from Rembrandt – are drawn by the narrator/narrated, who repeatedly inscribes himself into this venerable Christian tradition and creates ludicrous fantasies of the philosophical and Christian life, to undermine not only the *ratio* of the 'I' but its most pious pretensions.

### Pim's *Paideia*: Anathematic *Logos*

Plato's parable of the cave offers a metaphor of 'our nature in respect of education [*paideia*] and its lack [*apaideusia*]' (*Republic* 7.514a). As ignorance and ill-breeding, *apaideusia* stands in opposition to *paideia*. Chapter 2 followed Beckett's allusion to this archetypal Western allegory in *How It Is* when his narrator/narrated likens his life in the underworld of mud to a fly's attempt to emerge from excrement into life in the light:

> [. . .] that fly perhaps gliding on the pane the counterpane all summer before it or noonday glory of colours behind the pane in the mouth of the cave and the approaching veils. (113–15)

The fly that once glimpsed the light above is condemned to live below in a world of shadows and ignorance. Similarly, I proposed, confronted with the veils across his cave that screen out the glorious light beyond, the 'I' reverts to his Pythagorean education in hope of finding the mathematical key that would open the way to the 'ideal' plenitude. He aspires towards the panorama that later schools termed *theoria* – from the verb to observe and contemplate – the ecstatic revelation of divine order comprehended as an intellectual vision. A potent idea in the Western mind, *theoria* was taken up within the different teleological systems of Plato, Aristotle and the Ancient Stoics, then assimilated into early Church theology and typified in the New Testament account of Paul's blinding revelation of the light on the road to Damascus (Acts 9:1–31, 22:1–22 and 26:9–24).

Beckett's 'I'/eye is veiled and returned to the darkness of the cave, the lower realm of *apaideusia*. Here Socratic ideals receive their gothic twist: on his journey the 'I' encounters a formless being named Pim. He teaches Pim how to behave and speak, first by blows and tortures, then by scraping letters into Pim's back and backside. The 'I' conceives of his journey as one link in a great chain of beings who alternate between torturer and victim – in the next rotation of the cosmic circle the 'I' will be the 'victim' of his 'master' behind, and Pim 'master' to his 'victim' ahead. The circle is universally predetermined and eternally repeats a sadomasochistic representation of teacher and student, where ignorance is inscribed from generation to generation.

Socratic method was conceived as the ideal instrument of the *paideia*, its controlled maieutic dialogues of question and answer drawing out of students their reasonable faculty, learning how to acquire knowledge rather than being inscribed within it. *How It Is*, however, is steeped in rancid Platonism: Pim is savagely attacked until he comes to understand the behavioural responses desired by his pedagogue, whose motivation for training Pim in his language, literally scratching letters into Pim's back, is to satisfy himself with a sadistic ritual of question and answer which ends the ordeal. The only 'Good' of this encounter is the pleasure the pedagogue derives from the student's answer when it becomes a cry of pain: 'face in the mud nose mouth howls good' (129; 2.129). The sadistic application of the Platonic ideal of developing the mind's autonomous 'consent' to goodness reverses upon itself in the final scene of *How It Is*; the 'I' inflicts this exhausting ritual of question and answer upon himself:

how was it then no answer HOW WAS IT screams good

[. . .] my name no answer WHAT'S MY NAME screams good

[. . .] so that's life here no answer THAT'S MY LIFE HERE screams good

[. . .] die no answer DIE screams I MAY DIE screams I SHALL DIE screams good. (191–3; 3.301–14)

The Socratic horror realises itself most completely when the dialogue of torture/education has been internalised.[2] The 'I' releases his own 'scream' on seven occasions, eliciting, as in the note registered after the 'howls', the sadist's contentment: 'good'.

Beckett's spoof of pedagogical idealism undermines the *paideia* that was, for Plato as much as for Aristotle, the means by which a human becomes a creature endowed with *Logos*. According to Aristotle (*Politics* 1.1260b), even slaves should not be denied reason. *Paideia* is the vehicle of the *Logos* through which humans realise their potential: 'reason and intelligence are for us the end of our natural development' (*Politics* 7.1334b). Aristotle set out to systematise Plato's ideal of the philosophical life within the formality of his own system, the 'theoretic' life. In the *Nicomachean Ethics*, the virtue of the intellectual life is its moral self-perfection through the constant activity of 'Working' (1117 12): the development of self-sufficient scientific reason. Scientific contemplation is achieved through detachment, by overcoming one's lower instincts in the passage towards the higher realm.

In 'Part 1' of his *History*, 'The Philosophy of the Greeks', Windelband sanctifies the *dianoëtic* virtues of Aristotle's *theoria* in the history of Western thought:

The highest perfection of its development finally is achieved by the rational nature of man in *knowledge*. The *dianoëtic* virtues are the highest, and those which bring complete happiness. The activity of theoretical reason [. . .] is directed to the immediate apprehension of the highest truths [. . .]

But knowledge of these, the full unfolding of the 'active reason' in man, is again designated by Aristotle as a 'beholding' θεωρία [theoria]; and with this beholding of the highest truth man gains a participation in that *pure thought*, in which the essence of the deity consists, and thus, also, in the eternal blessedness of the divine self-consciousness. For this 'beholding' which exists only for its own sake and has no ends of will or deed, this wishless absorption in the perception of the highest truth, is the blessedest and best of all. (W 154)

Following this logic, Beckett notes how the Stoics explored this 'wishless absorption' through their notion of *apatheia* – not 'apathy' but a notion closer to the *accedie*, or total indifference, of the Sullen and Slothful in Dante's *Inferno* 7. Despite Beckett's debt to *Inferno* 7, and the narrator/narrated's ironic self-image as the indolent Belacqua, the apparent suspension of will in the past-I's 'quotation' of his *ancient voice*, is far from disinterested. Even editorial intrusions within the *ancient voice*, such as 'my life last state last version', are self-reflective, forming part of the past record of the narration, infinitely repeated within the closed loop of circular narrative.

The present-I's editing of the *ancient voice* assumes an ironic posture with respect to his former intuition of events and the nature of the cosmos, but as an ethical position his submission accords with his intuition of an anti-Aristotelian, potentially Stoic cos-mology. He expresses the law of narrative events as the 'natural order', a phrase recurring frequently, and variously, in his discourse of Part 1, and which is echoed again in Part 3 (151, 171). This expresses the concept of a harmonious, linear and underlying logic that determines and unites the cosmos, the journey, generic narra-tive and its recitation. The present-I claims to relinquish his will and subdue his passions to the obligation to recite faithfully this order: 'I say it my life as it comes natural order my lips move I can feel them it comes out in the mud my life [. . .] things so ancient natural order the journey the couple the abandon all that in the present' (21). Pim's education delivers him into this natural order, his 'dressage' assimilating him into his master's 'moral plane bud and bloom of relations proper' (71). Indeed, bringing pedagogical 'relations proper' into accord with the cosmic natural order charts a Stoic path to virtue.

Diogenes Laërtius defines this route as the practice of 'living consistently with nature' (*Lives* 7.87). Virtue, according to Plutarch, is held by Zeno of Citium,[3] Chrysippus and Ariston of Chios to be: 'reason consistent and firm and unchangeable' (*On Moral* 441 C). Zeno's notion of correct behaviour is, following Diogenes Laërtius, the virtuous harmonising of the self with nature: 'living consistently with nature is living in accordance with virtue, since nature leads us to virtue' (*Lives* 7.87). The Stoics did not believe living consistently to be a prescription for moral action; rather, the innate nature of humans determines their action. 'Nature' here is both a human and cosmic order, and human reason is nature's crowning virtue. It is the realisation into action of the *Logos* immanent in all things: 'Therefore, the end turns out to be living in agreement with nature, taken as living in accordance with one's own nature and with the nature of the whole' (*Lives* 7.88). The *telos* of the Stoic *paideia* is learning to listen to the natural order. Hence Beckett's 'I' hopes to learn the *natural order* dictated by his master/God through will-less listening: 'je le dis comme je l'entends dans l'ordre [. . .] je l'apprends dans l'ordre [. . .] l'ordre naturel' (20; I say it as I hear natural order [. . .] I learn it natural order [. . .] natural order 21).

## Nature/Order: Stoic Ethics

The importance to Beckett of the thought of the seventeenth-century Occasionalist, Arnold Geulincx, in particular his doctrine of the *inspectio sui*, has been recognised in recent scholarship. Beckett perhaps encountered Geulincx before he ventured into the Reading Room of Trinity College Dublin in early 1936 to read his *Ethics* in Latin, yet his appreciation of Geulincx (see Chapter 5), like that with Spinoza (Chapter 7), was preconditioned by his studies of Aristotle's 'wishless absorption in the perception of the highest truth' as transformed by the Stoic dictum of the 'withdrawal of the individual':

> Virtue (control of passion by reason) is the sole good, Vice (control of reason by passion) the sole evil. All other things & relations are in themselves indifferent.
>
> This *withdrawal of the individual personality into itself*, which all these Greek epigones considered the mark of the wise man, was

nowhere so valuably supplemented as among the Stoics. <u>Scepticism</u> *never desired such a positive supplementation*, Epicureanism sought it in a direction which expressed in the sharpest form the subordination of ethical interest to individual happiness. But when *the Stoics iden-tify the rational with the natural*, as the Cynics did, they arrive, not at the Cynic <u>Sensuous</u> determination of morality, but at the *Aristote-lian <u>reasonable</u> determination*. For <u>Nous</u> is not only the world-,[4] it is the individual soul. The virtuous self-withdrawal of the individual is also in subordination to the World-Nous, <u>Providence</u>, with which the individual soul is consubstantial. (TCD MS 10967/114v, underlining is Beckett's, emphases are mine; W 169–70)

This passage represents a submission to the 'natural order' identified as the Stoic 'relations proper' in *How It Is*. Windelband acknowledges in a footnote an indirect debt to Diogenes Laërtius, a crucial section of the *Lives* that indicates why the narrator/ narrated's philosophical deliberations are suspended in the act of recitation ('I quote'): that is, because the nature of his submission is itself the ethical inheritance of his rational deliberations upon such issues. His attitude oscillates between the Sceptics' detached 'non-committal condition of suspense'[5] which Molloy referred to as 'my old ataraxy' (*TN* 42) – where one holds that nothing matters so as to focus on what matters supremely – and the congruence of a Stoic ethic of *apatheia* with his sense of the cosmos as one great interpenetrated body, in which space and movement are incorporeal. This 'stoic love' suggests ironically that the relationship between 'I' and Pim is of the same order as that (homosexuality) practised between Ancient Greek masters and students, a bizarre understatement given that Pim has 'stoi-cally' endured his teacher's sadistic anally-fixated advances.[6]

Beckett draws upon the popular cliché for the notion of the 'virtuous self' derived from the Roman Stoics as epitomised in Seneca's avowal of endurance. In his letter 107 to Lucilius, Seneca councils Lucilius not to lament his slaves running away because such events are to be expected; they are as inevitable as getting dirty when walking through mud. In Justus Lipsius' account, Seneca does not offer a principle of affirmation, but rather looks fate in the eye and prescribes steadfastness, *optimum est pati*: one should suffer what one cannot alter, *patere igitur, quod non emendas* (Lipsius, *Senecae* 631). Seneca advises meditation upon future evils as preparation for what may come: 'It is not possible to change this condition of things; but it is possible to take on a noble soul worthy of a good man, thereby courageously enduring chance (*fortiter fortuita patiamur*) and being in harmony with nature' (Seneca, *Letters* 107.7). For Seneca, as for Chryssipus, to go against the natural order of things is to contravene both divine will and human reason. Beckett's dystopia of 'stoic love' is administered by a master who, like Seneca, believes that his suffering in the inferno of mud prepares one for life's trials, and for life in the light. The cosmological model of alternating sadist and victim suggests Beckett's blackly comic deduction of Stoic (and Leibnizian) theodicies, where evil is apportioned its place within the divine harmony, to be endured like the loss of a slave for Seneca, as unavoidable as walking through the mud.

Windelband identifies the 'double sense' (*W* 172) of Nature for the Stoics: firstly, the creative, cosmic world-power which acts to teleological ends; secondly, humanity's moral subordination to the law of Nature. This accords with the narrator/narrated's expressions of the 'natural order': firstly, as the linear sequence of events and cosmic order of time and space; secondly, of his withdrawal into the self, relinquishing the power to disrupt the narrative in its recitation. His expressed purpose, in which he assuredly and comically fails, is to interfere as little as possible with the voice of World-Reason, his intuited *other above in the light* and ultimate orchestrator of the *ancient voice*.

The status of the voice is the most recalcitrant problem. The narrator/narrated identifies its source as either *the other above in the light*, the figure of *Nous*, God-Author and universal Reason, or equally, the 'I' in his former life to whom memories of the past are attributed. This latter self is often assumed to be autobiographical, while the former has received little critical attention. Childhood images that return in Part 1, such as the boy kneeling and praying under his mother's 'severe love', may be attributed to Beckett's memory, which implies that attempts to reach himself through his characters pass into pure fiction. Yet elsewhere this 'life' of the past-'I' is an obvious fabrication (his former wife Pam Prim falling out a window, thus repeating the fall of his father, that of his dog, Skom Skum, or that of humankind).

Part 3 offers a clear account of how voices separate out within the narrative:

> and this *anonymous voice self-styled quaqua the voice of us all* that was without on all sides then in us when the panting stops bits and

scraps barely audible *certainly distorted* there it is at last *the voice of him who before listening to us* murmur what we are *tells us what we are* as best he can

*of him to whom we are further indebted for our unfailing rations* which enable us to advance without pause or rest. (183, my emphases)

The *voice quaqua* is 'self-styled' (in French, *'se disant'*); it is the self-saying, the autonomous voice recreated in the act of recitation apart from the transcendent voice. As the chorus of 'us'[7] existing 'on all sides', it is analogous to the cacophony of a singular subjectivity; the noise of consciousness rehearsing past experience. The world of extension is equated with the material voice, embodied in mud, *quaqua*.[8] This voice contrasts with 'the voice of him', which Beckett deliberately obscures by delaying recognition that it is modified: 'when the panting stops bits and scraps barely audible certainly distorted *there it is*'. The French reads: 'quand ça cesse de haleter à peine audible *dénaturée* certainement la voilà' (182, my emphasis). Here 'the voice of him' is that of a monotheistic deity, which in the next paragraph becomes the voice of 'unfailing rations', the economy of Beckett's diction dispatching the *constant reason* of the Stoic 'ratio' before it becomes *dénaturée* into its piecemeal 'rations'. Within this version of 'give us this day our daily bread' and 'manna from heaven', Beckett assimilates the Greek *paideia* into Christianity.

In Book I of *Émile, ou de l'Éducation*, Rousseau discusses how a child is 'dénaturée' when entering into society;[9] nature must be tamed so that harmonious social relations may be maintained. In *Comment c'est* Pim's education is his 'problème du dressage' (70), which is the issue of his 'training' (71). The French assumes the training of an animal, but its pejorative tones imply a pedagogical discourse for bringing a student to execute mechanically what the master expects of him (*Trésor*); Pim's *paideia* is thus more the breaking in of a horse than the merely coercive sense of the English 'dressage', or the gentle Socratic method. This crushing of a wild nature is advanced as a prerequisite for accommodating the *Logos*, yet it animates a pedagogical regime as brutal as any uncivilised nature; hence Beckett's delightful irony when *dressage* is equated with 'moral plane bud and bloom of relations proper' (71; 2.38). The 'stoic love' of master and slave inverts the communication of *Logos* to a higher nature, understood as uncorrupted, rational order. In *How It Is*, distortion arises in the disharmony of the one below, whose constant 'panting' interrupts the *ancient voice* with its expiring slather.

Beckett reiterates that the voice of *ratio*/nature exists prior to its discordant translation: the voice of him 'who *before listening to us murmur* what we are *tells us what we are*' (quoted above, my emphasis). This revision is immediately undermined with the narrator/narrated's ironic quip, 'of him who God knows who could blame him'. Despite the attempt to distance 'God' from 'him' the reader appreciates, rather, the amusing tangle which a seemingly unconscious figure of speech produces. However, when such figures are so precise and so apt, they seem neither accidental nor unconscious but the work of 'him' who is construed by the text as synonymous with the World-Reason, 'him' who is within the novel's metatextual schema, the *other* one *above in the light*. This figure is the poet-without-subject who moonlights as an anthropomorphic deity, the transcendent author who lives under 'the lamps' (19 passim). Subverting his character's discourse, he ushers himself into the scene not as himself but theatrically, as a character, playing himself in the role of an author. Less the poet expelled from the *Republic* than a truant from *apaideusia*, he is the mocker of false teaching.

When Beckett encountered Windelband's enthusiasm for Stoic ethics, his natural inclination was to cock an ironic brow:

> To the Stoic ethics belongs the glory that in it the ripest & highest which the ethics of antiquity produced attained its best formulation. The intrinsic worth of moral personality, the overcoming of the world in the overcoming of self, the subordination of the individual to the world-mind,[10] his disposition in an ideal union of spirits & at the same time his dutiful participation in the actual world – all these constitute one of the most powerful & pregnant creations in the history of conceptions of human life. Tra-la-la-la. (TCD MS 10967/116v; W 176)

Beckett's sceptical 'Tra-la-la-la' is a rare incursion of his own opinion into the 'Philosophy Notes', but may be the seed of the 'Stoic' parody in *How It Is*. This mocking voice, like the subversive other in *How It Is*, unstitches any diligent quotation of the *ancient voice*.

Just as the narrator/narrated polarises his cosmos between Aristotelian and Stoic physics with no intention of generating a dialectical resolution, so too a dialogue between the active 'Working' reason

of Aristotelian ethics and Stoic *apatheia* induces his personal sac-
cadic telotaxis through the mud. A Stoic 'withdrawal into the self'
is needed to break the iron links of hylomorphic causation induced
by Aristotle's sense of 'Working' relentlessly towards the thought of
thoughts and light of reason: 'ascending heaven at last no place like
it in the end' (131).

With his 'ten yards fifteen yards push pull' the 'I' once dragged
a sack full of hope, but having done with his dogged calculations,
attempting to reconcile his schooled beliefs that his portion is to
'advance' with linear 'rations', and harmonising his motor with a
just, teleological destiny, his final position face down in the mud
betokens, rather, a *rational* opposition to the logic of quest and
progress. Nietzsche's path through philosophy finally champions
the escape from reason – embodied in his 'irrational' carriage
of fragmentary and epithetic exposition – the narrator/narrated
finally claims no longer to 'quote' the *ancient voice*. A pantheistic
or even mystical communion with the World-Reason is assuredly
not his fate, though his immobility and tongue in the mud may
suggest a final triumph of his Stoicism: his entry into one continuous present and the search within nature for its 'order'. But if the
narrative has instilled anything, it is that this resolution is liable
to be equally transient, just as the *ancient voice* may return with
its red-hot spike. Submission is part of the enformed habits of a
*ratio* that cannot escape the power of the *paideia*, and the dialectic
between these two rational conceptions of ethical action (active
and passive) is the heart of the Aristotelian-Stoic dialectic in *How
It Is*. Indeed, the 'I' of *How It Is* becomes wrapped around his
Stoic solipsism, for as soon as he liberates himself from the *ancient
voice* he returns to Part 1 to tell his tale in the present, the point to
which he returns incessantly. If this manifests his withdrawal into
the self and liberation from will, his loop in the continuous present
will never manifest a divine natural order of *Logos*, for it is condemned to the ill-hearing which is, for Beckett, an epistemological
condition of being in language: the only reasonable constancy in
nature is this discordant noise of the *ratio*, consciousness itself.

### The '*Élysée Visuelle*': *Theoria* in the Desert, via Rembrandt and the Painted Image

The ideas (and angels) which in Philo's gnosis mediate the gulf
between God and the world are indebted to the Stoics' *Logos*.
Beckett's notes record the 'attempt to reconcile apostolic tradition

with Greek philosophy, & to change <u>faith</u> into a special mode of <u>knowledge</u>' (TCD MS10967/144r). Attempting to reconcile the voice *above in the light* and the *voice quaqua*, the narrator/narrated repeats the error of Beckett's acolyte of Manichean intellectual transgression, Krapp, the mediator of Spirit (light) and Sense (dark). Beneath the post-/Cartesian costume of Part 3, the narrator/narrated struggles towards a reasoned theology, revealing the neo-Platonic lining to his Christianity. While his journey through the mud might evoke the extreme rites of Mani's cult, his persistent self-image in ascesis develops from the Christian asceticism that grew out of opposition to an Alexandrian intellectualisation of faith. The narrator/narrated reveals the enduring dialectical opposition in his thinking, not that between various reasoned interpretations of the cosmos (Plato v. Democritus, Aristotle v. Stoics), but his attraction to, and repulsion from, transforming his act of faith into 'a special mode of <u>knowledge</u>' (above). In resisting a reasoned or theological interpretation of his journey, he desires, above all, to escape the anthropomorphic parameters of reason itself.

Scribe and witness, Krim and Kram are slippery figures. Their diminutive form suggests less the presence of the Deity as his angelic descendants from the light; like neo-Platonic mediators they form a syzygetic (homo-)couple, while also fulfilling the judicial function of a Kantian court of reason.[11] During the theological 'formulation' of Part 3, they interrupt a direct communication with the transcendent unities, World-Reason and Author: Kram is accused of having 'eliminated' the 'ear' (181), symbol of God's uncorrupted listening (as in the Bible and Augustine). Still within the anthropomorphic parameters of his Christian education, the narrator/narrated frets when unable to find a coherent answer to his question: 'me sole elect'. Either he finds salvation in 'an intelligence somewhere a love', and can 'assign an ear like ours' (anthropomorphism), or die a meaningless death: 'otherwise desert flower' (181), a traditional image of blooming and dying unseen employed by Leopardi and Thomas Gray, for instance. At this stage of Part 3, the Stoic, pantheistic solution proposed by the narrator/narrated is rejected with an ascetic counter-thesis: the 'I' is cloaked in 'this black air that breathes through our ranks and enshrines as in the 'Thebaïd' our couples and our solitudes as well of the journey as of the abandon' (183; 3.263).

The 'Thebaïd' (or 'Thebais') was a Greek epic poem in hexameters, originally attributed to Homer; like the *ancient voice*, it survives only in fragments. The Roman poet, Statius, took up its theme in his twelve-book epic, the *Thebaïd*.[12] In this epic of fraternal strife the two sons of Oedipus, Eteocles and Polyneices, are unable to rule Thebes together, so alternate the throne every year. The narrator/narrated's sense of the 'black air' of his underworld suggests that the narrator/narrated, if not Beckett himself, has been exposed to a classical education. Beckett's delicate art of balancing comic with philosophical and religious motifs is witnessed when, in the early manuscripts 'ms', the 'couples' in the 'Thebaïd' were first enshrined in their *'véritable désert'*, revised in 'TxI' to *'un véritable <riant> désert'*, before 'TxI' decides the matter: *'un désert <une thébaïde>'* (579; 3.263). Striking out *désert* for *riant*, or gaiety, establishes the quixotic comedy of the brothers, but in losing the arid *désert*, Beckett erased a crucial allusion, the ascetic practice of the Desert Fathers, which he partially recovered by opening their 'Thebaïd'. The early Christian hermits, who from the third century sustained the Christian monastic culture, offer the narrator/narrated an alternative to his fate as the 'desert flower' which dies unseen by God.[13] The Desert Fathers retreated into the Egyptian desert, where they practised extreme asceticism, either alone as hermits (anchorites) or in communities (cœnobites). Many followed the example of St Anthony of Egypt, greatest of anchorites, but finding the hermetic life too challenging they entered under St Pachomius into nine cells in the desert, thereby forming the first monasteries. Beckett had read *La Tentation de Saint Antoine*, Flaubert's account of St Anthony's life.[14]

Flaubert's *Tentation* opens in the 'Thebaïd' and explores the metaphysical dualism between *Matière* and *Esprit*, the derivation of multiplicity from unity, and the regression towards *prima materia*.[15] While St Anthony was reputed illiterate, his '170 Texts on Saintly Life' council a Stoic constancy with subjection of the passions, echoing metaphors and phrases from Epictetus' *Encheiridion*. At the end of Part 1, ironically referring to the example of Christ, the narrator/narrated takes his 'last meal the last journey' (59), preparing not for the *Via Dolorosa* to Mount Calvary but rather his own mundane 'gleam of hope frantic departure' (59). Setting out towards his prophetic future, his journey imitates the flight of the Holy Family's into the desert (Matthew 2:13–23). This disputed chapter of Christ's life may have been invented by Matthew, his record of Jesus' life thus parallel to Moses' journey into the desert. In Matthew the Holy Family escapes after Herod instigates his plan to kill the baby Jesus after hearing the prophecy of the wise men, claiming that the Messiah had been born. St Anthony's journey is therefore his imitation of those faced by Moses and Jesus. In manuscript 'ms' of *Comment c'est*, the narrator/narrated hopes explicitly that his own quest will continue the tradition of solitude and mortification quickened when his '*étincelle d'espoir*' ('gleam of hope') was first conceived by Beckett as '*la prière à St-Antoine*' (388; the prayer to St Anthony). He varies the theme, imagining the suffering Pim: 'an oriental [. . .] he has renounced I too will renounce I will have no more desires' (69). This 'dream' (69), or aspiration, echoes his self-comparison a few pages before with Gautama Buddha, the 'extreme eastern sage' (65) and ascetic upon whose teachings Buddhist monasteries were founded.

Krim and Kram are also shrouded in a monastic aura. The narator/narrated figures them into a paradoxical image of the 'generations' of his *ancient voice* transmitted through monastic praxis, by focusing on hermeneutic revelation in their act of scriptural copying and recitation:

> all alone and the witness bending over me name Kram bending over us father to son to grandson yes or no and the scribe name Krim generations of scribes keeping the record a little aloof sitting standing it's not said yes or no samples extracts. (103)[16]

Echoes of Biblical begetting and the *homoiousios* of Father and Son (though extending this line becomes questionable) mingle with a Trinitarian triangulation with Krim hermeneutically engaged with the 'extracts' generated by the communication of *Logos* between generations. Having departed from their unity in the divine light, Krim and Kram's 'mediation' is less neo-Platonic than cœnobitic, issuing forth fragments where the narrator/narrated inevitably loses the 'ninetenths' (105).

When towards the end of Part 2, the narrator/narrated searches for a 'little scene' in the early manuscript 'ms', he draws from his mind an image which derives from one of the great masters of seventeenth-century painting:

> lumière lumière du jour *lumière* de la nuit petite scène ICI jusqu'au sang et quelqu'un à genoux ou accroupi dans un coin *d'ombre par exemple* n'importe prière sans paroles rest on the <round> flight début de petite scène dans la pénombre ICI ICI jusqu'à l'os l'ongle s'en casse vite un autre dans les sillons ICI ICI et hurlements coup [. . .] dans l'aire noire la boue de vieil enfant inétouffables bon recommençons (498; 'ms' 2.255)

light light of day *light* of night little scene HERE to the quick and someone kneeling or huddled in a corner *in the gloom for example no bother prayer without words rest on the <round> flight* start of little scene in the gloom HERE HERE to the bone the nail breaks quick another in the furrows HERE HERE *and* howls thump [. . .] in the black air and the mud like an old infant's never to be stifled good try again.[17]

As a student and lecturer at Trinity College Dublin, Beckett often made a short walk to the National Gallery of Ireland, where he was impressed by Rembrandt's brooding *Rest on the Flight into Egypt* (Knowlson, *Damned* 57–8).[18] Above, unsure of its correct French appellation he keeps the English. Notes to *Comment c'est* register the translation/memory problem: 'français pour 'rest on flight' (fin II) repos en Egypte – Fuite en Egypte' (201). On 21 September 1959, Beckett wrote to MacGreevy: 'What is the French for "Rest on the Flight", can't for the life of me think of it' (*LSB* 3, 244).

Rembrandt's painting depicts the solitude, anxiety and unknowing experienced by the Virgin and Child: the obscurity of the figures intimates the impenetrable dark in which they are cloaked, and the peril of their journey into the desert. They are visible only through the intensely bright light of the fire, whose radiance illuminates the figure of Joseph at the side of the more visible Virgin and Child. The flames entrance the ass, while a small figure reaches towards the fire. In the manuscript revisions, Beckett changed his 'rest on the flight' to 'rest on the <round> flight', amusingly referring to a self-conscious *aller retour* of images between mind and mud, memory and creation/recitation. This desire to interrupt or obscure the source of the image continues through revisions until the published text makes no reference to the source of its *'petite scène'* (124, twice repeated). Explicit reference to the 'rest on the flight' is erased, though Beckett retains its character; in the final chiaroscuro effect of 'light of day light of night' the figure looking into the fire is abstracted into 'someone kneeling or huddled in a corner' (125; 1.255).

Nixon argues that during the latter half of the 1930s, Beckett became increasingly disillusioned with Rembrandt's display of technical expertise (*German Diaries* 153–4). Both he and Knowlson instead emphasise Beckett's special affection for Adam Elsheimer, the German spotlight painter and master of the miniature, arguing

Figure 3  Rembrandt van Rijn, *Rest on the Flight into Egypt*, 1647, National Gallery of Ireland

Figure 4  Adam Elsheimer, *Die Flucht nach Ägypten* [The Flight into Egypt], 1609, Alte Pinakothek, Munich

that he continued to regard highly Elsheimer's moody landscapes and scenes of peasant life, while shunning the virtuosity of Rembrandt's hyperactive mastery (Knowlson, *Damned* 196, 234, 244; Nixon, *German Diaries* 122, 133, 143, 159–61). In February 1937 when visiting the Alte Pinakothek Gallery in Munich, Beckett's developing appreciation of Elsheimer led him towards Elsheimer's celebrated painting, *The Flight into Egypt*, this painting being a major point of reference for Rembrandt's version of Matthew's story. Indeed, Beckett was already familiar with Elsheimer's work and no doubt keenly anticipated seeing it, for Knowlson reports that he had borrowed the catalogue to the Alte Pinakothek from Morris Sinclair a year earlier to study its collection (*Damned* 256).[19]

Elsheimer's *Flight* is celebrated for its accurate depiction of the constellations, perhaps the first successful such attempt in the history of painting. The silver moonlight of Rembrandt's version washes over exactly this feature of the canvas, replacing Elsheimer's innovation with his castle and its interior light. Whereas Elsheimer balances Biblical motifs with an appeal to the light of cosmic order and reason, Rembrandt appeals to the light of the human heart and hearth. In Rembrandt's piece, time has moved on, the Holy Family has reached the camp, the moon is almost overhead. Rembrandt's castle is a prominent divergence, but less noticeable is the figure in the middle ground, seen only by the faint light of his lantern. In both versions of this painting and in *How It Is*, the small crouching figure reaches towards the fire.

As he etches his 'memory' into Pim's back, 'ICI', the 'I' participates in the recreation of a 'Thebaïd' narrative by invoking its historical evolution in the visual arts, to exemplify its cœnobitic circulation within his *ancient voices*. In so doing, this allusion to the ascetic voyage becomes not only the flight from a sadistic master (Herod), but an artistic practice evoked as a form of religious *praxis*. In the paragraph immediately preceding this one, the narrator/narrated claims that his voice is either exclusively his, or '*autre chose cela va sans dire pour un témoin attentif <comme il faut>*' (497; something else that goes without saying for an attentive witness <as it must>). Between 'ms' and typescript 1661, this 'attentive witness' becomes less God's emissary than the '*observateur idéal*': '~~autre chose cela va sans dire~~ <dernier exemple> ~~pour~~ <~~aux yeux d'sous les projecteurs d'~~> ~~un témoin attentif comme il faut~~ <*sous les feux de l'observateur idéal*>' (498; ~~something else that goes without saying~~ <last example> for <~~to eyes under the projectors~~

of> an attentive witness as it must <under the lamps of the ideal observer>). Here, he is explicitly contemplating Berkeley's idealism, where to exist is to be perceived: one's voice is either one's alone, or one perceived by the 'ideal observer', the Ancient of Days. In his 'Thebaïd', either the 'I' is observed by God or he does not exist, a philosophical variation on the theme of the 'desert flower'. Quite literally in the dark (and mud), 'under the ideal observer's lamps' (125), and with a Manichean sense of the divide between spirit and matter, Beckett's chiaroscuro lighting refracts Berkeley's philosophical concept, prompted by his memory of Rembrandt's style.

The 'lamps' of the 'ideal observer' at the end of Part 2 are a refraction, both imagistically and philosophically, of the lost '*lanterne magique*' (304) in the *Comment c'est* manuscript. Beckett exploits the metaphor of the 'projector' – the magic lantern was a precursor to the slide machine or cinematic projector – by reversing the perspective of Plato's cave as light and images come from above and are beamed into the 'I', who transmits them onto Pim, like the perverted images projected onto the cave's wall. Beckett appears to link with imagination the magic lantern (an emblem of consciousness in Proust) and the journey of moral suffering (in imitation of Christ); and hence, perhaps, the more prominent lanterns in Rembrandt's other versions of this scene in ink, for instance *Fuite en Egypte* and *Repos pendant la fuite en Egypte,* displayed in the Louvre, each with the same barely noticeable figure carrying a lantern as it does in the painting of the same title in the National Gallery of Ireland.[20] In *Fuite en Egypte*, Joseph's lantern guides the Holy Family and ass through the wilderness like the light of divine Providence revealing its safe passage. In the *Repos pendant la fuite en Egypte*, the lamp is the source for Rembrandt's spotlighting effects, its comfort protecting Jesus from the enveloping darkness. The Rembrandt in the National Gallery of Ireland depicts, in the middle ground, and visible only by the faint glow of his lantern, a lonely figure who makes his way through the grey-black of a no-man's land, awaiting the warmth of fire and the beatific presence of Christ/fire/*Logos*. He is perhaps a shepherd, though his lantern and direction establish a visual trajectory from the castle upon the hill, with its room internally lit, to the fire. Viewed through the frame set by *How It Is*, Beckett invites the reader to see this figure as pacing towards the '*Élysée visuelle*', carrying his *flammèche* down from his own little castle. He is led as he will be in the afterlife, according to Plato, by his 'tutelary genius'.

Crowned by the artificial light of the moon, Rembrandt's castle appears to be governed by a prevailing sense of isolation: rather than being located in the world of Herod's gruesome slaughter, or suggesting the monastic course of humanity's desert pilgrimage (for that route is surely ahead of the family), its lit interior is a reminder of the nocturnal workings of the mind. The image of man generating his own fire when the universal *Logos* fades goes back to Heraclitus: 'A man strikes a light for himself in the night, when his sight is quenched' (Fragment 90; Kahn, *Art* 71). The light in Rembrandt's castle is the figure of an abstracted intellect, much like Milton's image for the cultivation of reason by the midnight oil in his poem of 'divinest melancholy', 'Il Penseroso', or in Samuel Palmer's painting of *The Lonely Tower*, which Yeats adored. Rembrandt's dialogue between forms of light intimates the emerging oppositions of the Renaissance, categorised in post-Cartesian philosophy as that between the light of divine revelation and the *lumen naturale* (light of reason), the supernatural light which shines through the rational mind – like the *Logos* of the Stoic 'natural order' – allowing one to assent to clear and distinct ideas – like Plato's rational mind consenting to the Good in things. Beckett's imagination connects Berkeley's idealism with the practice of the early Christian ascetics, who will either be united with the Lord in a beatific vision, becoming one with Him, the subject of his 'lamps' and 'sole elect'; or who will perish unobserved, as desert flowers.

When *Molloy* remembers himself at the house of Lousse – a return to his mother's room or womb, perhaps – he envisages a 'rest on the flight' scene:

> And the confines of my room, of my bed, of my body, are as remote from me as were those of my region, in the days of my splendour. And the cycle continues, joltingly, of flight and bivouac, *in an Egypt without bounds*, without infant, without mother. (66, my emphasis)

Molloy's Cartesian journey into and out of the confines of his body and region (a theme discussed earlier) is blended with Rembrandt's painting. Molloy has left behind his past learning and now makes his way, without a lantern, through the darkness. He casts himself, perhaps, not as the figure bearing the lantern, nor as Joseph, but rather the ass that carries the Virgin and child.[21]

Towards the end of Part 2 of *How It Is*, images of the journey, crucifix, ass, cattle, shepherds, peering eye, migrating family and the vision of light are poetically distributed between Homer, Aristotle, Matthew, Rembrandt/Elsheimer, Dante and Beckett himself. The narrator/narrated sketches himself and Pim: 'like two old jades harnessed together' (119). These old nags are, in French, *'canassons attelés ensembles'* (118), continuing the theme of the horses that appear after the *atelier* scene ten paragraphs earlier. There, the 'I' remembers himself as a child enclosed in what appears to be a Christian workshop, where hammers and chisels manufacture Catholic icons: 'crosses perhaps or some other ornament' (115). The child *'à quatre pattes'* (114; 'I crawl' [literally, on all fours]) is therefore linked with the small crawling figure of the *Rest on the Flight* paintings. The ensuing journey begins when the child crawls to the door of this workshop, spying through a *'fente'* (114), which suggests in French an opening or gap in nature, and which in *How It Is* becomes a 'chink' (115), like a weakness in the armour of his reason. In the early 'ms' manuscript, peering through this hole, the 'I' first lays his eyes upon what is termed the *'Élysée visuelle'* (484), the beatific vision of Christianity, becoming One in the light of the Divine. This vision of God, known to Christian asceticism as *theoria*, is afforded once the 'I' has left behind the Catholic noise of fabricated theological symbols and his castle of reason and theology. The Elysian Fields were for Homer as they are in Beckett's text 'the world's end' (115), though the French *'au bout du monde'* (114) figures this space as reconstituted *boue* (mud). The Homeric context is a reminder of the genealogical history whereby this Christian *theoria*, or vision of Elysium, found its passage into Christianity via Aristotle and the Stoics and the Church Fathers (discussed in the next chapter), and located by Dante in Limbo, abode of the virtuous pagans.

The vision through the hole (compare Dante's escape from the *Inferno*) inspires the narrator, still on all fours to declare:

> so I would go to the world's end on my knees [. . .] up the gangways between decks with the emigrants // homer mauve light [. . .] creaking of wheels [. . .] coming home but the hooves in that case. (115)

This might stand for a going back in time, from the Christian to the pre-Christian era, from Renaissance representation back to its Christian inspiration, all these in turn indebted to the narratives of a classical education which mixes themes from his classical texts with Christian doctrine and practice and images from Renaissance art.

### Beckett's *Risus Purus*

Beckett connected *Rest on the Flight* with Aristotle in *Watt*, where the ascetic voyage is trivialised as another form of reason's *ars combinatorio*:

> We shall be here all night,
> Be here all night shall we,
> All night we shall be here,
> Here all night we shall be.
> One dark, one still, one breath,
> Night here, here we, we night,
> One fleeing, fleeing to rest,
> One resting on the flight. (46)

Arsene's ditty refigures the narrative of the 'flight into Egypt', represented so differently in the history of art, to fit his jolly rhyme, which leads immediately into a passage that twists Aristotle's teleological doctrine into a cosmic comedy:

> the mirthless laugh is the dianoetic laugh [. . .] It is the laugh of laughs, the *risus purus*, the laugh laughing at the laugh, *the beholding*, the saluting of the highest joke, in a word the laugh that laughs – silence please – at that which is unhappy (47, my emphasis)

This term, *beholding*, derives from the English version of Windelband's *History*, which uses it to translate the Aristotelian *theoria*, or the divine unity with the transcendent One, for Beckett/Arsene the 'highest joke'. Neither hollow, nor bitter, the mirthless laugh simply laughs at that which is unhappy, a principle that could be both Stoic (steadfast) *and* comic. Nietzsche writes:

> The Olympian vice. – . . . I would go so far as to venture an order of rank among philosophers according to the rank of their laughter – rising to those capable of *golden* laughter. And if gods too philosophize . . . I do not doubt that while doing so they also know how to laugh in a new and superhuman way – and at the expense of all serious things. Gods are fond of mockery; it seems they cannot refrain from laughter even when sacraments are in progress. (*Good and Evil* [no. 294, 199])

When the religious longings and practices of the 'I' of *How It Is* are mocked as the inheritance of education and a confusion of *ancient voices* Beckett's laughter liberates them from seriousness. But Nietzsche's 'golden laughter' is too strong a term, because Beckett's mockery is rarely distant and never superhuman.

Simon Critchley argues that Beckett's *risus purus* is ethical precisely because 'the object of laughter is the subject who laughs' (*On Humour* 50). In laughing at oneself one's mockery does not violate the other, and this form of laughter resists nihilism. This is challenged by Shane Weller, who believes that Beckett's comic 'il faut', the dogged, and today clichéd, 'you must go on' (*TN* 414), opens a space which cannot be reduced to the dialectics of difference and alterity, but which is rather 'anethical', a kind of affirmation that precedes all negation and value judgements (*Beckett, Literature* 194). This is a cogent response to Beckett as artist rather than philosopher, and Weller distinguishes Beckettian 'indecision' from 'ignorance' and 'indifference'. Weller strives for a new vocabulary with which to discuss Beckett's debts to ethical philosophers – 'ignorance' and 'indifference' are two key Stoic concepts reformulated by Geulincx – without reducing Beckett's writing to statements of ethics. This does justice to Beckett's post-World War II writing, which tries to free itself from inherited forms of thought. For Weller, Beckettian 'indecision [. . .] is an occasion for invention, not of a new art or a new ethics, but rather of ways in which the experience of the disintegration of both art and ethics might be rendered visible – or audible – on a page or a stage' (*Beckett, Literature* 194).[22] Indeed, the very absence of the possibility to 'decide' which voices will haunt one's subjectivity drives the narrative and form of Beckett's novels after *Watt*; as a consequence, he chose not to evacuate ethical ideas from his work nor endorse them.

The claim to annihilate any source of authorising values in the final climax of *How It Is* mirrors the positive development of the narcissistic subject described in Freud's late essay of 1927, 'Der Humor'. Humour in this process is generated when the super-ego separates itself from the ego and elevates itself to a position from which to perceive the ego's trivial comic nature. I have elsewhere argued that the circularity of the narrative of submission and domination in *How It Is* undercuts this otherwise healthy development, and thus Beckett's rejection of a Freudian 'solution' (Cordingley, 'Psychoanalytic'). This investigation attests to the depth of ethical content in Beckett's oeuvre but denies it an ethical outcome, for his writing resists the affirmation of a broad ethical agenda. The 'Rest on the Flight' motif shows Beckett's reappropriating ethical content to express his personal relationship to artistic creation. His ethical – his obsessive autofictionalising ('il faut') and 'syntax of weakness' – might itself be formatted, unconsciously or otherwise, from his own inculcation in the historical dialectic between reason and piety.

In Arsene's ditty, Beckett mocks 'One resting on the flight' as much as any artist's schooled *beholding* in the 'hyper excellent'[23] representation of divine fire, the '*Élysée visuelle*'. He was probably attracted to Rembrandt's reworking of Elsheimer because it differs from works of technical precociousness which Beckett found inauthentic. Rembrandt's painting is, rather, a poetic departure from the traditional myth of Rest on the Flight, and its image in *How It Is* contrasts with other more explicit references to painting. One such allusion which was *not* obscured through revision occurs just before his 'memory' of the *Flight* image. The 'I' is in the grips of an 'image not for the eyes made of words not for the ears . . . head in the sack the arms round it' (57). The 'image' is one of Jesus, stylised in the garb of clichéd representations of *theoria* from illustrated Biblical stories for children: 'raise the eyes look for faces in the sky animals in the sky fall asleep and there a beautiful youth meet a beautiful youth with a goatee clad in an alb wake up in a sweat and have met Jesus in a dream' (57).

In its French version, this dream was provoked by the *unconscious* habits of learning, language and memory: the sleeping head was 'sur' (on) a 'sac' (sack) stuffed with images/words/mud which infuse the mind with visions as if by osmosis, or rather, habit. Beckett's translation denies such fancy, for the English head is brutally 'in the sack'. This revision may be part of the self-effacing and ironic commentary of the self-translator, whose English head is now similarly wedged in his French *sac*. The rhetoric of translation states how the images of Christian and Renaissance painting circulate, from the outset, throughout the mud of *Comment c'est*, and are deliberately reworked by the narrator/narrated in the present. One can here distinguish between Beckett's flavouring the narrator/narrated's discourse with purely derivative forms of representation (such as the celestial Jesus veiled in a white robe) and the complex interlacing of 'rest on the <round> flight' motifs below the visible surface of the text. Beckett's habit of effacing the sources of his references is a self-conscious procedure, which forces him to extract his head from his 'sack' of *ancient voices* and breathe originality into his work. The strategy protects him against the danger that the inevitable reconstitution of his *boue* (mud) will merely terminate in the excremental products of obsessive narcissism. Indeed, Beckett transforms this anxiety into satirical emblems of the creative process, which like the dianoetic laugh, smiles at its own desire to transcend its textual *boue* – the self-reflexivity marks Beckett's awareness of habit, within which he recognises his own internalisation of the pedagogical imperative. The narrator/narrated's evocation of the crouching infant of Rembrandt's *Rest on the Flight* was immediately preceded by an image of Freud's defecating child – 'the mud like an old infant's never to be stifled' (125) – and a series of allusions to the formation of narcissistic tendencies which lead to adult neuroses (Cordingley, 'Psychoanalytic'). In Beckett's irreverent imagination, Freud's child then crawls into Rembrandt's painting, continuing his journey on all fours to the fire of *Logos* and the Holy Family, then goes on his merry way under Homeric skies. The narrator/narrated claims this child to be his memory of himself, which is typical of Beckett's playful tendency to mock what he feared might be his narcissistic self-writing. But when Beckett cocks an ironic regard towards his text by pulling a Freudian grimace, he is led naturally to see in his reflection not the face of his own childish obsession, but that of the most famous case of relentless self-portraiture in history: Rembrandt.

While Beckett might distance himself from Rembrandt's technical bravura, the Dutchman's lifelong production of some fifty self-portraits[24] is a project that Beckett's oeuvre was beginning to resemble. Rembrandt's self-portraits are often highly comic, with the painter frequently posing as a historical or mythical figure from another of his works, or recycling his own image between works, as when his etched *Self-portrait* of 1639 became the basis of the 1640 painting in which he posed as the 'Titian of Amsterdam' (in the London National Gallery and frequently visited by Beckett). Like Rembrandt, Beckett often deforms and mutilates past 'images' of his comic, self-deprecating self.

This chapter has built on the three previous in mapping out important coordinates underlying the dialectic between reason and asceticism that animates the oppositions within the narrator/narrated's thinking. Manuscript versions of *Comment c'est* and Beckett's 'Philosophy Notes' afford a chink through which to spy on Beckett's backstage carnival. From this perspective one may glimpse the antics of the metanarrative, the comedy within the comedy, and the chorus of characters who support the stylised gags of the staged clown. In *How It Is* the comedy of the narrator/ narrated's farcical participation in a quixotic 'Thebaïd' becomes all the more significant when one attends (in the gray canon) to what has been left out of the published narrative, where the silent engineering of Beckett's *risus purus* is differently displayed. While Beckett may parody the striving for sincere, rectilinear authority or assume a stance that can be described as 'anethical' – indifferent to ethical considerations – his last novel acknowledges the impossibility of his narrators escaping the religious character of their aesthetic as much as existential compulsion to *go on*. Within this state of affairs, where to struggle, to smite and to suffer is purely and simply *how it is*, and where violence arrogates reason, the Beckettian universe differs from that of de Sade – 'sadism pure and simple no since I may not cry' (79) – for not only is its violence ritualistic and devotional, but its total compulsivity and unconditional acceptance is one more permutation of the pedagogical apparatus. More complex still, within this religiously formatted universe, alternative praxes present themselves to the narrator/narrated as legitimate options to escape from the tortures of philosophical and theological ratiocination (above all, as it were, his paradigmatic question: 'me sole elect'). The next two chapters turn to the narrator/narrated's entanglement within the praxes of Christian devotion that claim to circumvent the reasoning mind, as articulated by and filtered through the early Church Fathers, neo-Platonists and seventeenth-century mystics and rationalists.

### Notes

1. Using different philosophical coordinates, Ackerley describes Beckett's scepticism as developing out of the Protagorian dictum: 'Man is the measure of all things', arguing that Beckett's impulsive rejection of anthropomorphism is, ironically, his experience of the 'romantic agony' (Ackerley, 'Anthropomorphic').
2. Duffy writes of the coercive dimension to Platonic philosophy with respect to *The Unnamable*'s Worm (*Prisoners* 65–6). Dowd further observes the Socratic inversion in *How It Is* (*Abstract* 175–6), taking a cue from Abbott, who senses that *How It Is* 'turns the Platonic structure of western thought on its head' (*Author* 92). These observations stop short of identifying the centrality of the pedagogical imperative within the novel and its relationship to the philosophy to which it alludes.

3. Not to be confused with Zeno of Elea, philosopher of the famous paradoxes.

4. Beckett's hiatus (the text has World-Nous). Windelband uses 'world-purpose' and 'world-reason' in this section, which Beckett summarises rather than transposes.

5. 'Happiness the highest good zwar [sic], but happiness presupposes a knowledge of the nature of things which cannot be acquired. Hence happiness is not possible, or only possible in a non-committal condition of suspense, suspension of judgement, reserve of opinion. Only possible happiness <u>ataraxy</u>' (TCD MS 10967/122r).

6. Strictly speaking, the Ancient Stoics abrogated homosexuality, which adds another layer of irony.

7. Cf. end of Part 2: 'the voice of us all when the panting stops' (129).

8. This is not Berkeley's radical nominalism, yet the material existence of the world is equated with its consciousness in language.

9. Beckett mentions *Émile* in a letter to MacGreevy of 16 September 1934 (*LSB 1*, 228).

10. 'World mind' is in Windelband 'divine law of the world' (W 176).

11. The narrator/narrated makes an oblique allusion to his 'aeons my God' (179) as the generations of time/discourse which separate him from unity of voice. Like aeons, Krim and Kram descend upon the 'I' from 'above in the light' as emissaries from Oneness, or Alexandrian neo-Platonists: 'Alexandrians attempted a system of evolution in the <u>theogonic process</u> of <u>Basileides</u>. Sections from both systems appear in <u>Valentinus,</u> where *Æons are at once an elaboration of the dark & primordial depth & a series descending toward imperfection.* This series of <u>syzygy</u> (internal pair of male & female deities). These with the sacred eight (Æons), from which others proceed, to form entire Pleroma. In no other schools are dualistic & monistic elements so unified as in the Valentinian' (TCD MS 10967/139v–140r, my emphasis; W 243).

12. Beckett would have been familiar with Statius through his appearance in Dante's *Purgatorio*, as the prodigal poet who accompanies Dante and Virgil from the level of the avaricious and the prodigal up to the Earthly Paradise (Dante drew from Statius' *Thebaïd* for his *Inferno*). Statius' poem was also a popular text for teaching Latin and Beckett could have encountered it in this way. He may have seen Gherardo Starnina's (di Jacopo) *Thebaïd* at the Uffizi gallery where he 'spent many days looking at the vast collection of paintings' (Knowlson, *Damned* 75).

13. The fact that *'fleur du désert'* (with its echo of Leopardi) already existed in the earlier paragraph 251 of Part 3 in the 'ms' manuscript suggests that Beckett always had Desert Fathers in mind, and that the detail was not just a consequence of his subsequent revisions.

14. Among Beckett's other debts to Flaubert, *Mercier et Camier* is a sustained engagement with *Bouvard et Pécuchet*, and Flaubert laboured over its companion piece *La Tentation de Saint Antoine* for a great portion of his life.

15. For discussion of this see Griffin ('Flaubert' 18–33).

16. I have discussed *How It Is* in terms of its tropes of early graphic and manuscript culture, and of spoken and silent reading within monastic reading and transcription ('The Reading Eye'). Beckett used such terms to Tom MacGreevy of his isolation at Ussy while writing *Comment c'est*: 'Back in the quiet now with great relief I cannot say . . . They'll have me in a monastery in the end' (21 September 1959, *LSB 3*, 244).

17. My translation is made with the help of Beckett's version of the French text's final paragraph.

18. The National Gallery of Ireland purchased the work in 1883 (White, *National* 92–3). It also has Guiseppe Maria Crespi's gruesome depiction, *Massacre of the Innocents*, and Jan de Cock's *Flight into Egypt*, composed in a more gentile Flemish style (White, *National* 28, 39). In *Dream*, Belacqua ponders 'the dehiscing, the dynamic décousu, of a Rembrandt, the implication lurking behind the pictorial pretext threatening to invade pigment and oscuro' (138).

19. A miniature of Elshiemer's work is displayed in the Louvre today, as is a version by Peter Paul Rubens (itself the work of one of Ruben's copyists).

20. Knowlson writes of the influence of the old masters on Beckett's writing: 'he could draw on these images at will in his own writing – just as naturally, perhaps even as unconsciously, as he did on his memories of Dante or Milton, Racine or Leopardi, Shakespeare or Hölderlin' (196). Pilling identifies the Rembrandts in *Dream* with those in the Louvre, when Lucien is likened to 'Rembrandt's portrait of his brother' and placed beside 'the Selbstbildnis' (138, self-portraits). Ackerley identifies, also from the Louvre, Rembrandt's *The Evangelist Matthew Inspired by the Angel* as the source of 'the cute little Saint Matthew angel' in *Murphy* (215) and the Unnamable's inability to write (*TN* 301; Ackerley and Gontarski, *Faber Companion* 481). While writing *Comment c'est*, from late June to late July 1959, Beckett spent nearly a month in Ireland and 'saw quite a lot of Tom MacGreevy' (Knowlson, *Damned* 469), then director of the National Gallery, where Beckett had the chance to revisit his old favourites.

21. An ass appears in Beckett's notes to *Comment c'est*: '*l'âne et noria*' (203; the ass and the noria). The noria is a device for gathering water; buckets attached to a wheel fill with water from a well or river, to be deposited into a container as the wheel turns. The ass, tied to the wheel, is sometimes blindfolded.

22. That Beckett's writing offers an experience of disintegration beyond inherited categories of value offers a useful way of drawing his writing into dialogue with contemporary art movements of his day.

23. In his 'German Diaries' Beckett describes Rembrandt's style as 'hyper excellent painting' (GD2, 6/12/1936; quoted in Nixon, *German Diaries* 154).

24. Once thought to have been around ninety self-portraits, the figure is today thought to be around fifty – this reflects the difficulty in identifying original Rembrandts, as he often had his students paint them.

5

# Mystic Paths, Inward Turns

> Words and images run riot in my head, pursuing, flying,
> clashing, merging, endlessly. But beyond this tumult there
> is a great calm, and a great indifference, never really to be
> troubled by anything again. (*TN, Malone Dies* 198)

The mind's static maddens Beckett's wandering anti-heroes.
Colliding words and images loom as a threshold, which, if crossed,
promises spiritual calm. *How It Is* establishes an inseverable link
between the noise of individual consciousness and the pedagogical
processes that inculcate reason. Beckett thinking about quietening
the reason-ridden mind passes through a multitude of influences,
from Democritus' ideal of philosophical peace to Schopenhauer's
appeasing of the Will, the experience of the *Nichts* (Nothing), a
peace beyond reason, calm of spirit, deep rest and serenity (*World as
Will*, I, 531). The trope echoes the 'post tempestatum, magna sereni-
tas' in Thomas à Kempis' *De Imitatione Christi*, 'after the storm, a
great calm' (III.vii.5; Ackerley, *Demented* 197). Stronger, more reso-
lute and more provocative than in any other work by Beckett, this
spiritual longing in *How It Is* fuels an unrelenting comic allegory of
the mystic's quest. Beckett's 'I' returns time and again to bodily and
mental impoverishment, as well as a dissolution of self, the stripping
away of its particularity, to become one with what sustains him, the
mud: 'the terrain the terrain try and understand no accidents no
asperities' (179). Alluding to his journey as a personal imitation of
Christ's suffering and humility, he frequently mixes mystical motifs:
'here all self to be abandoned' (107).

Steven Connor (*Material Imagination* 133–7) identifies three
broad ways in which scholars have interpreted the plethora
of religious material in Beckett's texts: firstly, the persistence of
religious belief within the works, which affirm the possibility of a
religious salvation they cannot fully articulate; secondly, the ironic

use of religious material to deny a religious interpretation to the work itself; thirdly, to separate the mystical from the Christian, privileging the *via negativa* of negative philosophy so that the form of Beckett's negation guarantees the religious character of his thought. In his 'religion beyond belief', patterns of belief persist but 'belief is actually beside the point' (135). This last way of reading indicates how religious material plays a key role in shaping Beckett's narratological invention of the first person 'I' that relinquishes ownership of his own discourse. The text's engagement with the Psalms, the early Church Fathers, Gregory of Nyssa, Augustine and Christian mystics offered Beckett a mythology to conceptualise the journey of voice from author to character and subsequently back to the author within the fictional realm. The text responds to Augustine's counsel of inward listening and the *verbum cordis*, God's originary discourse of the heart. Augustine's legacy and the neo-Platonic cosmologies that influenced much Christian mysticism during the medieval period constellated anew within the rationalism of seventeenth-century philosophers Nicolas Malebranche and Arnold Geulincx. In its dialogue with rationalist philosophy and reasoned theology, Beckett's 'I' follows modes of asceticism forged at the nascence of the Christian Church. Augustine's commentary on recitation conceptualises his acts of 'quotation'. The 'I' attempts to heed his warning against (1) deriving pleasure from self-inflicted penitence (masochism) and (2) seeking a pantheistic solution to life in the mud. His persistent hope for a beatific vision of *theoria*, explored in the last chapter, is here defined within the specific praxes of Christian mysticism, and his acts of spiritual recitation and self-denial are framed by the mystic's inward turn, to the 'Internus homo', or 'inward man' (*Dream* 63; *Dream Notebook* 83; à Kempis, *Earliest* 41).

In her 1981 book on Beckett's mysticism, Helene L. Baldwin maintained that the progressive stripping down of the self in Beckett's works is not just a search for self, but 'the "negative way" of mysticism, whose object is to break through the bonds of time and place and to find what Eliot has called the still center of the turning world' (*Real Silence* 6). Beckett could not affirm that Christian God, but, as Ackerley observes, 'the Christian mystical tradition with its goal of spiritual enlightenment and metaphor of ascent to the light offered Beckett a paradigm of the inverted journey of his various protagonists toward their inner darkness' ('Perfection' 32). Inge's *Christian Mysticism* offered the motif of the *scala perfectionis*, the soul's ascent to God (9–10; Ackerley, *Obscure Locks* #15.8, 44.8, 45.1),[1] but also that metaphor's reversed trajectory, the falling or sinking into the earth that symbolises the dissolution of self and the becoming one with God (*Christian Mysticism* 110–11). The *Comment c'est* manuscripts reveal that notions derived from mysticism and negative theology were more explicit at earlier stages in the novel's genesis, creating a dialogue with other philosophical and theological preoccupations or connecting the dialectical oppositions between the Ancient and Modern periods, from the tension between Ancient *paideia* and *ascesis* to the new ways of conceptualising both divine, transcendent reason and self-negation that emerged from the Renaissance. A significant tradition of early-twentieth century modernism was founded upon the desire to *make it new* by rupturing traditional forms of aesthetic representation, splintering a simple correspondence between subject and object, and complicating national and disciplinary traditions. *How It Is* projects a subject worn down by the 'humanities'; it relinquishes the desire to remake the tradition within which it has been formed, enacting rather Beckett's later vision of consciousness as the incessant patterning of culture's *ancient voice*. This renders even the novel's most radical formal disruptions of Christian tropes or its burlesque treatment of irrational mysticism susceptible to interpretation as the next iteration of religious patterns of thought and action that persist in the absence of their Godhead.

## Christian Praxis, Spiritual Metamorphosis

The narrator/narrated, alert to a Manichean reading of the divisions to life in the mud, inherits two methods to overcome any possible lapse into Gnosticism. Firstly, before inclining towards his apathetic posture at the novel's end, he listens to the *ancient voices* of his Hellenistically grounded Christian education, sensing a nexus between philosophy and reasoned theology that invests his 'Thebaïd' with the faith to transform himself, to rise out of the mud by emulating Christ's Passion. The formation or *morphosis* of the human personality through the *ascesis* of the Greek *paideia* became with Paul the Christian *metamorphosis* – becoming like God (Jaeger, *Early* 97–8). Gregory of Nyssa, the fourth-century Archbishop of Constantinople, reconciled the Platonic discourse of the self-perfecting ascent towards the Good with St Paul's sense of the Christian athlete and the moral training in bodily asceticism: life is a metamorphosis whose stages are a progression of the individual towards *theoria* (beatific vision), initiating the philosophically informed tradition of Christian asceticism within which the 'I' sets off on his journey towards an '*Élysée visuelle*' (484).

The second means of overcoming a Gnostic divide involves an act of faith that needs no reasoned 'formulation' to expound the Christian *Logos* or calculate a universal, divine harmony, but rather draws upon the Christian *praxes* that hold out the promise of a beatific vision of God. The historical fact that the rules governing Christian praxes were themselves indebted to the Greek philosophical tradition implicates the narrator/narrated in more circuitous problematics which, given his saturation in *paideia*, undermine the innocence of his pious practice – his ultimate rejection of his *ancient voice* cannot be naïve or without theological motivation.

In the following episode, the 'I' is again on his knees, but this time his praxis does not pass through *paideia* but via Christian education. He is afforded a memory of 'himself' as a boy reciting with his mother the 'Apostles' Creed':

> the huge head hatted with birds and flowers is bowed down over my curls the eyes burn with severe love I offer her mine pale upcast to the sky whence cometh our help and which I know perhaps even then with time shall pass away
>
> in a word bolt upright on a cushion on my knees whelmed in a nightshirt I pray according to her instructions
>
> that's not all she closes her eyes and drones a snatch of the so-called Apostles' Creed I steal a look at her lips
>
> she stops her eyes burn down on me again I cast up mine in haste and repeat awry. (15)

The scene is a self-reflexive metonym of witnessing and memory, reproducing the image of a well-known photograph (c. 1908), shown in Bair's *Biography* (115), in which the young Beckett is kneeling piously before his mother. This artifice of historical witnessing and the contingencies of its present reproduction, evidently prone to 'repeat awry', frame the precariousness of both the theological doctrine and the affirmation of God's word. When the 'I' names the Apostolic dimension of the Creed 'so-called', he indicates his awareness that the fifth-century myth of the Creed as dictated by twelve Apostles under inspiration from the Holy Spirit was contested by the tradition, also expounded in contemporary texts (including Augustine's), that the 'Creed' should be learnt by heart and never consigned to writing.[2] Not as incidental as it might seem, the reference to the Creed intimates the narrator/narrated as attempting to overcome irreconcilable dichotomies between life in the *mud* and life in the *light*: the Apostles' Creed affirms the Holy Trinity in the face of Gnosticism. For if the oral record when passing into human speech is subject to the same distortions of memory and recitation that plague the repetition of his own 'ancient' discourse, then heavenly dictation can only ever be 'ill-said'; thus, as he says, he will 'repeat awry'.

In the *Confessions*, Augustine restores that loss by distinguishing between the temporal language of humanity and that of his eternal Spirit, the inner and the outer word (13.29.44). A potent force in Augustine's theology, the idea is developed in *De trinitate* (*On the Trinity*) and *De doctrina christiana* (*On Christian Doctrine*). The inner is the ineffable Word before it becomes sound, existing outside human speech (*De trinitate* 15.10.19). This inner Word appeals to the senses and is expressed – ill-said – to the outer word, the Word made flesh. So that God's Word may impress itself upon others, the mind as much as the heart remains awash with God's eternal discourse: our words carry the *inarticulated* presence of God's inner Word. This part of the inner Word was not made flesh: 'For both that word of ours became an articulate sound, and that outer Word became flesh, by assuming it, not by consuming itself so as to be changed into it' (*De trinitate* 15.11.20). Augustine holds that no link should be made between the outer and inner Word, nor should one seek for the inner Word. God is fully self-present in his inner Words, but He lives fragmentarily in the human outer word. Behind the outer words of humanity is the *verbum cordis* or original speech of thought, ineffable and immaterial (*De trinitate* 15.10.19), through which the textual signs become but a partial reflection of an inner speech.

The transmission of *ancient voice* to the 'I' parallels this situation, even before it enters the hermeneutic text. The 'bits and scraps' of *How It Is* register only the outer word of the *ancient voice*; the listening of the 'I' shifts over the course of the novel from his past active listening, and his searching for the *Logos* within the words transmitted to him, to his final 'will-less' recitation (*apatheia*), the claim to cast off his pedagogical narratives. This final manoeuvre resonates with Augustine's directive to forgo all anticipation and, in Part 2 of the novel, the role of recitation in a Christian alternative to *ratio* converges with Augustinian motifs as the narrator/narrated remembers the Psalms of his youth:

> mamma none either column of jade bible invisible in the black hand only the edge red gilt the black finger inside the psalm one hundred and something oh God man his days as grass flower of the field wind above in the clouds the face ivory pallor muttering lips all the lower. (101)

Psalm 'one hundred and something' was in the earlier 'ms' manuscript, 'psaume 157? (citer)' (463; 2.164; Psalm 157? (quote)). Returned to his source, Beckett rediscovered not only that the Psalms culminate in a vision of *theoria* (at 150) but also the reference to man as transient: 'As for man, his days are as grass: as a flower of the field, so he flourisheth. For the wind passeth over it, and it is gone' (Psalms 103, Authorised version, 15–16; cf. Bryden, *Beckett* 103–4). The intention of *citing*, noted in the 'ms' manuscript, is abandoned for a deliberate imprecision, allowing Beckett to complicate Psalm 103's benign vision of ephemeral nature through other allusions to man 'as grass', as in one of the *canticum graduum*, or 'songs of degrees' and pilgrim-songs, Psalm 129: 'Let them be as the grass upon the housetops, which withereth afore it groweth up.' This Psalm includes another verse pertinent to *How It Is*: 'The plowers plowed upon my back: they made long their furrows.' This image of the unbeliever's plough gouging the promised land shadows the sadistic inversion played out in *How It Is*, when letters are grafted into Pim's back. The malice of the 'I' mocks the pious pretensions of the earnest masters who whipped him into church, and of his mother, who enforces Church teaching with her disciplinary gaze. Here, corruptions of force-fed religion spoil his innocence, as much as Pim's (like Israel's soil prior to its being *dénaturée*).[3]

In his *In inscriptiones psalmorum* (*On the Inscriptions of the Psalms*), St Gregory of Nyssa divides the Psalms into five sections, ascending in their spirituality,[4] from the first step towards virtue until the pilgrim finally achieves blessedness in likeness with God, the eschatological union of human and angelic natures, the *theoria* described in Psalm 150. The Christian *paideia* is the *imitatio Christi*, Christ taking form in oneself; the goals of the *paideia* combine with the phenomena of revelation, and David's prophecy contrasts with an uncomplicated notion of the Holy Spirit speaking to the heart, as expressed in speech. With David, the 'secret instruction' by the Holy Spirit is 'simultaneously' articulated (2.114). However, the menacing context in which the narrator/narrated recites the Psalms belies the value of repetition in his spiritual education. His mother's eyes 'burn with severe love' and when he casts his gaze to the sky 'whence cometh our help' he has borrowed from the fifteenth of the 'Songs of Ascent', Psalm 121: 'I will lift up mine eyes unto the hills, from whence cometh my help.' While this Psalm affirms the Lord's guarantee of protection to the faithful, the 'I' knows now, as then, that with time that 'help [. . .] will pass away'.

The narrator/narrated alludes effortlessly to the Bible; his language is steeped in its imagery, and the biblical rhetoric embedded within the discourse of this indoctrinated subject contrasts with the bric-à-brac of his 'humanities' that litters his speech and more obviously appeals for interpretation. Yet this language is no less important and the inscription in Pim's flesh may be partly allegorical (the Christian subject singing an orthodox song), for Gregory uses a similar analogy when interpreting the Psalms. Adapting the Aristotelian analogy of enforming matter to the possession of the body by the Word, Gregory argues, 'the psalms have been formed like a sculptor's tools for the true overseer who, like a craftsman, is carving our souls to the divine likeness' (Gregory of Nyssa 2.117).[5] The Psalms are tools used by a craftsman who has need of different instruments to 'produce the statue' (2.117). Gregory suggests that no one questions the order of the Psalms' conception just as '[t]he craftsman has no concern to enquire carefully which tool was forged before the other, so that the first prepared might also be the first to assist with the carving' (2.117). He emphasises the totality of the Psalms' vision: the effectiveness of each tool is its role in shaping the statue. The evocation of psalmody reflects the narrator/narrated's hope that his interrupted temporal discourse might reveal an eternal order or *Logos* orchestrated from his, like Gregory's, 'true overseer'. Gregory's counsel to accept the divine plan and relinquish the rational impulse to reorder the Psalms according to a perceived order of past, present and future resonates with the Stoic doctrine of *apatheia*, where the absence of will allows one to enter into the continuous present and receive the natural order of the divine *Logos*.

The religious experience in the Psalms is like a voice which carries a spiritual presence from an inferior to a superior state of the divine presence. Gregory's explication of the Psalms becomes a complete portrait of the life of the Christian mystic, who concentrates his efforts upon his welcome into the divine world. The mystic confirms the 'steps' towards the holy voice of '*théognôsia*', enacting the parable of the perfect Christian's incremental 'metamorphosis'. Gregory's lifelong interest in the institution of the monastic life and his continual efforts to fill it with the Holy Spirit reflect the practical nature of his educational zeal: in his theology Christianity is understood as perfect education (Jaeger, *Early* 95).

The mother's 'drone' of the 'Apostles' Creed' was in French her '*psalmodie*' (14; 1.71). The 'psalmody' within the son's education mobilises the imperative of St Gregory of Nyssa's *praxis*, the act which receives and serves Christ: while *theoria* restores one's original nature (love) in the vision of God, *praxis* tests love with actions that lead to God's love. Yet the narrator/narrated's 'severe' instruction in the production of a monotonous, liturgical recitation seems to be a factor contributing to his sadistic 'carving' of Pim and the elicitation of Pim's song. The mechanics of recitation schooled within the Christian *paideia* have gone haywire in a being starved of love, rendering him covetous for a sign that he is God's 'sole elect'. The archetypal event in *How It Is*, Pim's instruction, is structured as a pedagogical allegory in which education would lift the larval subject out of its mineral existence toward light and unity with the One above.[6] Yet the education is flawed, its methods indulgent, and the subject metamorphoses into nothing but the demagogue of its own little world.

From his fallen corrupt flesh, the 'I' awaits God's Word, an originary discourse like the *verbum cordis* of Augustine's inner Word. The rational voice of the 'natural order' (Stoic or otherwise) and the Aristotelian hierarchy of species is bypassed when his tongue finds direct communication with God's ear:

> fallen in the mud from our mouths innumerable and ascending to where there is an ear a mind to understand a means of noting a care for us the wish to note the curiosity to understand an ear to hear even ill these scraps of other scraps of an antique rigmarole
>
> immemorial imperishable like us the ear we're talking of an ear above in the light [. . .] in that untiring listening to *this unchanging drone* the faint sign [for us][7] of a change some day nay even an end in all honour and justice. (177, my emphasis)

Like the '*psalmodie*' of his apprenticeship in piety, the 'unchanging drone' of the 'I' is his recitation, which is in French his '*antienne*' (176). This is a refrain, or antiphon: a verse sung alternately by two choirs in worship. It suggests, furthermore, the monotonous *praxis* of the self-translator. Beckett casts this repetition of voice in terms of the religious antiphon, whose Ancient Greek form was assimilated into the Christian Church, where Psalms and canticles were introduced with a corresponding antiphon; the words of this short plain-song elicit the evangelical or prophetic meaning of text (Sadie and Tyrrell, *New Grove* 1: 735–48). Like Augustine's borrowing of Hellenistic thought to shape his Patristic doctrine, here the narrator/narrated's prophetic chant will reach God's ear as well as ending 'in all honour and justice'; that is, in the ideals of Greek ethics. Here, the 'I' is still engaging with his *paideia*, and his ratiocination of the *telos* of his journey cannot shake its hope for a dianoëtic *theoria*. Yet his ultimate conclusion awaits a purely Christian eschatology of Christ's salvation for the 'fallen in the mud'. Rather than the anti-Aristotelianism of à Kempis' (or Luther), this discursive axis in his thinking evokes a reasoned theology opposed to unquestioning piety or shapeless religious irrationalism.

### The Mystical Plane

By advocating the abandonment of all prior beliefs or assumptions about the divine, Gregory of Nyssa left the way open for the *via negativa* of the mystical passage to God.[8] In the 'Whoroscope Notebook', Beckett noted 'Omnis determinatio est negatio' from Inge's *Christian Mysticism* (121), which he read at the Trinity College Library in the early 1930s at the suggestion of MacGreevy. Inge describes the negative theology whereby the fact that 'God can only be *described* by negatives' means that 'He can only be *reached* by divesting ourselves of all the distinctions of personality, and sinking or rising into our "uncreated nothingness"' (111). Inge's discussion of 'apathy' is less sophisticated than the complex permutations of *apatheia* channelled into *How It Is*, yet the narrator/narrated avails himself of protean images of sinking to evoke the possibility of mystical experience. The second of the six *Comment c'est* notebooks contains a fascinating digression on the nature of the mud as a pantheist substance, and points to specific mystical ideas that subtend the narrative discourse (MS HRC SB/1/10/2/9r–13r). Crucially, this passage immediately precedes the section extracted from his manuscript that Beckett published as *L'Image*, commonly read as a parody of seventeenth-century rationalism and especially the Occasionalist doctrines of Arnold Geulincx and Nicolas Malebranche (the latter mentioned explicitly). Yet the Occasionalist dimensions to *How It Is* have not been appreciated as entering into dialogue with the novel's diverse allusions to theology, Christian praxes and mysticism. The novel's limpid parody of Occasionalist logic is prefaced in the *Comment c'est* manuscripts by an episode that evokes negative theology and mystical notions of sinking into the earth.

This episode, which I term the 'mystiques' passage, evolved into several related sections of the published text:

[#139] to speak of happiness one hesitates those awful syllables first asparagus burst abscess but good moments yes I assure you before Pim with Pim after Pim vast tracts of time good moments say what I may less good too they must be expected I hear it I murmur it no sooner heard dear scraps recorded somewhere it's preferable someone listening another noting or the same never a plaint an odd tear inward no sound a pearl vast tracts of time natural order

[#140] suddenly like all that happens to be hanging on by the fingernails to one's species that of those who laugh too soon alpine image or speluncar atrocious moment it's here words have their utility the mud is mute

[#141] here then this ordeal before I go right leg right arm push pull ten yards fifteen yards towards Pim unwitting before that a tin clinks I fall last a moment with that

[#142] enough indeed nearly enough when you come to think of it to make you laugh feel yourself falling and hang on with a squeak brief movements of the lower face no sound if you could come to think of it of what you nearly lost and then this splendid mud the panting stops and I hear it barely audible enough to make you laugh soon and late if you could come to think of it

[#143] escape hiss it's air of the little that's left of the little whereby man continues standing laughing weeping and speaking his mind nothing physical the health is not in jeopardy a word from me and I am again I strain with open mouth so as not to lose a second a fart fraught with meaning issuing through the mouth no sound in the mud. (29–31)

Various images in #139 refract Beckett's personal mystical vocabulary. 'Never a plaint' initiates the theme of silent suffering, the 'odd tear inward' and the 'pearl' are iterations of the later 'marguerites from the Latin pearl' image (99). Ackerley ('Thomas' 83) identifies this play on the Latin word for pearl (*margarita*) as an allusion to the humility of Christ's suffering, the pearl/tear in Ingram's translation of Thomas à Kempis' *De Imitatione Christi*: 'a precious margaret & hid from many' (Kempis 108; 'pretiosa margerita, a mul tis abscondita' 3.xxxvii). The thematic of the pearl as a motif for Christ-like humility will incorporate Pascal's asceticism (see the next chapter), expanding the broader mystical contexts present in the *Comment c'est* manuscript (ms) and its revisions, as well as the typescript (1661) with its autograph emendations.

In addition to the images of silent suffering, pearl and inward tear, the first fragment above (#139) contains the image of the 'first asparagus', the variety cultivated in Europe that emerges from the soil white because it is denied photosynthesis. Its stretching towards the light above dialogues with other mystical symbols evoking the ascent towards God and the vision of divine light, *theoria*, but immediately contrasted with motifs of sinking into the ground. In the 'ms' manuscript the fresh asparagus is likened to the abscess that bursts after forty days: 'les premières asperges de la saison, l'abcès qui perce au bout de quarante jours' (312; first asparaguses of the season, the abscess that bursts after forty days). The Biblical echo evokes the journey of Moses, who climbed Mount Sinai and fasted for forty days and nights before descending with the Ten Commandments inscribed by God (Exodus 34:28), this a prefigurement of the New Testament forty days Christ spent in the wilderness. The narrator/narrated contemplates a forty-day ascetic rite that aspires to these. In Gregory of Nyssa's *On the Life of Moses* the journey of the Christian ascetic into the 'Thebaïd' mirrors the three stages of Moses' metamorphosis. In the first, the soul is purified and illuminated by the story of the Burning Bush; the second involves the sequestration of the soul from the world, the traversing of the desert and the passing through the cloud; then, finally, the darkness of Sinai, where the soul awaits further challenges in its growth towards God (*Vita Moysis* §162). Moses' journey is an allegory of how one loses life in order to find it, which Gregory blends with the story of Christ's Passion to form the archetypical narrative to be emulated in the life of Christian metamorphosis.

The narrator/narrated evokes this tradition, even if the analogy between his journey, spiritual metamorphosis and Christ's passion is immediately mocked by the abject, phallic image of an abscessed asparagus, spiritual aspiration reduced to a gratuitous, masturbatory epiphany.

Christian mysticism here presents itself as an illicit temptation to distract the 'I' from his rational path to self-perfection, the Aristotelian striving articulated within a reasoned theology. In the second *Comment c'est* notebook, the text proceeds down the recto, with Beckett using the verso for notes, testing sentence formulations and doodles. Opposite this passage he inscribed 'insoutenable l'hypoth l'hypothèse de la fosse d'aisance, lieu ou alors de la merde divine' (MS HRC SB/1/10/2/10r; untenable the hypoth the hypothesis of the ditch of comfort, place or rather of divine shit'). This idea, which is not reproduced in O'Reilly's genetic edition until it appears in the 1661 typescript, evokes an overly indulgent theological relaxing, an easy renunciation of self that falls too readily into negative theology, even pantheism. According to Inge (*Christian Mysticism* 110), Proclus introduced into Christianity mystical images that were popularised by later authors, such as 'sinking into the Divine Ground' and 'forsaking the manifold for the One'. Beckett's *ditch of comfort* and *divine shit* recast this idea while remembering from *Dream* Belacqua's 'delighting . . . in swine's draff' (46), which alludes to Thomas à Kempis' *De Imitatione Christi*: 'I sawe hem delite in swynes draf', for the husks of grain were fit for swine only (Ackerley, 'Thomas' 83; Ackerley and Gontarski, *Faber Companion*, 227). Belacqua's laxity is criticised as a regression, when he emerges from 'the two months odd spent in the cup, the umbra, the tunnel' (46). The failed quietism of the 'dud mystic' (186) is framed as infantile, narcissistic and anal, as when his mind goes 'wombtomb' (45). Just before the 'mystiques' section in the *Comment c'est* manuscript, the narrator/narrated reflects upon the mud and his journey through 'ce long tunnel vers le silence et le noir meilleurs' (309; this long tunnel towards better silence, better dark).[9] This recalls Belacqua's mystical tunnel, holding out the promise of a superior silence and darkness through the loss of individuation as he enters the mud. Equally, it might prove nothing more than a digestive, anal parturition, emptying him into the mud as he devolves into the *voice quaqua* (caca). The phrase was revised in the typescript: 'du silence de ce noir tunnel cette noire trouée vers un noir et un silence un peu meilleurs' (310; silence of ~~this black tunnel~~ this gaping/punctured black towards a little better dark, a little better silence). This quiet designates the absence of *ancient voice* in the moments of 'panting': 'les blancs sont les trous sinon ça coule' (108–9; the gaps are the holes otherwise it flows). The holes in the flow of *ancient voice* offer hope of a better silence and dark than that experienced in his moments of breathing. Tunnels and gaps open up within the mud, which is referred to in the published version of this paragraph as 'black sap', where 'a tin clinks first respite very first from the silence of this black sap' (27). Jacob Boehme's mystical notion of the world organism offers a point of comparison: for Boehme, 'the world is a tree which from root to flower and fruit is permeated by one life-giving sap, and which is formed and ordered from within outward by its own germinal activity' (367). This echo is consistent with the way the narrator/ narrated mocks his own journey by corrupting mystical motifs. The clinking tin implies God's intervention into the clockwork universe, like the Occasionalist's little miracle (discussed below) that precipitates a mystical moment outside the willing of the narrator/narrated. Yet, because he is reliant on images inherited from an education in mystical theology, his speculations return him to the discourse of his pedagogues and *ancient voice*, interfering with the purity of any holy, mystical silence.

The 'mystiques' passage in the 'ms' version begins at #139 with descriptions of the mud as neither lukewarm nor cold; it is sticky and does not dry upon the skin, while the air is vaporous but not mephitic. This is a variation on the emetic salvation prophesied in *Revelation* 3:16: 'So then because thou art lukewarm, and neither cold nor hot, I will spue thee out of my mouth'. The 'I' hesitates to 'Parler de Bonheur [. . .] on veut y voir du positif' (312; Speak of happiness [. . .] see the positive in it), but proceeds with negativity and self-abasing images. His sensation of falling is both 'alpine' and 'speluncar' before the 'atrocious moment' precipitates. A note in parentheses appears to record the intention of adding to the passage an '(image alpine) ou spéléologique)' (313). This mental note was itself integrated without parentheses into the revised typescript, the text's genesis thus incorporated into its evolution, sustaining a narrative voice that articulates the writing yet maintaining the verisimilitude of a composing voice listening to its *ancient voice*, quoting and inscribing it anew. While this process is visible only through a genetic reading, the published text nevertheless signposts the record when it affirms: 'someone listening another noting or the same'. Despite its lack of specificity, the *image alpine ou spéléologique* evokes the motif of the eremite, the solitary monk who isolates himself or herself on a mountain or in a cave. In his 'PIM' notebook, which forms part of the *Comment c'est* manuscripts, Beckett inscribed the neologism 'Ontospéléologie' (200), a term that conflates *being* and *caving* to evoke both subterranean space and the form of being specific to that space. In an early typescript of *Watt*, Beckett had used the term 'auto-speliology' [sic] of Watt's delving deeper into his mind (Ackerley, 'Geology' 152); *Comment c'est* extends this idea to mysticism and eremitic practices. Rather than emerge from the darkness of self-inspection, like the proverbial asparagus or abscess to which he alludes, the self might lose its specificity and descend into the mud, becoming One in being with God.

In the pre-fragmented *Comment c'est* manuscript reference to the 'image alpine ou spéléologique' proceeds directly into #140:

> je ne **xxx** tenais plus à mon espèce, celle des **m** seigneurs de la création, que par le bout des ongles (image alpine̶) ou spéléologique), c'était alors que les mots avaient leur utilité <sup><se <me> refuser à <être> cette majestueuse</sup>
> boue> <conformément au principe de la mutité de la matière,> < ? [conformément/en provenant] ?? au principe de la
> surdité de la matière> j'en avais encore malgré tout un certain nombre plus à [sic] moins à ma ~~disposition~~ discrétion, je n'étais pas encore arrivé comme malheureusement depuis la volatilisation de Pim tout à fait au bout de ma glossolalie. (313; MS HRC SB/1/10/2/11r)

On facing pages are three key phrases, written in blue ink and crossed out in red, to be integrated into the typescript, their position indicated (above) by the supralinear insertion.

conformément au principe de la mutité de la matière,

se <me> refuser à <être> cette majestueuse boue

conformément/en provenant—en principe de la surdité de la matière (313; MS HRC SB/1/10/2/10v)

(in accordance with the principle of the deafness of matter

to refuse me from becoming this majestic mud

in accordance with the principle of the deafness/absurdity of matter)

The narrator/narrated is gripping onto his 'species', to resist being stripped of his particulars and plunge into the 'splendid mud'. Words may stave off his fall for he has not yet arrived, he quips, at the end of his 'glossolalia'. This ironic reference to his own speaking in tongues, the intermixing and looping voice of narrator with narrated, evokes a reprieve from that cacophony for a religious ecstasy as silent, divine equanimity. He conceives of the mud as either inert, neither hearing him nor speaking to him, or, in the absence of *ancient voice* as majestic, a potential plane of mystical immanence into which he sinks. This ontological shift is stated more explicitly as the passage progresses, when the 'I' contemplates his fall in #142:

> c'est *drôle* si on y pense, se sentir ~~qui~~ *lâcher* **xxxx** *prise* enfin (ontologiquement[10] parlant <quoi qu'il ~~y ait de~~ <soit possible que> certaines choses ~~qui~~ retiennent,> ~~si aucun rapport avec la~~ <pas question de> ~~vie et de mort)~~ et s'accrocher ~~au moyen~~ en donnant de la langue, si on y *pense*, à ce qu'on allait *quitter, me refuser à être* cette boue splendide, ~~à présent heure~~ *heureusement qu'à présent ça ne dépend plus de moi, je tombe, on parle, la boue est sourde, je reste, à plus tard les détails, plaçons* <donc> *ici un incident de ce genre, la boîte ayant tinté.* (314)

> it's funny if you think about it, to feel ~~that~~ yourself falling caught at last (ontologically speaking) <while there ~~is~~ <be a chance that> certain things ~~that~~ hold back,> ~~if no relationship with the~~ <no question of> ~~life and death)~~ and to hang on ~~to the means~~ using the tongue, if you think about it, about what you were going to leave, hold back from being this splendid mud, ~~at the moment~~ luckily that now it no longer depends on me, I fall, one speaks, the mud is deaf, I remain, later the details, let's then put here an incident of this nature, the tins having clinked

The narrator/narrated speculates what it would be like to feel oneself falling until one is suspended 'ontologically speaking'. On the brink of becoming one with the 'splendid mud' he contemplates all that he would 'leave', which becomes all that he would 'lose' in the typescript revision. This fall from 'species' (#140 above) can be staved off by continuing to speak, but that is now beyond his volition ('ça ne dépend plus de moi') as he falls and witnesses the loss of subjectivity: '*je tombe, on parle*' (I fall, one speaks). The scientific metaphor of his devolution is paralleled by the mystical trope of losing one's individual subjectivity, dissolving into a divine plane/plain. Within a passage containing densely interconnected mystical tropes, the 'I''s falling into all nature/mud, his loss of species, ontological metamorphosis and loss of subjectivity points, in sum, to his contemplation of negative theology and a temptation to anticipate one's sinking into self-annihilated Oneness with God. This produces a false epiphany, for the mud is deaf.

The author-narrator of this early manuscript continues, 'je reste, à plus tard les détails, plaçons <donc> ici un incident de ce genre', as if to remind himself that in the next revision another, perhaps even a more successful (mystical), episode of this kind should be inserted. Curiously, when rewriting this scene in typescript 1661 Beckett again chose to maintain the illusion of a composing author contemplating a mystical episode (*incident*) to be inserted, for he retained the reference in the paragraph: 'plaçons donc ici un incident de ce genre, la boîte ayant tinté' (UoR 1661/15r; 314). He even crossed this out and reworked an alternative formulation in blue pen in the left margin: 'plaçons donc ici la boîte ayant tinté un incident de ce genre et n'en parlons plus' (UoR 1661/15r; 314; let us put here the tin having clinked an incident of this nature and speak no more of it). The direct link between the clinking tin and the mystical fall was worked into a new paragraph (#141), then inserted before the present one. This new fragment contains the phrase in *How It Is*, 'a tin clinks I fall last a moment with that'. The chime of the tin initiates the body's movement and its fall. The mystical episode is provoked not by the individual will but through extra-corporeal, probably divine intervention: 'ça ne dépend plus de moi, je tombe, on parle'. Suspicions that the narrator/narrated's mind has turned to mystical motifs are confirmed when the passage continues in the 'ms' manuscript into what will become paragraph #143 of the published text:

> est-ce au contraire pour des raisons difficilement imaginables ce bruit vaguement de cloche, voilà que ça arrive, difficile à se représenter, chercher chez les mystiques et lire boue <=> à la place de Dieu, échappement à vue d'œil de tout ce à quoi nous devons de pouvoir rester debout en riant, en pleurant et en disant ce que nous pensons, très difficile **xx** rien de physique en tout cas, <sup>léger refroidissement des extrémités à la rigueur,</sup> la santé n'est pas menacée, sensation assurément unique en son genre, un mot de moi et ~~je reste au bercail,~~ revis comme devant. (MS HRC SB/1/10/2/12r; 315)

is on the contrary for reasons hard to imagine this bell-like noise, here
it comes, difficult to picture, look up the mystics and read mud <=> in
place of God, escape in sight of all that we owe to be able to remain
standing, laughing, crying and saying what we think, very difficult xx
nothing physical in any case <sup>slight chilling of the extremities at most,</sup> health not under
threat, a sensation, certainly unique, a peep out of me and ~~I remain
with the fold,~~ I live again back where I began

The opposition between the laughing Democritus and the weeping Heraclitus is an example of the reason-ridden dialectics from
which the self must extract itself, and upon which it should look
with a Quietist's passivity. His escape into the mud follows the
*via negativa*, manifested here as a form of self-inspection, where
one observes all emotional states (laughing, crying), but denies
all physical sensations and repressive expressions of self, unless
a word from himself were to send him back to where he began,
within the '~~bercail~~' or fold of passive sheep.

The narrator/narrated states his intention to 'look up the
mystics', to verify his memory of the source for the mystical
equation of mud with God. Inge's *Christian Mysticism* is one such
source, but closer to home was the Marne mud of Ussy, where
Beckett composed this passage in 1959; though his intention to
consult a reference work and 'look up the mystics' might have
led him to Windelband, or perhaps his 'Philosophy Notes' from
three decades before. In the typescript revision of the phrase that
declares the stripping of subjectivity and negative epiphany, the
mud expands to become all of nature, '*ça ne dépend plus de moi,
je tombe, on parle, la ~~boue~~ <nature> est sourde*' (314). The specific
equation of mud and nature intimates a pantheism, which, in the
novel's mechanistic universe, evokes the rationalist philosophy of
Baruch Spinoza with his *Deus sive Natura* (God is Nature). In his
'Philosophy Notes', Beckett sketches Spinoza's negative theology,
then surmises his pantheism:

> God consists of countless attributes Deus sive omnia ejus attributa:
> similarly attributes of countless modes. Thus Spinoza adopts natura
> naturans and natura naturata of Cusanus and Bruno. God is Nature: as
> the universal world essence, natura naturans; as sum total of individual
> modes of this essence, natura naturata. This is Spinoza's unreserved
> pantheism. (TCD MS 10967/188r; W 409)

The distinction between *natura naturans*, God as nurturing Nature,
and *natura naturata*, God as nurtured Nature, is one between the

whole and its parts, between the active God along with his attributes
and what follows necessarily from them, defined as 'all the modes of
God's attributes insofar as they are considered as things that are in
God, and can neither be nor be conceived without God' (Spinoza,
*Ethics* Ip 29s). Book 1 of Spinoza's *Ethics* defines Nature as the totality of all modes in the world; it exists necessarily, is indivisible and
uncaused; in sum, Nature is God. Spinoza was heavily influenced
by the Ancient Stoics and his philosophy reflects their opposition
to Aristotle's teleological purposeful universe working towards 'final
causes'. Beckett's notes from Windelband demonstrate his appreciation of this lineage:

> Teleology consequently set aside (victory of Democritus over Plato &
> Aristotle). Bacon counted teleological mode of regarding Nature as
> an Idola Tribus. Explanation of nature is physics if it concerns only
> causae efficientes (formales), metaphysics if it concerns causae finales.
> Descartes also will have nothing to do with final causes. Still keener is
> Spinoza: polemic against anthropomorphism of teleology. (TCD MS
> 10967/186r; W 401)

The alignment made here by Windelband of Spinoza with Democritus against Plato and Aristotle emerges within the arranged
fragments of philosophical dialectics in *How It Is*. In Chapter 2
I explored how the materialism of Democritus was for Beckett a
foil to Plato, and in Chapter 3 how Aristotlean teleology was challenged by ancient Stoic pantheism (a philosophical dialectic noted
by Beckett from Windelband). Within the narrated/narrator's more
mystical moments, this pantheism takes on a distinctly Spinozist
character: everything exists in Nature, is determined inexorably by
Nature, and outside Nature there is nothing. The universe moves
according to God's essences: 'Nature has no end set before it [. . .]
All things proceed by a certain eternal necessity of nature' (*Ethics*
I, Appendix).[11] To anthropomorphise God or believe in miracles is
foolish and ignorant, Spinoza writes:

> All the prejudices I here undertake to expose depend on this one: that
> men commonly suppose that all natural things act, as men do, on account
> of an end; indeed, they maintain as certain that God himself directs all
> things to some certain end, for they say that God has made all things for
> man, and man that he might worship God. (*Ethics* I, Appendix)

The interpenetrating bodies within *How It Is* evoke a pantheistic
world body, undermining the narrator/narrated's plotting of corpora

in space and time according to the Aristotelian logic that has governed his hylomorphic journey of upward self-improvement. Here, in the 'mystiques' episode, he considers becoming one with the mud, now conceived as a divine substance and equated briefly with all of 'nature' before being revised back to the *boue*.

After expressing his intention to 'look up the mystics' the narrator/narrated needs an image to capture his abject take on mystical sinking: an 'image de vidange' and 'déperdition' (315; an image of draining, waste). The act of listening inwardly and self-observation provokes a 'sensation assurément unique en son genre' (sensation that is surely one of a kind), an idea that is carried into the next typescript, where it becomes 'l'articulation de sons s de sons [sic] significatifs par dessus le marché avec menace de metamorphose' (315; the articulation of significant sounds on top of that with threat of metamorphosis). This voice overlaid with meaning might provoke the larval ascetic's metamorphosis, a spiritual ecstasis important to patristic thought, though Inge does not define it as such.

In 1932, and perhaps again in 1959, Beckett read in Windelband's *History* (225–7) that in Hellenistic philosophy divine revelation was a 'supplement for the natural faculties of knowledge' (257), unlike the Church, for which the Old and New Testaments validated all claims to prophecy and revelation. Authors of the sacred texts were believed to be in an inspired state of pure receptivity to the divine, and any claim of revelation verified in accordance with their prophecies.[12] Hellenistic philosophy lacked the authority of the Church and its sacred texts; hence the notion that revelation was a 'supra-rational apprehension of divine truth', albeit a rare and fleeting one. This experience of the divine had no claim to be historically authenticated revelation and its authority did not apply to all. Windelband states that 'this extant *Neo-Platonism is the source of all later mysticism*' (227). John Updike disapproved of the atmosphere in *How It Is* of Hellenistic philosophy, which he termed its 'rancid Platonism' (166), yet the richness and depth of the text's Hellenistic themes is impressive. When the narrator/narrated contemplates a mystical short cut to the divine, which sets him in opposition to his orthodox Christian education, his relinquishing of self and the inward turn of his 'I' participates in broader philosophical narratives than those commonly identified by Beckett scholars, such as Arnold Geulincx's quietism and Arthur Schopenhauer's philosophy of will-lessness.

Indeed, the dialectic of *How It Is* with neo-Platonism might (as Windelband suggests) originate in the mystical conception of unity with the divine in the teachings of Philo, who believed that 'knowledge of God consists only in the renunciation of self – in giving up individuality, and in becoming merged in the divine Primordial Being', and for whom 'the soul's relation is entirely passive and receptive; it has to renounce all self-activity, all its own thought and all reflection upon itself' (W 227).

Philo insisted on the quietening of all voice, even the *Nous*, reason itself, which 'must be silent in order that the blessedness of the perception of God may come upon man' (227). Beckett's 'I' must silence his own *ancient voice*, the voice of reason, to enter the divine oneness of his 'splendid mud'. Windelband characterises the Alexandrians' conception of mystical ecstasy as a '"deification" of man from the standpoint of his oneness in essence with the ground of his world' (228), that transcendence is an ecstatic unity of man with his *ground*: 'It is a sinking into the divine essence with an entire loss of self-consciousness' (228). This trope of sinking into the divine Windelband identifies as hallmarking the division between Christian and neo-Platonic theories of revelation. While the Christian has recourse to historical authority through the scriptures, the neo-Platonist relies upon 'the process in which the individual man, freed from all eternal relation sinks into the divine original Ground' (229).

*How It Is* opens with the 'I' already sunk in the 'boue originelle', 'primeval mud' (8, 9), though in the 'mystiques' passage this substance is potentially all nature, an immanent divinity. Textual fragments reveal the equation of the 'majestueuse boue' (313; majestic mud) with 'la merdre divine' (310; divine shit), attributing to it the laxity of apophatic theology (the *via negativa*), which tempts the 'I' with the prospect of a mystical fall and provokes in him a loss of individuation ('species') and consciousness. This is equated with silence, the absence of sound that comes when the 'I' ceases to hear either the *ancient voice* or his own panting in the mud. This passage into a better silence, a better dark, will not ultimately affirm the ecstatic experience of the divine, yet he is drawn to Spinozist pantheism because it eliminates the transcendental jury which humanity set over itself when it anthropomorphised the divine, an image derived in *How It Is* from the earlier *Texts for Nothing*.

This contemplation of a pantheistic dissolution of self through apophatic theology praxis informs the text's detached signifiers, which refuse to relate while continuing to do so. More simply, the published text reads:

> you laugh feel yourself falling and hang on with a squeak brief movements of the lower face no sound if you could come to think of it of what you nearly lost and then this splendid mud the panting stops and I hear it barely audible enough to make you laugh. (29)

Even so, the *risus purus*, the laugh that laughs at itself, cannot entirely conceal the sense that beyond this series of non-sequiturs is a mind that was thinking *ontologiquement*, a hint of the 'I' listening (with difficulty) to its *ancient voice*. The calm that intervenes in the brief moments when the *panting* overpowers the noise of the *voice* tantalises the 'I' with the idea of escaping into a mystical ecstasy. Yet its *Nous* returns incessantly 'tout bas', barely audible, a phrase so significant that Beckett even contemplated using it as the work's title,[13] provoking the narrator/narrated to mock his mystical fantasies as laughable. Moreover, the easy mystical resolution to his predicament in the mud brings with it not only his self-derision but Augustine's censure.

## Augustine's 'Glue'

In his *Dream Notebook* Beckett registered from Book 4 of the *Confessions*: 'let not my soul be riveted unto these things with *the glue of love*, through the senses of the body' (4.10.15, my emphasis). Pilling links the phrase, which Beckett drew from Pusey's translation of the *Confessions*, to *Dream* (66, 70, 141) and *Malone Dies*: 'love regarded as a kind of lethal glue, a conception frequently to be met within mystic texts' (262). In *How It Is* both 'glue' and 'cleave' derive from the single French verb 'se coller' in *Comment c'est*. Augustine prayed not to be *glued* to the sensual realm so he may devote all his love to God, but when the 'I' and Pim are 'at last glued together' in a 'vast imbrication of flesh' (*vide* the Stoics), Beckett equates mystical love with the Christian love of God, two united in a curious Oneness. He further subverts, by an antithetical ambiguity, the Lord's natural order: 'Therefore shall a man leave his father and his mother, and shall *cleave unto his wife*: and they shall be one flesh' (Genesis 2: 24, my emphasis), for the word *cleave* is a Janus-word that embodies its antonym, intimating first unity then separation, and not without a sadistic touch of cruelty (a 'cleaver').

In Part 2, before his turning inward at the end of Part 3, the 'I' compounds theological error with absurdity, equating God's love with his love of Pim. A convoluted syntax enacts his descent into confusion and the abrogation of sense:

> God in heaven yes or no if he loved me a little if Pim loved me a little yes or no if I loved him a little [. . .] *glued together love each other* a little love a little without being loved be loved a little without loving answer that leave it vague leave it dark. (95, my emphasis)

Again, he finds himself entangled with Pim: 'my head against his my side glued to his' (67); 'a mouth an ear sly old pair glued together' (101); 'bodies glued together mine on the north' (117). The Stoicism of these corpora is sensed when this Augustinian mingling generates repetition and sameness: 'Bem had come to *cleave to me* see later Pim and me I had come to *cleave to Pim the same thing*' (139, my emphasis; cf. 85, 119).[14] The infinitely splitting edges of Stoic bodies are present: 'he's there still *half in my arms* cleaving to me with all his *little length*' (119). The body's extremity is characterised by infinite regress and infinitesimal quantities that generate the figure of interpenetrated bodies comprising one pantheistic body. This dualism appears elsewhere: 'his mouth against my ear our hairs tangled together impression that to separate us one would have to sever them' (119);[15] a sentiment that evokes Zeno's sorites paradox of the 'baldhead'.

Augustine's sense of the spatial dimension and temporal present is close to that of the Stoics: 'Place there is none; we go backward and forward, and there is no place' (*Confessions* 10.26.37). Augustine's space is accorded an eternal temporality reminiscent of the Stoics' continuous present: 'a *present* of things past, a *present* of things present, and a *present* of things future' (11.20.26, my emphasis). For Augustine the eternal existence of the soul, its 'present', is cloaked by human myopia which divides time into a three-part narrative.[16] The eternality of the soul in the unlocatable present does not, for Augustine, justify a belief in pantheism, for when the 'I' re-enacts Augustine's sensual corporeal penetration he repeats the Manichean sin and expresses a Stoic-Spinozist pantheism steeped in theological error. For Augustine, life on earth demands an intense, restless activity of the will, channelled into fighting Evil for Good; its reward in heaven is the 'God-intoxicated contemplation' (W 287), the rest and absorption in divine truth. Augustine maintains the transcendence of the deity but does not rule out communication of *Logos* through the Inner Word of the heart, the ineffable *cœur* of human speech.

Augustinian images subvert the pretensions of Beckett's 'I', who aims to find valid grounds for his theatrical calculation of divine justice when extrapolating into a mechanistic theodicy his model of the transferral of voice as inscriptions in the flesh between alternating torturers and victims. Christian orthodoxies compel him to self-censor from that account his neo-Platonic and mystical temptations to conceive of his journey as a mystical sinking into divine mud. Yet Augustinian and mystical images coexist with other allusions to divine intervention still to be explored, weaving into the novel's gruesome narrative of pedagogical torture competing Christian and philosophical accounts of revelation, divine inspiration and its expression. The tension between these ideas fuels the metafiction, *How It Is*, its fictionalising the act of authorship and the perils that can sabotage the passage of voice between author above in the light and creature below, reiterating its words in the fictional realm. The author's word is, like God's (or Augustine's) *verbum cordis*, ineffable; while it resides within subjects it is differed by them perpetually. Yet if Beckett's intention was to affirm a Derridian truth with respect to the language of the text or a Barthesian intuition about the language of authorship, he would not have gone to such pains to construct a pseudo-cosmological fiction that engages so deeply with Western humanist and religious traditions. Nor would he have needed to employ such a breadth of religious and mystical ideas or filter the journey of his 'I' through motifs of monastic life. He would not have fictionalised the process of fragmenting and decomposing a dialectic between self-denial, inward listening and the eremite's desert journey, on the one hand, and the individual's *paideia* or will to self-perfection, on the other. Rather, when composing *How It Is* Beckett confronted the philosophical and theological traditions that would invest his act of writing with significance, loading his pen with ethical freight. The question abides as to how he positions himself with respect to the humanist traditions that followed the Ancient Greek and early Christian thinkers, while yet honouring the internal man. I turn therefore to the text's dialogue with the Quietist tradition and seventeenth-century rationalism.

## From Quietism to Rationalism

By the end of the novel, the 'I' has passed through the gruelling trials of the *ratio*, the tortured effort to offer a logical account for how a passage of voice and its reasoned output might reflect the narrative of 'life above in the light' and thus elevate him from *apaideusia*, the ignorance of life below in the mud. Exhausted, he appears to give up all hope in any such account, offering rather an inexpungible and enduring self-image, face down in the mud with his arms spread wide, alone and self-contained, in imitation of Christ and as a singular, perhaps delusory emblem of Quietism or a literal interpretation of Thomas à Kempis' *De Imitatione Christi* (c. 1418–27). The 'I' claims to have cast off his *ancient voice* and its libidinal apparatus of pleasure and pain to which he has been subjected, as well as its learning and theological disputes, to have found peace in the acceptance of a solitary, suffering existence. In Inge's *Christian Mysticism*, Beckett read of the seventeenth-century beginnings of Quietism when Miguel de Molinos advocated passivity and abandoning the self as the means of finding God. Chris Ackerley has written of Beckett and à Kempis, and of the latter as a forerunner to Quietism, a doctrine of 'extreme asceticism and contemplative devotion teaching that the chief duty of man is the contemplation of God, or Christ, to become independent of outward circumstances and sensual distraction' ('Thomas' 88).

Mary Bryden contends that Beckett rejects 'an abject and self referring quietism' in favour of 'humanistic quietism' (*Beckett* 29), borrowing this term from Beckett's title to his 1934 review of MacGreevy's *Poems*. Ackerley reformulates this by noting Beckett's oxymoronic title, arguing instead for his rejection of the Christian of the *Imitatione*: 'his ethic remains more self-referential (or isolationist) than humanist' ('Thomas' 86).[17] Ackerley stresses the importance of Beckett's remarkable letter of 10 March 1935, in which, alone in Berlin, he responds to MacGreevy's advice to find consolation in à Kempis' *De Imitatione* by replying that he has already twisted it into 'a programme of self-sufficiency' while rejecting its non-secular attributes. Beckett typically downplays his own 'quietism' as the:

> quietism of the sparrow [. . .] An abject self-referring quietism indeed [. . .] but the only kind that I, who seem never to have had the least faculty or disposition for the supernatural, could elicit from the text,

and then only by means of a substitution of terms very different from
the one you propose. I mean that I replaced the plenitude that he calls
'God', not by 'goodness', but by a pleroma[18] only to be sought among
my own feathers or entrails. (*LSB 1*, 257)

Like an apostate Quietist, Beckett devines by haruspicy ('feathers
or entrails') his ethical and aesthetic commitment to a moral code,
the supernaturalism of which he cannot accept. Nor can he assert
the rational deity of Greek monotheism ('goodness') as a proxy for
à Kempis' God. In a complementary article, Ackerley ('Perfection')
shows how Beckett integrated Thomas' Quietism with that of
Geulincx by sensing the doctrine of *humilitas* central to each. In
his letter, Beckett expresses his inability to comprehend how such
secondary virtues as 'goodness & disinterestedness' in the *Imitatio*
could relieve the 'sweats & shudders & panics & rages & rigors
& heart burstings' which moved him to undergo psychotherapy
with Wilfred Bion at the Tavistock clinic, London, from December
1933, and helped him locate the 'specific fear and complaint' in its
prehistory, 'a bubble on a puddle'. Disillusioned with psychotherapy,
Beckett discontinued his sessions with Bion after 1935, but his
letter to MacGreevy offers a Freudian analysis of both his physical
symptoms and his tendency towards self-isolation, intimating that
both are rooted in his neurotic belief of his own superiority.[19] These
problems gnaw away at Beckett's writing, until with one swift blow
at the end of *How It Is* the narrator/narrated expels not only the
transcendent author-God but also his Freudian overlord, although
the necessity to do so reveals Beckett's persistent need to come to
terms with both.[20]

## François Fénelon: Who Holds the Old Feather?

From Beckett's first to his last novel, the relationship between
'Quietist' ethics and Freudian thought is crucial. Belacqua's Proustian sensibility rejects coordinates assumed to be psychologically
*real* in his striving for a self-styled *ideal*. He declares, 'I can only
know the real poise at the crest of the relation rooted in the unreal
postulates, God-Devil, Masoch-Sade (he might have spared us
that hoary old binary), me-You, One-minus One' (28). The narrator does *not* spare the reader the 'hoary old binary': Belacqua's
claim to profound indifference straddles the examples of Christ,
the accused masochist and the Frica, the 'nightmare harpy' (179),

who clutches 'Sade's *Hundred Days* and the *Anterotica* of Aliosha G. Brignole-Sale' (179).[21] Belacqua imagines himself to transcend the binary illusion and become:

> The *hyphen of passion* between Shilly and Shally [. . .] the modus vivendi, poised between God and Devil, Justine and Juliette, at the dead point, *in a tranquil living at the neutral point*, a living dead to love-God and love-Devil, *poised without love* above the fact of the royal flux westerly headlong. (27, my emphasis)

His indifference will find its ideal real by bridging such opposed 'unreal postulates'. In preparation for writing *Dream* Beckett made notes from the entry on 'Mysticism' from the 11th edition of the *Encyclopaedia Britannica* (Beckett, *Dream Notebook* 88). Belacqua's aspiration to be the 'hyphen of passion [. . .] tranquil living at the neutral point [. . .] poised without love' takes its point from the *Encyclopaedia*'s definition of 'Quietism':

> Hence the first duty of the Quietist was to be 'passive'. So far as was possible he must numb all his spontaneous activities of every kind; then he could fold his hands, and *wait in dreamy meditation until inspiration came.* [. . .] the shortest road to passivity was to suppress all desires [. . .] Then he would be dead to hope and fear; he would be icily indifferent to his fate, either in this world or the next. Thenceforward no human tastes or affections would stand in the way of his performing the will of God. He was, as Fénelon said, like a feather blown about by all the winds of grace. His mind was a mere *tabula rasa*, on which the Spirit printed any pattern it chose. Hence arose the great Quietest *doctrine of disinterested love*. '[. . .] In this sentence of condemnation they generously acquiesce; and thenceforward having nothing more to lose, *they stand tranquil* and intrepid, *without fear and without remorse*. This is what the quietists call the state of *holy indifference*. Their soul has lost all wish for action, all sense of proprietorship in itself, and has thereby reached the summit of Christian perfection' (André, *Vie du Père Malebranche*, ed. Ingold, Paris, 1886, p. 271). (22: 749, my emphases)

Belacqua, the ultimate dreamer, claims to be 'untouched by the pulls of the solitudes (. . .) indifferent to the fake integrities' (*Dream* 28). Yet Beckett's treatment is ironic, and like the gushing of poetic *enthusiasm* in his impassioned discourse, Belacqua remains 'too ecstatic a spectator' (11) to achieve the passivity of the Quietest's disinterested love. His 'flux' delivers him unattractively Christ-like upon the thorny 'crown of the passional relation' (28). Belacqua's fantasised 'hyphen of passion' is mocked by the narrator: 'Ain't he advanced for his age!' (28), which would surely meet the approbation of both Polar Bear's Jesuit interlocutor and the psychoanalyst.

The *Imitatio* of à Kempis influenced the seventeenth-century Gnostics, and Quietist teachings were spread by Miguel de Molinos. The movement attracted the condemnation of Innocent XI and passed into its final phase during the reign of Louis XIV in France, generating a controversy through the actions of a theologian, writer and tutor at the court, François Fénelon, whose first theological tract of 1688, *Le Traité de l'existence de Dieu et de la réfutation du système de Malebranche*, opposed the rationalist's path to the divine. Fénelon advocated Quietist passivity in his *Explication des maximes des saints sur la vie intérieure*, and he contentiously defended Madame Guyon, who had railed at the militant ecclesiasticism of the Jesuits by promoting Quietism and an ecstatic communion with God. Despite Beckett's direct allusions to Malebrache in *How It Is* and the more potent dialogue with Arnold Geulincx, it is important to appreciate the range of Quietism in the novel. For instance, the 'mystiques' episode in Part 1, with its themes of falling into a pantheistic plane of mud and glossolalia, is varied in this scene, a little later in Part 1:

> vite la tête dans le sac où révérence parler j'ai toute la souffrance de tous les temps je m'en soucie comme d'une guigne et c'est le fou rire dans chaque cellule les boîtes en font un bruit de castagnettes la boue glouglousse sous mon corps secoué je pète et pisse en même temps

> jour faste dernier du voyage tout se passe le mieux du monde la plaisanterie mollit trop vieille les soubresauts s'apaisent je reviens à l'air libre aux choses sérieuses [. . .]

> quick the head in the sack where saving your reverence I have all the suffering of all the ages I don't give a curse for it and howls of laughter in every cell the tins rattle like castanets and under me convulsed the mud goes guggle-guggle I fart and piss in the same breath

> blessed day last of the journey all goes without a hitch the joke dies too old the convulsions die I come back to the open air to serious things. (46–7)

The convulsions of the mud, the *glouglousse*, varies the mystical theme introduced in the tropes of *glue* and *glossolalia*, among others. The child-like rotation of sounds and infantile language signal the dynamics of regression with reference to *Dream*'s Belacqua and his tunnel towards the womb or a 'better dark', though now the narrator/narrated imagines himself once more suspended over a mystical plane of mud, '*la boue glouglousse sous mon corps*', 'under me convulsed the mud goes guggle-guggle' (46–7). The movement is precipitated again by external (divine) intervention symbolised by the clink of tins, though unlike in the earlier 'mystiques' passage, here they take on a mocking theatricality rattling 'like castanets'. The '*glouglousse*' generates a bilingual pun on Augustine's mystical 'glue', designating, in Beckett's lexicon, sensuous love and a mysticism steeped in theological error. The mystical contexts of the 'I''s sinking is enriched in Beckett's English through its reference to the 'convulsions' that open a *via negativa* to God's grace, 'back to the open air' (46–7) above, provoking a self-conscious reflection that these are more 'serious things'. The manuscript version of the first 'mystiques' passage contained the remarkable admonition '~~search~~ <look> up the mystics and read mud <=> in place of God', in effect picturing the writer bailed up at Ussy with limited access to books turning to his well-thumbed *Encyclopaedia*. In its entry on 'Mysticism' the *Encyclopaedia* refers to the dispute between Fénelon and Bossuet and the controversy of the disowned Jansenists known as the '*Convulsionnaires*' (Convulsionaries). Should Beckett's interest have been piqued by the reference to the Jansenists (he was already a devoted reader of Racine and Pascal), he would have found in the entry on 'Jansenism' a description of their infamous 'apocalyptic prophecy and "speaking in tongues"', of how they 'worked themselves up, mainly by the use of frightful self-tortures, into a state of frenzy, in which they prophesied and cured diseases' (*Encyclopaedia* 4: 154; cf. Sainte-Beuve, *Port-Royal* 4: 234–5). Textual allusions to convulsions, glue, *glossolalie* and *glouglousse* constellate around themes of Quietism, theological laxity and the mystical escape hatch.[22] The next chapter will explore the pertinent Port-Royal contexts, but here the questing 'I' is shown as 'suffering, failing, bungling, achieving', before finally claiming to reject mystical speculations. His clawing in the mud opens no tunnel to 'paradise' (25) if the mud is but an archive of the tired residua of theological dialectics: 'the mud yawns again that's how they're trying to tell me this time' (25).

Beckett uses motifs of mysticism and Occasionalism and their conceptualisation of free will to thematise artistic originality and the agency of narrative voice, its relationship to the authorial voice. The narrator/narrated contemplates the source of his voice in the first 'mystiques' episode, wondering if its origins are divine, inspired or human. After he evokes the ontological fall, the intention to 'look up the mystics' and communication with the mud, he poses the question:

> et si comme ce serait compréhensible vous vous demandez qui tient la veille plume que voici et la retient de tomber, ~~je n'en sais pas plus que vous,~~ ^je me demande avec vous,^ un quelconque chie-copie dans la paix de la campagne probablement, dans ses moments de relaxation (314)

> and as if it were understandable you ask yourself who holds the old feather and stops it from falling, ~~I know no more about it than you,~~ ^like you I ask^ someone shit-copies in the countryside probably, in his moments of relaxation.

Who holds the old feather, who commands the quill? And who stops it from falling not into a mystical union with God but a confusion of tongues? These questions express the Quietist's dilemma as formulated in the *Encyclopaedia*'s entry on 'Quietism': 'The question in this relation to God is – how to know the voice of God from the vagaries of our own imagination' (22: 749), to which Beckett adds, and how can we know that our imagination is our own? The *Encyclopaedia* gives Fénelon's answer: in relinquishing all desires, tastes and affections, the Quietist is 'like a feather blown about by the winds of grace' (above). These questions express the narrator/narrated's anxiety with respect to his *ancient voice*. How does one know who holds the old quill? Who speaks? Where does imagination begin and *ancient voice* end? Satirically, Beckett acknowledges the auto of his autofiction, writing himself into his narrative of the composition of the work at hand as 'un quelconque' who 'chie-copie' in his country peace. Yet within this abject autofiction, the author's spiritual relaxation, inward listening and copying of his inner voice resembles more the ataraxy of the sceptic than the ecstasy of the Quietist.

The mention in the *Encyclopaedia* of Fénelon and the Convulsionaries may have suggested for Beckett Fénelon's celebrated classic, *Les Aventures de Télémaque* (*The Adventures of Telemachus*). Written for the education of the Duc de Bourgogne, this popular pedagogical novel for children of 1699 was usually seen as a subversive political satire of Louis XIV's monarchism. In this version of the archetypal myth of the post-mortem journey with its 'tutelary genius', like Dante led by Virgil, Telemachus, the son of Ulysses, is guided through Ancient Greece by his Mentor, making a *katabasis* or visit to the underworld (the *glouglousse* and convulsions of *How It Is* occur during Lazarus' visit to 'Abraham's Bosom' [47], an outpost of Limbo). Telemachus (the duke) and his Mentor (Fénelon) encounter many problems, which are resolved by the young hero by imitating the passivity of his Mentor, who epitomises above all *calm listening* and embodies the virtue of passivity in Fénelon's Quietist theology (Niderst, 'Le Quiétisme' 205–16). The motif of Dante's onwards (Aristotelian) journey in *How It Is* may be shadowed by the Quietist's listening, as in Fénelon's novel.

In *Dream*, the Polar Bear charged Christ with an egoism like that of doers of 'good works' for interfering with Lazarus' fate, for which he is criticised by the Jesuit. In *How It Is*, those who induce their speaking in tongues are ludicrous failures: 'convulsed the mud goes guggle-guggle I fart and piss in the same breath [. . .] convulsions die' (47). The sentiment is inherited from Schopenhauer's criticism of the doctrine of good works: whenever such deeds are performed in the hope of doing God's will the individual's motivation, or *will*, must be egoistic (*World as Will* I. §70). Similarly, for the Quietist, God's election is assured only through relinquishing all 'sense of proprietorship' over one's good actions; in the words of the *Encyclopaedia* entry, 'the more they came from a source outside of himself – the surer might he be that they were divine'. The *Encyclopaedia* makes a remarkable observation: 'the great object of the Quietist was to "sell or kill that cruel beast self-conscious will"' (22: 749). In the savage inversion of the self upon itself at the end of Part 3 of *How It Is* the 'I' relinquishes all former proprietorship over his voice: 'only me yes alone yes with my voice yes' (193); he takes responsibility for it and assumes a 'Quietist's' posture, 'the arms spread yes like a cross no answer LIKE A CROSS no answer YES OR NO yes' (193). His *imitatio* is unconditionally patterned by the *ancient voice* into the cross from which his own behaviour is inextricable. This is the inevitable legacy of his Christian *paideia*, how it is. A 'hyphen of passion', he remains face down in the mud, his listening no longer directed towards the 'other above in the light'. He attempts to induce its bubbling *glouglousse* but listens from within his ego's abjection, having taken control of his voice. When the circular structure returns him to Part 1, with his tongue in the mud he may find proof of his sole election, but this takes on entirely new significance. With a method indebted to that of the Quietist, and which acknowledges its genealogical 'natural order' from Stoic *apatheia*, he grapples with the Quietist's dilemma: who now holds the old feather? The plume is not carried by spiritual winds but the profane, for the subjugated will listens not for the voice of the Divine but the voice within itself. Looped back upon itself he listens for a unique grain of voice within that of his ancients that recomposes itself anew: imagination dead imagine.

The novel proceeds as an act of listening to one's internal voice and articulating its contents as faithfully as possible. Subjects that figuratively and literally come to a head, such as divine intervention, individual will, personal agency, or how to conceptualise self-deprivation and inward listening, establish a dialogue with the way that Quietism and rationalism intersect in seventeenth-century philosophical discourses. The novel contains only one limpid allusion to the rationalist philosopher Nicolas Malebranche, but an array of images and concepts evoke a rationalist world view or cosmology informed by the ideas of Pascal, Spinoza and Leibniz.

## Malebranche and Scientific Optimism

The 'Mystiques' section of the *Comment c'est* manuscript leads into an episode that begins with the 'I' observing his limbs as he claws through the mud, which he probes with his tongue, chewing it over until a narrative emerges. He recovers a memory from when he was a youth, climbing a mountain with a girlfriend. Beckett extracted this section from his 'ms' manuscript, reworked it in another manuscript version and two typescripts before publishing it as the short text *L'Image* (xxi–xxii; corresponding with paragraphs 150–71 of Part 1 of *Comment c'est* and *How It Is* 33–7). This libidinous episode is recounted humorously, as if the lovers inhabited a mechanistic universe where their bodies act and react as automata. Specifically, when the 'I' glosses the scene as 'Malebranche less the rosy hue' (35) their movements are governed by an Occasionalist logic, an apparently whimsical reference to 'Malebranche' the signature of a more intricate world. The passage is typical of Beckett's comic mode of exposition, a parody of rationalist logic filtered through an analytical geometry.[23]

> we let go our hands and turn about I dextrogyre she sinistro she transfers the leash to her left hand and I the same instant to my right the object now a little pale grey brick the empty hands mingle the arms swing the dog has not moved I have the impression we are looking at me I pull in my tongue close my mouth and smile
>
> seen full face the girl is less hideous it's not with her I am concerned me pale staring hair red pudding face with pimples protruding belly gaping fly spindle legs sagging knocking at the knees wide astraddle for greater stability feet splayed one hundred and thirty degrees fatuous half-smile to posterior horizon figuring the morn of life green tweeds yellow boots all those colours cowslip or suchlike in the buttonhole
>
> again about turn introrse at ninety degrees fleeting face to face transfer of things mingling of hands swinging of arms stillness of dog the rump I have
>
> suddenly yip left right off we go chins up arms swinging the dog follows head sunk tail on balls no reference to us it had the same notion at the same instant Malebranche less the rosy hue the humanities I had if it stops to piss it will piss without stopping I shout no sound plant her there and run cut your throat. (35)

The name *Malebranche*, apparently a valueless token within a circulating economy of recycling residua, intimates, ironically, the authorial voice investing its narrative with the pretension of Occasionalism, of a divine cause orchestrating the appearance of causation between the two lovers and the dog, when each is acting without volition yet according to God's will and plan. These pretentions are deflated when the dog licks itself, providing a bathetic reflection of the couple's petting. Similarly, the apparent causation between their actions and the dog's motion is mocked by the Occasionalist idea that the actions of all parties were orchestrated elsewhere – 'no reference to us it had the same notion at the same instant' – which locates, comically, the source of the dog's abject idea in the mind of God (Beckett was fond of the dog/God inversion). Similarly, the dog cannot control the stem of its own urine and the will of the 'I' to shout produces 'no sound'. For Malebranche, one has no direct control over one's body; there are no efficient causes other than God, who intervenes between mind and body, and between bodies, to affect all changes in the world. The injunction to 'run cut your throat' is thus an affront to Malebranche, who like Geulincx[24] and the Stoics before him, affirmed the immorality and futility of suicide (a theological paradox, as it must concede the congruence of macrocosm and microcosm, Beckett's 'Big' and 'little' worlds).

Beckett may be mixing different Occasionalist ideas under the rubric of 'Malebranche'. David Tucker argues in *Beckett* that the historically more influential philosopher becomes in *How It Is* 'Geulincx's Occasionalist understudy' (154). He offers a detailed treatment of Beckett's use of Geulincx's philosophy, building upon the explorations of Chris Ackerley, which were followed by others who profited from access to Beckett's now published notes on Geulincx, such as Matthew Feldman, Mark Nixon and Anthony Uhlmann. For Tucker, Geulincx offered Beckett a profound architechtonic device for *How It Is*, and the phrase 'Malebranche less the rosy hue' is less an ironic affirmation of the rationalist priest's rose-coloured view of divine orchestration and salvation than a reference to his body in death (its pallor). He justifies this claim by reference to the apocryphal story of Malebranche's death, as related by Beckett's Trinity College tutor, A. A. Luce, in *Berkeley and Malebranche: A Study in the Origins of Berkeley's Thought* (Tucker, *Beckett* 152–3): a passing said to have been provoked by the excitement caused by the intensity of a philosophical argument with Berkeley. There is no evidence that Beckett read this text, as he had left his teaching post at Trinity two years before its publication in 1934, but Tucker nonetheless believes that Luce's version of this story resonates through this passage as well as Beckett's short prose work of 1946, *La Fin* (*The End*), in which a tutor who gives the narrator a copy of Geulincx's (spelled Geulincz) *Ethics* is found dead on the floor of his water closet. However, there is no reference to Malebranche in *The End*, where the tutor is simply 'struck down by an infarctus' (91), presumably an *infarctus cerebral*, a stroke, though the term can also refer to a heart attack.[25] The primary irony of the philosopher's death in Beckett's story is that he met his destiny, struck down by an Occasionalist God after passing on the *Ethics* of Arnold Geulincx, a staunch believer in the inexorable and divinely ordained destiny of each human. His *Ethics* becomes, ironically, an instrument that occasions God's fatal intervention.

Beckett need not have read Luce's text to know about the story of Malebranche's death, for it is one of the commonly recounted anecdotes of the period, concluding the otherwise brief entry on Malebranche in the 1911 *Encyclopaedia Britannica*. There is little doubt that the primary sense of the rosy hue in *How It Is* is the optimism of Malebranche's rationalism. The phrasing in *Comment c'est*, 'Malebranche en moins rose' (34), is clearer: to see something 'en rose' means to see it through rose-tinted glasses,[26] and the *Comment c'est* manuscripts (334) show how Beckett oscillated between 'optimiste' and 'rose' in successive revisions of this passage, with him even contemplating a less 'souriant', smiling or cheerful, Malebranche, before settling on 'en moins rose'.[27] They also confirm that it is not the person of Malebranche but his doctrine that is evoked: '*on dirait* du Malebranche, moins *l'optimisme*' was revised to '*c'est* du Malebranche', the meaning in both instances being like Malebranche, but without his optimism. Ironically, this scepticism may even support Tucker's thesis that 'Malebranche' cloaks the more specific reference of Geulincx, whose name cannot be used because it comes with too much baggage, having been employed by Beckett in previous texts. By alluding to a less optimistic version of Malebranche's Occasionalism, Beckett can refer to a more pessimistic critique of Occasionalism, such as Geulincx's, or to an Occasionalist-like universe stripped of all hope or possibility of God's salvation to which the text otherwise alludes: 'that strange care for us not to be found among us' (181).

Malebranche's 'rosy hue' is his belief in the salvation by divine Reason, through which humans can raise themselves from their wretched state and error. He believed that original sin has deprived humans of reasonable cognition: man's fall is a fall from intelligence, and our capacity for thought has become limited by our bodies. Bodies are not the real cause of pleasure, and we commit a grave theological error when we think they are, for God alone is cause. Yet by listening to the teaching of reason, His voice, humans can make amends:

The Master who teaches us inwardly wills that we listen to Him rather than to the authority of the greatest philosophers. It pleases Him to instruct us, provided that we apply ourselves to what he tells us. By meditation and very close attention we consult Him; and by a certain inward conviction and those inward reproaches He makes to those who do not submit, He answers us. (Book 1, chapter 3; 13)

Whereas Augustine counselled against searching within oneself for God's word, the *verbum cordis*, in *The Search for Truth* Malebranche optimistically believes that humanity can restore its faulty cognition and achieve inner peace by turning inward, ignoring the vexatious distraction of philosophical logic and listening for the voice of Reason. This listening will permit union with God, the only true cause and author of all our thoughts. There is therefore a parallel between Malebranche's theological position and the narrative structure of *How It Is*, where Beckett's 'I' avows his submission to the voice of his master above, listening within himself for its 'natural order', however disrupted by the imperfections of his own cognitive capacities (ill-hearing, ill-saying). In the passage with the two lovers, whose bodies tick like Occasionalist clocks,[28] the 'I' demonstrates a cast of mind capable of tending towards seventeenth-century rationalism: the optimistic faith that everything is knowable and will soon be known, and that should empiricists set limits to human knowledge those limits would soon be reached. A sharp break from precedence was universally perceived; these moderns felt they uniquely were doing something right and doing it systematically, the results justifying the preoccupation with the discovery and articulation of method (Lennon, 'Malebranche and Method' 8).

The narrator/narrated is, or probably once was, well aware of the dialectics of seventeenth-century scientific method and reason. While he dissents from Malebranche's *rosy hue*, he nonetheless sketches a scientific model of a mechanistic universe that evokes Newton, Leibniz and Spinoza; one that has a theological pay-off because it will account for the equation of 'souls' with 'sacks' in his universe. Beckett encountered in Windelband a synopsis of what Lennon describes as the 'pandemic' of 'extreme epistemic optimism' in the 'belle époque of method' (8). He noted from Windelband:

> Importance of mathematics as ideal of demonstrative science is as an axiom for all epistemological investigations far into 18th century, and became a lever for scepticism and mysticism (Pascal, mystic Poilet, sceptic Pierre Daniel Huet: 1630–1721, Bish. [Bishop] of Avranches: Censura Philosophiæ Cartesianæ; Traité de la Faiblesse de l'Esprit Humain; Autobiographie.) (TCD MS 10967/184r-v; W 395)

Pilling and Knowlson maintain that in *How It Is* '[m]athematics appears to offer the kind of refuge in which suffering may be subsumed into abstract patterns, but it is exposed here as a myth which is quite as illusory as the religion it has supplanted' (75). This is true, though the text engages assiduously with both Hellenistic and seventeenth-century paradigms in which mathematics supports rather than supplants religious belief. *How It Is* bears witness to this leveraging of mathematics by post-Cartesian philosophers, whose presence in the narrator/narrated's thoughts as he builds a rational explanation for his universe in Part 3 testify to the legacy of ideas that Beckett had noted three decades before: 'Positive beginnings towards transformation of Cartesian method into <u>Euclidean line of proof</u> are found in Port-Royal logic', as carried into the 'logical treatises of <u>Geulincx</u>; but [the] system of <u>Spinoza</u> [was] the first to perfect this methodical schematism' (TCD MS 10967/184v; W 395–6). Beckett follows Windelband's account of how 'Descartes' disciples confused his mathematical philosophy with Euclidean rigidity of demonstration and elaborated its monistic methodology into an *ars demonstrandi*' (TCD MS 10967/184r; W 395). Such 'Euclidean rigidity' underlies the entire 'Malebranche' episode, which begins with the distant observation by the 'I' of its body, moves into the exposition of the clockwork universe, in which scaling a hillside refashions the *scala perfectionis* and ends with the satisfactory creation of the image, albeit one that is a bawdy mocking of Occasionalist metaphysics. The passage is a microcosm of the whole mechanistic universe in which the 'I' meets Pim, tortures and trains Pim, leaves Pim, only to assume the position of Pim. His 'formulation' of such a cosmology in Part 3 might be read within this Occasionalist context. Most obviously, the reference to Malebranche (a parenthetical citation without parentheses) reflects with a malicious irony the sadistic, mechanistic universe of *How It Is*. Yet the 'I' must also signify his journey through other Christian *praxes*, such as rituals of recitation, practised *apatheia*, inward listening for God's word or, as the next chapter will discuss with reference to Pascal, by inducing miracles.

Beckett may have been more interested in Malebranche than scholars have assumed. According to Knowlson, when at the École Normale he first read 'Descartes and later Cartesians like Geulincx and Malebranche' (*Damned* 334). Twenty years later, on 4 January 1948, he wrote to MacGreevy, inviting a discussion: 'Have you read Malebranche? I have been too restless and nervous to read anything this long time, but feel the old lust for study stirring in me again' (*LSB* 2, 72).[29] If these stirrings did indeed lead Beckett to (re)read *De la recherche de la vérité* or *Éclaircissements*, he would have encountered Malebranche's quasi-phenomenological investigations expressed in a highly engaging prose style. These may have suggested an alternative frame through which to engage imaginatively with ideas circulating around the Parisian intellectual scene, such as the Husserlian *epoché* and its strategy of objectifying material bracketed in the mind.

Malebranche's name indicates that Beckett in *How It Is* had in mind the reasoning found in his first elucidation, and iterated elsewhere, which sets out his Occasionalist argument for the absence of causation between bodies. Beckett's 'I' consistently observes his body as if it were an object dissociated from his consciousness. Its movement, and especially that of his hands, appears not to have been provoked by his will. This in turn fuels the analogy between his fictional universe and the relations described by Occasionalist thinkers. Tucker (*Beckett* 160) notes this coincidence with Malebranche's preferred metaphor for causation, yet follows Geulincx's less prominent reflections on the movement of his hands, following Hugh Kenner (*Samuel Beckett* 83), while admitting that Beckett's notes on Geulincx do not mention this.

Malebranche's discourse on his hands is striking and plays a key role in his logical refutation of Descartes' connection between mind and body in the pineal gland, as mocked by Beckett in *Murphy* and elsewhere. Malebranche writes:

> In vain do I touch my face or my head. I feel my body and those surrounding me only with hands whose length and figure I do not know. I do not even know for sure that I really have hands; I know so only because when it seems to me that I am moving them certain motions take place in a certain part of my brain, which according to current belief is the seat of the common sense. But perhaps I do not even have this part of the brain about which so much is said and so little known. At least I am not aware of it within me, whereas I am aware of my hands. Consequently, I ought to believe that I have hands rather than that I have this little gland that is constantly the object of controversy. But I know neither the figure nor the motion of this gland, yet I am assured that I can learn only by means of them the figure and motion of my body and those surrounding me. (*Search* 571)

The doubting tone of this voice, advancing prepositions only to retract them, typifies Beckett's post World War II prose. In *L'Œuvre* Bruno Clément identified this rhetorical feature of Beckett's writing as the chiasmic rhetorical structure known as *epanorthosis*.

Familiar, too, is Malebranche's manner of narrating his own corporeal inspection. In this passage, because one cannot use one's will or senses to arrive at knowledge of the pineal gland (which would bridge mind and body), Malebranche charges Descartes with circular reasoning (cf. W 417). For Malebranche, only God, and not sense impressions, can lead to knowledge and truth. The citation 'Malebranche' in *How It Is* alludes specifically to this enquiring voice, heard as it probes its own body. It also recalls the sixth proof of the fifteenth elucidation, the oft-cited account for which Malebranche was ridiculed, where he doubts his ability to affect his body's motion: 'I deny that my will is the true cause of my arm's movement, of my mind's ideas, and of other things accompanying my volitions, for I see no relation whatever between such different things' (669). He affirms that God has established a 'union' between his mind and his body, that his arm will be moved 'not by my will, which in itself is impotent, but by God's, which can never fail to have its effect' (670).

Beckett's 'I' uses his tongue like a proboscic instrument to search the mud for evidence to answer his existential and theological question, 'me sole elect' (11), a literalised metaphor for language and enquiry that is dependent on language use. At the same time, the 'I' objectifies his own body, which is subsumed into this ostensibly dualist, quasi-scientific inspection. His hands, like those of Malebranche, are subject to detached self-inspection but are also a recurring preoccupation:

> rosy in the mud the tongue lolls out again what are the hands at all
> this time one must always try and see what the hands are at well the
> left as we have seen still clutches the sack and the right

> the right I close my eyes [. . .] and finally make it out way off on the
> right at the end of its arm full stretch in the axis of the clavicle I say
> it as I hear it. (33)

I will return to this concern in the next chapter with reference to Pascal, who believed that the optimism of the philosophers of his age exhibited the sin of egotism, for as man's true condition was wretched the task of philosophical ratiocination was to reveal his limitations and offer appropriate remedies.

Beckett satirises the phenomenologico-rationalist pretensions of his reasoning 'I' throughout the novel, long before the *L'Image* passage in which the name 'Malebranche' appears. Early in Part 1 the 'I' reasons in a similar fashion:

> my hand won't come words won't come no word [. . .]

> the hand clawing for the take instead of the familiar slime an arse on his belly [. . .]

> [. . .] free play for the leg which leg [. . .]

> I turn on my side which side the left it's preferable throw the right hand forward bend the right knee these joints are working the fingers sink the toes sink in the slime [. . .]

> push pull the leg straightens the arm bends all these joints are working the head arrives alongside the hand flat on the face and rest

> the other side left leg left arm push pull the head and upper trunk rise clear reducing friction correspondingly fall back I crawl in an amble ten yards fifteen yards halt. (19–21)

This disjunction between the moving body and the consciousness that observes it argues not for any specific allusion but rather for a generalised Occasionalist world view within the whole novel. Tucker accordingly mounts the argument that Beckett's dialogue with Geulincx shapes the universe of *How It Is* and the novel's narrative structure.

## The Currency of Arnold Geulincx in *How It Is*

In the seventeenth-century Occasionalist philosophy of Arnold Geulincx Beckett found a justification for self-analysis and Quietist reclusion, which he integrated into his personal, agnostic ethics. Geulincx aimed to revive the ancient approach to ethics by injecting it with Christian principles, which, he believed, surpassed the imperatives of Aristotle's ethics for the striving for excellence and the practice of virtue. Though Geulincx framed his ethics within the virtue of humility, he came close to advocating a form of Stoic ethics within a Christian veneer. This is felt, for instance, in the *Ethics'* arguments against suicide, its pessimistic rejection of one's capacity to influence one's fate and achieve enduring peace, and above all in the way Geulincx embraced the idea 'that human happiness could not be based on primary experience, but had to be found through a process of rational reflection that might deliver the soul from the automatism of its subjective illusions' (Van Ruler, 'Introduction' xvii). Like Spinoza, Geulincx repudiated Stoicism, yet the theory of morals that each developed came finally to resemble Stoic moral philosophy. Uhlmann details the importance of Geulincx for Beckett's works, albeit without reference to *How It Is*, and especially Geulincx's inversion of Descartes' *cogito ergo sum* into *cogito nescio*, an epistemology premised on the affirmation of the self's ignorance and incapacity to achieve understanding (*Philosophical* 86–113).

Geulincx is a rich source of images in *How It Is*, many having appeared in earlier works. Among these is Geulincx's figure of humanity's limited freedom, the 'sadly rejoicing slave' in *Molloy* who exercises his freedom by crawling across the ship's deck (west to east), while chained to the ship's inexorable course (east to west).[30] This figure resurfaces in *Malone Dies* and then in *The Unnamable* as the 'galley-man';[31] his voyage inevitably halts at the ship's stern, leaving him to contemplate its wake. The image is linked in Beckett's thinking to Geulincx's axiom, repeated frequently throughout his *Ethica* and *Metaphysica Vera*, *Ubi nihil vales, ibi nihil velis*, which Beckett translates in *Murphy* as: 'Where you are worth nothing, there you should want nothing'.[32] Tucker argues (*Beckett* 134) that this motif of freedom constrained within stasis is volatilised within the following fragment from Part 1 of *How It Is*, an 'old [Geulingian] dream': 'old dream I'm not deceived or I am it all depends on what is not said on the day it all depends on the day farewell rats the ship is sunk a little less is all one begs' (47).

The shipwreck is Homeric, and not obviously related to Geulincx, but the French version of this paragraph explicitly contemplates whether the 'I' physically walks or not: 'vieux songe je ne marche pas ou je marche ça dépende' (old dream I don't walk or I walk it depends). A Geulingian frame implies the Occasionalist ideas of the limits of human will and the nature of God's intervention in human decisions. This scepticism might otherwise be an expression of Descartes' infamous argument for doubting the extended world because one may be deceived by an evil demon, which might compromise the 'I' who recites the words of his *ancient voice*; or a fleeting allusion to Berkeley's idealism, where the physical world exists only in the experiences perceived by the mind. A French reader might be even less inclined to recognise the Geulingian image because in *Comment c'est* 'adieu rats naufrage est fait' means, literally, *good bye rats shipwreck is done*, but equally, *good bye rats ruin is done*. The proverbial rats that flee a sinking ship are figures of reason, known for their gnawing, cunning, but pestilent, intellects. When possible sources multiply through the dialogue between French and English versions, the uncertainty of the philosophical referent for this *deception of voice*, which may change somewhat whimsically ('it all depends on the day') is performed by the rhetoric of the self-interrogating bilingual oeuvre.

A second allusion to the 'galley-man' comes in Part 2 of *How It Is*, when the narrator/narrated imagines himself sitting at a ship's stern:

> sea beneath the moon harbour-mouth after the sun the moon always light day and night *little heap in the stern it's me* all those I see are me all ages the current carries me out the awaited ebb I'm looking for an isle home at last drop never move again a little turn at evening to the sea-shore seawards then back drop sleep wake in the silence eyes that dare open stay open live old dream on crabs kelp
>
> *astern receding land of brothers* dimming lights mountain if I turn water roughening he falls I fall on my knees crawl forward *clink of chains perhaps* it's not me perhaps it's another perhaps it's another voyage confusion with another what isle what moon you say the thing you see the thoughts sometimes that go with it disappears the voice goes on a few words it can stop it can go on depending on what it's not known it's not said. (111, my emphases)

Tucker argues that here Beckett weaves his personalised Geulingian tropes into the imagery derived from Dante's *Commedia*, as identified by earlier critics (see Caselli *Beckett's* 160). The 'I' sits at the stern of his vessel, carried out by the ebb, and contemplates the ship's wake, like the 'galley-man' in chains. If so, Beckett intimates a Geulingian interpretation only for his narrator/narrated to reject this overtly philosophical explanation as a 'confusion'. This 'land of brothers' scene may recall Christian Brothers scouring the hills with their lanterns in search of courting couples, precisely as the narrator on board ship fantasises in *Dream*. I have elsewhere argued that it offers, furthermore, a self-referential trope of narcissistic self-reflection and self-projection ('all those

I see are me') within Beckett's parody of a Freudian diagnosis of his own neuroses (Cordingley 'Psychoanalytic'). *Comment c'est* makes the narcissistic autonomy of its 'terre de frères' felt even more strongly, as heard to emerge not from an intimate (Irish) or mythical (Homeric) external world or philosophical narrative (with Geulingian echoes) but out of a self-conscious rhetoric of invention. Its phonic combinations recast the haunting pedagogy of *ancient voice* within a novel poetics of assonance and sonic association: 'à l'arrière qui s'éloinge terre de frères et lumières qui s'éteingent' (110).

A Geulingian frame of reference allows Tucker to interpret some of the more opaque details, as, for instance, in the following: 'we can drag ourselves thus by the mere grace of our united net sufferings from west to east towards an inexistent peace we are invited kindly to consider' (*Beckett* 189).

The movement from west to east effects a stasis that may recall Geulincx's slave moving across the ship's deck, in the opposite direction to its course. This is consistent with my emphasis on fragments of knowledge that circulate in the discourse and sustain vestiges of an Aristotelian dialectic that coerce the 'I' and his narrative into a forwards motion. Interpreting these fragments can be perilous, and some of Tucker's braver attempts are somewhat strained, as for instance when the following statement is held to evoke the divine intervention of Occasionalism: 'huge cymbals giant arms outspread two hundred degrees and clang clang miracle miracle the impossible do the impossible suffer the impossible' (*Beckett* 81–3). Here, in Part 2, the 'I' is simply saying that he cannot make Pim do things of which Pim is not capable, even were he to take two cymbals and clang them together. The image colours the idea, *I can't perform miracles*, without explicitly suggesting Occasionalism, although it offers a distant and ironic echo of 1 Corinthians 13:1, Paul's celebrated: 'Though I speak with the tongues of men and of angels, and have not charity, I am become as sounding brass, or a tinkling/clanging cymbal.' The 'tinkling' of the *King James Version* is translated by most other Bibles as 'clanging', rendering more accurately the sound of two pieces of hollow brass being struck. The irony of Beckett's echo derives from Paul's words, which continue: 'And though I have the gift of prophecy, and understand all mysteries, and all knowledge; and though I have all faith, so that I could remove mountains, and have not charity, I am nothing.' Tucker probably follows Knowlson and Pilling's suggestion that the 'little miracle' in *How It Is* is the one 'Occasionalist philosophers thought only God could perform' (*Frescos* 68), with close affinities to the Malebranche scene discussed earlier:

> if I was born it was not left-handed the right hand transfers the tin to the other and this to that the same instant the tool pretty movement little swirl of fingers and palms little miracle thanks to which little miracle among so many thanks to which I live on lived on. (43)

The 'little miracle' according to the 'two clocks' theory may be one of the 'many' constant miracles of divine intervention. Curiously, in the *Comment c'est* 'ms' manuscript this miracle denotes the conquest over reason's paradox.

> tout ce qu'on peut dire c'est qu'elles [les mains] font chacune la moitié du chemin qui les sépare, se rencontrent au milieu, <par les doigts et les ~~ma~~ paumes alors donc le voir un miracle littéralement ce n'est pas trop dire, tourbillon indescriptible le temps d'un éclair> (349)

> all one can say is that they [the hands] each make half the distance that separates them, meeting in the middle, <by the fingers and palms then so see in that a miracle literally it's not too much to say, indescribable whirlwind at the speed of lightning>

The miracle is one's capacity to overcome the infinite divisibility of the space that separates the two hands, like that between the two cymbals. In Chapter 7 I will discuss the philosophical consequences Leibniz drew from his calculus of infinitesimals, which effectively overcame the sorites paradox and accounted for the infinitesimal gap that terrified Pythagoreans and remained unresolved by mathematicians for centuries. The 'tourbillon' (whirlwind) that arrives with the speed of an 'éclair' (lightning) may evoke Leibniz's belief that God radiates throughout the universe as 'continual fulgurations of the Divinity from moment to moment' (*Monadology* §47), but what may seem to be an Occasionalist idea signifies less obviously its opposite: Leibniz rejected the 'two clocks' metaphor for a notion of pre-established harmony in which God set the clocks in motion according to his will once and for all, absolving him of any need to intervene further in the mechanical universe. This example typifies the need to approach *How It Is* not from a single perspective but with respect to the range of its references, for Beckett took great care to undermine any capacity of his images to point to a single referent only. A purely post-modernist strategy would pastiche philosophical material without regard for its deeper significance, but Beckett's late modernist poetics seeks to deny his text the capacity to affirm its referents and confer upon them a foundational role yet all the while relying upon them for its meaning.

Encouraged by the discovery of the perceived 'residue of earlier inter- and intratextual references' (150) Tucker argues that Geulincx's philosophy is instrumental for the structure and meaning of *How It Is*. Where others have identified the novel's tripartite order ('before Pim with Pim after Pim') as engaging with the prevailing trope of literary Romance, the guiding sequentiality of reason or the philosophical logic of the event, he perceives Geulincx's seven ethical obligations divided into the categories of death, life and birth, surmised by the philosopher as 'coming hither, being here, or departing hence' (Geulincx, *Ethica* 350; Tucker, *Beckett* 159). He acknowledges that the text confounds such categories, yet reads in the novel's 'boundaries and borders' Geulincx's description of the physical universe. He therefore argues that the realm of mud is less Dante's *Inferno* than Geulincx's 'fourth region', a zone divided into the upper region of plants and animals, and a lower region of metals, stones and minerals. He quotes Geulincx: 'My body is a part of the world, an inhabitant of the fourth region, and claims a place among the species who walk over it' (329–30); interpreting this to mean that the philosopher inscribes his own body into both upper and lower parts of the fourth region, not unlike Beckett's 'I' above in the light and below in the mud. This understanding hinges upon on a grammatical ambiguity, requiring the final *it* in the quotation from Geulincx to refer not only to the surface dividing upper and lower parts of the fourth region but to 'my body', which is then presided over by animals and plants. This is contrary to the immediate sense of the English translation as well as the Latin original that Beckett transcribed, which contains no such ambiguity.[33] The description of the fourth region makes no mention of mud, but Tucker reinterprets Geulincx's statement 'once we have in mind *Comment c'est/How It Is*' (157). This suggests a solipsistic process, reading Geulincx through *How It Is* then ascribing this meaning to Geulincx, which subverts the assertion that Geulincx's philosophy offered Beckett a structuring device. The novel's landscape cannot be equated exclusively with the topography of Dante's *Inferno*, but before it was mud the 'I''s habitat might have been described as a mixture of the primal writing scene and the sands of desert mysticism.

Little evidence supports Tucker's assumption that in *How It Is* Beckett adopts Geulincx's cosmology. Even in Part 3, when the 'I' elaborates a hypothetical cosmos that parallels scientific models of a mechanistic universe, from Newtown to Leibniz, Beckett carefully leaves that system open to a plurality of interpretations that frustrates any one reading. The wealth of allusions to mystical inward turns that complicate the text's evocation of listening to the divine *Logos* in accordance with the Hellenistic tradition testifies to the impossibility of naming Geulincx as a privileged 'source' for the narratological structure of the will-less 'I' reciting its *ancient voice*. Nonetheless, Geulincx's ethical doctrine of the *despectio sui* (disregard of oneself) appealed to Beckett, and influenced the states of abjection experienced by the 'I' of *How It Is*.

### 'Here All Self to be Abandoned': The *How It Is* of Beckett's *Despectio Sui*

*How It Is* contains many affirmations of impotence including this limpid variation on Geulincx's motto: 'in the dark the mud hearing nothing saying nothing capable of nothing nothing' (77). Tucker notes this 'fragmentation' (149) of Murphy's axiom: *Ubi nihil vales, ibi nihil velis* (TCD MS 10967 189v; Where you are worth nothing, there you should want nothing). The affirmation participates in the text's rhetoric of nothing. The word 'nothing' occurs 107 times in *How It Is* and 'nothingness' once. 'Nothing' habitually signifies the absence of voice or movement, as opposed to the regime of *ancient voice* that is marked with its *humanities* and narratives of human progress. This dualism is endemic: 'my life a voice without quaqua on all sides words scraps then nothing then again more words more scraps the same ill-spoken ill-heard then nothing' (175). As in Democritean materialism, *nothing* is regularly affirmed as substantial *within* the underworld of mud, perhaps constituting that world entirely. This has the effect of making every instance of the word suspicious, as if *nothing* can always be *something*: 'nothing too to be sure often nothing in spite of everything' (123); 'to the effect it is leaving me like the others then nothing nothing but nothing' (123); 'the mud that one day come back to myself to Pim why not known not said from the nothing come back from the nothing' (129). These reflections on and permeations of *nothing* position the 'I' as a veritable student of nothingness, as he acknowledges at one point: 'monster silences vast tracts of time perfect nothingness reread the ancient's notes' (105). Here, when returning to the notes of the ancient (or former) self, the 'I' studies different forms of nothingness (perfect or imperfect) and *perfects* nothingness (learning its definitions).[34]

Beckett's wry acknowledgement of the potent philosophical heritage to his trope of nothing focuses, elsewhere, on the Geulingian axiom.[35] The *Ubi nihil* shapes the form of the 'I''s expressions of nothingness: 'in a word my voice *otherwise nothing therefore nothing* otherwise my voice therefore my voice so many words strung together to the effect first example' (123, my emphasis), even if this echo is subsumed into fragmented iterations of philosophical exposition – [x or y] *therefore* [y or x] *therefore* [x etc.] *to the effect first example* [. . .]. Like Derrida's description in *Mal d'archive* (*Archive Fever*) of the functioning of the archive, the novel's circular structure and self-repeating discourse, where every speech act occurs within the dynamic of ill-hearing and ill-saying, corrupts the archive of *ancient voice*, a process that perpetually distances the 'I' from the contents of the *ancient's notes*. The transcendent voice in *How It Is* is the verbatim voice of an uncorrupted archive, to which the 'I' at one point refers as the voice recorded in 'the yellow book that is not the voice of here' (107). Here he makes his most explicit reformulation of Geulingian ethics: 'here all self to be abandoned say nothing when nothing' (107). The equation of self with nothing through the act of self-abandonment is a classic Geulingian manoeuvre, the inward self-examination of the *inspectio sui* evolving, crucially, into the *despectio sui* or *disregard of oneself*. Beckett's *ancient notes* from Windelband's *History* state this clearly as the telos of Geulincx's ethical system:

> Geulincx reduces self-activity to immanent mental activity of man. The 'autology' or inspectio sui is not only epistemological starting point, it is also ethical conclusion of his system. Man has nothing to do in outer world. Ubi nihil vales, ibi nihil velis. Highest virtue humility – despectio sui. (TCD MS 10967/189v)

Beckett transcribed in Latin sections of Geulincx's *Ethics*, here translated into English:

> The second part of Humility is *Disregard of Oneself* [. . .] The Disregard consists in the abandonment of myself, altogether relinquishing, transferring, and yielding myself to God, from whom [. . .] I have my whole being (in coming hither, acting here, and departing hence).

> I must be led by no regard for myself, I must put away all care and study of myself; and as one who has no right over anything, not even over myself, also claim nothing by right. I must have a mind not for what suits me, but for what God commands, and I must labour not over my own happiness, blessedness, or repose, but over my obligations alone. ('Beckett's Notes'; Geulincx, *Ethics* 337)[36]

Beckett jams into his 'occluded'[37] trope of nothing layers of philosophical fragments, from Democritus' *nothing* of ontological materialism with its absent Godhead to Geulincx's ethical affirmation of the self as nothing. Geulincx counsels one to follow the ascetic trajectory, shun materialism, take the inward turn and disregard one's will and self.

> In order that I may not care about myself, I inspect myself, and because in doing this I see that I can do nothing, neither do I will anything (and the parts of Humility are observed, one of them being called inspection of myself, the other, disregard of myself). In order that I may rightly perceive Reason, I keep company with it, I dedicate myself to it [. . .] I break the habit of doing what men dictate [. . .] I consider the nature of things [. . .] When I listen to Reason, I at length perceive what it says, and become wise [. . .] When I do what Reason dictates, I am free, and now no longer serve any man [. . .] I do enough, and am fulfilled [. . .] When, not caring about myself, I abandon myself, God Himself accepts me (and this is the reward of humility). (Geulincx, *Ethics* 296)

Following a Geulingian trajectory, the 'I' abandons his will and submits to a voice that he equates with reason, listening within it for its 'natural order'. This dynamic is portrayed as a voice that feeds the 'I' with *rations* of its *ratio*:

> [. . .] the voice of him who before listening to us murmur what we are tells us what we are as best he can
>
> of him to whom we are further indebted for our unfailing rations which enable us to advance without pause or rest. (183)

The 'voice of him' remains nonetheless forever estranged, misquoted, confused and, ultimately, ineffable. Its narrative has morphed into the one before the reader: the tale of an innocent's submission to a cruel master, learning the master's language and the logic of his commands so that it can go on to perpetuate the master's will. This internal narrative mirrors its narrative frame of dictating voice and submissive, speaking subject. This dynamic evokes a variety of Augustinian, mystical and rationalist praxes, yet the portrayal of extreme self-abandonment through self-abasement brings the text closer to Geulincx's imperative of *despectio sui*.

Even more than *Murphy*, *How It Is* offers Beckett's most sustained engagement with Geulingian ethics. Not only does its 'I' affirm his nothingness, debase and abandon himself to the voice of a transcendent overlord and a postulated voice of inner reason, but he claims no agency over his voice or its content. The structure of this ethical situation influences the narrative that he produces – the novel itself – in which Pim submits completely to the one inscribing its *Logos* within him. Beckett's sense of the dialectic between Geulincx's impotent, abject negation of self and Spinoza's affirmation of the self's capacity to comprehend the majestic divine through certain kinds of understanding concurs with an awareness emerging in recent scholarship of the relationship between these two philosophers.[38] Beckett corrupts the Geulingian narrative of *selflessness* and its assumption of divine grace with a comedy of human *selfishness*, of the gratuitous pleasures that pedagogues derive from inflicting their reasonable discourse upon their victims. These include Christian discourses that school pupils in the hope of divine salvation through the submission of the will, as well as rationalist dictates that mould the self to reason in the traditions of *paideia*. Beckett presents the intersection of these discourses within Western culture as a self-perpetuating cycle that subjugates the individual, formats its consciousness and, in turn, enslaves its master. In *How It Is* Pim must divine with his own resources the *ratio* of his teacher, before that bearer of voice is himself reduced to ignorance, and like his erstwhile student and victim, attempt to come to terms with the logic inscribed within him.

Moving towards its final climactic scene, the novel maintains a palpable narrative tension, in which the narrator/narrated articulates his voyage with his *ancient voice*, which struggles to negotiate Augustinian and mystical traditions that seek a direct experience of the divine through the renunciation of self, and those of its Ancient philosophical *paideia*, which counsel him to emulate the divine through self-perfecting education. At that climax, the 'I' assumes the position of Pim prone in the mud and is struck with a new idea that is presented as a moment of anagnorisis. He claims to cast off the yoke of his transcendent authority, its voice and declare its whole narrative to which he was beholden to be a fabrication:

> but all this business of voices yes quaqua yes of other worlds yes of someone in another world yes whose kind of dream I am yes said to be yes that he dreams all the time yes tells all the time yes his only dream yes his only story yes
>
> [. . .] all balls yes [. . .]
>
> never any Pim no nor any Bom no never anyone no only me no answer only me yes. (191)

With this act of superlative affirmation, the 'I' claims to liberate himself from the programming of his authoritarian voice(s) and strike out for himself, cutting all ties between himself and the *ancient voice*. In repudiating his overlord, the novel closes with the 'I' finally victorious: 'end of quotation after Pim how it is' (193).

There are some troubling hitches to this. Firstly, the 'I' frees himself through a stunning psychic shift whereby he assumes the voice of the sadistic master and subjects himself to a form of self-interrogation whose violence mimics that of the tormentor. As such, there is no suggestion that he has liberated himself, for he appears to have simply internalised and now reproduced the sadism of his malignant deity/pedagogue. If so, he will carry on as always, subjugating his next *pupil* or *victim*. Secondly, the text offers unequivocal proof that this resolution should be considered to be part of the narrative dictated by the *ancient voice* itself, for the final scene is prefaced by a solution 'more simple by far and by far more radical': 'a formulation that would eliminate him completely and so admit him to that peace at least while rendering me in the same breath sole responsible for this unqualifiable murmur [. . .]' (189). The 'I quote' of the speaking voice claims at this stage still to be speaking within a regime that cites its *ancient voice*. As such the solution to do away with 'him', the dictating voice, is dictated by that voice itself. And this dictation includes its own rejection, comprising everything prior to the novel's last line: 'end of quotation'.

One may object to these two critiques, by arguing that the voice of the 'I' has already corrupted its record, so that what is heard is never the verbatim account of *ancient voice* but the fragmented record of its original dictation looped into the circular narrative that is further corrupted and estranged in each iteration of the 'I' retelling his narrative. I have anticipated this objection by examining the psychoanalytic content of the novel, which indicates that the narrator/narrated continues to reiterate his own neuroses even into this final 'solution', maintaining his sadistic fantasy in this next permutation of his performative masochism (Cordingley 'Psychoanalytic'). As such, there never was a pure voice above or an overlord, and the one constant of the novel is way that the 'I' projects his neuroses into a paranoid cosmology of domination and submission, to end on a note of false salvation in the *reductio* of a Geulingian *despectio sui*.

His final posture, lying face down in the mud with arms outstretched, forms an emblem of the symbolic rejection of the entire discourse of *ancient voice*, the traditional Western dialectic between the *Logos* of philosophical reason or that of Christian love, between the striving of a positivist, self-perfecting and the renunciation of will in a self full of humility. Ultimately, the presence of any one rationalist world view – Descartes, Malebranche, Geulincx, Spinoza or Leibniz – is less important than the fact that the narrator/narrated's geometric method is manifest as a form of pedagogical automatism. The 'I' has internalised methods of tutorly discipline into a regime of self-mastery, one replete with rituals of interrogation that echo those he was taught to perform upon Pim:

> flat on my belly yes in the mud yes the dark yes nothing to emend there no the arms spread yes like a cross no answer LIKE A CROSS no answer YES OR NO yes. (193)

The itinerant 'I' of *How It Is* must first overcome attempts to assemble logically the divine order of his universe and remodel it within Newtonian-rationalist mechanics before he may throw his hands in the air ('all balls') and abandon self and will. This final, spreadeagled interpretation of the Quietist's posture, *De Imitatione Christi*, is a self-conscious emblem of Christian suffering and humility, but one inscribed within a regime of self-criticism and debasement. If it follows the Geulingian trajectory of the *despectio sui* there is, nonetheless, a hesitation ('no answer') and reluctant lower-case assent ('yes') to acknowledge that the voice of Geulincx has become one among the many voices constituting the *ratio* of the narrator/narrated, which continues to bedevil him. He must admit that he still interprets his resistance within the heritage of his *Bildung*, as one position within a spectrum of possibilities spanning from the reasoning advance of his *paideia* to a will-less self-abased renunciation of self, or a nihilist's *despectio sui*. His ultimate posture seeks to reject God, the ratio, *paideia*, *Bildung*, indeed the entire positivist and anthropomorphic world view that is perpetually inscribed into youthful bodies as they pass through institutions of education and religion. He wishes to repudiate the very dialectic that would posit piety in opposition to reason, yet he must admit that he is formed within this tradition and can do nothing but accept his degeneration within it: 'arms spread yes like a cross no answer LIKE A CROSS no answer YES OR NO yes' (193). If this is the telos of his *despectio sui* he comes no closer to a voice of original Reason but rather generates one more iteration of his self-perpetuating, self-estranging *ancient voice*. Indeed, none of the hypotheses the 'I' entertains as he journeys in the mud is as disturbing as that affirmed by this final scene, which implies that consciousness itself is imprisoned within predetermined patterns of inculcated pedagogy. The narrator/narrated's awareness of this means that he cannot, finally, believe in Geulincx's programme, nor indeed that of any philosopher. Indeed, his attempts to cast his journey as the ascetic path of *homo internus* generates a self-parody that finds its apogee in the way he emulates the seventeenth-century theologian, philosopher and mystic, Blaise Pascal, to whom I now turn.

## Notes

1. 'The mystic, as we have seen, makes it his life's aim to be transformed into the likeness of Him in whose image he was created. He loves to figure his path as a ladder reaching from earth to heaven, which must be climbed step by step. This *scala perfectionis* is generally divided into three stages. The first is called the purgative life, the second the illuminative, while the third, which is really the goal rather than a part of the journey, is called the unitive life, or state of perfect contemplation' (Inge, *Christian Mysticism* 9–10).

2. While scholars have not neglected Beckett's use of Augustine, nothing has been written on the *verbum cordis* or inward listening; nor has any affinity between Augustine and *How It Is* been explored. Mary Bryden (*Beckett* 89–96) discusses Beckett's references to the *Confessions* in *Dream* as constituting a 'tribute' (79) rather than

parody. Olney (*Memory* 857–80) offers a stimulating analysis relating narrative breakdown and memory in Beckett and Augustine. David Houston Jones ('Que Foutait' 185–98) shows how the 'paradoxical art' of each 'encounters and promotes a radical openness to the creative power of language' (196). Wolosky's *Language Mysticism* (51–134) traces the work of language negativity in the mystical elements of Beckett and Augustine, albeit quite differently from my line and without reference to *How It Is*. Elizabeth Barry ('Rhetoric of Dying' 72–88) details similarities in the rhetorical strategies of each author and their common theme of death, with special reference to Augustine's *City of God*.

3. The memory of the grass and wind also evokes Psalm 147 (perhaps confused with Psalm 157); Beckett's inability to pinpoint the precise Psalm in effect blending from memory recurrent motifs of the Psalms, which does not invalidate the real point, namely the inversion of holy psalmody.

4. The value of a Greek education was essential for Saint Gregory, who transformed Origen's theology into a Christian *paideia* (Jaeger, *Early* 81–96). Gregory was an important defender of the Nicene Trinitarian doctrine and an influential figure in *pneumatology*, the theology of the Holy Spirit. Christian virtue cannot be attained without divine help, yet Gregory introduced the Christian notion of divine grace into the classical *paideia*. He understood grace as the cooperation of the Holy Spirit with the efforts of man (Jaeger, *Rediscovered* 86). Gregory is the only Greek Father who followed Athanasius (Inge, *Christian Mysticism* 100–1).

5. In Gregory's analogy, the Word (*Logos*) works upon base matter, stone – that which lies below the mud – and which he associates with Evil and materialism.

6. Inge offers another mystical context for this vision of larval metamorphosis when his discussion of Dionysius and neo-Platonism leads into a citation of Amiel's *Journal* that recounts the experience of a mystical trance: 'All my faculties drop away from me like a cloak that one takes off, like the chrysalis case of a larva. I feel myself returning into a more elementary form' (Amiel quoted in Inge, *Christian Mysticism* 99). Ackerley analyses the purgatorial predicament of Beckett's creatures, denied metamorphosis and condemned to return to the 'mineral' from which they emerge, as in Genesis 3:19, 'for dust thou art, and unto dust shalt thou return'. This, he argues, expresses Beckett's rejection of 'the impulse towards anthropomorphism' ('Inorganic' 83).

7. The genetic-critical edition indicates this variant in the Grove edition.

8. Paul's epistle to Timothy expresses negative definitions of God, distancing Him from humanity. For Paul, as an example of apophatic theology with mystical tendencies God is incomprehensible in His

essence, 'dwelling in the light which no man can approach unto; whom no man hath seen, nor can see' (1 Timothy 6:16).

9. On the facing page of the manuscript notebook Beckett tested this formulation and left a trace that suggests the proximity between the ideas of the voyage and the tunnel: 'ce long ~~voyage~~ <tunnel> ~~vers un~~ <~~le un~~ le> noir meilleur' (309).

10. Magessa O'Reilly's critical edition renders this word as 'tautological' (314), incorrectly as it begins '(ont[. . .]' rather than 'taut[. . .]'. His transcription of typescript 1661 recognises 'ontological' (314).

11. Nadler clarifies Spinoza's equation of Nature and God: 'The phrase 'God or Nature' is intended to assert a strict numerical identity between God and Nature, not a containment relationship. God is not 'in' Nature in such a way that nature contains, in addition to its natural contents, a distinct divine and supernatural content. There is no supernatural divine spark or spirit or juice either in natural things or in or under Nature as a whole' (Nadler, *Spinoza's* 118).

12. 'The *proof from prophecy*, which became so extraordinarily important for the further development of theology, arose accordingly from the need of finding a criterion for distinguishing true from false revelation. Since man is denied knowledge of the future through natural processes of cognition, the fulfilled predictions of the prophecies serve as marks of the inspiration, by means of which they have propounded the doctrines' (W 226).

13. Robert Pinget's unpublished 'Sur Beckett (extraits de journal)' notes that Beckett contemplated 'TOUT BAS' as the work's title at 17 August 1960 (PNG 354/3/46). A letter to Barbara Bray confirms that the running title of the work at 21 September 1960 was 'TOUT BAS DES BRIBES or TOUT BAS' (*LSB* 3, 357). Pinget adds on 28 November 1960 that Beckett's publisher Jérôme Lindon renounced the title he prefered 'Tout Bas, des Bribes' for 'Comment c'est' (PNG 354/3/47).

14. One notes the parody of academic ratiocination within the authorial interpolation 'see later'.

15. Caselli argues that 'our hairs tangled together' is a reference to Dante's *Inferno* 32, 'due sì stretti / che 'l pel del capo avieno insieme misto' (41–2; two who were pressed so close together that they had the hair of their dead intermixed; Caselli, *Beckett's* 158). If so this is another case where Beckett's reading of the *Inferno* supplied him with images ready to accommodate his philosophical and aesthetic interests.

16. Olney writes of the Augustinian dimension to the time in *Waiting for Godot*, emphasising Augustine's comments with respect to memory ('Memory' 857–80).

17. Beckett's 'quietist impulse' was mentioned in Knowlson's discussion of Beckett's reading of à Kempis (*Damned* 172–4). Nixon and Feldman have extended research into Beckett's 'quietist' influences

during the 1930s (Proust, Rousseau, Leopardi and Schopenhauer). In addition, Nixon charts Beckett's taste for Quietism in German literature during the later half of the 1930s, Beckett having read deeply in Hebbel, Grillparzer and Gœthe (*German Diaries* 37–59, 60–83). Feldman argues for an 'agnostic quietism' growing out of Beckett's exposure to Geulincx, Schopenhauer and Fritz Mauthner, noting his interest in *Unaninisme*, Jules Romains and Pierre-Jean Jouve in his final year at Trinity College Dublin, as well as more arguable 'quietists', such as Dante, Keats, the later Augustine, Burton and Dürer (Feldman, '"Agnostic Quietism"' 181–200).

18. Beckett's *Dream Notebook* records 'pleroma' as the 'totality of divine attributes' (198), from Inge's *Christian Mysticism* (81). On the following page Inge discusses the 'degenerate mysticism' of early Gnosticism, its 'oscillations between fanatical austerities and scandalous licence, and its belief in magic and other absurdities' (82).

19. Nixon gives a detailed account of the relationships between psychoanalysis, Quietism and bodily/literary waste in the years following Beckett's treatment by Bion (*German Diaries* 37–59).

20. I have analysed the text's dialogue with Freud in 'Psychoanalytic Refuse in *Comment c'est/How It Is*' and in my PhD, 'Samuel Beckett's *How It Is*: A Philosophy of Composition'.

21. Beckett corrects the title to '120 Days' in 'A Wet Night' (*More Pricks Than Kicks* 50). 'Aliosha G. Brignole-Sale' blends the piety of the youngest of Dostoevsky's brothers Karamazov with Anton Giulio Brignole Sale (1605–62), flagellant and writer of lascivious satire whom Beckett had encountered in Mario Praz, *The Romantic Agony* (37).

22. The manuscript version of Part 1 paragraph 120 contains a convergence of the thematics of God's intervention (tins clinking/rattling) and the mystical 'glue' with its '*boîtes englouties*' (314, my emphasis; devoured tins).

23. Beckett's 'Philosophy Notes' contain the following clarification: 'Sensations for Descartes are psychic signs for geometrical structures. Task of physical research is to elicit latter from former. Locke later designated real (geometrical) qualities as <u>primary</u>, those sensuously perceived as <u>secondary</u>. Descartes allowed as primary qualities only shape, size, position & motion, *identifying thus physical body with mathematical*' (TCD MS 10967/186v, my emphasis; W 403–4).

24. Han Van Ruler notes in his introduction to *Ethics* that Geulincx 'was obsessed with suicide' (xxxi; cf. Geulincx, *Ethics* 160–1, 246, 258, 267).

25. The tutor is 'foudroyé' (Beckett, *Nouvelles* 97) by the infartcus, Beckett employing a verb used for lightning strikes, hence the substantive, *la foudre*, or lightning, as a metaphor of God's causal intervention in the world. This does not appear in Malebranche's *The*

*Search After Truth* or *Elucidations on the Search After Truth*, nor in Geulincx's *Ethics*, but it is Leibniz's figure for God's continuous creation in the *Monadology*: 'all created derived monads are productions and are born, so to speak, by virtue of continuous lightning flashes of the divinity from moment to moment' (§47).

26. It also offers the humorous insinuation that this erotic scene is a less *rose*, or *soft porn* version of Malebranche, an amusing irony given that Malebranche famously riled against the abuse of the passions (for more on this theme see Cordingley 'L'ordre naturel').

27. Beckett wrote in his manuscript, '*on dirait* du Malebranche, moins *l'optimisme*'; he types this out and revises it, 'on dirait <*c'est*> du Malebranche, moins l'optimisme, <en moins *optimiste*>'; he then writes it out again by hand, 'Malebranche en moins rose *optimiste*'; and types then revises until he hits upon his final formulation, 'Malebranche moins souriant rose' (334).

28. Beckett describes Malebranche's Occasionalism and Geulincx's 'two clocks theory' in the 'Philosophy Notes' (TCD MS 10967/189r; W 307; cf. Ackerley *Demented*, #178.9) and notes to Geulincx (332–3). The implication here is that the movements of the couple and the dog are synchronised despite the absence of physical causation between them, as mind is to body.

29. This reading would have supplemented the earlier study he made at the École Normale.

30. 'Now as to telling you why I stayed a good while with Lousse, no, I cannot. That is to say I could I suppose, if I took the trouble. But why should I? In order to establish beyond all question that I could not do otherwise? For that is the conclusion I would come to, fatally. I who had loved the image of old Geulincx, dead young, who left me free, on the black boat of Ulysses, to crawl towards the East, along the deck. That is a great measure of freedom, for him who has not the pioneering spirit. And from the poop, poring upon the wave, a sadly rejoicing slave, I follow with my eyes the proud and futile wake. Which, as it bears me from no fatherland away, bears me onward to no shipwreck' (*TN, Molloy* 51).

31. The galley-man is in the French of *L'Innommable* the *galérien*: 'The galley-man, bound for the Pillars of Hercules, who drops his sweep under cover of night and crawls between the thwarts, towards the rising sun, unseen by the guard, praying for storm. Except that I've stopped praying for anything. No no, I'm still a suppliant. I'll get over it, between now and the last voyage, on this leaden sea' (*TN* 336).

32. Uhlmann glosses the different translations of Geulincx's phrase in his introduction to Beckett's notes on Geulincx ('Introduction' 305).

33. 'Interim *corpus meum* pars hujus mundi est, incola quartae plagae, et inter species gradientes sibi locum vindicat; *ego* vero minime

pars hujus mundi sum, utpote qui sensum omnem sugiam, qui nec
videri ipse, nec audiri, nec manu tentari possim' (Geulincx *Opera*
III [Treatise I. Chapter II. Section II. §2], 204). Beckett's notes to
Geulincx form an appendix to the English edition of the *Ethics*,
translated by Han van Ruler.

34. Marius Buning ('Samuel Beckett's' 136) points to the long lineage
in mystical thought of the affirmation of nothing when he connects
the late medieval mystic Meister Eckhart's 'self-naughting' with
Beckett's rhetoric of nothing and project of the 'unword'.

35. Shane Weller (*Literature* 81–5) discusses Adorno's interpretation of
Beckett's *nothingness* as 'nihilistic mysticism' (*nihilistische Mystik*)
whose ethical dimension invites further comparison with *How It Is*,
for Weller affirms that it 'constitutes a radical rejection of the world
as it is, a world of institutionalized torture which it is ethically justifiable to see as "radically evil"' (83).

36. The injunction to self-abandonment is repeated elsewhere in Geulincx's *Ethics* (e.g. 176, 277, 291, 292) and in Beckett's reading notes
(344, 352).

37. See the discussion in Chapter 1 of Uhlmann's notion of Beckett's
'occluded' philosophical image, which symbolises unresolved aporia
in the history of philosophy (*Philosophical* 68–9).

38. Uhlmann draws attention to the important work of Bernard Rousset,
who shows that Geulincx and Spinoza responded to each other's work
in a productive but antagonistic fashion: 'He [Rousset] argues that
Geulincx represents, in effect, a kind of anti-Spinoza: beginning with
quite similar understandings of physics, derived largely from Descartes,
they reached widely diverging positions, because Geulincx embraced
the transcendence of God, the immortality of the soul and the primacy
of mind over brute extension, while Spinoza embraced immanence, the
dissolution of our mortal mind with our mortal body and the paral-
lelism of thinking and extension. The other main element which distinguished the two, and that which, for Rousset, is the most telling, is
that Geulincx bases his entire ethical system on human ignorance and
powerlessness while Spinoza offers the potential, at least, of becoming
eternal through knowledge of a certain kind and recognises the power
of all beings (through his understanding of conatus) as a key compo-
nent of his system. In short, Geulincx is a philosopher of negation and
ignorance (representing, for Rousset, the most extreme example of
this position in the history of philosophy) while Spinoza is the extreme
example of a philosophy of affirmation' (Uhlmann, *Philosophical* 98).

# 6

## Pascal's Miraculous Tongue

Quelle chimère est-ce donc que l'homme ? Quelle nouveauté,
quel chaos, quel sujet de contradiction ? Juge de toutes choses,
imbécile ver de terre ; dépositaire du vrai, amas d'incertitude ;
gloire, et rebut de l'univers.

Blaise Pascal, Penseés ([1905] 186)

What sort of a monster then is man? What a novelty, what a
portent, what a chaos, what a mass of contradictions, what
a prodigy! Judge of all things, a ridiculous earthworm who
is the repository of truth, a sink of uncertainty and error; the
glory and scum of the world.

Blaise Pascal, Pensées ([1962] 169)

Pascal's vision of the impoverished human condition finds its
comic, atheistic incarnation in Beckett's post-World War II novels. In the *Pensées*, Pascal condemns humanity's faith in reason as
an absurdity and its aspirations to material happiness as worthy
of nothing but pity. These sentiments chimed with Beckett, who
rejected Pascal's unwavering fideism yet continued to count him
among his select 'old chestnuts' into his old age (Knowlson,
*Damned* 653). Pascal's influence on Beckett's writing has attracted
relatively little attention.[1] His extreme asceticism and belief in
miracles offered Beckett the perfect caricature of one striving over-
zealously for the Quietist's humility. This chapter will first account
for Beckett's knowledge of Pascal, and chart Pascalian figures common to *L'Innommable/The Unnamable* and *Comment c'est/How
It Is*. The historical figure of Blaise Pascal, as much as his *Pensées*,
emerges as a source of inspiration for Beckett, who uses both to
implicate his characters in ever-deeper philosophical conundra. By
exploiting eccentric episodes in Pascal's life and writing, Beckett
could mock his characters' pious aspirations and their desire to

escape the residue of their learning and experience through miraculous transportation.

Beckett's intertextuality has been theorised variously as his
'poetics of unknowing' (Nixon, *German Diaries* 181), 'poetics of
ignorance' (Van Hulle, '*Faust* Notes' 291) and 'poetics of residua'
(Caselli, 'The Promise' 249), all these formulations intimating a
method of composition whereby to write he needed to first divest
himself of his erudition, of what he called in his short poem 'Gnome'
the 'loutishness of learning'. He neutralises his learned languages
by deploying references privately, so that rather than affirm their
source meaning they become the raw material for his own creation
(poetics). As Beckett commented to Israel Shenker in 1956: 'The
more Joyce knew the more he could. He's tending toward omni-
science and omnipotence as an artist. I'm working with impotence,
ignorance' (quoted in Federman and Graver, *Samuel Beckett* 148).
Beckett reiterated this to James Knowlson shortly before his death
in 1989:

> I realised that Joyce had gone as far as one could in the direction of
> knowing more, [of being] in control of one's material. He was always
> adding to it; you only have to look at his proofs to see that. I realised
> that my own way was in impoverishment, in lack of knowledge and in
> taking away, in subtracting rather than adding. (*Damned* 352)

This became for Beckett an aesthetic principle, influencing not
only his use of learning but his style. He wrote to Barbara Bray on
11 March 1959, early in the genesis of *Comment c'est*:

> I'm struggling with the new moan, trying to find the rhythm and
> syntax of extreme weakness, penury perhaps I should say. Sometimes
> I think I'm getting on, then realise how far I am from it still. This is
> the fifth or sixth version of the opening. (*LSB* 3, 211)

Beckett's sparse, fragmented style can be viewed as a desire for
linguistic asceticism, which he expressed to Herbert Blau (quoted
in Coe, *Samuel* 14) and Lawrence Harvey (*Samuel Beckett* 196)
as motivating his move to write in French after World War II. His
sense of the absurdity of his own *ascesis* is transformed into the
content of *Comment c'est*, partly as a parody of Pascal's asceticism
revealed when images are charted through early manuscripts to
their fragmentary remnants in the published text, or where allusive

discourse is volatilised, leaving a 'residua' of tropes, shadows and comic images.[2]

The evidence suggests that Beckett saw in Pascal a figure onto whom he could project his perception of the absurdity of his own exploitation of 'ignorance'. In so doing, Beckett's self-referential discourse revives the question of memory and the status of its contents, and thus his sustained interest in Proust. Beckett's burlesque treatment of the miracles and asceticism affirmed by Pascal enters into a discourse with his concern for originality in voice and his identification of the mystical in Proust. Beckett's desire to escape the habitual formations of thought informs his (mis)use of allusion and leads him to explore the paradoxes of 'involuntary memory', not simply to efface his erudition but to use it with maximum economy. His Pascalian/Proustian images are crafted with a Vorticist-like intensity, yet unlike Pound who funnelled Tradition into the Image, Beckett subverts such a possibility, lacing his images with paradox and self-cancellation. Beckett's late modernist, post-Joycean poetics offers his alternative to the Tradition.

## Two Mystical Conversions, or '*Pascal Fou!*'

Pascal became increasingly implicated in the Jansenist controversies in seventeenth-century France. The Jansenists were a radical branch of the Catholic Church who stressed the theological consequences of human sin, predestination and divine grace. Accused of Calvinism and condemned for heresy, the movement is remembered for the remarkable concentration of literary talent connected with its schools and monasteries at Port-Royal. As well as Pascal, its members and affiliates included Jean Racine, Antoine Arnauld and Pierre Nicole. Unlike Arnauld's, Pascal's fideism never allowed him to integrate into his theological beliefs Cartesianism and a rationalist faith in reason. He claimed to have experienced two mystical 'conversions' and was a staunch defender of the Jansenists' claims that miracles had taken place at Port-Royal. From adolescent mathematical genius to quasi-philosopher and Jansenist apologist, Pascal became increasingly reclusive at Port-Royal and ended his days practising an extreme and arguably absurd asceticism.

Beckett had a keen eye for the eccentricities of literary figures to whom he was intermittently attracted: he enlisted Descartes' peculiar habits when casting him as narrator of his early poem, 'Whoroscope'; and the idiosyncrasies of Samuel Johnson when embarking on an aborted play, 'Human Wishes'. In *The Unnamable* and *How It Is*, Beckett litters his narrators' discourse with allusions to Pascal's life, drawing many details from the twenty-nine-page biography entitled, 'Notice sur Blaise Pascal', which prefaced the edition of the *Pensées* in Beckett's library at his death.[3] The first page of the 'Notice' mentions the vertiginous event that provoked Pascal's 'first conversion' to Jansenism: in 1648, while crossing a bridge at Neuilly just outside Paris, Pascal's horses bolted, nearly launching his carriage into the Seine: 'la commotion de cet accident fut si forte qu'elle changea complètement sa vie ; il se réfugia près de ses amis de Port-Royal dont il devint le redoutable défenseur' (1; the shock of this accident was so great that it completely changed his life; he took refuge near his Port-Royal friends, whom he defended vigorously). Pascal interpreted his survival as a miracle, and the event assumed a life of its own, as Beckett's well-thumbed *Encyclopaedia Britannica* confirms, referring to the 'anecdotic embellishments of the act which are too famous to be passed over'; namely, that Pascal 'would have been plunged in the river but that the traces fortunately broke', and 'the tradition (due to the abbé Boileau) that afterwards he used at times to see an imaginary precipice by his bedside, or at the foot of the chair on which he was sitting' (20: 879).

The biographical 'Notice' also describes the 'second conversion', Pascal's 'nuit de feu' or mystical communion with the divine, to which his fragmentary ecstatic poem, 'Mémorial', bears testimony. Pascal is believed to have sewn his original poem and a copy into the lining of his coat; the 'Notice' refers to '*fragments étrangers aux* Pensées, *tel que l'*écrit trouvé dans l'habit de Pascal après sa mort' ('fragments which are not part of the *Pensées*, such as the *piece of writing found in Pascal's clothing after his death*'; 26). The *Encyclopaedia* calls this the fabled story of 'Pascal's amulet'; the parchment slip ('Memorial') he carried about him constantly was discovered on his death, sewn into the lining of his coat (20: 879).

These 'conversions' are contested, but form part of the apocryphal mythology of Pascal's life. They are contextualised in Beckett's copy of the *Pensées*, which includes editorial commentary on Charles Augustin Sainte-Beuve's celebrated history, *Port-Royal*, and its '*pénétration*' (13) into the mystery of 'Mémorial'. This commentary cites Pascal's detractors, such as Cousin, who claims that Pascal fell prey to '*une* dévotion ridicule et convulsive' (15), and Lélut, whose *De l'amulette de Pascal* of 1846 is credited with a footnote. The commentary rejects the scepticism that eighteenth-century intellects imposed on Pascal's religiosity, but concedes that the hypothesis of Condorcet and Lélut has at least '*le mérite de la logique: Pascal fou!*' (17).

### The 'Miracle of the Holy Thorn': Pascal and Proust, and the Spectre of Saint-Beuve

Pascal's plunge and amulet enter Beckett's writing, as images that evoke another 'miracle' that the biographical 'Notice' refers to when discussing the bibliographical history of 'les pensées relatives au miracle de la Sainte-Épine et à la polémique qui s'y rattache' (23; the 'thoughts' relating to the miracle of the Holy Thorn and the polemic associated with it). This event is described in Sainte-Beuve's *Port-Royal* as 'le coup de tonnerre qui suspendit tout' (III, 173; the clap of thunder that suspended everything). The 'miracle' was experienced by Pascal's eleven-year old niece, Marguerite Périer, a resident of the convent at Port-Royal who suffered from what was believed to be a fistula of the eye. The details are known from the letters of Mother Angélique, also reproduced in Sainte-Beuve's history, saying that Marguerite's fistula was exuding pus and causing her pain, but doctors had declared it incurable. At this time the convent at Port-Royal was offered a holy relic, a thorn from Christ's crown. During a ceremony in which the nuns venerated the thorn, kissing it and singing, Sister Flavie took the holy relic and touched Marguerite's eye with it. That night the swelling went down and the pus disappeared. A miracle was declared, and later affirmed by four doctors (Sainte-Beuve, *Port-Royal* III 173–7). Thus, in the face of their Jesuit and royal persecutors, the Jansenists were confirmed of their election in the eyes of the Lord.

Pascal salutes this miracle in the *Pensées*, reasoning that if God continuously revealed himself to humanity there would be no merit in the act of faith, hence the importance his momentary, miraculous revelation. Beckett's edition footnotes further background information: 'Cette Marguerite Périer est celle que l'on appeleait, a l'époque du miracle de la sainte épine, *la petite miraculée*' (236; This Marguerite Périer is she known at the time of the miracle of the Holy Thorn as *the little miracle-child*).[4] The edition includes a remarkable letter to Mademoiselle de Roannez, in which Pascal explains how a member of the convent (Marguerite) was healed by a miracle arising from devotion to the Holy Thorn. He affirms that the Holy Spirit resides invisibly in the relics of those who die by grace, which renders the relics worthy of veneration (348).

Beckett's 'Pascalian' imagery suggests that his reading about Pascal extended beyond the *Pensées* and the *Encyclopaedia* to Sainte-Beuve's classic, *Port-Royal*. The 'Notice' recommends this history for a thorough account of the 'Miracle' (3), and footnotes it frequently. Sainte-Beuve's history was the greatest work of the most important French literary historian of the nineteenth century, an essential resource for anyone wishing to know about Port-Royal and its authors.[5] Beckett studied Racine at Trinity, and his knowledge of the period is witnessed in the notes of his student Rachel Dobbin (née Burrows) to his 1931 lectures on Racine and Gide, when he briefly returned to Trinity College Dublin as a lecturer. Beckett observes gaps in the knowledge of Racine's life and makes historical inferences: '1675–77. Not religious revival – return to Jansenism perhaps'; 'Reconciled himself with Jansenists in Port Royal in this play [*Phèdre*] – probably thought Jansenists would pay him better shelter than Louis XIV. Essence of Jansenism exasperated sense of sin' (Dobbin, TCD MIC 60/79r). Beckett differentiated Pascal from the more dogmatic Port-Royalists, commenting, for instance, that 'Jansenism – limits main free will. Pascal wrote against it' (TCD MIC 60/9r), and connecting this sensibility with Gide's 'Characteristic strain – almost Jansenistic' (TCD MIC 60/9r, 10v).

On 5 December 1932 Beckett wrote to MacGreevy, discussing his rereading of the first volume of Proust's *Le Temps retrouvé* and its allusions to Balzac, then continuing in the next paragraph: 'I have a great admiration for Sainte-Beuve & I think his was the most interesting mind of the whole galère [crew] but I can't help regretting that it was applied to criticism' (*LSB 1*, 145). Beckett praises Sainte-Beuve's novel, *Volupté*, comparing it to Rousseau's *Rêveries* but expressing regret that his critical writing had developed 'a rather horrible process of crystallisation into a plausible efficiency of method' (I, 145). Beckett's movement from Proust to Sainte-Beuve is curious, for his disdain of Sainte-Beuve's 'clockwork' (I, 145) scholarship mirrors the contempt that Proust reserved for his biographical method. Proust conceived aspects of the *Recherche* as an elaborated riposte to Sainte-Beuve's reductive vision of literature, and as early as 1908 was working towards his volume, *Contre Sainte-Beuve*. Proust's attack on Sainte-Beuve was published only in 1954, yet it is the source of numerous passages of the *Recherche*. Beckett's 'Foreword' in his 1931 *Proust* reveals his Proustian hostility to biographical criticism as declared in his first words: 'There is no allusion in this book to the legendary life and death of Marcel Proust, nor to the garrulous old dowager of the Letters, nor to the poet, nor to the author of the Essays' (i). Later letters comment further on Sainte-Beuve: on 14 May 1937 he tells MacGreevy of his lunch with the Irish poet, Brian Coffey, who 'Talked most of the time about Saint[e]-Beuve and the critical function' (*LSB 1*, 497). On 5 June 1937 he mentions to MacGreevy that he had read Coffey's article on Sainte-Beuve (503). Writing to Mary Manning Howe on 22 May 1937 he evokes Proust's opposition to Sainte-Beuve: 'Someone once wrote <u>La Jeunesse de Sainte-Beuve</u>. Who will write <u>In Search of Morton</u>?'[6]

## 'The Affaire is Thorny:' Pascalian Echoes in *L'Innommable/The Unnamable*

In a letter to MacGreevy dated 18 October 1932, Beckett discussed his own writing in terms of a tension between bodily secretions and their refinement by the mind:

> There is a kind of writing corresponding with acts of fraud & debauchery on the part of the writing-shed. The moan I have more & more to make with mine is there – that it is nearly all trigged up, in terrain, faute d'orifice, heat of friction and not the spontaneous combustion of the spirit to compensate the pus & the pain that threaten its economy, fraudulent manoeuvres to make the cavity do what it can't do – the work of the abscess. I don't know why the Jesuitical poem that is an end in itself and justifies all the means should disgust me so much [. . .] I suppose I'm a dirty low-church P. even in poetry, concerned with integrity in a surplice. I'm in mourning for the integrity of a pendu's emission of semen, what I find in Homer & Dante & Racine & sometimes Rimbaud, the integrity of the eyelids coming down before the brain knows of grit in the wind.
> Forgive all of this? Why is the spirit so pus-proof and the wind so avaricious of its grit? (*LSB 1*, 134)

Pus, semen and grit are authentic elements in Beckett's economy of poetry: the 'grit' the irritant that provokes it; the 'semen' of the hanged its involuntary but generative force; and the 'pus' the protean substance emerging from the pain, becoming its expression.

His spirit is 'pus-proof', it cannot combust the pus, so 'faute d'orifice' he fabricates inauthentic poetic records that feign the work of the abscess. In the same letter Beckett finds some value in his poems, 'Alba', 'Dortmunder' and 'Moly', which have 'something arborescent or of the sky'. If his other work is 'facultatif' (optional) these poems do not give him 'the impression of being "construits"' despite having been drawn 'from the really dirty weather of my "private life" [. . .]' (134). Having emerged from an abject body the poems lack the 'staged drama' of Wagner or the 'false mimesis' of clouds on wheels; they are 'written above an abscess and not out of a cavity', 'a statement' rather than 'a description of heat in the spirit to compensate for pus in the spirit' (134). To deny the pus in the spirit, unsavoury but real, would be to falsify, as would a fanciful 'description of heat in the spirit', instead of the unmediated expression of the thing itself.

This tropology of the abject body predates Beckett's psychotherapy with Wilfred Bion, which began in December 1933 and was designed to treat the 'causes' of his psychosomatic problems, including anal abscesses, welts and rashes. Beckett found a thoroughly Freudian analysis in his reading of Ernest Jones, who likened the treatment of a single neurotic 'aberration' to trying to cure a 'riddling abscess by tapping superficial pockets of pus instead of thoroughly draining entire system of connected cavities' (TCD MS 10971/8/21r).[7] Beckett criticism has generally framed such psychosomatic symptoms within a mind/body dualism that has been assumed to play upon the Cartesian heritage in modern subjectivity. It has not, however, considered Pascal's role within this seventeenth-century dialectic, a fact exacerbated by Beckett's tendency, after *Murphy*, to echo and refract, rather than directly allude to the rhetoric or images of his intertexts. For instance, the following passage from *The Unnamable* blurs Cartesian and Pascalian tropes while focusing on the problematics of original voice:

That one day on my windpipe, or some other section of the conduit, a nice little abscess will form, with an idea inside, point of departure for a general infection. This would enable me to jubilate like a normal person, knowing why. And in no time I'd be a network of fistulae, bubbling with the blessed pus of reason. Ah, if I were flesh and blood, as they are kind enough to posit, I wouldn't say no, there might be something in their little idea. They say I suffer like true thinking flesh, but I'm sorry. (*TN* 353)

The 'fistulae', or cysts, imperfectly convey bodily waste, the pus of reason not of poetic spirit. There is an obvious Cartesian architecture: Descartes had argued that the connection between immaterial mind and physical body was located in the conarium, or pineal gland. He later abrogated this argument for a mysterious rapport between the innate ideas God puts in the mind and the extended world of the body, an idea refined by the Occasionalists, such as Malebranche and Geulincx. For Descartes, God as *Logos* was perfect reason, hence his valorising geometric and mathematical truths and postulating these as the language which the immaterial mind shares with God.[8] This informs the Unnamable's speculation that his fistulae have corrupted the flow of reason from those whom he terms his 'ancestors' or 'pedagogues', his Masters. The Unnamable's ironic image of the weeping 'blessed pus of reason' echoes Beckett's private discourse (above) from some twenty years earlier about 'the work of the abscess'; a rhetoric that is consistently engaged with Pascal.

While Descartes' God conversed with humans in a reasonable language through the immaterial mind, Pascal's Augustinianism led him to believe that God spoke with an ineffable language through the human heart. Pascal's ideal of the heart brimming with Grace and the voice of God (*Logos*) contrasts with that clogged with 'Muck' in Beckett's translation of a fragment from the *Pensées*:

> how hollow heart and full
> of filth thou art
>> *Que le cœur de l'homme est creux et plein d'ordure.*
> (*Poems* 200)

Beckett's letter to Barbara Bray of 12 September 1973, written from Morocco, reveals: 'Wondered about Pascal's Pensées doggerelised.' On 10 October 1973 he jotted on a postcard to Bray: 'Found a 2nd hand Pascal (Pensées) annotated in Arab hand', adding, 'Nothing doggerelisable so far.' Nearly six months later, on 31 March 1974, he sent Bray an early version of the poem: 'Still stuck in poem. Found from last year in Pascal's Pensées.' The fragment was included in the *Collected Poems* (1977) under the title, 'Huit Maximes' and attributed to Sébastien Chamfort, the eighteenth-century French poet.[9]

Hiding his 'doggeralising' of Pascal may be playful or erroneous, yet there is a strange recurrence in doggerel of references to bodily eruptions in an early manuscript draft of *Comment c'est*. The '*je*' begins to compose a ditty: '*Les mots se mettaient à chanter, quand j'ava [sic] lorsque j'avais mon cancer <sarcome> au sinus*' (292; Words began to sing, when I had when I had my cancer <sarcoma> in the sinuses). As the 'I' contemplates his capacity for such change, in its next manuscript revision ('Tx1') the ditty expands into a more elaborate, bawdy doggerel:

> *Les mots se mettaient à chanter,*
> *Lorsque j'avais mon sarcôme [sic] au sinus*
> *Un soir je m'pends après l'espagnolette*
> *J'en avais aussi au trou d'l'anus*
> *On m'sort de là en m'disant, Sois pas bête*
> *vingt fois, je les aurais écoutés toujours, ils s'arrêtaient soudain*
> *<pile > au milieu d'un hémistiche.* (292; 'Tx1': 1.95f)

> The words began to sing,
> When I had a sarcoma in my sinus
> One night I hanged myself from the window-bolt
> I also had one on the ring of my anus
> They got me out of it, saying, 'Don't be a dolt'
> twenty times, I might have heard them still, they stopped suddenly <dead> in the middle of a hemistich. (my translation)

Like the Unnamable's abscess, the sarcoma (a malignant and embryonic tumour) of the 'I' does not confirm his own identity and originality but passes into the abject. In the published text of *How It Is*, the narrator revisits such ideas differently: 'to speak of happiness one hesitates those awful syllables first asparagus *burst abscess* but good moments [. . .] never a plaint *an odd tear inward* no sound *a pearl* vast tracts of time natural order' (29, my emphasis).

From fistula to cancer to sarcoma in the sinuses to inward tears, there is good reason to believe that Beckett echoes the 'miracle' at Port-Royal. Sainte-Beuve's analysis of Marguerite's fistula of the eye, for example, discovers that: 'en bonne médicine, en bonne pathologie, la petite Marguerite avait non pas précisément une fistule, mais une tumeur lacrymale causée par l'obstruction du canal des larmes' (3: 178; in proper medicine, proper pathology, the young Marguerite did not have a fistula precisely, but a lachrymal tumour caused by an obstruction of the tear duct). That is, Marguerite's tear duct was not entirely blocked by the tumour, but part of the tumour was exposed, and when dislodged and lanced by the Holy Thorn the body's natural reaction to produce tears, the interconnection of the lachrymal and nasal passages explains the immediate disappearance of symptoms and thus the miracle (3: 178–80).

The 'burst abscess' and 'pearl' are equated with the 'tear' because a *marguerite*, or daisy, is etymologically derived from the Latin word for pearl. Beckett invests these flowers/tears/pearls with aspirations to a miraculous discourse with the spectral voice of 'the other above in the light'. The 'inward tear' remembers the hope of divine ablution and respite from the ceaseless cacophony of cancerous voices which infect the pure discourse between the 'I' in mud/text and the voice from the spectral author/God. As Sainte-Beuve explains with *bonne pathologie*: 'Il suffit que [. . .] le libre écoulement des larmes se rétablisse à l'intérieur, pour que tous les désordres cessent presque à l'instant même' (3: 179; The free flowing of tears has only to be restored internally for all disorders to cease at almost the same instant). In *Comment c'est/ How It Is*, Pim does not shed the masochist's tear; rather, the path of the 'inward tear' is towards the humility of the Quietist. Yet Beckett cannot entirely embrace Geulincx's Quietist ethic, for he is aware that piety can become both dogmatic and, in the case of Pascal, indulgent.

The heart clogged with 'filth' in Beckett's translation of the fragment from Pascal was, in the draft sent to Barbara Bray on 31 March 1974, the heart filled with 'muck'. In *How It Is* 'muck' is a synonym for 'mud', like the Unnamable's abject 'blessed pus of reason'. The 'I' of *How It Is* also calls his 'mud' the *voice quaqua*, his discharged *ancient voice*, the voice of past experience and learning materialised into excremental residue (quaqua/caca). When the Unnamable's fistula spreads from his throat it offers, unlike Marguerite's benevolent and divine thorn, an opportune moment for punishment by his malignant deceiving demons. Before his digression on the fistulae he says: 'They mentioned the roses. I'll smell them before I'm finished. Then they'll put the accent on the thorns [. . .] The thorns they'll have to come and stick into me, as into their unfortunate Jesus' (350). The Unnamable evokes the crown of thorns, but he is in a bar and attended by one Marguerite. He confuses her name with Madeleine, Gœthe blended with Proust, but not relinquishing the association of Proust and Sainte-Beuve that leads to Pascalian miracles. The Unnamable denies that he needs anyone to stick a thorn into him: 'No, I need nobody, they'll start sprouting under my arse, unaided, some day I feel myself soaring above my condition' (350). Curiously, the 5 December 1932 letter on Sainte-Beuve mentions Beckett's 'deep-seated septic cystic system!!' (*LSB 1*, 144). Cysts on the rump (as Beckett was all too aware) are like sitting on the Unnamable's 'billybowl of thorns' (350), with its biblical echo: 'For as the crackling of thorns under a pot, so is the laughter of the fool: this also is vanity' (Ecclesiastes 7:6).[10] Pascal's extravagant asceticism and his extreme, arguably perverse, psychic engagement with the 'Miracle of the Holy Thorn' is intimated in the 'Notice' in Beckett's edition of the *Pensées*: '*une austérité incroyable*' (2). Sainte-Beuve tells of Pascal's sister, Madame Périer (whose short 'Vie de Pascal' has prefaced many editions of the *Pensées*), who revealed that in later life the 'Spartiate chrétien' (Spartan Christian) would strap on a belt of nails over his bare skin; and whenever he suspected himself of vain or pleasurable thoughts would violently drive his elbows into the belt (3: 320–1).

In *The Unnamable*, the larval Worm emerges (like white asparagus) from the slimy mud, 'without voice or reason' (347). Like Pim, Worm is a potential vehicle of the Unnamable's voice, acting in a process not unlike the 'miracle' of the 'burst abscess' of *How It Is*. Worm's birth into the light avoids his pedagogical voices: 'Well if they ever succeed in getting me to give a voice to Worm, in a moment of euphory, perhaps I'll succeed in making it mine, in a moment of confusion' (348). Worm's only feature as he assumes form out of chaos is his singular 'weeping eye' (359); curiously, after the 'Miracle of the Holy Thorn' Pascal changed his seal and coat of arms to a single eye surrounded by a crown of thorns (Sainte-Beuve, *Port-Royal* 3: 184). Be that as it may, Worm is implicated in what Pascal called *l'esprit géométrique* (a concept discussed by Beckett in his 1931 lectures and which titles Pascal's *De l'ésprit géometrique*) as the Unnamable contemplates the voices controlling Worm (and thus himself): 'A-t-on vraiment besoin d'eux pour qu'il puisse entendre, d'eux et de fantoches analogues? Assez de concessions, à l'esprit de géométrie' (120, Are they necessary that he may hear, they and kindred puppets? Enough concessions, to the spirit of geometry, 359). Pascal identified *l'esprit géométrique* – both the 'geometric mind' and the 'spirit of geometry' – with not only the limitations and arrogance of human reason but with Cartesian philosophy. Reason alone would deprive humanity of the graces the passions afford. Pascal contrasts the *esprit géométrique* with the *esprit de finesse* of mind against heart; like Augustine, he valorised the heart above all as the organ through which God speaks to humanity (in a language beyond human words and representation). Beckett's reference to 'l'esprit de géométrie' is ironic because the figures/voices above have no 'pedagogical' function, yet they practise 'the catechist's tongue' (356), that of one who imparts the teaching of the faith. In the Unnamable's imagination, their attempt to extract an exalted song from him gives birth to Worm, yet they regard Worm as if his eye were but a fistula, hoping to 'dislodge' him with their crooked 'gaffs, hooks, barbs, grapnels' (359).[11] The Unnamable pictures them as reaching Worm through 'a small hole for the eye, then bigger ones for the arms, they can make one bigger still for the transit of Worm, from darkness to light' (357). Their Cartesian brutality centres on not the pineal gland but the eye, like a knife twisting in the 'Miracle of the Holy Thorn'.

Despite the machinations of the reasonable voice of 'l'esprit de géométrie', the Unnamable maintains a longing for the miracle of *theoria* – the vision of God as divine light – of 'the voice of the blest interceding invisible' ... 'perhaps it's the light of paradise' (359). This could be interpreted as a Romantic agony, a desire for his words to transcend their limited capacity for representation. However, miracles and transcendence are never endorsed by the texts. In the absence of divine vision, the Unnamable's discourse becomes ironic: 'Nothing much then in the way of sights for sore eyes' (360); 'Decidedly this eye is hard of hearing' (361). Bored with inherited philosophical dialect and the images it produces in the mind, he finally regrets 'this tedious equipoise' (362). A Pascalian valency to these images enriches the influences that Mark Nixon identifies as Beckett's 'poetics of the eye' (*German Diaries* 172–5), extending to the minimalist imagery of Beckett's late theatre: an old man holds a needle to his eye in an unfinished dramatic manuscript from 1980 (UoR 2930). Erik Tonning connects this image with Beckett's cataracts and his early reading of mysticism in Inge's *Christian Mysticism* and Schopenhauer (*World as Will* 223–39). His reading is compatible with the broader issue of divine vision in *Comment c'est/How It Is*, though the presence of lachrymal cancers rather than cataracts blurs the distinction.

The Unnamable's 'synthesis' of philosophical-theological dialectics is directed not towards a philosophical solution, but to a unique poetic transformation of inherited ideas. Should Worm see a face, he suggests, it would be 'Worth ten of Saint Anthony's pig's arse' (362). Meditating in the desert, St Anthony was attacked by Satan in guise of a pig, which was spared a roasting by the ascetic's resistance to temptation.[12] For his saintly restraint, Anthony was bathed in God's beatific light, and the pig turned into a porcupine. The Unnamable hopes for a like miracle of *theoria* and conversation with divine *Logos* (à la Pascal's poem, 'Mémorial'), precipitated by something akin to touching an abscess with a divine thorn. Rejecting this inherited dialect, the Unnamable produces a marvellously poetic image: he is not a participant in St Anthony's holy vision of light, and he does not avail himself of any beatific *imitatio* of Pascal/Marguerite, but he imagines his body pricked with thorns, piercing his own cancerous sores of reason, while below thorns will 'start sprouting under [his] arse, unaided', until he is 'soaring above [his] condition' (350) in a splendidly absurd transcendence.

Beckett's comic use of inherited dialectic in *The Unnamable* animates his narrative, as with a roll of his eye Worm pursues his Pascalian version of desert asceticism, strewn with a rhetoric of the Augustinian/Pascalian heart: 'his heart that is, on its waltz', 'within reach of the heart, happy expression that, of the heart crying out' (363); 'across the desert, it's a desert [. . .] not necessarily the Sahara, or Gobi, there are others [. . .] As long as he suffers there's hope' (367).[13] Christian metamorphosis offers hope for Beckett's larval ascetics: 'instead of suffering less than the first day, or no less, he suffers more as time flies, and the metamorphosis is accomplished' (367). The tropism of this metamorphosis is towards *theoria*. Through imagination the Unnamable thwarts the controlling voices and the 'blessed pus of reason'; he enacts his own interpretation of the Oedipal and Freudian myths, a metaphorical piercing of the eye/'I' to escape 'ancestors', 'pedagogues' or the Id. But the 'metamorphosis' can only be temporary and, as the Unnamable admits, 'The affair is thorny' (367).

## The Pascalian Tropology of *Comment C'est/How It Is*

*The Unnamable* treats less the specific doctrines of Descartes and Pascal than the dynamics through which pedagogical voices inculcate themselves within the articulating subject. Indeed, the manuscripts of *L'Innommable* bear witness that the allusion to

Pascal's 'l'esprit de géométrie' was earlier 'l'esprit de Descartes' (MS HRC SB/4/1/06v). Beckett often effaced clear revelations of the philosophical content that informs his fiction, but that he chose to add a contradictory dimension to his image is extraordinary. To maintain that the Pascalian allusion is a veiled reference to Descartes would be to fall into a teleological reading of textual genesis, ignoring the way that ideas shift and may become more complex in their revising and rewriting. This detail confirms Beckett's technique of using philosophical material with little regard for orthodoxy but with an eye to inscribing paradox within his images. Not only may they point to numerous philosophical 'sources' simultaneously but to 'read' them one must accommodate those internal contradictions, suspending the understanding that would issue from the identification of any one referent. Beckett views the history of philosophy as a narrative ridden with paradox and incoherence, against which the voice of reason regularly posits the arational logic of Christian asceticism. Indeed, he perhaps conceived his own attempts to forge a 'syntax of extreme weakness' in the writing of *Comment c'est* in relation to asceticism and the narratives of that tradition. This involved a dislocation and fragmentation of his prose from the 'strength' of its supporting contexts more radically than in *The Unnamable*, deepening his exploration of 'impotence' and 'ignorance', though making the text notoriously resistant to interpretation. Beckett's discourse with Pascal is typical of such rarefied intertextual poetics, but by divulging and then disfiguring allusive matter (and memory) over the composition process, the text can assume a more removed or 'ignorant' perspective, freeing it to be reused continuously as the raw material for new poetic forms.

The bawdy doggerel about the sarcoma in the sinus halted on the 'hémistiche' (or 'half-stitch'), the 'I' between the 'hem' and the 'stich' suggesting to an Anglophone eye, like a symbol to a *symboliste*, the Holy Thorn in Beckett's imagination, and the more so given that Pascal offered a comic example of misguided devotion by sewing his poem of ecstatic revelation, 'Mémorial', into the lining of his coat. Just as the Unnamable fails splendidly in his *imitatio* of Marguerite, the 'I' of *How It Is* confuses and transforms ludicrous details from the life of Pascal; the sarcoma in the sinus progresses into the 'I' hanging himself from a window-bolt: '*un soir je m'pends après l'espagnolette*'. Beckett's 'I' tries to find a sign of his divine election by recreating Pascal's ecstatic 'first conversion', his supposed hanging over the bridge at Neuilly. Pascal's mysticism and negative theology is a condition for the ascetic's divine vision. With the pathos of Yeats climbing his tower to induce his epiphany, the words of Beckett's 'I' are half-born into verse, despite the voices of reason that interrupt his vision when their sage or sceptical advice is delivered by the fistulae in his anus: '*Sois pas bête*' (Don't be a dolt). They correct his desire for a mystical short cut away from their voice of reason, and echo eighteenth-century voices from the *Âge de lumières*, such as those of Voltaire and Condorcet, who derided Pascal and in whose writing: 'Pascal y est présenté comme victime d'une superstition sordide; sa piété vive et tendre disparaît sous l'étalage des bizarreries' (Sainte-Beuve, *Port-Royal* 3: 412; Pascal is presented as a victim of sordid superstition; his raw and tender piety disappeared under bizarre displays). Beckett thus distances himself from the 'philosophers of light', whose sparkling intellects are subsumed into his farcical dialectic between piety and reason.[14]

While he was 'above in the light' the 'I' had a wife, Pam Prim, from whom he tried to induce a miracle like that of Marguerite:

Pam Prim [. . .] *she fell from the window or jumped* broken column

in the ward before she went every day all winter she forgave me . . .

the flowers on the night-table she couldn't turn her head *I see the flowers* I held them at arm's length *before her eyes* the things you see right hand left hand before her eyes that was my visit and she forgiving *marguerites from the latin pearl* they were all I could find

*iron bed* glossy white two foot wide all was white *high off the ground vision of love in it see others' furniture* and not the loved one how can one

*sitting on the foot of the bed* holding the vase bile-green flute the feet dangling the *flowers between the face* through them that I forget what it was like except intact white as chalk *not a scratch* or my eyes roved *there were a score of them.* (99, my emphasis)

Pam Prim embodies Burton's 'column of quiet', a phrase recorded in Beckett's *Dream Notebook* (#916), the good wife who comforts a scholar in his labours. She is 'broken', so has suffered greatly, and the act that she 'forgave' is somehow linked with her 'falling from the window'. Despite his faulty memory, he remembers himself perched on the edge of her bed, like Pascal on the verge of his precipice. He sees, 'white as chalk', those cliffs; but his 'vision of love' (the exact definition of *theoria*) has nothing of the fire of Pascal's 'Mémorial', for it is not the 'loved one', let alone Pascal's One of divine love. He cannot recall the flowers ('a score of them'), save that they were marguerites (or daisies), all that he could find; but he recalls her face, 'white as chalk' but intact, with 'not a scratch' from her fall, in which by memory he is implicated.

In the *The Legend of Good Women* Chaucer refers to the etymology of *daisy* as 'dayeseye', the *eye of day* (prologue ln. 43, 184; cf. Beckett, *Dream Notebook* #1163), a figure of perfect wifehood, as, for instance, when Alcestis is transformed into a daisy, or in the French tradition of 'Marguerite' poems and Jean Froissart's *Le Dittié de la Flour de la Margherite*. Chaucer named the women of his *Legend* 'Cupid's Saints' (xxi) because they died for love, but in the poem he defends himself from an imagined charge of misogyny, of which Love has accused him. In the scene from *How It Is*, when the daisies are held in front of Pam Prim's eyes ('right hand left hand'), something strange happens. The narrator's lament, 'marguerites from the latin pearl they were all I could find', far from being a fantastical transformation or the miraculous vision of a Marguerite, entails a memory of guilt or regret, perhaps for his assault of Pam Prim, forming another disingenuous image in the interwoven fabric of his learning. His Chaucerian 'vision of love' equally implicates Ingram's translation of *De Imitatione Christi*: 'a precious margaret & hid from many' (à Kempis 108; 'pretiosa margerita, a multis abscondita' 3.xxxvii), turning it into an image of abjection. This has been anticipated in *How It Is* by 'a little pearl of forlorn solace' (53). While the inward course of this first 'pearl' – 'never a plaint an odd tear inward no sound a pearl' – is more consistently engaged with the other Marguerite, she of the 'burst abscess', the second reference to it accommodates another stitch in my Pascalian haberdashery, but one best addressed in its Proustian *couture* of involuntary memory.

### The Work of an 'Unruly Magician': A Poetic Solution to the Cul-De-Sac of Involuntary Memory

In his lurid ditty about the sarcoma and window-bolt the 'I' implies that his words might have continued to 'sing' some 'vingt fois' ('twenty times') had they not been interrupted by the censuring voice ('Sois pas bête'). In the section just discussed, the 'eyes' of the 'I' roved: 'there were a score of them', while in French: 'mon regard errait elles étaient bien une vingtaine' (98), that is, 'twenty something'. In the earlier ditty from the 'ms' manuscript, Beckett chose the term, '*da capo*' (292), for 'vingt fois', neatly intimating in English a musical score. He may have wanted to 'weaken' a term from his early writing that signalled Proust's 'mystical' composition, the ironic connection made in his essay *Proust* between mystical experience and a '*da capo*' motif, 'a testimony to the intimate and ineffable nature of an art that is perfectly intelligible and perfectly inexplicable' (71). In musical notation, *da capo* is an instruction placed after a later section to indicate a return to the beginning or a notated earlier section. Beckett appropriates the term to refer to the musical transportation in the work of Proust, which he expressed in mystical terms, whereby 'the recurrent mystical experience' is Proust's 'purely musical impression' (*Proust* 71). This is related to involuntary memory, as if an image, word or sensation functioned like the *da capo* instruction, returning to a flood of earlier sensations, as when the celebrated *madeleine* unexpectedly provokes the euphoric return of childhood experiences. Beckett links this kind of 'mystical' experience to Pascal. Defining Proust's involuntary memory, he states that for Proust there is no difference between the memory of a dream and that of reality, just as a creature of habit makes no distinction between the *Pensées* and a soap commercial (19–20). Beckett thus responds to Pascal's comments on habit in the *Pensées* while evoking Pascal's mysticism and the nature of miracles, and relating these to Proust's involuntary memory. Why associate Pascal with the dream state, which, if taken for reality, might save one from the banality of habit? Beckett states that involuntary memory is the 'accidental and fugitive salvation' that surpasses the deadening effects of habit: 'But involuntary memory is an *unruly magician* and will *not be importuned*. It chooses its own time and place for the performance of its *miracle . . . its climax in revelation*'; Proust has, like Pascal, 'adopted this *mystic experience* as the Leitmotiv of his composition' (*Proust* 35, 20–1, 22, my emphasis).

Involuntary memory is an abiding concern in Beckett's writing, despite his increasing distrust of its capacity for 'salvation'; its familiar motifs include hawthorn flowers (their cascading form), the Proustian vase and verbena (Ackerley and Gontarski, *Faber Companion* 248–9, 604–5). 'Verbena' flourishes in *How It Is* (15; 1.68), and in the section recently discussed the 'I' awaits an involuntary 'miracle' as he stares into 'the vase', but its 'bile-green flute' offers little hope of escape from sequential, habitual time. The flowers hold promise, since it is 'through them that I forget what it [the vision] was like'; but they are drained of colour, 'white as chalk', impotent, 'not a scratch', and cannot flood this instant with past sensations. Memories are like the 'recordings on ebonite' evoked later (compare Krapp's tapes): 'a whole life generations on ebonite . . . mix it all up change the natural order . . . the voice we're talking of the voice' (137; 3.27–8). Yet no willed or voluntary images will transport the 'I' out of the tyranny of sequential time, that habitual rather than *da capo* repetition, and he is left reiterating the 'before Pim with Pim after Pim' empty mantra of his *ancient voice*.

The figure on the edge of his bed is evoked again in Part 1, a touching, pathetic image consumed by the narrator/narrated's zealous appropriation, consciously mapping a Pascalian image over that of himself in his past life 'above':

> deterioration of the sense of humour *fewer tears* too that too they are failing too and there another image yet another a boy sitting on a bed in the dark or a small old man I can't see with his head be it young or be it old his head in his hands *I appropriate that heart.* (19, my emphasis)

The Pascalian heart within this familiar figure opens up new possibilities in Beckett's late drama. In *Hey Joe*, Joe is on the edge of his bed, the drama unfolding as his pathos is channelled into a tear. The liturgical 'Nacht und Träume' features a seated figure with head in hands as the consolation of Christ. Beckett's use of Schubert in 'Nacht und Träume' is 'characterised by an aspect of modification as opposed to a mechanical doubling or "da capo"' (Maier, 'Two Versions' 98). The Quietist or holy aura of such works is far from the mockery of *How It Is*, where the spectre of a '*da capo*' repetition offers Beckett the chance to satirise farcical religiosity.

A self-consciousness poetics of residual learning follows the reference to the 'precipice' in manuscript 'ms': '*Foin <donc> maintenant <dorénavant> de détails, tout ce qui n'est pas écurie <perles et broderies,>*' (385; Let's skip <thus> now <henceforth> details, all that isn't stable <pearls and embroidery>).[15] Within the matrix of allusions to early Church history, the pun on hay ('*foin*') evokes the horse/ass and manger ('*écurie*'), recalling the Unnamable's sense of being outside the stable door:

Perhaps Marguerite has come and gone [. . .] It is not a night like other nights. Not because I see no stars [. . .] it is a silent place, at night. I am half-deaf. It is not the first time I have strained my ears in vain for the stables' muffled sounds. All of a sudden a horse will neigh. Then I'll know that nothing has changed [. . .] Perhaps I am still under the tarpaulin. (*TN*, *The Unnamable* 344)

Excluded from the miraculous vision the Unnamable, during the silent holy night, neither sees the star above nor hears the voices within, but his mystical zeal leads him into a comic epiphany of faith confirmed by the neighing horse inside the stable, thus sustaining his belief in the beatific scene behind its door. Beckett's penchant for drawing out the literal in idiomatic expressions – the French interjection, 'foin', as 'let's skip', the unstable '*écurie*' – gives way to 'pearls and embroidery', reworking traditional Biblical allusions of hay and stables into the pearls and tears embroidered in the text. The dialectic of reason and its abandonment of miraculous discourse is thus played out through the texture of images lining and interweaving the narrator/narrated's discourse.

After Pam Prim and the failure of the flowers and memory to generate a miraculous discourse, the 'I' inserts an image from the past (a voluntary memory) into his narrative. He returns to a scene of religious instruction and *praxis*, learning to recite the Psalms: 'mamma [. . .] jade bible [. . .] psalm one hundred and something' (101). Augustine's commentary on the recitation of the Psalms stresses their potential for spiritual transportation, though the Unnamable debased such notions when he conflated pedagogues and catechists within *l'esprit de géométrie*. In such sequences, with their obsessive focus on the primal scene of their composition, Beckett explores the bind within his 'poetics of ignorance'. The problem can be restated variously: how can one move beyond the habits of memory, the forms of thought forged not in the smithy of the soul but by the institutionalised transmission of his masters' voices?[16] And what is so miraculous about involuntary memories if they consistently lead one into loops with voices not one's own, or voices no longer so? Can one find a different shape for these thoughts and so expurgate the 'blessed pus of reason', and make them one's own? The core of Beckett's poetics of ignorance entails the use of the imagination to refigure experience and reshape the content of habitual as much as involuntary thought. By refiguring the mind's return to its past learning and

the scenes of its acquisition, Beckett unwinds the prescriptive formations of his *Bildung*, his constitution in reason, which frees him
to appropriate its content for his poetics. Largely unconcerned
with philosophical coherence, Beckett uses philosophical images
as raw material, refiguring them in the continuum of creation
(where past works revisit present manuscripts that are in turn
revised until ready for self-translation) into that a-philosophical
poss of Cartesian and Pascalian tropes that turned the Unnamable
into Pascal's ludic porcupine of (un)reason.

### 'bubble in the head all dead now': Paradox in the Involuntary, Philosophical Image

For Beckett, these problems are ultimately provocative, rather than
paralysing, though they first require a conscious engagement with
the contents of memory and its erudition. In *How It Is* he layers his
Pascalian tropes with Zeno's paradoxes of reason concerning the
impossibility of motion in space and time, drawing their absurdity
into discourse with the vertiginous matutinal awakenings Pascal
experienced after his first 'conversion': 'sudden quasi-certitude that
another inch and I fall headlong into a ravine or dash myself against
a wall though nothing I know only too well to be hoped for in that
quarter this tears me from my reverie' (51).

When the 'I' is torn from his 'reverie', Zeno's absurdity
of reason is identified: logically, a man should not walk off a cliff
or touch a wall because every measure forward can be infinitely
halved. Yet Pascal's precipice (here, a ravine), a cliché of the sublime, is evoked knowingly, by one aware of Rousseau's rêverie.
The implicit pun on 'tears' evokes the miraculous lachrymal Pascalian associations elsewhere in this section of the text. Torn from
his mystic's hope, the 'I' is the precipitate of his memories of this
very hope itself, the platitudinous vision of the sublime that his
reverie might have afforded dashed against the junk of past learning. The irony is complex: if involuntary memories of a schooling
in philosophy disturb best intentions of falling into the trans-pre-
cipitous Oneness, then involuntary memory may equally scupper a
Romantic reverie or mystical vision à la Marguerite. The Unnamable's abscesses of past learning are lanced when the 'bubble in the
head' is terminal: 'all dead now' (51). Hence the reflection: 'always
understood everything except for example history and geography
[. . .] forgave nothing [. . .] never loved anything' (51). The futility

of a Christian education in forgiveness and love is compounded with 'humanities', a forced feeding that distracts the mind in later life and drains the 'I' of mystical enthusiasm: 'such a bubble at such a time it bursts the day can't do much more to me' (52).

The ensuing deliberation on the 'little pearl of forlorn solace' (53) – identified by Ackerley ('Thomas' 83) as referring to à Kemp-is's Imitatio – immediately encounters Pascal's 'precipice' (57). Yet between 'pearl' and 'precipice' lies a digression that offers more than a trace of Marguerite's relic:

> to the scribe sitting aloof he'd [the witness] announce midnight no two in the morning three in the morning Ballast Office [. . .] it's my words cause them it's they cause my words [. . .]

> the dust there was then the mingled lime and granite stones piled up to make a wall further on the *thorn in flower* green and white quick-set mingled privet and *thorn*. (57, my emphasis)

The 'I' hears in his own voice the announcements of the writerly dyad – witness and scribe – tolled in the sequential time (two, three . . .) of the Dublin Ballast Office. Beckett's image evokes his comment in *Proust*, 'Habit is the ballast that chains the dog to its vomit' (19).[17] Less habitual is this 'épine en fleur', the 'thorn in flower' (55–6). In the 'ms' manuscript the image is more clearly that of the Proustian 'miracle' (involuntary memory): 'une haie d'aubépine' (382) or hawthorn hedge. The 'stones piled up', evoking the detritus of habitual time, yet the published text obscures the Proustian echo when the hawthorn becomes 'the thorn in flower'. Compare Beckett's short story, 'The End', which finishes with its narrator en route to the ascetic's cave: 'We followed the quiet, dustwhite inland roads with their hedges of hawthorn . . . The ass carried me right to the mouth of the cave' (*Complete Short* 88). Here the hawthorn is a portent of *theoria* or, perhaps, a misplaced belief in that 'divine vision'.

In *How It Is*, tropes of asceticism define the journey through the desert of mud. Shortly after the section quoted above, which in the manuscript 'ms' references the 'hawthorn' and thus Proust's invol-untary memory, Beckett flirts with a *'prière à St-Antoine'*, which becomes the *'<étincelle> d'espoir'* (388; 'prayer to St Anthony;' 'spark of hope'), aligning Proust's 'mysticism' with the ascetic's hope to transcend the habitual repetitions of his body and mind. Such a release from the self transports the ascetic into a communion with the divine, 'the other above in the light'. The theme of desert asceticism is more clearly present in this early manuscript, which includes several paragraphs erased from the final text in which the 'I' is visited by 'visiteurs' and those who 's'enfuient dans un endroit désert' (247; flee into a wilderness), like St Anthony and his followers, or the Holy Family of Rembrandt's *Rest on the Flight into Egypt*. The 'I' charts his journey into the self, likening himself to other ascetics who bloom and die in the desert unseen by God, the 'thorn in flower' now a variety of 'desert flower' (181).

In the 'ms' manuscript the trope of desert mysticism is developed as the 'I' betrays his attempt to practise a will-less *reduction*. That 'I' finds himself within a desert wilderness and affirms his ascetic practice: 'la majeure partie de ce qui se passe autour de moi, comme des idées et des sentiments qui naissent spontanément en moi, je dois l'ignorer complètement' (251; the greater part of what happens about me, like the ideas and feelings that arise spontaneously within me, I should ignore completely). Yet this character is writing a text which appears to be the text the reader is reading (or would have read but for the subsequent revision and fragmentation). Beckett thus casts an ironic eye over his attempt to bring an 'ignorant' perspective upon his *ancient voice[s]*, equating the writing of his 'I' with the kind of ascetic practices that he might admire but in which he could not, fundamentally, believe. The published text alludes to its compositional processes, offering a textual scar or what Dirk Van Hulle terms a 'figure of script' (*Manuscript Genetics* 155–6) that remembers its genesis, even when that figure is replaced by the self-conscious inscription of its absence: deleting the manuscript episode of the desert 'visiteurs', Beckett wrote in its place, 'ni de visiteurs dans ma vie cette fois nulle envie de visiteurs' (10; nor callers in my life this time no wish for callers (11)). Following the genesis of the text the 'I' has moved from a desire to 'ignore' his own sentiments and body to the assertion that he has relinquished all agency over them. His ultimate claim to having abandoned his self and will consists in his lying face down in the mud, attempting to 'quote' his *ancient voice*.

In *Comment c'est/How It Is* the false hope offered by Proust's 'miracle' is linked to the ascetic's hope for a communion with the divine Author, one beyond the limited capacity of his own thought and language. 'Pascalian' motifs, such as the 'bubble in the head', affirm the vortical patterning of the intertextual thorn, even as Beckett prunes his text of its Pascalian foliage. A reader unfamiliar with Beckett's private vocabulary of images might interpret the text by drawing on others: 'The End', for instance, features the Glastonbury thorn (a hawthorn bush or hedge), which flowers in spring but also in mid-winter and was therefore considered a miraculous confirmation of God's benediction. Yet in the same paragraph of the 'ms' manuscript where Beckett alluded to 'une haie d'aubépine', he further obscured his Proustian evocation of the hawthorn by inscribing the name 'Hamilton' (382). Antoine Hamilton was, like Beckett, an expatriate Anglophone (an Anglo-Irishman of Scottish heritage), who wrote in French in the early eighteenth century. He is known for his highly original ironising of the traditional *conte de fées*, mixing it with the *conte oriental* (in the manner of the *Thousand and One Nights*). His long tale, *La Fleur d'épine* ('the flower of the thorn') is muddled by the 'I' of *How It Is* as '*l'épine en fleur*' ('the thorn in flower'); in turn the '*troènes épines confondues*' of *Comment c'est* become 'mingled privet thorns' of *How It Is* (56).

The footnoting habits of the academic animal die hard, and Beckett despised the derivative nature of his own discourse unless it was poetically transfigured. A degree of academic sabotage ensues when he laces allusions to one intertext (Proust) with another (Pascal), contemplates disguising them with a third (Hamilton), mocks his Anglophone self writing in French, and then recedes from the page by throwing out pointed decoys. This sabotaging of allusion with allusion shows Beckett struggling to make his language 'ignorant' of habitual shapes of thought and deaf to his *ancient voice*. He thus allows an accessible reference to the Glastonbury thorn to prick a wary reader, but this may entrap the prize allusion hunter. He frames the reader in a manner not unlike Thomas Browne's doubting the scientific veracity of the miraculous Glastonbury thorn in the *Pseudodoxia Epidemica*: 'strange effects, are naturally taken for miracles by weaker heads, and artificially improved to that apprehension by wiser' (2.6.12–14; 1.150). If such thorns exist in memory but are experienced anew with each return of *ancient voice*, one may well ask which is the signified to the textual signifying thorn? Uncertainty mediates and motivates Beckett's use of Pascal, involving his badinage with Proust and Sainte-Beuve and thus questioning memory, biography and, indeed, the very reading of literature. Anyone seeking empirical certainties of clear and distinct ideas will find uncomfortable Pascalian thorns under the folds of Beckett's skin.

## Notes

1. Jacquart (*Le Theatre* 92) argues that Beckett dramatises Pascal's 'wager' in *En attendant Godot*. Nelson ('Three Orders' 79–85) ruminates on similarities between Pascal's cosmic order and that of *Fin de partie*. Morot-Sir ('Cartesian Emblems' 61–82) offers a profound reflection on Beckett and Pascal but limits his discussion to the nature of language and a comparison with Wittgenstein.

2. This chapter will not consider the influence of Pascal's unique prose style on Beckett's French. That important question requires a separate study beyond the scope of this book.

3. The works in Beckett's Library at www.beckettarchive.org include the 1670 Port-Royal edition, published by Flammarian and undated, though first published in 1905.

4. Sainte-Beuve recalls that Margot Périer became known as Marguerite only after the 'miracle' (3: 177).

5. T. S. Eliot's introduction to a 1958 English edition of Pascal's *Pensées* attests to the international reputation of Sainte-Beuve's history at this time. For details of Pascal's involvement in Port-Royal and the Jansenist's defence from the charge of heresy, Eliot recommends, 'the best account, from the point of view of a critic of genius who took no side, who was neither Jansenist nor Jesuit, Christian nor infidel, is that in the great book of Sainte-Beuve, *Port-Royal*' (x). Eliot adds: 'And in this book the parts devoted to Pascal himself are among the most brilliant pages of criticism that Sainte-Beuve ever wrote' (x).

6. I thank Mark Nixon for bringing this reference to my attention, and for identifying Morton, mentioned in Beckett's letter to MacGreevy of 10 March 1935, when he writes that he has given his mother a copy of Morton's *In the Steps of the Master*. This work recounts Morton's journey through the desert Holy Lands.

7. Baker (*Samuel Beckett* 6–7) and Nixon (*German Diaries* 58) discuss Beckett's use of the psychoanalytic 'draining'.

8. In his 'Philosophy Notes', Beckett records this distinction (TCD MS 10967/186v).

9. Genetti ('Molto' 171) noticed that one of the eight translations was of Pascal, rather than Chamfort.

10. I thank Chris Ackerley for this Biblical echo.

11. Ackerley and Gontarski (*Faber Companion* 363) see the stick with a hook that fishes out Worm as an allusion to the 'pot-hook of memory', or '*Häkchen*', derived from Fritz Mauthner. This implies an even greater complexity to Beckett's fusing of tropes and images of memory and language, and demonstrates his practice of erasing a clearly signified allusion or 'memory' but leaving the traces.

12. Anthony is the patron saint of pigs and, appropriately, skin diseases. The runt, or 'Tantony', of a litter is traditionally offered to monks. Beckett's copy of Pierre Gustave Brunet's *Curiosités Théologiques* contains the underlined words 'Le cochon de saint Antoine' within the following passage: 'Le cochon de saint Antoine n'était d'abord qu'un symbole qui signifiait la victoire remportée sur le démon et sur la chair ; la clochette attachée au cou de l'animal désignait encore plus nettement son esclavage ; mais ce sens symbolique ne fut pas longtemps compris' (34–5, www.beckettarchive.org; Saint Anthony's pig was first only a symbol that signified victory the demon and the flesh; the bell attached to the animal's neck indicated its slavery even more clearly; but this symbolic meaning was for a long time not understood.)

13. Sainte-Beuve often draws upon the rhetoric surrounding the 'désert des champs', the site of the Port-Royal monasteries (*Port-Royal* III: 188).

14. The 'Notice' in Beckett's edition of the *Pensées* discusses their publication history and the role of Condorcet and Voltaire, prompting the reflection: 'Nous assistons à la lutte de l'esprit philosophique contre l'esprit de foi' (11; We are witnessing the struggle of the philosophical mind against the spirit of faith).

15. Beckett's use of 'écurie' is a piece of bilingual horseplay, as if his searching for another way of saying 'n'est pas stable' (is not stable) was translated, via English, into 'n'est pas écurie'.

16. Beckett's self-directed study, particularly in the 1930s, desired equally to de-compose the influence of 'authority' on his thought.

17. The Ballast Office also echoes Joyce's *Ulysses* and Bloom's sense of the discrepancy of time between Greenwich and Dublin.

# 7

# Spinoza, Leibniz or a World 'less exquisitely organized'

To read *How It Is* closely is to engage in the intensive hermeneutic activity usually associated with reading poetry, and poetry of the erudite, modernist kind. It reconstitutes the discourse lost to the gaps between surviving fragments of the narrator/narrated's ratiocination, and obliges the reader to participate in the writing process. My final chapter explores how this process is thematised through an engagement with mathematics, and especially the problem of the infinitesimal 'gap' (see Chapter 2) that the calculus of Newton and Leibniz resolved. Many rationalist philosophers understood mathematics as a symbolic system that represented eternal truths of humanity's relationship to God. One paradigm immediately evident in Part 3 of *How It Is* is the attempt to construct a cosmology that resembles the mechanistic universe of seventeenth-century rationalism. The narrator/narrated becomes hopelessly embroiled in his elaborate but confused 'formulation', the chain of bodies locked in a perpetual cycle of meeting, colliding, training, torturing and leaving one other. Working through the relationship between Occasionalist ideas and his attraction to pantheistic or mystical solutions to his predicament he touches on Spinoza (see Chapter 5). I now return to *How It Is* and Spinoza's *Ethics*, to discover a deep affinity between Beckett's text and Spinoza's uncompromising attack on the Judeo-Christian transcendentalism and anthropomorphism that informs a counter-narrative to the transcendentalism that powers the will of the 'I' to ascend to the light. I examine the crucial influence of Leibniz's *Monadology* and his theory of perception and knowledge, and I suggest his calculus of infinitesimals as a source of the vocabulary of philosophical concepts that Beckett drew on to reconfigure into an original, poetic order many of the problems witnessed in my previous chapters. Such interrogations of the nature of reality and the divine, and the claim to represent mathematically the relationships between them, offered Beckett a language to express the complex and often para-doxical aesthetic questions of authorship, character and textuality.

### The Spinoza 'Solution'

Beckett's library contained, at his death, an English translation of Spinoza's *Ethics*, their first nineteen pages heavily marked up and annotated. The book was awarded to Beckett's friend A. J. ('Con') Leventhal as a Latin prize in 1911–12, so the annotations may be his or Beckett's. Initially frustrated by this translation, Beckett abandoned it for an edition of the original Latin text with a French translation on facing pages offered to him by Brian Coffey. On 19 September 1936, he wrote to MacGreevy:

> [Coffey] lent me Brunchwiff's Spinoza et ses Contemporains, the Ethica in the Classiques Garnier with Latin en regard, of which I have had time only for enough to give me a glimpse of Spinoza as a solution & a salvation (impossible in English translation). (*LSB 1*, 370–1)

The 1923 Brunschvicg ['Brunchwiff'] edition of *Spinoza et ses contemporains* remained in Beckett's library, probably the copy Coffey had lent him. Five months after receiving it Beckett wrote in his 'German Diaries': 'propound the Spinoza formulation – solution congruence as the Hauptsache [main thing]' (GD, 18 February 1937; quoted in Nixon, *German Diaries* 163). That 'formulation' of Spinoza's belief in divine harmony resurfaces in the *humanities* in *How It Is*. Like Geulincx, Spinoza played a crucial role in developing Beckett's ethical sensibility. Nixon has noted that 'Spinoza was very much on [Beckett's] mind during his journey through Germany' (*German Diaries* 163). He recounts from the 'German Diaries' a conversation with Axel Kaun on 15 January 1937, during which Beckett stuttered out his 'distortions of Spinoza & Leibniz'. Nixon does not speculate on the Spinoza 'solution', that is on Spinoza's refutations of the anthropomor-phised God of Judeo-Christian theology who underwrites their ontological and ethical systems. Autograph underlining in the introduction to Beckett's English edition of the *Ethics* notes:

> Spinoza denied final causes, or purposes at work in nature, and that, in their ordinary sense, he denied the immortality of the soul, free-will,

and moral responsibility [. . .] he identified nature with God, and taught that all things, whether in the eyes of men they were good or evil, mean or noble, were integral parts of the divine being. (vii)[1]

For Spinoza, 'Nature has no end set before it, and all final causes are nothing but human *figmenta*' (I, Appendix). Residua of Spinoza's rejection of a teleological universe can be detected in the muddy deposit of past learning in *How It Is*. These register Spinoza's incredulity *vis-à-vis* the belief in a divine order wherein things happen according to God's purpose, for God does not reveal Himself to mortals, dispense grace, reward the good and punish sinners. To claim that He does or appeal to His benevolence is to succumb to the fictions of superstition, to enslave oneself to irrational passions.

While Spinoza rejects the psychologically and morally endowed deity of the Judeo-Christian tradition, he offers the possibility for individuals to achieve a finite apprehension of the infinite. This is outlined in his theory of knowledge, which distinguishes between three kinds of ideas. Firstly, ideas may be confused and appear randomly, determined by contact with the external world. Secondly, they may be 'adequate', acquired through the faculty of reason, for which Spinoza's geometric method was essential. Beckett noted from Windelband that this method 'knows no other causality than that of "eternal consequence"; real dependence should be conceived neither mechanically nor teleologically, but only logico-mathematically' (TCD MS 10967/190r; W 419). Spinoza argued that adequate ideas unveil the essence of a thing, its causal connections, the purpose of its existence; that although it is impossible to perceive all connections in their entirety at once, the perfection of adequate ideas reveals their necessary character, offering a glimpse of the infinite. He went further than Descartes in claiming that one can know the perfection of God: 'The knowledge of God's eternal and infinite essence that each idea involves is adequate and perfect' (II Pr46); 'The human Mind has an adequate knowledge of God's eternal and infinite essence' (II Pr47). The third type of idea arises when this knowledge is grasped not through logical operations of inference and discursive reason but by intuition, seized immediately in the mind.[2] Spinoza's *Ethics* asserts that 'The intellectual love of God, which arises from the third kind of knowledge, is eternal' (V Pr33), an idea that resurfaces in Beckett's best-known use of Spinoza, the epigraph to chapter 6 of *Murphy*: 'Amor intellectualis quo Murphy se ipsum amat' (107; the intellectual love with which Murphy loves himself). Ackerley summarises the issue and Windelband as its source:

> This subverts Spinoza's *Ethica Ordine Geometrico Demonstrata*, V §35, in which is affirmed: 'Deus se ipsum amore intellectuali infinito amat' [L. 'God loves himself with an infinite intellectual love'], such intellectual love consisting in the understanding of His perfections and rejoicing therein, with the implication that the more the human mind understands the divine love the less it will be subject to emotion. (Ackerley, *Demented* #107.1)

In the 'Philosophy Notes' this is equated with Malebranche's 'raison universelle' (TCD MS 10967-188r; W 410), but when Murphy practises his self-love he evidently inverts the rationalist dictum and positions himself as the false god of his narcissistic universe.

Beckett noted from Windelband (W 400) the use of seventeenth-century mechanics as a methodological principle, by which corporeal phenomena were traced to spiritual causes, this resulting in a view of nature as despiritualised atoms in motion. Beckett used Zeno to support Democritean materialism, as when the paradox of motion undermines the transmigration of the soul (see my Chapter 2), confounding the distance that separates a body from a corpse. Mathematical paradoxes of infinity challenge the theory of atomism, as when advocates of Stoic physics employed Zeno's paradox to maintain that limits of all bodies split into infinity. When Beckett followed Windelband's discussion of Descartes' corpuscular theory, where the elements of *res extensæ* are indivisible spatial particles, or corpuscles, he noted that they are, however, 'mathematically infinitely divisible', which led Descartes to posit the 'impossibility of empty space and infinitude of corporeal world' (TCD MS 10967/187v; W 407). Bodies are therefore 'parts of space, limitations of the universal extension' (TCD MS 10967/187v); they are apprehended by an act of limitation (*determinatio*) in perception or imagination (W 406–7). Malebranche made the analogous claim for the mental world, whereby individual finite minds are modifications of the infinite, and therefore become attributes of God. As Windelband states, 'God is in so far the "place of minds" or spirits, just as space is the place of bodies', and 'human insight is a participation in the infinite Reason' (W 407). Making the finite mind disappear into the infinite divinity landed Malebranche in trouble with the Catholic Church (*vide* the Malebranche-Arnauld controversy) and unable to account for human freedom. Beckett noted how Spinoza extended this line of thought 'to its farthest consequences' (TCD MS 10967/187v; W 407–8), and how his dualist model comprised a consciousness and the corpuscular world, an insight that informs the model of interacting corpora in Part 3 of *How It Is*: 'He adheres to qualitative and causal dualism of spatiality and consciousness. The endless series of bodies, modes of extension, and endless series of minds, modes of consciousness, are absolutely heterogeneous and independent' (TCD MS 10967/187v; W 408). The 'I' generates variations on the image of an infinity of corpora: 'a procession without end or beginning languidly wending from left to right straight line', or 'a procession in a straight line with neither head nor tail in the dark in the mud with all the various infinitudes that such a conception involves' (161). He perceives the world through ideas like those of Spinoza's first category, in a confused and irrational fashion, yet employs his own version of the geometric method to elaborate calculations representing the true number of bodies and the nature of their causality. He works towards a mathematically correct 'formulation' to open a finite perception of the perfection of the eternal, infinite truth of his cosmology. His geometric representation of the straight line of bodies that stretches infinitely in both directions becomes in the great 'formulation' of Part 3 the image of a *procession* along a 'closed curve', whose parts he perceives as the 'great' or 'greatest' chord (151). This limited representation of the curve of bodies is a finite perception of the circle's infinity.

These calculations strive to apprehend the infinite mind, while evoking mystical or Spinozist tropes of sinking into divine nature and so embracing a negative theology. This *vidange* into the bowels of his world merges with tropes of transcendentalism, as when he is 'shat into the open air the light of day the regimen of grace' (161). This notion of *grace* is foreign to Spinoza's anti-anthropomorphism, with its hostility to teleological monotheism and the notion of a deity who presides with judgement over humanity. Beckett's blurring of philosophical and religious motifs is typical of the pastiche of *humanities* in the discourse, but the thundering conclusion to *How It Is* denounces the anthropomorphic fantasy of a human God: 'all this business of voices yes quaqua yes of other worlds yes of someone in another world yes whose kind of dream I am [. . .] an ear listening to me yes a care for me [. . .] all balls' (191). When the juridical function ascribed to the deity falls away – 'ability to note yes all that all balls yes' (191) – an ethics based upon divine reckoning is no longer tenable.

Perhaps the 'glimpse of Spinoza as a solution & a salvation' that impressed the younger Beckett as he acquainted himself with the Latin-French edition of the *Ethics* and Brunschvicg's companion inspired the prospect of eliminating not only the transcendental jury that humanity had set up to preside over itself but also the end to religious divisions. The Anglo-Irish Beckett, fleeing his religiously-divided country of birth, encountered in the stirring conclusion to Brunschvicg's chapter on Pascal an account of the opposing tendencies in Spinoza, or more precisely, of the Old Testament God of Pascal pitted against the Christ of Spinoza. As Brunschvicg affirms, Spinoza creates no church for himself; his *Ethics* develops the spiritual content of the New Testament without regard to the accidents of history, allegorical form or theological commands. He writes:

> The Christ of Spinoza put an end to the sects that have divided men; he elevated them 'above the Law'; he united them in the intelligence of the infinitely infinite substance, in interior peace, in fraternity of spirit; he founded a religion that carries neither exception nor exclusion, that is truly Catholic, because it relies upon philosophy. (211)[3]

The Christ of Spinoza's human fraternity, founded upon sound rationalist principles, surpassed theological schisms and released the true spirit of the New Testament. If Beckett's narrator/narrator betrays Spinozist fantasies in his vision of clockwork corpora within his rationalist *formulation* in Part 3, this vision competes with his voice's evocation of Pascalian asceticism and different modes of submission to an awe-inspiring God. Brunschvicg concludes his chapter on Pascal by comparing 'Mémorial' – encountered in my Chapter 6, the record of Pascal's 'night of fire' when the Old Testament God revealed Himself, as 'God of Abraham, God of Jacob, not of the philosophers and the learned' – to Spinoza's philosophy, and in particular to Spinoza's interpretation of Christ as the philosopher *par excellence* (335). When the narrator/narrated lies face down in the mud at the end of *How It Is*, his *imitatio Christi* rejects Pascal's vengeful God, even if he cannot resist interpreting his rejection of a transcendent deity by the example of Christ's suffering. Spinoza offered Beckett a model of Christ the philosopher within a philosophy that rejected the presumption of a universe moving towards final ends, with humans under constant surveillance from their transcendent personification of justice.

If Beckett was impressed by Spinoza's philosophy as a potential 'solution' and 'salvation', this hope was short-lived given his overarching scepticism of all rationalist pretensions to explain the human condition. The Spinozist voice that ascends periodically within the *humanities* of *ancient voice* is heard by the 'I' from his Quietist position. Those fragments nonetheless offer the prospect of a 'miracle' of their own, a rationalist's *via negativa* whose great aspiration, Brunschvicg suggests, is to silence the voice of consciousness. For Spinoza, who rejected all notion of miracles as fantasy, 'there is indeed a miracle "as great as the demystifying of Chaos": it is "to overcome the impressions of habit", to erase false ideas, which fill the minds of men before they are capable of judging things for themselves' (Brunschvicg, *Spinoza* 210).[4] If this sentiment provokes the bilious rejection of *ancient voice* by the 'I' at the climax of *How It Is*, the text affirms only that the 'I' cannot know if his desire to 'silence the voice of consciousness' is its own or if it is part of the implicit patterning within the pedagogy of his mind (which must reiterate his past reading of and about Spinoza). The finite consciousness is able neither to dissociate itself from the confusion of its received ideas nor align its thinking with an image of pure reason (the immanent, uncorrupted archive). This captures a distinctly late modernist predicament in Beckett's positioning of the narrative subject *vis-à-vis* the grand narrative of Western philosophy: the subjective voice cannot escape the voices of Tradition but nor can it affirm them and thus edify that Tradition. His situation does not deny it the possibility of originality, only that his voice can never be one of radical alterity, purely other, free of the *blessed pus of reason*.

## Leibniz and Transcendentalism

The narrator/narrated of *How It Is* constructs an allegory of *ex nihilo* creation in which a creature emerges out of nothing, finds its voice and gains its species as it aspires to rise towards its transcendent juror *above in the light*. Critics were quick to argue that this allegory took inspiration from Leibniz's hierarchy of monads, and that the cruelty and violence presided over by the novel's deity makes 'a savage parody of the Leibnizian idea that this is the best of all possible worlds' (Pilling, *Samuel Beckett* 119). Indeed, *How It Is* damns the impulse to rationalise human life into a theodicy, to accommodate evil within a logical schema then attributed to the mind of God. Dowd (*Abstract* chapters 3–4) established the profound connections between Beckett and Leibniz, and the *Monadology* as origin of the larval creatures in *The Unnamable* and *How It Is*, who labour under a presiding tribunal of reason in hope of transcendence. He notes two evolutionary requirements of Leibniz's monad: firstly, the capacity for apperception, the consciousness of one's conscious states, 'the force to gather [. . .] indistinct perceptions and to marshal them beyond the threshold which marks the distinction in Leibnizian terms between the possession of mere consciousness and the possession of powers of "apperception"' (*Abstract* 154). Dowd argues that Worm and Pim, like the 'I' of *How It Is*, are denied both this facility and the monad's second evolutionary requirement, a capacity for archiving. Without memory the synthetic operations of apperception are worthless. Dowd notes the disjunction between the voice of the subject who has lived above, and its reception in the 'I' below who, like Worm, 'can only think of himself/itself in the role of the mobile partition as such, the tympanum which receives vibrations, the organless body without locality, without a capacity to cross the threshold into the realm of reason' (*Abstract* 153). For Dowd (168), Worm and the 'I' embody the *monade nue*, the lowest monad in Leibniz's hierarchy, for the 'I' cannot archive voice, has no memory and fails to acquire reasoning through the pedagogical mechanisms of voice to which it is subjected. This 'I' cannot 'speak his own mind' (172).

Dowd accords the three-part narrative of *How It Is* with, firstly, the 'travelling days'; secondly, the 'Greek phase' of coming together in community; and, thirdly, the final phase in which the vision of the mud as a plane of immanence is challenged by the possible world represented by a plane of transcendence, a Platonic-Leibnizian pre-arranged hierarchy (188). This useful schema should be revised in light of the philosophical material identified in this study within the discourse of the 'I', of 'Greek' dialectics within the voice that mobilise theories of materialism, mysticism and ontologies of immanence, bringing them into contact with rationalist teleologies structured by Ancient Greek metaphysics, Christian theology and seventeenth-century philosophical rationalism. This consistent source of narrative tension erupts finally, I have argued, into the attempted cosmological proof in Part 3, which fails, and leads to the purported but ultimately unsuccessful rejection of *ancient voice*. This complicates Dowd's claim that the 'solution' with which the novel ends returns the 'I' to the plane of immanence, with the mud simply 'the abstract plane where pre-individual singularities emerge, where points of intensity can be discerned, where incompossible times and places enter into dissonant arrangements' (*Abstract* 191). With recourse to Deleuze's characterisation of subjective states in Spinoza's plane of immanence, he asserts that there are no subjects but 'individuating affective states of the anonymous force' (191). While this aptly describes the subjectivity of the 'I', who remains a cypher of the discourse without ever achieving his independent existence as a character, one must ask: what is this *force*? I have maintained that the mud is the materialisation of ancestral residue, the *voice quaqua*, the excreta of *humanities* (the expenditure of past voice in the pursuit of learning, and experience more generally); and that Beckett's 'I' is tempted, in the 'mystiques' episode and elsewhere, to perceive it as plane of immanence, of divine nature. The 'I' does not gain his own mind at the end of *How It Is*; but I question Dowd's belief that the text finally denies the existence of the tribunal of reason inherent in the Leibniz-Kant articulation of possible worlds.[5] This would negate the tribunal of reason, the act of rational self-examination and establishment of a set of principles from which action and opinions are judged. Their negation would effectively silence the *ancient voice*, yet this plenitude is denied the 'I', who is ineluctably patterned by his conscious voice to conceive of all life within the parametres of his *paideia*.

The rejection of *ancient voice* aspired to by the 'I' performs a mystical inward turn, the act of will-less listening that would bring about the 'end of quotation' (193). I have shown that the narrator/narrated is aware that even this act is imperilled because it too has been communicated from its *ancient voice* as a potential 'solution' (an arational praxis). The 'I'-in-text attempts such an act without being able to quieten the voices within. This takes it back to the beginning of his (the narrator *above in the light's*) narrative, where the 'I' below recounts again what it hears, namely the first person voice narrating its story of the journey of the 'I' below. This voice above purports to allow events from its life, events that are part of the world from where it composes *above in the light*, to infiltrate its 'I'-in-text under the *lamps*. The story of the *narrator*, his composing the narrative of his 'I' in the first person, is *narrated*, again in the first person, and that story narrates the composition of *How It Is*. Chapter 3 detailed how this structure and its circularity generate an infinite regression that estranges the narrative voice from any point of origin, and that this textual situation preoccupies the content of the metanarrative, populating it with paradoxes of the infinite divisibility of time and space. This imperils the capacity of the 'I' as monad or reasoning being to apperceive and archive coherently the impressions transmitted to it. There is a degree of self-evidence to this discussion of the absence of rationality within the 'I' below, for the text does not expect the reader to suspend disbelief to the point of ascribing to this nascent, not fully formed 'character' the consciousness of a human in a realist fiction. *How It Is* militates against verisimilitude and denies the anthropomorphism for which Beckett condemned representative or realist arts,[6] but the reader cannot be deaf to the overarching presence of an authorial voice fictionalising its life as journeying out into the dark in search of (narrative) company, and the failure thereof. The act that in times past involved searching within one's *ancient voice* for fervently disputed images within the *humanities* to engender one's tale with significance is now suspended – the reader is told – and the narrator is compelled to journey out into the mud trying to discover new forms that lie ahead. The desire of this fictional form to liberate itself from the stranglehold of its author and the infernal consciousness ascribed to it drives the drama of its 'Thebaïd'. Beckett offers no absolute alternative to the existential, but rather accentuates the epistemological bind where without the *ancient voice* there can be no fiction.

I have identified the voice of a *poet-in-text*, the authorial other who frequently discloses its presence through overt self-referencing or in a too-perfect ironising of the voice of the 'I'. The following passage encapsulates its self-inscription as an auctorial voice within an autofiction.

> say say part one no sound the syllables move my lips and all around all the lower that helps me understand
>
> that's the speech I've been given part one before Pim question do I use it freely it's not said or I don't hear it's one or the other all I hear is that a witness I'd need a witness
>
> he lives bent over me that's the life he has been given all my visible surface bathing in the light of his lamps when I go he follows me bent in two
>
> his aid sits a little aloof he announces brief movements of the lower face the aid enters it in his ledger. (19)

This tongue-in-cheek portrait of the birth of the author for the life of its character (*he lives bent over me that's the life he has been given*) is framed within the double imperative, 'say say', where the *narrated* who commands the *narrator* is itself instructed by another narrator. Beckett exposes writing's mechanisms of iteration, reflecting here the double-speak of the self-translator at work in a way described by Deleuze in 'Bégaya-t-il . . .' (He Stuttered): 'It is no longer the character who stutters in speech; it is the writer who becomes a stutterer in language. He makes the language as such stutter: an affective and intensive language, and no longer an affectation of the one who speaks' (107).[7] When this *say say* occurs amid discussion of how *freely* the 'I' may use his own tongue, the imperative voice that commands its feigning in the imperative tips the reader to an intervention by the mischievous *poet-in-text*, the one who offers a self-parodic vignette of himself 'bathing in the light of his lamps', resembling less the mighty Monad of Monads than the judge of a small claims tribunal, armed with the accoutrements of his petty bureaucracy (aid and ledger).

The veracity of memories of *life above in the light* supposedly attributed to the 'real' narrator who lived a life on earth is constantly undermined. Outrageous coincidences and suspicious namings render images of life above highly suspect; others, however, foreground their own poetic composition to the point of making them sound entirely invented. A salient example is the scene recalling a photo that Beckett kept, depicting himself around the age of three, kneeling under his mother's 'severe' gaze (see Chapter 6). This image betrays an acutely self-conscious lyricism:

> we are on a veranda smothered in verbena the scented sun dapples the red tiles yes I assure you

> the huge head hatted with birds and flowers is bowed down over my curls the eyes burn with severe love. (15)

The verbena, like the pink hawthorn at the outset of Proust's *Recherche*, triggers the epiphany, and the phrase 'yes I assure you', by echoing the 'doch I assure thee' of 'Enueg II', affirms its validity. Its harmonic variation, from *veranda* to *verbena* to *severe*, and intoxicating synaesthesia, the lyrical *scented sun*, is, however, undercut with self-conscious irony. The writer mocks his temptation to fabricate such effects from his *verbis* as an oedipal perversion (*vide* the forbidden fruit when the *su*[/o]n [d]*apples*), for this scene recalls the moment in *Dream* when Belacqua returns to that veranda:

> [...] to plunge his prodigal head into the bush of verbena [...] to swim and swoon on the rich bosom of its fragrance, a fragrance in which the least of his childish joys and sorrows were and would for ever be embalmed. (145)

In *How It Is* the discourse of the narrator/narrated is a 'pell-mell' of primary sources 'blue yellow and red' (107), which he would separate into three notebooks: one for observations on 'the body', one for overheard 'mutterings verbatim', and another for his own 'comments' (106–7). Yet this is a fantasy, for each is interpenetrated with the other by infinitesimal degrees, producing a discursive spectrum of intermingled variants and echoes. I turn now to how Beckett drew from Leibniz's coherent metaphysical system to fictionalise his obsession with the epistemology (the know/nohow) of narrative voice.

### Infinitesimal Calculus and Midget Grammar

I close this study of *How It Is* by returning to the ancient dialectic from which the discussion of philosophical intertexts began, namely the disjunction between perception of reality and its mathematical representation as paradox. The relationship between the perception of a definite point in space and time and its capacity to be a chasm of infinite divisibility was for millennia a crux of philosophical dispute. This paradox was shown in Chapter 2 as underlying Beckett's presentation of the dialectic between the limited and the unlimited, as well as atomism and Platonic forms, of materialism, immanence and transcendentalism; and in Chapter 3 as an Aristotelian conception of the physical cosmos and nature of time versus a 'Stoic' alternative. In Chapter 4 I offered a perception of the absurdity of that reason central to the ethical choices Beckett offers; and their rejection, or an acquiescence to their incomprehensibility, is charted in Chapters 5 to 7. From this, amid the diverse philosophical influences within the *ancient voice*, a central philosophical question has emerged with uncanny persistence. The kernel of this problem is stated by Ackerley in 'Samuel Beckett and the Physical Continuum', even as he underscores Beckett's attraction to a monadic expression of this paradox.

> Though continua are potentially as infinite and as variegated as the minds that conceive them (spectra, numbers, length, memory, time, consciousness, narrative . . .), two qualities are common to all: first, their dual existence as both physical object (different wavelengths of the colour continuum) and subjective experience (colour experience differing with each individual); and second, their paradoxical identity as simultaneously continuous and discrete (wave and particle). One might divide the continuum of colour into 'yellow', 'orange' and 'red' into discrete entities, yet admit that each blends into the others with imperceptible continuities; memory might represent a long continuum, yet be invoked in discrete units or as continuous; and time might be considered as an unbroken *durée* or as a continuum infinitely divisible into discrete units, a process Bergson called 'spatialisation'. To reduce complex phenomena to one fundamental sound: Windelband's sense of the *petites perceptions* as unconscious mental states let Beckett's aesthetic move from an attractive but unsatisfactory Atomism to a monadic awareness in which indivisibles are simultaneously limited (indivisibilities of substantial form) and unlimited (a continuum infinitely divisible). The advantage of the Monad over the Atom, with respect to ancient disputes over the nature of the continuum, or its existence as discrete or continuous, was that he need not commit himself to either the physical or the metaphysical, as the continuum could be simultaneously 'both' and/ or 'not'. (125–6)

*How It Is* reveals an abiding concern for exactly this problem of the relationship between the finite speech acts of the 'I' and the infinitude of its circulating *ancient voice*; of the limits of its body and those of its 'region'; of the 'I''s sense of journeying within a space-time continuum and its intuition of the futility of this journey given the unknowable magnitudes that defy reason. Ackerley identifies the importance of Leibniz's *'petites perceptions'*, gleaned by Beckett from both Windelband's *History* and Latta's commentary to his edition of the *Monadology*.[8] For Leibniz *petites perceptions* are impressions of the world in the soul, or monad, of which it is not conscious. Leibniz criticised Descartes for failing to account for them within his notion of clear and distinct ideas. As imperceptible quantities they express the integration into Leibniz's metaphysics of the infinitesimal quantities of his calculus that are larger than zero but not finite, or smaller in absolute value than any positive real number without being zero. Beckett noted from Windelband that the *petites perceptions* are Leibniz's response to Locke's argument that there cannot be innate ideas of which one is not conscious. For Leibniz, the 'Genetic process of psychical life consists in the changing of unconscious into conscious representations, in the taking up of perceptions into the clarity of self-consciousness' (TCD MS 10967/205r; W 463). One might identify such a process within the 'I' below, yet to describe the consciousness in *How It Is* as monadic is not without complication.

Beckett's understanding of the monad is indebted to Windelband's discussion of Leibniz's doctrine of the *virtual innateness of ideas*:

> Nothing comes into one from without; that which it consciously represents has been already unconsciously present. On the other hand, the soul cannot bring forth anything in its conscious ideas which has not been in it from the beginning. Thus, in one sense (unconsciously) all ideas are innate, & in another (consciously) none are innate. (TCD MS 10967/205v; W 463)

This is an accurate description of the voice of the narrator/narrated in *How It Is* (rather than just the 'I' below), with confused impressions apperceived by the subjective consciousness as they arise within itself, except that the voice appears to assert the opposite, consistently varying the string of words, 'voice once without quaqua on all sides then in me' (3 passim), which affirms its externality and so a process of its internalisation. Beckett leaves unresolved the source of the voice *now within*, suggesting that it is transmitted from the 'I''s past self represented as on high (*in the light*) while also being reingested from the detritus of its past selves in the mud below (*quaqua*). Both sources may be interpreted as metaphorical expressions of the Leibnizian reality of hermetic subjectivity, where the interior world of the monad already contains within itself the exterior world, where its perceptions are prearranged by its past and the future set out for it. This interpretation is supported by a series of allusions to Leibniz set out below. Emphatically, the problem of innate ideas is thematised in the novel, and Pim's back is the site that memorialises the philosophical disputes of the seventeenth century. Pim's acquisition of ideas through the impressions thumped, engraved and inscribed with letters on his back and buttocks unmistakably caricatures Locke's *tabula rasa*.[9] With Part 2 just begun, Pim exhibits 'modesty perhaps the innate kind it can't have been acquired' (63). This underlines a general absence in Pim's mind of innate properties, within a governing regime of sensationalism. Yet as his presence is finally rejected as a fabulation, and the 'I' returned to its solitary acoustics, this Lockean sensationalism assumes the appearance of a predetermined system of actions and responses. Indeed, when Beckett registered Locke's sensationalism in his 'Philosophy Notes': 'Locke had appropriated the Scholastic nihil est in intellectu quod non fuerit in sensu', he observed, 'Leibniz adds nisi intellectus ipse' (TCD MS 10967/205v; W 464); that is, there is nothing in the mind that was not first in the senses, except the mind itself.

Beckett's notes relay Windelband's gloss on the concept of the monad:

> The force-substance he [Leibniz] calls monad. Each monad is, with reference to the rest, perfectly independent, unable to exercise or experience influence. Their 'windowlessness' is expression of their 'metaphysical impenetrability'. Monad a purely internal principle, psychical not physical, – therefore substance a force of immanent activity. States of monad are representations & principle of its activity an impulse (appetition) to pass over from one representation to another. Each monad a 'mirror of the universe', i.e.: indistinguishable by the content they represent. But yet each is individual, there are no 2 substances alike. Hence their idiosyncrasy can only consist in the different degree of clearness & distinctness with which they 'represent' the universe. (TCD MS 10967/191r-v; W 423)

Untangling some of the puzzling characteristics of the narrative voice and its imagery is to recognise how Beckett integrated into *How It Is* the Leibnizian concept of the windowless monad as a mirror of the universe impregnated with *petites perceptions*.

Leibniz respected Pascal, who was obsessed with the fallen nature of man and the notion of human limits. In *De l'esprit géometrique* Pascal had argued that the study of mathematics confronts infinities of scales great and miniscule, whose magnitude is beyond human comprehension, and so mocks the limitations to human knowledge. He believed that the plenitudes of infinity opened up by mathematics offer grounds for resisting scepticism and relativism, as well as speculative optimism (the *rosy hue*) of his rationalist peers. Leibniz agreed that human sensory capabilities were inadequate for grasping their potential, but algebraic analysis and infinitesimal algorithms offer humans the means to extend their faculties and surpass the limited pictorial representation of geometric analysis. In his 'Preface to the General Science' (1677), 'Preface to a Universal Characteristic' (1678–79) and other writings on the *characteristica universalis*, he heralds his project to create a universal language of symbols capable of expressing, as Beckett noted from Windelband, 'philosophy in general algebraical formulae' (TCD MS 10967/185r; W 397). Beckett's allusions to Leibniz encompass this idea of a universal philosophical algebra within the narrator/narrated's aspirations to articulate a language of logical perfection. As he claims to speak in 'l'ordre naturel' (2 passim) of the French tongue he evokes discourses of the French Enlightenment that advanced the belief that the French language was the best vehicle to mirror the image of thought (Cordingley, 'L'ordre naturel'). Following Leibniz, Beckett identifies, in language that becomes the mark of the reasoning of an evolved monad, this ordering process with the clarity and distinctness acquired by *petites perceptions* as they undergo apperception and expression. Such attempts by the 'I' below fail, for he articulates only the 'bits and scraps' (3 passim) of a reasoning voice.[10] This voice arrives in English with 'little blurts midget grammar' (99), but in French it is encoded more explicitly with Zeno's paradoxes of the infinitely little, arriving as a 'petits paquets grammaire d'oiseau' (98). These tiny packets with their infinitesimal grammar need to be apperceived by the 'I' below, just as his tongue must find some reason within the immanent but unperceived past impressions contained within the *voice quaqua* or archive of mud. The *grammaire d'oiseau* returns in Part 3 as the *oiseau-mouche* or hummingbird; but in the 'ms' manuscript it was once literally a '*petits paquets des secondes*' (505; little packet of seconds), another emblem of *petites perceptions* to be discussed below. For the 'I', crawling in the dark, to crack the code of this *midget grammar* would be equivalent to Leibniz's discovery of infinitesimal calculus; he could account for the irrational or infinite remainder in his world view, and access the universal reason of his Monad of Monads. The 'I' continues to affirm that 'the gaps are the holes otherwise it flows' (109), accommodating in his own fallible way the unknowable blanks into his discourse signified by the repeated and varied string: 'brief movements of the lower face no sound' (29 passim). Newton and Leibniz resolved the gap that tormented mathematicians for centuries by defining mathematical limits and making absences present. The narrator/narrated's capacity for representation faces a comparable disjunction between reality and language; like a mathematician he must incorporate limit procedures to resolve the fundamental paradox of the gap between his words and their object. He is satirised by the *poet-in-text* for aspiring to the kind of universal *ordre naturel* that defines Leibniz's *characteristica universalis*, yet Beckett's prose places the reader in a similar position with respect to its *gaps* and lays a trap for the zealously rational who might fill them with literalist applications of an archival order.

Leibniz's philosophy took inspiration from contemporary developments in optics, notably the inventions of the microscope and the telescope. In his lifetime, telescope technology advanced from the refracting telescope that uses a lens, as developed by Galileo to facilitate the astronomy quickening the Scientific Revolution, to the reflecting telescope, like the one Newton presented to the Royal Society in 1668, which reflects light between a primary parabolic or spherical mirror and a secondary mirror. Windelband's exposition of Baconian method identifies the telescope with the optimism of the Scientific Revolution:

> A new epoch of civilisation seemed to be opened, and an exotic excitement seized upon men's fancy. Unheard-of things should succeed; nothing was to be impossible any longer. The telescope disclosed the mysteries of the heavens, and the powers of the earth began to obey the investigator. (387)

It symbolises a departure from inductive (Baconian) to deductive (Newtonian) modes of enquiry. The telescope's capacity to augment vision became Leibniz's preferred metaphor for his belief that the calculus extended the faculty of human reason. In the 'Preface to a Universal Characteristic' he proclaims that his own system of universal notation will be 'a new kind of tool, a tool that will increase the power of the mind much more than optical lenses helped our eyes, a tool that will be as far superior to microscopes or telescopes as reason is to vision' (*Philosophical Essays* 8). Leibniz's optimism radiates through his letter to John Frederick, Duke of Brunswick-Hanover in April 1679.

> [M]y invention comprehends the entire use of reason in its entirety, it is a judge of controversies, an interpreter of notions, a scale for probabilities, a compass to guide us through the ocean of experiences, an inventory of things, a table of thoughts, a microscope to

penetrate things near, a telescope for discovering things far away, a general calculus, an innocent magic, a non-chimerical Cabbala; a writing that each one will read in his tongue, and even a language that may be learnt in few weeks and will soon be adopted throughout the world. (*Sämtliche* Vol I, 2, 168, my translation from the French original)

In Autumn 1679, Leibniz still promises to deliver 'undoubtedly one of the greatest projects to which men have ever set themselves', a universal calculus he describes as 'an instrument even more useful to the mind than telescopes and microscopes are to the eyes' (*Papers and Letters*, 261–2). This project differs from micro-corpuscular reduction, for it involves perspectives on knowledge. Leibniz's interest in visual representation grew out of his attraction to the projective geometry of conic sections, developed by Desargues and Pascal, and of anamorphic perspectives, which concern the manipulation of images projected onto surfaces of different shapes or at different angles. From these studies came a desire to explore modes of representation that permit the perception of everything at once (Jones, *Good Life* chapter 5).

Beckett's first extended prose work, *Dream of Fair to Middling Women*, evokes this dialogue when Lucien alludes to the passage in the *Monadology* (§67, §68) of the microscopic mirroring of the infinitely small. Lucien draws on Leibniz when he 'compares matter to a garden full of flowers or a pool of fish, and every flower another garden of flowers and every corpuscle of every fish another pool of fish' (*Dream* 47). This poetic evocation of scalar invariance is more accurately a preformationism, whether ovism or animalculism, in which the end of all is immanent within the beginning of all. Beckett's monadic awareness has been catalogued by Ackerley, who demonstrates his sustained engagement with Leibniz; a 'deep respect' ('Monadology' 185) tempered by a recognition of the fundamental absurdity of the *Monadology* and an incapacity to believe in its transcendent Monad of Monads. While Ackerley is attentive to the use of Leibniz in *Murphy* and *Watt*, Erik Tonning has analysed the mindscapes of Beckett's later prose and drama in terms of the hermetic space of the monad (*Beckett's Abstract* chapter 6). I discuss the optical metaphors of *How It Is*, extending Dowd's pioneering work and highlighting a feature of Beckett's engagement with Leibniz that has not received critical attention.

### Petites Perceptions in Endgame

The stage of *Endgame* has often been compared to a skull, its hermetic action encased in a space with two windows for eyes. For this reason it has generally escaped comparison with Leibniz's 'windowless' monad. Two studies by Mori are the exception: the first recognises that windows in *Endgame* do not permit contact with the outside world, that its light does not reach Hamm, and that Clov's efforts to view the outside render the window suspect ('Windows' 358–62); the second maintains that the stage embodies characteristics of Leibniz's theory of dynamism ('No Body' 110–12, 114). The prominence of these windows focuses the dramatic action into a dialectic between inside and outside, within which their very capacity as windows is questioned, for they do not facilitate any communication. The theatrical space becomes as impenetrable as a monad, and its Leibnizian principles are accentuated when the images that Clov relays are said to have been invented by him, representing his interior world. When he hints at logical paradoxes of infinitude, his images themselves become instances of Leibniz's *petites perceptions*.[11]

Like Leibniz, Beckett employs a rhetoric of optical technologies, whose lenses and mirrors become reason's prostheses. Hamm insists that Clov 'Look at the earth [. . .] with the glass' (*CDW* 105). Clov resists this instrumentalising of his vision, turning the telescope into an object of slapstick humour, and playing on Hamm's blindness, before turning it onto the audience, 'I see . . . a multitude . . . in transports . . . of joy' [. . .] That's what I call a magnifier' (*CDW* 106). Clov's irony mocks Leibniz's conception of reflective harmony detailed in his metaphysics of divinity, a concept that encompasses the reflective nature of mind as detailed in his *Elements of Natural Law*:

> But as a double reflection can occur in vision, once in the lens of the eye and once in the lens of a tube, the latter magnifying the former, so there is a double reflection in thinking: for since every mind is like a mirror, there will be one mirror in our mind, another in other minds. Thus, if there are many mirrors, that is, many minds recognizing our goods, there will be a greater light, the mirrors blending the light not only in the [individual] eye but also among each other. The gathered splendour produces *glory*. (*Papers and Letters* 137)

For Leibniz, reflecting of light between the individual monad as mirror and the surrounding monads of the entire universe increases their goodness (Mercer, *Leibniz's Methaphysics* 219, 249). Clov's perception of multitudes in transports of *joy* institutes a negative dialectic with Leibniz's metaphysical *theoria*, whereby Clov situates himself within the monad but denies himself the comfort of Leibniz's optimism. He then climbs the ladder and turns the telescope onto the exterior world, but perceives 'Zero' (106), a figure that is affirmed substantively, three times. This number did not exist in pre-Socratic mathematics, which is ironic because Clov often alludes to paradoxes of pre-Socratic philosophy. Hugh Culik connects Beckett's understanding of zero within mathematics and other disciplines as 'a sign about signs, a meta-sign, whose meaning is to indicate, via a syntax which arrives with it, the absence of certain other signs' (Rotman quoted in Culik, 'Raining' 140–1). Zero is not nothing; rather, it indicates an absence, and named as such it draws attention to itself in relation to the way a signifying absence is conceived in semiotic systems, such as astronomy, astrology, neurology, phrenology, philosophy, finance, painting and music. As a sign, zero underscores how those systems rely upon semiotic systems of representation that are continuously evolving. Clov's telescope reveals to him not just an absence of things outside the window but a signifying of absence.

Clov then turns the telescope inwards and focuses on the body of the blind Hamm, declaring the outside 'corpsed' (106). His archaism intimates the extinction of the corpuscular realm, according to Enlightenment dialectics about the differences between mind (substance) and bodies (extension). Descartes believed that the body is spatial extension distinct from the mind: 'All things are either bodies or mind, res extensae or res cogitantes' (TCD MS 10967/187r; W 405). Leibniz rejected this view and circumvented the dualist problem by arguing that Descartes' corpuscles are infinitely divisible while his monad was a metaphysical point, animated by active force; unextended and distinct from space. Leibniz's aim, Beckett noted, was 'to substitute entelechies for corpuscles [. . .] to understand cosmic mechanism as the means & phenomenal form whereby living content of world realises itself. . . [cosmic] change became again for him active working, substances forces, God creative form evincing itself in mechanical system of motions' (TCD MS 10967/190v; W 420–1). Beckett's language and imagery suggest that the stage's monadic space, in which Hamm and Clov circulate like particles in motion, cannot be explained simply by mechanistic or corpuscular theories. It privileges a dialogue with Leibniz's notions of dynamism, infinitesimal calculus and *petites perceptions*. The tension between the two characters reflects the conflict between light and dark within the monad, as revealed in Beckett's despondent letter to Mary Manning Howe on 30 August 1937 (*LSB 1*, 546), when he likened himself to a 'monad without the conflict, lightless & darkless', one of Leibniz's *monades nues* that he calls the 'lugworms of understanding', far from the light of clarity and distinctness in 'a grey tumult of *idées obscures*'.

Clov is framed within this 'enlightenment'. Having pronounced the world to be 'corpsed', he looks out the opposite window and reports substantial negatives that cannot be equated with the total absence of light or number: the sea has turned to 'lead', the sun is again 'Zero' and all is 'Grey' (107). His empirical investigations, conducted with the scientific instruments of another era, provoke Hamm to suggest that he and Clov might be 'beginning to . . . to . . . mean something' (108). Hamm metaphorically inverts the telescope upon himself: 'Imagine if a rational being came back to earth [. . .] if he observed us long enough' (108). After the comic interlude of the crablouse, with attendant biological gags about the species regenerating from the infinitely small within Clov's lower region, Hamm offers a melancholic vision:

> One day you'll be blind, like me [. . .] a speck in the void [. . .] Infinite emptiness will be all around you, all the resurrected dead of all the ages wouldn't fill it, and there you'll be like a little bit of grit in the middle of the steppe. (109)

A microscopic quantity, Hamm is imperceptible to unaided human vision. His self-image as a 'little bit of grit' is the sorites image expressed more conventionally in *Molloy*: 'The black speck I was, in the great pale stretch of sand' (*TN* 74). Hamm's perception is reminiscent of the moment in Act 2 of Chekhov's *The Cherry Orchard*, when the bizarre sound of a string snapping in the distance magnifies everyone's already acute sense of their insignificance. Images of infinitesimal quantities proliferate in *Endgame*, evoking Zeno's sorites paradox and the integrations which Leibniz's calculus made to explain the *petites perceptions*, present within the monad but not perceived by it, a process Beckett alluded to in *Proust* as 'occult arithmetic' (91).

The tension between numerical zero and the something that is nothing increasingly assumes Leibnizian dimensions as the play draws towards its climax and attention returns to the 'windows'.

Again Hamm implores Clov to 'Look at the earth' (127) as if they inhabited another planet, whereas they endure as a planet within a planet, with all that is external already within them, reflected unconsciously. This alludes to Leibniz's two analogies for pre-established harmony. The first, the 'two clocks' image, in the thought of Geulincx and Occasionalism, represents two separate clocks perfectly aligned through God's constant miraculous inter-vention (his occasions). Leibniz believed, however, that the clocks were perfectly synchronised by God, always and forever, needing no further intervention. The analogy established the relationship between monads as metaphysically ideal and necessary. The second is the choir, whose independent voices sing in perfect choral har-mony, a metaphor of a universe of divinely coordinated monads. Latta affirms the choir analogy as better capturing the import of Leibniz's doctrine, and Ackerley locates this figure in the 'mixed choir' of *Watt* and subsequent works. These various images now materialise in *Endgame*. First, Clov appears with an 'alarm clock', which he hangs on the wall, watching over them as a polyvalent metaphor of pre-established harmony (the ticking) and imminent ending (the alarm). Then, as Clov moves towards the window he begins to hum, provoking Hamm's censure, 'Don't sing' (127).

Hamm is still smarting from the failure of his attempt to bask in sunlight, when, craving light, he made Clov wheel him to below one of the windows:

HAMM:      What window is it?
CLOV:      The earth.
HAMM:      I knew it! [Angrily.] But there's no light there! The
           other! [Clove pushes chair towards window left.] The
           earth! [Clov stops the chair under window left. Hamm
           tilts back his head.] That's what I call light! [Pause.]
           Feels like a ray of sunshine. [Pause.] No?
CLOV:      No.
HAMM:      It isn't a ray of sunshine I feel on my face?
CLOV:      No. (*CDW* 123)

According to Leibniz, 'The body is like a special lens through which the soul sees the universe' (Latta, 'Introduction' 122). Reclining in his chair, and adjusting his angle so that the lenses he wears over his blind eyes are aligned to receive external light, Hamm's bespectacled body assumes the form of a human telescope. He aspires to the warmth of spiritual light, but Clov must tell him that these windows afford him neither external impressions nor metaphysical comfort. The moral consequences of Hamm's spiritual darkness are made explicit through his insistence on opening the other window to hear the sea outside. When Clov informs him three times that this will be useless, Hamm still insists that he open it. Hamm's cruelty and the futile rituals that he imposes on Clov express the moral darkness that festers within this microcosm, and the stage in turn is a dystopic monad deprived of spiritual nourishment. Beckett's pessimism does not ascribe to God the power to bring light to this monad, nor does it endorse any source of light, immanent or transcendent.

The optical antics continue when Hamm orders Clov to fetch the 'glass' (129) and again look out the window. Clov retorts, 'You'd need a microscope to find this' (129), an absurdity that draws attention to the irrationality of Hamm's demand that he searches for infinitesimal quantities outside the window, having just made the frustrated outburst, 'Do you want me to look at this muckheap, yes or no?' (128). This invokes Zeno's paradox of the heap, or sorites paradox, with its attendant implications of infinites of space and time; but when Clov is next at the window, he reiterates 'Nothing . . . nothing . . . good . . . good . . . nothing' (130), until suddenly he claims to spy a small boy, as if the incremental nothings have suddenly precipitated into a something. Hamm immediately doubts the image's veracity, for within the darkness of his monadic state, even if he longs to feel the metaphysical light upon his face, he knows that he is an impenetrable, infinitesimal speck, living on the threshold of nothing. Clov's telescope augments his own rational faculty, allowing him to perceive these infinitesimal quantities; his eye's calculus endows the monad with apperception. The windows do not offer a perspective on the outside world but rather reveal literal projections of *petites perceptions* that exist within (the small boy may be an image of his earlier self that Hamm had projected). Beckett's use of optics and light suspends Hamm and Clov within the frame set by Leibniz, who combined the imagery of ancient dialectics, such as Plato's God as a sun emitting rays and Plotinus' moral struggle between light and darkness, with contemporary technologies for refracting and reflecting light, to capture the image of divine light as a moral force dwelling within nature.[12] But when Beckett held that frame up to his own sources of light, he perceived only its figures in negative.

## Stripping the Wings off Butterflies

Understanding Beckett's Leibnizian tropes is vital for comprehending the many images in *How It Is* that rely on optical technologies similar to those encountered in *Endgame*. At the outset of the novel the narrator/narrated observes an anonymous creature:

> life in the light first image some creature or other I watched him after my fashion from afar through my spy-glass sidelong in mirrors through windows at night first image (5)

The observer is an authorial figure *in the light* watching his creature. The 'image' he produces includes himself observing his creature 'sidelong in mirrors', as with a reflective telescope. He thus evokes the mirroring of spiritual light described in the *Monadology*, although the telescope is more an extension of his creativity than a rational faculty to observe his creation. He articulates:

> saying to myself he's better than he was better than yesterday less ugly less stupid less cruel less dirty less old less wretched and you saying to myself and you bad to worse bad to worse steadily
>
> something wrong there
>
> or no worse saying to myself no worse you're no worse and was worse. (5)

The phrase 'bad to worse bad to worse steadily' is a translation of 'suite ininterrompue d'altérations irréversibles' (4), a more explicit expression of an uninterrupted series of irreversible degradations/alterations. Leibniz rejected the Pythagorean notion of space as an aggregate of points and time as the accumulation of instants; his dynamic theory rested on a continuum of space and time, which he sought to harmonise with his metaphysics. Latta's 'Introduction' to the *Monadology* identifies Leibniz's central problem: 'How can that which is continuous consist of indivisible elements?' He surmises that Leibniz's notion of substance as non-qualitative and intensive developed from a critique of Spinozist and Atomistic characterisations. He rejected Spinoza's pantheism because it sacrificed the reality and integrity of the parts by emphasising the unity of the whole, but he demurred from the atomistic view of substance as 'constituting no true unity, "but only a collection or heaping up of parts *ad infinitum*"' (Latta, 'Introduction' 23). Latta may have sown the seed in Beckett's imagination of the dialectic between the pre-Socratics and Leibniz, as exemplified in the image of Zeno's sorites series to characterise Democritus' atomism.

A monad is a metaphysical point compelled to act, unlike Democritus' atoms which are material and indivisible. Leibniz's solution was to affirm that substance has no quantitative elements, or parts, but rather that 'each part must contain the whole within itself, each unit must include an infinite manifold' (Latta, 'Introduction' 31). His microscopic-telescopic dynamism stimulates the narrator/narrated's portrait of his creative activity. The reality of the monad cannot rely on its quantity, which will always be indivisible, and its indivisibility cannot depend upon spatial or temporal features, for these may form an aggregate but never a continuum. This led Leibniz to conclude that the reality of the monad's substance must be intensive, not extensive: 'the continuity of the whole must be not a mere empty homogeneity, but a continuity through infinite degrees of intension' (Latta, 'Introduction' 30–1). The infinitely repeating and self-estranging discourse of the narrator/narrated aligns his fictive universe with this principle. The multiple 'I''s of his series are intensive, continuous and definitive; he represents the 'you' of his 'I' as a reflecting point within an infinitely diminishing but uninterrupted series *and* continuum.

Again, the telescope has afforded no other perspective than a glimpse of the *petites perceptions* surfacing from the monad's unconscious mind, for, as Beckett read in Latta's commentary and in the *Monadology* itself, the monad contains the whole universe within itself; it contains all impressions of its past and is big with its future. Leibniz's law of continuity implies its inverse expression, known as the 'Identity of Indiscernibles', which is summarised by Latta:

> The number of Monads must be infinite: otherwise the universe would not be represented from every possible point of view, and would thus be imperfect. But if the number of Monads is infinite, and if every Monad differs in quality from every other, then the Monads must be such that they might be considered as a series, each term or member of which differs from the next by an infinitely small degree of quality, i. e. by a degree of quality less than any which can be assigned. ('Introduction' 37)

Not only does the narrator/narrator portray himself as a generator of a narrative that contains elements of the *Monadology*, but

Beckett positions him within a narrative in which the philosophy of the *Monadology* competes for ascendancy.

Leibniz offers the 'I' a potential solution to escape its lowly state in the mud through a reordering of perceptions. Its capacity to archive is, as Dowd (*Abstract* 188) has noted, faulty. Yet the 'generations' of his 'humanities' are available to him like Krapp's recordings of his past voice: 'recordings on ebonite or suchlike a whole life generations on ebonite one can imagine it nothing to prevent one mix it all up change the natural order play about with that' (137). To order perceptions requires apperception or self-consciousness, as Latta explains:

> The self-conscious soul or spirit does not merely connect its particular perceptions in the empirical sequence of memory; but, having a knowledge of eternal and necessary truths, it can represent things in logical order, that is to say, in their necessary rational relations. ('Introduction' 120)

Reordering perceptions into a logical order presents the 'I' with a key to his freedom, yet 'the degree of freedom belonging to any Monad depends on the degree of its intelligence, that is to say, on the degree of clearness and distinctness of its perceptions' (Latta, 'Introduction' 145). Latta concludes his exposition of the *petites perceptions*[13] by explaining that the realm of self-consciousness includes the whole of substance, which implies that a monad's consciousness contains an infinite variety of substances higher and lower than itself, that there exists infinite varieties of self-consciousness, and yet 'there are many substances in which its degree is infinitely little, that is to say, less than any degree that can be assigned or named' ('Introduction' 133).[14]

The English text less obviously evokes the metaphysical dimension to the 'suite ininterrompue de altérations irréversibles' (4), privileging rather the ethical implications of the diminishing moral force for good when the spiritual light that reflects between these mirrors renders the observer 'bad to worse steadily'. The *Comment c'est* manuscripts and typescripts reveal Beckett testing the terms 'dégradations' and the more morally inflected 'avilissements' before settling on 'altérations' (217), a word that encompasses a notion of incremental moral decline while also being the word in French that commonly means a change in a state of being, and which is the specific term in Aristotelian metaphysics to designate a qualitative shift in category; in musical notation it identifies a note that is a semitone or two higher or lower, a momentary departure from the key signature; and when used in relation to a voice, it is a modification often resulting from a change in emotion. In sum, 'altérations définitives' encapsulates this shift from 'light' above to 'night' below, imagined as a diminishing series of 'definitive' bodies (points), albeit without interruption, paralleled in the estrangement of voices between the two characters. At the level of body and voice, the series generates an inverted teleology of physical, moral and ontological degradation, *bad to worse steadily*. The comedic twist is generated by the irony that the 'you', the present creature within this series, declares the authorial 'I' to be worsened by his efforts to make him, the 'you', advance.

Each monad is *sui generis*, none is identical, and each is the logical consequence of its preceding state. Leibniz claimed that this law of continuity is founded on the doctrine of the mathematical infinite, with neither vacuum nor rupture, everything taking place by degrees, 'the different species of creatures rising by insensible steps from the lowest to the most perfect form' (*Encyclopaedia* XVI 388). Indeed, Leibniz's attempts to align his philosophy with his mathematics is a source of inspiration for the narrator/narrated, amplifying his Pythagoreanism (see Chapter 2), within which he envisions space, time, movement, speech and even thought as obeying an underlying ratio that regularly generates sorites series. The resolution of its 'gap', the 'irrational' and infinitesimal quantities, was found when Leibniz's calculus determined the relationship between unknown quantities or magnitudes by treating them as variables or as growing. By considering the velocity of points, themselves neither large nor small and for which 'no leap is needed to pass them', Leibniz claims the problem of Achilles and the tortoise is solved (Leibniz, letter to M. Foucher, quoted in Latta, Introduction' 81, fn. 1). Latta, employing a term from 'Psycho-physics', likens infinitesimal points to qualities that are 'on the threshold' ('Introduction' 82), following Windelband, who illustrated the continuity between Leibniz's mathematics and metaphysics – as well as with his theories of dynamism, perception and knowledge – in the *petites perceptions*, which he likened to the 'unconscious mental states' of modern psychology (W 424). This notion presented Beckett with a crucial link between Leibniz's philosophy and contemporary psychology, as noted by Ackerley (*Demented* #107.6, 'Monadology' 190, 'Physical Continuum' 125), and psychoanalysis (Feldman, *Beckett's* 97). Indeed, Latta repeats the word 'Ego' twenty-four times in his 'Introduction' to denote the monad, compared with the single instance of the word in his translation of the *Monadology* (265) itself, confirming this sequence.[15]

Immediately after the authorial 'I' has declared at the outset that he and his avatars form a monadic series that conforms to the principles of Leibnizian calculus and the law of continuity, he illustrates the idea with the following image:

> I scissored into slender strips the wings of butterflies first one wing then the other sometimes for a change the two abreast never so good since. (5)

Because the stripping of the butterfly's wings reflects the series of *definitive degradations*, the wings logically will be tranched into ever more slender strips, leaving (at ground zero) just its body plus an infinitesimal remainder. The image is parodic, because the 'I' is using the ancient geometric technique for aggregating the space below a curve by summing its sections and thereby approximating infinitesimal quantities. This is Archimedes' method of 'enumeration', a diagram of which is offered in a seventeen-page entry on 'Infinitesimal Calculus' in Beckett's copy of the *Encyclopaedia* (14: 535–52).[16]

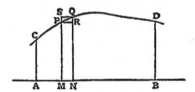

Figure 5 'Fig. 3', 'Infinitesimal calculus', *Encyclopaedia Britannica* 14: 536

Archimedes demonstrated an accurate approximation for the area below a bounded curve (the problem of quadrature) by aggregating the rectangles drawn within it. As the number of rectangles increases – the more slender the strip – the more accurate the approximation. At the limit, the approximation would be an exact calculation, except that such a geometrical demonstration can never reach its limit.[17] Integration in mathematics calculates the area of any curvilinear region between two limits by using strips or columns of an infinitesimally small width. The classic example is the graph that shows, on one axis, velocity, and, on the other, time. When plotting motion, the space below the curve represents distance travelled. Leibniz (and Newton) discovered the integral function of this relationship. Stated in general terms, the integral of any power (where r is not −1)

$$f(x) = x^r$$

is

$$x^{r+1}/_{r+1}.$$

In *How It Is* the juxtaposition of Leibniz's law of continuity with Archimedes' method of exhaustion rehearses the conflict between ancient and Newtonian geometrical demonstration versus Leibnizian infinitesimal algorithms and integral calculus. The natural philosophy of the seventeenth century and problems presented by the analytical geometry of Descartes led to new limiting processes in mathematics. The controversy around infinitesimals then hinged on the question of mathematical demonstration, of whether it is sufficient for the conclusion to a mathematical proof to derive from its premises (Euclidean geometry) or whether one should reveal how the conclusion was generated (the method of indivisibles). Descartes favoured algebraic proofs because they revealed transparently the steps to a conclusion, while geometric proofs often required a more circuitous path involving auxiliary proofs (Gaukroger, *Descartes* 172–81). With the introduction of infinitary mathematics the assumptions surrounding algebraic and geometrical proofs needed reformulation because the behaviour of infinitesimal quantities differed from previously defined arithmetical quantities (they generated the paradoxes of my Chapters 2 and 3). Beckett learnt from Brunschvicg (*Spinoza* 408–9) Leibniz's critiques of the 'circuitous' proofs of analytic geometry; like Descartes, Leibniz favoured algebraic proofs, which were direct, and where an unknown quantity could be represented symbolically and its relationship to a known quantity manipulated until the equation reflected the required relationship. Newton criticised algebraic proofs for this very reason; he objected to the way they left the concrete realm once the problem had been presented, eschewed its real entities during the demonstration, and returned to them only at the solution (Berkeley famously derided Newton's fluxions as the 'Ghosts of departed quantities'). Soon after its discovery in the 1670s he abandoned his calculus of 'fluxions', his infinitesimal calculus, for geometrical demonstrations that did not rely on it, appreciating that ancient geometers had a definite interpretation of geometrical constructions which always referred to something. This influenced the course of the Royal Society and mathematics, while science on the Continent advanced with Leibniz's calculus.[18]

Leibniz had reasons for omitting the steps of the proof. He considered that not only are our sensory capacities inadequate and thus an unreliable source for clear and distinct ideas, as Descartes and Malebranche had argued, but the reasonable capacity suffers from a kind of myopia. This led him to believe that in mathematical reasoning 'infinitesimal algorithms cannot be grounded in "natural" mathematical reasoning [. . .] our use of them must be "blind": it is they that guide us, we do not guide them' (Gaukroger, *Collapse* 141). Beckett's 'I' is in this situation; being quite literally blind he employs the remnants of his calculus to navigate through the mud, apperceive voice and sensation, and apprehend his unknown object. The specific forms of knowledge that Beckett reveals here may suggest a greater complexity in his work of what he termed in *Proust* the comedy of 'exhaustive enumeration' (71), such as Murphy's descriptions of his biscuits, Watt's matrices and linguistic permutations that approach the limit of exhaustion, Molloy's celebrated sucking stones (Latin *calculus*, a small pebble), or the enumerated bodies in *Quad*. The narrator/narrated wonders how he acquired his 'notions' of the phases of the development of infinitesimal calculus. If, as he admits, 'it's not said where on earth I can have received my education acquired my notions of mathematics' (51), the point is his admission, 'they have marked me that's the main thing' (51).

His need to find an algebraic formulation to escape being entrapped within a paradox of infinitude is expressed in an echo of this scene, in Part 3, when 'God's old clapper old mill threshing the void' is contrasted with the figure of Atropos, who cuts the thread of life: 'great shears of the black old hag older than the world born of night click clack click clack two threads a second five every two never mine' (135). Mori evokes these scissors as an example of the arbitrary when he asserts that the cosmological calculation in Part 3 in *How It Is* may be understood within Leibniz's doctrine of Striving Possibilities: 'What works here is the contingency, which makes Leibniz's pre-established harmony and the maxim of "nihil fiat sine ratione" ("nothing could be made without reason") sound inane' (Mori, 'Animal' 78). Yet, the snipping from two threads per second to five per two seconds initiates a geometric series (each term is multiplied by 2.5) that telescopes out towards infinity and is far from arbitrary. If there is an infinity of monads in the universe, Atropos will pursue them all, severing all threads, except that of the narrator/narrator – 'never mine' – for his infernal string is less than one but more than nothing, and escapes her ancient geometry.

The two wings of the butterfly, and its permutations, image the imperfect reflection of facing pages of the French and English versions of the self-translated text. The author's scissoring of his bilingual oeuvre generates a metaphor of translation as an infinitesimal and potentially infinite process, where the absence of formal equivalence between languages institutes a relationship of difference that may appear to open up like a gaping chasm or *reductio ad absurdum*. In *Comment c'est* the narrator/narrated identifies the noise in his mind as diminishing gradually forever, 'c'est moi le cerveau bruits toujours lointains toujours loins' (114); yet, in the midst of self-translation, this focuses into a figure of infinitely estranging sounds within the bilingual mind: 'I'm the brain of the two sounds distant still but less' (115). The stripping of the butterfly's wings is an economical and potent Leibnizian image, marshalling his theme of *degradations*, his law of continuity and calculus of infinitesimals, as well as the infinite steps of the ladder that separate a radiant and flourishing monad full of reflecting light and colour from its lowest form, the larval *monade nue* equipped with its unconscious *petites perceptions*. Latta adds a note in his edition of the *Monadology* from Leibniz's *Theodicy* to clarify his comments on metamorphosis: 'God has preformed things so that new organisms are nothing but a mechanical consequence of a preceding organic constitution; as when butterflies come from silkworms' (*Monadology* 304–5, fn. 33). This refutes the idea of metempsychosis, to affirm the imperceptible nature of change in the continuum of nature: 'no animal nor any other organic substance comes into existence at the time at which we think it does' (305). In *New Essays on Human Understanding*, appended to Latta's edition, Leibniz uses the example of 'when a caterpillar develops into a butterfly' (381) to illustrate the facility with which some will lapse into a belief in metempsychosis, the idea that the soul is preserved and journeys through each stage like the caterpillar's evolution into a butterfly. Such a conviction challenges his proof that 'a leap from one state to another infinitely different state could not be natural' (380), as in the maxim *'nature never makes leaps'* (376), which, he admits, restates his law of continuity. Hamm puppets this idea in an early corrected typescript version of *Fin de partie*:

'La Nature . . . la Nature . . . voyons . . . abhorre le vide [. . .]. Abhorre le vide . . . ne fait pas de sauts' (Nature . . . Nature . . . you see . . . abhors the void [. . .] Abhors the void . . . never leaps).[19] Beckett revised this to 'Nature has forgotten us' (*CDW* 97), then makes Hamm affirm the law of continuity, expressed with a false optimism that is contradicted by the diminishment of his monad: 'But we breathe, we change! We lose our hair, our teeth! Our bloom! Our ideals!' To which Clov replies, 'Then she [nature] hasn't forgotten us' (*CDW* 97). Clov intuits their status as that of base monads with faulty reason: 'No one that ever lived ever thought so crooked as we'; and likens himself to a blasted little quantity, 'A smithereen' (*CDW* 97). If the sorites logic of the play condemns it to motion, these *smithereens* by infinitesimal degrees will become imperceptible, less than one but more than zero. Hamm and Clov follow a trajectory not towards the light but to the confused and base state of the *monade nue*, a Leibnizian process that refracts differently in *How It Is* when the snipping and clicking of the scissors returns the butterfly – synecdoche for the narrator's aesthetic object, his 'I' – from its life above in the light back to its larval form. This presents a poetic variation on the process, detailed in Chapter 2, of the images of Democritean fire atoms becoming gradually but never fully extinguished, which counters Plato's transubstantiation of the soul and thus condemns the 'I' to an eternity of life below in the mud. Again, Beckett learned from Leibniz via Latta how paradoxes of infinitude might apply to the conceits of atomism.

Beckett's narrator/narrated subverts the latent optimism of his Leibnizian metaphors, deforming them and relishing in vulgar parody of their method. His perception of Leibniz's law of continuity provokes his self-portrait as scientifically regressive and violent, slicing the wings of a butterfly. His 'irrational' target, *Pi-m*, whose mathematical subtext was detailed in Chapter 2, likewise stimulates his sadistic rationalism. Other methods for apprehending his object enter into dialogue with the text's Leibnizian metaphors, with different methods for calculating the infinitesimal remainder generated by figures such as *pi*. What might seem to be the naïve empiricism guiding Pim's bloody *dressage* becomes a sadistic reversal of rationalist ideology. A similar dynamic underlies the return in Part 2 of the 'two clocks' metaphor for pre-established harmony, which rejects Leibniz for Malebranche and Geulincx, for whom the parallel and coordinated ticking of two clocks is the result of God's constant intervention.

The trope re-emerges when the 'I' recounts, with the pseudo-geometric rhetoric of the earlier 'two clocks' scene of the lovers climbing the mountain, their 'vistas' (see Chapter 5) and the time-piece in Pim's possession. As if the presence of this were an affront, the 'I' tortures Pim by taking his body for a human clock:

> I draw his arm towards me behind his back it jams ticking very greatly improved I drink it for a moment

> a few more movements put the arm back where I found it then towards me again the other way overhead sinistro until it jams. (73)

The object of the rationalist's proof of divine harmony has become the target of sadism in the being starved of metaphysical light. He assails Pim's body like one disfiguring Leonardo da Vinci's *Vitruvian Man*. One clock engages the other, just as the scissors attacked the butterfly. The scene continues: 'I finally have the watch to my ear the hand the fist it's preferable I drink deep of the seconds delicious moments and vistas' (73). In Part 2, these French 'secondes' (72) pun with cruel satisfaction on a temporal division (*contra* Leibniz's continuum) as well as a second helping, the *poet-in-text* now remixing the rhetoric of Part 1's vignette of the lovers in *rosy* Occasionalist harmony with the 'stoic' union of 'I' and Pim.[20] But when he is 'abandoned' by Pim to the 'unforgiving seconds', he 'derive[s] no more profit . . . no more pleasure' from the watch's 'distant ticking' (75). The watch or clock's rationalism is layered with his Aristotelian and Pythagorean motifs when its counting becomes a 'measure' of 'durations . . . frequencies' (75), none of which illuminate his solitude. He would destroy the watch but cannot, 'it keeps me company' (75); its rationalist tick like a metronome against which he measures his own thoughts.

The zeal with which the 'I' pursues his goal to make Pim *sing* offers a comparable twist on Leibniz's other metaphor for pre-established harmony: independent voices contributing separately to the harmony of the universal choir. The 'I' below is mute, starved of his own voice. The narrator/narrated is no longer content to observe his other through his spy-glass, but concocts an experiment where his 'I' extracts song from Pim to observe how that voice will participate in this chorus of divine harmony, amplifying his own case for a promotion towards the light. However, his spiritual darkness cannot abide such optimism, his solitude periodically overcomes him, and he despairs of Leibniz's solution: 'this voice these voices no knowing not meaning a choir no no only one but quaqua meaning on all sides megaphones possibly technique something wrong there' (137). The telescope is replaced by a megaphone, yet it cannot project his voice into harmony with distant monads. The key word here is *technique*, which the narrator/narrated knows he does not, or does no longer, master. His 'humanities' are, he admits, 'the humanities I had' (35, 53), but his compulsive attacking of Pim signals that the methods and rituals designed to promote his transcendence have given way to satanic ritualising. This act of bad faith betrays his more profound intuition, if not perverse enjoyment, of his entelechy's 'impenetrable dark' (9).

Within this pessimistic situation, the reader is constantly entertained, recognising that the trials inflicted upon the 'I', Pim, Bom and others take place within a satirical fabulation of philosophical idealism, and that a higher logic is pulling the strings from a place of relative safety. I have termed this intelligence the *poet-in-text*, an authorial voice not necessarily Beckett's but that of a character who assumes authorship and whose voice the reader perceives as constantly infiltrating and manipulating the interaction between the 'I' and the strata of its *ancient voices*. This character delights in subverting the concepts it bequeaths to its creatures in a string of Leibnizian images whose forms refract one another: the butterfly and scissors; Atropos with her shears; Pim's body and his watch; the abject attacking of Pim's buttocks with the can opener. Like a score of recurring themes and motifs, sounds and variations, these images constitute a series with terms that share formal qualities of shape and content, but which subject that content to Beckett's late modernist logic, whereby their traditional relations are volatilised, and philosophical concepts are no longer received as prescribed or completely knowable.

The capacity of these images to express philosophical meaning diminishes as the reader intuits their function within this alternative, poetic logic. Here, the perversity of equating one's attempts to apprehend the aesthetic object with a scientific method that translates into stripping the wings off a butterfly or pounding the buttocks of an innocent is, I admit, funny. Yet it is no more fanciful, Beckett suggests, than pretending to account for metaphysical complexity with a system of mirrors, light and the dream of a *characteristica universalis* or their modern equivalents, such as a psychoanalysis of *petites perceptions*. After reading the *Monadology* his first impulse was to designate Leibniz 'a great cod' (*LSB* 1, 172), yet his profound engagement with Leibniz's concepts and images in *How It Is*, figured as an abject obsession, testifies to a lasting fascination with the aspirations of rationalist thinking and the poetic beauty of systems such as those of Spinoza and Leibniz, which offered him a magnificent foil for his own chronic scepticism. Just before the sketch of an elaborate Leibnizian cosmology in Part 3, a beguiling image of this scepticism enters the scene. It presents an apt point of closure for this study of *How It Is*, typifying Beckett's technique of shaping poetic images into a complex of philosophical ideas, whose significance can be grasped only by understanding their position within a particular logic of poetic relations. This image is like a point in Leibniz's calculus, variable and on the threshold of being, yet mocking the assumption that anyone might calculate the meaning of its, or indeed our, infinitesimal existence.

## The Hummingbird of Apperception

At the beginning of Part 3, with Pim departed, the narrator/narrated's attention turns to his perception of the past and present. A familiar buzz returns to haunt him, under the guise of the 'oiseau-mouche', the bird-fly or *colibri*, known in English as the hummingbird:

> the vast past near and far the old today of the extreme old even the humming-bird known as the passing moment all that
>
> the vast past even the humming-bird it comes in from the left I watch it fly lightning semi-circle deasil then respite then the next then then or eyes closed it's preferable head bowed or not before the storm brief blanks good moments brief blacks then zzizz the next all that. (131)

A zoomorph of the momentary, the hummingbird interrupts the continuity of the undefined ('Stoic') present. The 'passing moment' suggests that it is of the order Passeriformes, but this knowledge, 'all that', is defective, for the hummingbird is not. Rather, its 'storm' arises like an involuntary memory in the present; its lightning wing-beats are phenomenally rapid and imperceptible, which provoked later nineteenth-century writers to compare the bird's speed to that of the telegraph and the speed of thought. The Irish 'deasil' remembers Joyce's thrice repeated 'Deshil Holles Eamus' in

*Ulysses* (II, 825), the word defined by Dan Gifford as: 'turning to the right, clockwise, sunwise; a ritual gesture to attract good fortune, and an act of consecration when repeated three times' (408). The hummingbird's thrice swooping distracts the 'I' and diverts him from his reasoned path, straight ahead. This hummingbird moves from being unconsciously to consciously perceived, but watching it intently and charting its course with a geometer's rigour ('semi-circle deasil') underlies the effort to measure its infinitesimal part, the 'zzizz' present in the 'brief blanks/blacks' before any consciousness of its return. This example of Leibniz's *petites perceptions* is rendered a portent of rationalist superstitions, a warning of the fantasy of impending 'calculations' (191).

From *Dream* through *Murphy* to *Film*, Beckett's exploitation of the issues surrounding apperception is well documented, but a remarkable and whimsical digression in the *Encyclopaedia*'s entry on the hummingbird augurs the tiny bird as a potent symbol:

> But there is no one appreciative of the beauties of nature *who will not recall to memory* with delight the time when a live humming-bird first met his gaze. The suddenness of the apparition, even when expected, and its brief duration, are alone enough to fix the fluttering vision on the mind's eye. The wings of the bird, if flying, are only visible as a thin grey film, bounded above and below by fine black threads, in form of a St Andrew's cross, – the effect on the observer's retina of the instantaneous reversal of the motion of the wing at each beat – the strokes being so rapid as to leave no more distinct image. Consequently, an adequate representation of the bird on the wing cannot be produced by the draughtsman. (13: 887–8, my emphasis)

Unanticipated or watched consciously, the hummingbird is an emblem of *petites perceptions*, an unperceived presence before one's eyes. The impossibility of capturing its wings incarnates anew the problem of the infinitesimal quantity that the 'I' attempts to measure through both his calculus and his geometry. The lyrical description of the hummingbird's flight as a 'thin grey film' suggests its capacity to represent an image of the mind, a *tertium quid* of its own physicality, or Lockean 'thought-thing', in which its filmic blur would be the 'veil of ideas' between itself and the perceiver.[21] Its X form recalls the image projected upon the 'approaching veils' (113) by the 'I' in his Platonic cave, the quincunx generated through his tetrakyt coding (see Chapter 2: the quincunx revered by Pythagoreans as the heart of the tetrakyt's triangle, itself representing divine harmony). The *Encyclopaedia*'s likening the wings of the hummingbird to St Andrew's cross presumably influenced Beckett's images, as just before the cross's appearance in *How It Is*, towards the end of Part 2, in the wake of the metamorphosing larvae – 'we're talking of a fly' (115) – the 'I' inscribes an 'E', then a 'Roman N' into Pim (beginning the E-N-D). But he is distracted: 'when suddenly too soon too soon a few more little scenes suddenly I cross it out good and deep Saint Andrew of the Black Sea' (115). Slashing his N into an X scores Pim with a St Andrew's cross, just as the three dives of the hummingbird in Part 3 implicated the crucifix, but these are complicated with infinitesimals: 'these last tracts they are the last *extremely little* hardly at all a few seconds on and off enough to mark a life several lives *crosses everywhere* indelible traces' (131, my emphasis). Ironically, the *Encyclopaedia*'s author seems unconcerned by his assumption that one could 'recall to memory' a *petite perception*.[22] Memories of life are like the veils of the hummingbird, estranged from their object that generates a vision of perception's failure (a fleeting cemetery of life's *crosses everywhere*). These polyvalent 'crosses' are in dialogue with the quincunx of Sir Thomas Browne, in whose *Pseudodoxia Epidemica* the hummingbird is an example of the 'extremely little', the barely perceptible which challenges human lust for visible proof, our need 'to understand in things invisible' (6.8.24–5; 1:497). While it is difficult to apprehend that which is the 'neighbour unto nothing', it is 'impossible truly to comprehend God, who indeed is all in all' (6.8.29–30; 1:497).

The compulsion towards a rational verification of the divine is staged in the quincunx of *Quad*, where the 'players' perform an intentional 'deviation' from the supposed 'danger zone' (*CDW* 453) at the heart of their universe, maintaining a collective blindness to the irrational points along their habitual traversing of the straight line that divides their perfect square. *Quad*'s players fashion their cross into an anthropomorphic blindness; like St Andrew's greater suffering, they overreach Christ's example and esteem their God and universe as equally rational and consistent (a neo-Platonism that Beckett had the perverse pleasure of projecting onto the inside surface of the twentieth-century's fetishised Plato's cave, the television set). Beckett's quincunxes in *How It Is* assimilate vast bodies of thought into their self-referential images of vortex, containing in themselves the appropriation of the Greek *paideia* into Christian theology, and the dialectics of Christian *praxis* and *ascesis*.

The *crosses everywhere* in Part 3 are, for the 'I', a negative epiphany as fleeting as the hummingbird; they register the redaction of an author engaged in 'formulations' of pre-established harmony. This erasure remembers the backslash delivered to the 'N' towards the end of Part 2, so it could be imagined as an X, forming the quincunx described by Browne in *The Garden of Cyrus* as St Andrew's cross and 'the Emphaticall decussation, or fundamentall figure' (chapter I). The *Oxford English Dictionary* defines 'decussation' as both the figure X and one of rhetoric: 'An arrangement of clauses, etc. in which corresponding terms occur in reverse order; chiasmus.' Like the narrator/narrated's ironic assertion that he articulates the 'natural order' although afflicted by chronic *hyperbaton* (compare Watt's speech; see Cordingley 'Beckett's Masters'), the quincunx unwinds a cosmic formulation that cannot account for either the unperceived or the arational.

At the beginning of Part 3 in the manuscripts 'ms' of *Comment c'est*, the narrator/narrated's grand formulation was prefaced not by the hummingbird but by a flying '*petits paquets des secondes*' (505; little packet of seconds). His swooping hummingbird in the published text, 'known as the passing moment', is a point that divides into the many, incorporating the imperceptible infinity within Zeno's fractions; for this '*petit paquet des secondes*' was formerly a string of '*petits trous*' (506), the little *holes* or *memory blanks* synonymous with Pythagorean *gaps*. In the published text, the hummingbird arrives in the perceptual field as 'lightning', which in the *Monadology* is a figure for God's continuous creation: 'all created or derivative Monads are products and have their birth, so to speak, through continual fulgurations of the Divinity from moment to moment' (§47). The mystic's experience of revelation (*alethia*) regards lightning as the form of *ratio cognoscendi*, as Leibniz explained: 'they know by means of the light, which the thing brings with it, which shines and flashes in their souls' (*Die* V, 34; Cristin, *Heidegger and Leibniz* 27). Leibniz's desire to ground his system of mutually-interrelated things in a principle outside the system required him to 'gloss over', as Latta claims ('Introduction' 176), the intractable problems of explaining the monad's relationship to the world. Beckett was receptive of Leibniz's poetic solutions to philosophical problems, as when this problem was resolved in the 'producing of created Monads by continual fulgurations of Divinity' (Latta, 'Introduction' 176). Indeed, for Leibniz the world is created and mirrored in the divine infinite; by fulguration, microcosm and macrocosm are fused in the perspectivity of God. Latta likens these '"flashings" or "sudden emanations"' to 'the Stoic λόγος [*Logos*] which Cleanthes calls a "stroke of fire"' (Leibniz, *Monadology* fn. 74, 243). Latta's commentary draws attention to how Beckett's use of the *Monadology*'s metaphor of lightning connects with his thematics of fire as divine reason, which, in Chapter 3, were engaged with Stoic *Logos* doctrine. The capacity of the hummingbird to represent both a Leibnizian fulguration and the intermediate term in a triadic account of aesthetic perception is underlined when Latta identifies this lightning as 'a middle term between creation and emanation' (Leibniz, *Monadology* fn. 75, 243).[23]

Beckett's paradoxical hummingbird as flying veil (*tertium quid*) and infinite geometric series (*petit paquet des secondes*) suggests that the narrator/narrated is revisited, or rather mocked, by Leibniz's idea of God as the central light of the cosmos around which an infinity of 'living mirrors' is arranged (*Monadology* §83). Each monad is a mirror which reflects its own perspective and primary reality (like the lightning seen by each), while the unity of all monads' perspective closely approximates the absolute infinity (*Monadology* §47; Brunschvicg, *Spinoza* 407). This notion is indebted to Leibniz's interest in projective geometry, whose principles were first used in Renaissance perspective drawing: 'the art of representing solid objects by a plane drawing which affects the eye as does the object itself' (*Encyclopaedia* 21: 257). *Sight lines* extending from the artist's eye traverse the canvas's picture plane to the horizontal reality plane upon which the object lies. Similarly, projective geometry involves transforming points and lines from one plane onto another plane by connecting corresponding points on each plane with parallel lines. In Chapter 2 Beckett's 'I' was shown to generate his Euclidean zigzag by triangulating his advance with constant lengths and right angles, plotting two parallel lines upon a flat plane. 'Parallel projection' challenges Euclid's proportional segments theorem, which states that a line parallel to one side of a triangle divides the other two sides proportionally. When these line segments are projected onto another plane the angles change, and lines converge on a place of infinity beyond that plane. In perspective drawing, the artist's eye occupies that infinite point, standing before the picture plane.

In Leibniz's *Monadology* this infinite source of light is God. As a fulgurating veil of *petits trous*, Beckett's hummingbird augurs the return of Leibniz's infinitesimal calculus and highlights the very absence of a non-Euclidean geometry in the narrator/narrated's attempted cosmology. The latter acknowledges his limitations: 'the humanities I had' (35, 53), 'the anatomy I had' (67), 'the anatomy the geometry' (69). While the zigzag of the 'I' delimits his reiterated 'straight line' (51, 59, 159, 165) – the parallelogram that cuts a plane through the amorphous mud – the hummingbird's hyperbolic swoops threaten his blind Euclidean advance with the mathematics pioneered in the nineteenth century by Monge, Riemann and Gauss, Lobachevsky and Bolyai, and then Beltrami, who developed the first rigorous geometry that was not based upon Euclidean principles. The hummingbird's filmic picture plane, pierced with *petits trous*, telescopes the perspective of an eye from another dimension, one belonging to an undefined infinite who is not the *other above in the light* or Leibniz's *Monas Monadum* (Monad of Monads) but Beckett's truant, the *poet-in-text*. The *poet* shapes cognate figures, like when the subject-'I' observes his object-'I' through the lens of this spy-glass or studies his own body through a layered optometry, with sight lines that converge behind his eyes: 'what are the hands at [. . .] the right [. . .] I close my eyes not the blue the others at the back and finally make it out way off on the right at the end of its arm full stretch in the axis of the clavicle' (33). This blending of imagination and geometry recalls the way that Beckett's personae in the 'trilogy' regularly contemplate their own bodies in an alienating regressive perspective, whose extremities are no longer within reach of their hands, and thus approach the ever-narrowing horizon of their experience.[24] Yet the 'I' generates his version of the *Monadology* without the insight of Leibniz's critique of Cartesians, that in the realm of abstract relations and necessary truths humans may use analytic algebra and analytic geometry to exhaust their object but concrete reality implicates them in a present infinity whose resolution resides only in God, whose intuitive understanding has no need for such resolution. And, for all monads other than the central monad, the transformation of perceptions from confused to distinct is never, *contra* Spinoza, accomplished completely (Brunschvicg, *Spinoza* 410–11). For Beckett's knower, *the anatomy*, *the geometry* and *the humanities* each denotes an abstract system of knowledge as well as the immaterial extension of his mind's interior life, his unknowable anatomy and manifold humanity.

He begins Part 3 in a state of near exhaustion, yet he remains committed to his 'calculation' of the Aristotelian ethical impulse, reformulated within Spinoza's theological context, for whom, man, endowed with intelligence, has an ethical obligation not merely to admire the divine harmony, its natural order, but actively to change his destiny, modifying the point of application of the universe upon himself. The narrator/narrated's attempt to resolve his cosmic puzzle and ascend to his next category enacts Spinoza's dictum that man must aspire to the liberty of God's will, albeit within the transcendentalism of Leibniz's hierarchy of monads as working *force*. Yet after more than 150 paragraphs of 'formulations', the 'I' despairs at the futility of his act. Surrendering the machinery of the *ratio*, his posture assumes not only Geulincx's relinquished will – 'The Fruit of Obedience is Freedom' (Beckett, 'Geulincx' 323) – but Leibniz's 'patient' and 'victim' of the universe from the end of the *Discourse on Metaphysics* (cf. Brunschvicg, *Spinoza* 430).

While his speech might evoke Leibniz's warning to cosmographers, the rudimentary nature of the narrator/narrated's 'formulation' reveals that he has long forgotten the meaning of much of his philosophical discourse. Punished for his ignorance of Leibniz's counsel, the hummingbird is a figure of his own critical blindness, an emissary from an external director. The quincunx as *tertium quid* is the work of a ludic science, its clashing philosophical colours the signature of its departure from an inherited genus. A token of the non-Euclidean imagination, this *petit trou* is another of the poet's fatal holes pricked into the narrator/narrated's best-reasoned argument, or rather flying through its gaps. From outside the torturous contest of historical dialectic – of reason/piety and their respective flocks – it manages that small space of 'divine forgetting'. Far from inherited clichés, generic narrative or the pedantic and unnatural orders to cross one's t's in a correct and orthodox grammar of ideas, through a dot in the eye the *poet* envisions his world as 'less exquisitely organised' (189).

## Notes

1. Traces of this reading are evident in the images of this text in the 'Beckett Digital Library' (www.beckettarchive.org).

2. Beckett noted from Windelband Spinoza's '<u>Negative Theology</u>' 'God All – & Nothing' (TCD MS 10967/188r; W 409). Windelband adds in a footnote: 'To this corresponds also his *theory of cognition* with its three stages, which sets "intuition" as the immediate apprehension of the eternal logical resulting of all things from God, as knowledge *sub specie æternitatis*, above perception and the activity of the intellect' (409). In *Samuel Beckett and the Philosophical Image*, Uhlmann connects Beckett's *images of thought* and the philosophical tradition of the immediate apprehension of knowledge that runs from the Ancient Stoics, through Geulincx and Spinoza to Bergson and Deleuze.

3. 'Le Christ de Spinoza a mis fin aux sectes qui divisaient les hommes ; il les a élevés "au-dessus de la Loi" ; il les a unis dans l'intelligence de la substance infiniment infinie, dans la paix intérieure, dans la fraternité de l'âme ; il a fondé une religion qui ne comporte ni exception ni exclusion, qui est véritablement catholique, parce qu'elle repose sur la philosophie' (Brunschvicg, *Spinoza* 334).

4. 'Pour Spinoza il y a bien un miracle "aussi grand que de débrouiller le Chaos" : c'est de "surmonter les impressions de la coutume", d'effacer les fausses idées, dont l'esprit des hommes se remplit avant qu'ils soient capables de juger des choses par eux-mêmes' (Brunschvicg, *Spinoza* 332–3).

5. Dowd (*Abstract* 188) quotes the preface to Kant's the *Critique of Pure Reason*, which describes the role of the tribunal as: 'a call to reason, again to undertake the most laborious of all tasks—that of self-examination, and to establish a tribunal, which may secure it in its well-grounded claims, while it pronounces against all baseless assumptions and pretensions, not in an arbitrary manner, but according to its own eternal and unchangeable laws. This tribunal is nothing other than the Critical Investigation of Pure Reason.'

6. Beckett often derided anthropomorphism in aesthetic representation, notably in his 'Cézanne letter' to MacGreevy in September 1934: 'What a relief the Mont Ste. Victoire after all the anthropomorphised landscape – van Goyen, Avercamp, the Ruysdaels, Hobbema, even Claude, Wilson & Crome Yellow Esq., or paranthropomorphised by Watteau [. . .], or hyperanthropomorphized by Rubens [. . .], or castrated by Corot; after all the landscape "promoted" to the emotions of the hiker, postulated as concerned with the hiker (what an impertinence, worse than Aesop and the animals) [. . .] Cézanne seems to have been the first to see landscape & state it as material of a strictly peculiar order, incommensurable with all human expressions whatsoever. Atomistic landscape with no velleities of vitalism, landscape with personality à la rigeur, but personality on its own terms' (*LSB 1*, 222).

7. In 'Bégaya-t-il . . .', Deleuze claims that Beckett makes language
   stutter when his characters are apparently unaware of the linguistic
   problems they enounce, '[c]e n'est plus le personnage qui est bègue
   de la parole, c'est l'écrivain qui devient bègue de la langue' (Deleuze,
   'Bégaya-t-il . . .' 135).
8. The term *petites perceptions* appears three times in the 'Philosophy
   Notes' (TCD MS10967/191r, -205r, -205r; W 424, 462, 463).
   Feldman also discusses them and, following Windelband, connects
   them to the unconscious mind of Freudian psychoanalysis (*Beckett's*
   64–5, 97).
9. And Freud's *mystic writing pad*. There is no space here to explore
   that connection, but allusions to Leibniz's doctrine of *petites perceptions* as unconscious mental states suggest the direction that this
   argument might take . . .
10. Beckett read in Latta's introduction to the *Monadology* of the prin-
    ciples unifying Leibniz's various lines of enquiry: 'This project of the
    Logical Calculus or philosophical language connects the mathematics
    of Leibniz with his theory of knowledge, while the Calculus of Infini-
    tesimals finds immediate application in his revision of Descartes'
    theories regarding matter and motion' ('Introduction' 86).
11. This impenetrable theatrical space allows Beckett to leverage much
    metatheatrical humour in the play as Beckett offers the audience
    the privilege of penetrating into the dramatic space, entering into
    a relation with the characters and thus rupturing their otherwise
    hermetic monad.
12. For further discussion of Leibniz's metaphysics of light, technology
    and morality see Mercer (*Leibniz's Metaphysics* 249).
13. Ackerley suspects that Beckett read this passage closely, because the
    term *petites perceptions* appears not in Latta's edition of the *Monadol-
    ogy* but in Windelband's *History* and Latta's commentary. This point
    is strengthened by Latta's ('Introduction' 149) acknowledgement of his
    debt to Windelband.
14. Beckett also read the entry on Leibniz in the *Encyclopaedia* (Ackerley,
    'Monadology' 187, fn. 15), which emphasises the connection between
    mathematics and metaphysics in Leibniz and details how Leibniz criti-
    cised Descartes for ignoring the infinite grades of perception, cogni-
    sance of which is called apperception, and every monad a microcosm
    whose degree of its activity determines the distinctness of its represen-
    tation of the universe. Between the monade nue and the Monad of
    Monads 'there is room for an infinite diversity' (XVI 387).
15. In the ancillary texts appended to the *Monadology* Latta uses 'E/ego'
    twice in the 'New System of the Nature of Substances . . .' (310, 311),
    once in Leibniz's letter to Fucher (321), once in his own 'Prefatory
    Note' to Leibniz's 'On the Ultimate Origination of Things' (337), and
    once in Leibniz's 'Principles of Nature and Grace' (412).

16. The authority of the *Encyclopaedia*'s entry on 'Infinitesimal Calculus' is affirmed by Latta ('Introduction' 80), who directs his reader to it (albeit in the 9th edition) for further information. He opens his *Monadology* with an acknowledgement in the 'Preface' of the 'remarkably clear, but brief, account of [Leibniz's] philosophy' (v) written by Professor Sorley (who also wrote the entry on 'Infinitesimal Calculus') in the *Encyclopaedia Britannica*. This was a source of inspiration for Beckett. Curiously, soon after the entry on 'Leibniz' is that for 'Lens' with no fewer than twenty-two optical diagrams, closely followed by that on 'Lepidoptera' with seventy-six illustrations of moths, butterflies and larva laid out over fifteen pages. In a book that comprises many dense pages but few illustrations, these visual connections are striking.

17. The *Encyclopaedia* details how Archimedes' method of formulating the problem of quadratures accounted for infinitesimal quantities geometrically, but imperfectly. Leibniz's integral calculus improved on this: 'The method [of Archimedes] leads to a definition of a definite integral, but the direct application of it to the evaluation of integrals is in general difficult. Any process for evaluating a definite integral is a process of integration, and the rules for evaluating integrals constitute the integral calculus' (XIV, 536).

18. My understanding of the relationship of Leibniz's calculus to that of his peers is indebted to Stephen Gaukroger's *The Collapse of Mechanism and the Rise of Sensibility* (chapter 3).

19. This detail from the *Fin de partie* manuscript (no. I, leaf 9, Ohio State University (III)) was noted by Yoshiyuki Inoue and relayed by Mori ('No Body' 114). In the *New Essays* Leibniz discusses 'nature's abhorrence of a vacuum' (*Monadology* 387).

20. In a letter to Simon Foucher (1695), translated by Latta and appended to his edition of the *Monadology*, Leibniz emphasises the clock not as a whole but an aggregate, a point he made while refuting the 'two clocks' theory of divine harmony that Foucher was supporting: 'The unity of a clock, which you mention, is in my view quite other than that of an animal; for an animal may be a substance possessing a genuine unity, like what is called ego [moi] in us ; while a clock is nothing but an aggregate [assemblage]' (321).

21. The *tertium quid* is an intermediary object directly perceived between the subject and the intended, indirectly perceived object. It stands between perceiver and object. Thomas Reid famously evoked the 'veil of ideas' in 1764 to criticise what he believed to be the habit of rationalist philosophers since Descartes of taking ideas in the mind as the direct and immediate objects of perception, rather than the external world itself: 'that there must be some image of them in the mind itself, in which, as a mirror, they are seen' (Reid, *Philosophical* 1.226). Here, the filmic *blur* of this *tertium quid*, the image of the hummingbird, reflects an early twentieth-century notion of film.

22. This is compounded by the fact that the hummingbird, found only in the Americas, would always have been mediated, for Beckett, by its image from Flaubert's *Madame Bovary* or *Hérodias*. Flaubert completely overlooks the bird's uniquely American character, whereas other French writers do not, including Chateaubriand and Leconte de Lisle.

23. 'Fulguration means that the Monad is not absolutely created out of nothing nor, on the other hand, merely a mode or an absolutely necessary product of the Divine nature, but that it is a possibility tending to realize itself, yet requiring the assistance, choice or will of God to set it free from the counteracting influence of opposite possibilities' (*Monadology* fn. 74–5, 243–4).

24. A process reminiscent of Austrian physicist and philosopher Ernst Mach's famous self-portrait known as 'view from the left eye' from his 1886 *Beiträge zur Analyse der Empfindungen* (The Analysis of Sensations), used to illustrate his ideas about self-perception.

# Acknowledgements

Writing this book for over a decade, I have accumulated debts to more people than I can ever acknowledge. Research was conducted principally at the University of Sydney and the Université Paris 8 – Vincennes-Saint-Denis, and while teaching at the Université Paris 3 – Sorbonne Nouvelle and the Université de Rouen. I am deeply grateful for the encouragement and generosity of my colleagues, in particular those at Paris 8's TransCrit research group and the Department of English at the University of Sydney. My thinking about bilingual writing, self-translation and textuality has been shaped also by working with colleagues at the Institut des textes et manuscrits modernes (ITEM) in Paris.

Initial research was funded by an Australian Postgraduate Award and a French Government Postgraduate Scholarship. I am thankful to the Australian Research Council, the Université Paris 8 Labex Arts-H2H and the Research Foundation – Flanders for financial and material support. This book owes an inestimable and otherwise unacknowledged debt to the patience, scrupulousness and magical intellect of Dr Bruce Gardiner, who guided the doctoral project from which this book emerged. Professor Dirk Van Hulle generously supported post-doctoral research at the University of Antwerp's Centre for Manuscript Genetics; his work continues to be a source of inspiration. The generosity and collegial support of Professor Chris Ackerley has been inestimable; his revisions to my final manuscript saved me from innumerable blunders, and his commentaries have enriched it significantly. I am especially grateful to Professors Bruno Clément, Jean-Michel Rabaté and Anthony Uhlmann for inspiration and guidance.

Research in Dublin would have been impossible without the hospitality of Katie Long, whose warmth and fine humour helped me to survive many a long day at the TCD archives. In London, I thank especially Natalie Silk and Tom Baker, whose English rarity is as beguiling as any I found on level one of the British Library. During return visits to Sydney, I was lodged by dear friends, Sam McGuinness and Bianca Spender, Kimberley Crofts and Tom Carolan. I am most grateful to friends who have proofread parts of this book at one time or another: John Attridge, Mark Byron, Emma Carmody, David Large, Mark Fitzpatrick, Marc Jones, Philippe Lagadec, Nicholas Manning, Tom Newman and Will Noonan.

With gratitude, I acknowledge the precious assistance from library staff at the Bibliothèque Nationale de France; the British Library; Fisher Library, University of Sydney; Harry Ransom Center, The University of Texas at Austin; University of Reading Library; and, above all, Paula Norris and the staff of the Library of Trinity College Dublin.

Stan Gontarski was the first person I approached with this manuscript; I could imagine no better home for it than within his 'Other Becketts' series. I am honoured to be part of his exciting initiative. Professional staff at EUP have been a pleasure to work with, and I thank in particular my editor Jackie Jones and assistant editor Ersev Ersoy.

Portions of this book have appeared elsewhere in their more juvenile form: Chapter 2 in *Comparative Literature* 65.4 (2013), a section of Chapter 3 in *Samuel Beckett Today/Aujourd'hui* 22 (2010) and Chapter 6 in *Journal of Modern Literature* 33.4 (2010). I thank the publishers for permission to reprint, and alert readers to the fact that this material is developed differently here.

I thank particularly Edward Beckett and the Samuel Beckett Estate for the generous permission to quote from unpublished material by Samuel Beckett.

Finally, I am profoundly grateful for the understanding and compassion that my parents have offered their wandering, absent son. My brothers, Matthew and Nicholas, Greg Hyde, and my extended families in Australia and France should also be commended for suffering my peculiar obsessions, with magnaminity. No one has borne them more heavily or with more grace than Mathilde, to whom, with my deepest admiration and love, I dedicate this book.

# Bibliography

## Unpublished Sources

Beckett, Samuel. *Comment c'est* manuscripts and typescripts. MS HRC SB/1/10–11, MS HRC SB/2/1–3. Harry Ransom Center, The University of Texas at Austin.

—. 'German Diaries.' 6 notebooks. Beckett International Foundation Archives. University of Reading Library.

—. Letters to Barbara Bray. MS 10948. Manuscripts Department, Library of Trinity College Dublin.

—. Letters to Thomas MacGreevy. MS 10402. Manuscripts Department, Library of Trinity College Dublin.

—. 'Notes on Philosophy.' MS 10967. Manuscripts Department, Library of Trinity College Dublin.

—. 'Notes on Psychology.' MS 10971/7-8. Manuscripts Department, Library of Trinity College Dublin.

—. 'Sottiser Notebook.' RUL MS 2901. Beckett International Foundation Archives. University of Reading Library.

—. '*Whoroscope* Notebook.' MS 3000. Beckett International Foundation Archives. University of Reading Library.

Dobbin (née Burrows), Rachel. Notes to lectures by Samuel Beckett on Gide and Racine at Trinity College Dublin (1931). MIC 60. Manuscripts Department, Library of Trinity College Dublin.

'Term and Examination Returns.' 1925. TCD MS Mun V/30/82-85. Manuscripts Department, Library of Trinity College Dublin.

## Works Cited

Abbott, H. Porter. *Beckett Writing Beckett: The Author in the Autograph.* Ithaca: Cornell University Press, 1996.

—. 'Beginning Again: The Post-narrative Art of *Texts For Nothing* and *How it is.*' *The Cambridge Companion to Beckett.* Ed. John Pilling. Cambridge: Cambridge University Press, 1994.

—. 'Farewell to Incompetence: Beckett's *How It Is* and *Imagination Dead Imagine*.' *Contemporary Literature* 11 (1970): 36–47.

—. *The Fiction of Samuel Beckett: Form and Effect*. Berkeley: University of California Press, 1973.

Abbott, T. K. *The Elements of Logic*. 2nd edn. London: Thomas Nelson and Sons, 1885.

Ackerley, Chris. *Demented Particulars: The Annotated* Murphy. 2nd edn. Tallahassee: Journal of Beckett Studies Books, 2004.

—. 'Inorganic Form: Samuel Beckett's Nature.' *AUMLA* 104 (2005): 79–102.

—. 'Monadology: Samuel Beckett and Gottfried Wilhelm Leibniz.' *Beckett/Philosophy*. Ed. Matthew Feldman and Karim Mamdani. Stuttgart: ibidem Press, 2015.

—. *Obscure Locks, Simple Keys: The Annotated Watt*. Tallahassee: Journal of Beckett Studies Books, 2005.

—. 'Perfection is Not of This World': Samuel Beckett and Mysticism.' *Mystics Quarterly* 30.1–2 (2004): 28–55.

—. 'Samuel Beckett and Anthropomorphic Insolence.' *Samuel Beckett Today/Aujourd'hui* 18 (2007): 77–90.

—. 'Samuel Beckett and the Bible: A Guide.' *Journal of Beckett Studies* 9.1 (1999): 53–125.

—. 'Samuel Beckett and the Geology of the Imagination: Toward an Excavation of *Watt*.' *Journal of Beckett Studies* 13.2 (2004): 150–63.

—. 'Samuel Beckett and Mathematics.' *Cuadernos de literatura Inglesa y Norteamericana* 3.1–2 (1998): 77–102. www.uca.edu.ar/uca/common/grupo17/files/mathem.pdf (accessed 13 April 2017).

—. 'Samuel Beckett and the Physical Continuum.' *Journal of Beckett Studies* 25.1 (2016): 110–31.

—. 'Samuel Beckett and Science.' *The Blackwell Companion to Samuel Beckett*. Ed. S. E. Gontarski. London: Blackwell, 2010, 143–62.

—. 'Samuel Beckett and Thomas à Kempis: The Roots of Quietism.' *Samuel Beckett Today/Aujourd'hui* 9 (2000): 81–92.

—. 'The Uncertainty of Self: Samuel Beckett and the Location of the Voice.' *Samuel Beckett Today/Aujourd'hui* 14 (2004): 39–51.

Ackerley, Chris and S. E. Gontarski. *The Faber Companion to Samuel Beckett*. London: Faber, 2006.

Addyman, David. 'Different Spaces: Beckett, Deleuze, Bergson.' *Deleuze and Beckett*. Ed. S. E. Wilmer and Audronė Žukauskaitė. London: Palgrave Macmillan, 2015.

—. '"Speak of Time, without Flinching . . . Treat of Space with the Same Easy Grace": Beckett, Bergson and the Philosophy of Space.' *Beckett/*

*Philosophy*. Ed. Matthew Feldman and Karim Mamdani. Stuttgart: ibidem Press, 2015.

Adelman, Gary. 'Torturer and Servant: Samuel Beckett's *How It Is.*' *Journal of Modern Literature* 25.1 (2001): 81–90.

Albright, Daniel. *Beckett and Aesthetics*. Cambridge: Cambridge University Press, 2003.

Alexander, Archibald. *A Short History of Philosophy*. Glasgow: Maclehose & Sons, 1907.

Aristotle. *Aristotle in 23 Volumes*. Trans. H. Rackham. Vol. 21. Cambridge, MA: Harvard University Press; London: William Heinemann, 1944.

—. *Aristotle's Metaphysics*. Trans. W. D. Ross. 2 vols. Oxford: Clarendon, 1924.

—. *De Anima: Books II and III (with Passages from Book I)*. Trans., intro. and notes D. W. Hamlyn. Oxford: Clarendon, 1968.

—. *Nicomachean Ethics*. Trans. W. D. Ross. Oxford: Clarendon, 1908.

—. *Politics*. In *Aristotle in 23 Volumes*. Trans. H. Rackham. Vol. 21. Cambridge, MA: Harvard University Press; London: William Heinemann Ltd, 1944.

—. *Posterior Analytics*. *The Basic Works of Aristotle*. Ed. Richard McKeon. London: Random, 1941.

Arnim, Hans Friedrich von (ed.). *Stoicorum veterum fragmenta*. 4 vols. 1903. Lipsiae: Teubner, 1924.

Arthur, Kateryna. 'T. S. Eliot, Samuel Beckett, and Dante.' PhD diss. University of Sussex, 1982.

Augustine. *The Confessions of St. Augustine*. Trans. E. B. Pusey. London: Dent, 1907.

—. *De trinitate: libri XV*. Ed. W. J. Mountain and Fr. Glorie. Turnholt: Brepols 1968.

—. *On the Trinity*. Trans. Arthur West Haddan. *From Nicene and Post-Nicene Fathers*. First Series, Vol. 3. Ed. Philip Schaff. Buffalo: Christian Literature Publishing Co., 1887.

Badiou, Alain. *On Beckett*. Ed. Alberto Toscano and Nina Power. Trans. Bruno Bosteels, Nina Power and Alberto Toscano. London: Clinamen, 2003.

Bair, Deirdre. *Samuel Beckett: A Biography*. London: Picador, 1978.

Baker, Phil. *Samuel Beckett and the Mythology of Psychoanalysis*. London: Macmillan, 1997.

Baldwin, Hélène L. *Samuel Beckett's Real Silence*. University Park: Pennsylvania State University Press, 1981.

Baroghel, Elsa. '*Comment c'est* et *Les 120 Journées de Sodome.*' *Samuel Beckett 4. La violence dans l'oeuvre de Samuel Beckett: entre langage et corps*. Ed. Llewellyn Brown. Paris: Lettres Modernes Minard/Classiques Garnier, 2017.

—. 'My God to Have to Murmur That': *Comment C'est/How It Is* and the Issue of Performance.' *Samuel Beckett and BBC Radio*. Ed. David Addyman, Matthew Feldman and Erik Tonning. London: Palgrave, 2017.

Barry, Elizabeth. 'Beckett, Augustine and the Rhetoric of Dying.' *Beckett and Death*. Ed. Steven Barfield, Matthew Feldman and Philip Tew. London: Continuum, 2009.

Baudelaire, Charles. *Les Fleurs du mal*. Trans. Richard Howard. Boston: David R. Godine, 1982.

Beaufret, Jean. *Dialogue avec Heidegger*. I. *Philosophie grecque*. Paris: Minuit, 1973.

—. *Introduction aux philosophies de l'existence: De Kierkegaard à Heidegger*. Paris: Donoël/Gonthier, 1971.

—. *Leçons de philosophie*. I. *Philosophie grecque, Le Rationalisme classique*. Paris: Seuil, 1998.

—. *Notes sur la philosophie en France au XIXe siècle: De Maine de Biran à Bergson*. Paris: J. Vrin, 1984.

Beckett, Samuel. *Beckett's Dream Notebook*. Ed. and annot. John Pilling. Reading: Beckett International Foundation, 1999.

—. *The Collected Poems of Samuel Beckett*. Ed. Seán Lawlor and John Pilling. London: Faber, 2012.

—. *Comment c'est, How It Is* and/et *L'Image: A critical-genetic edition/ Une édition critico-génétique*. Ed. Édouard Magessa O'Reilly. New York: Routledge, 2001.

—. *Company/Compagnie; and, A Piece of Monologue/Solo*. Ed. Charles Krance. London: Garland, 1993.

—. *Company/Ill Seen Ill Said/ Worstward Ho/ Stirrings Still*. London: Faber, 2009.

—. *The Complete Dramatic Works*. London: Faber, 1986.

—. *The Complete Short Prose, 1929–1989*. Ed. S. E. Gontarski. New York: Grove, 1995.

—. *Disjecta: Miscellaneous Writings and a Dramatic Fragment*. New York: Grove, 1984.

—. *Dream of Fair to Middling Women*. London: Calder, 1993.

—. *Eleuthéria*. Paris: Minuit, 1995.

—. *En attendant Godot*. Paris: Minuit, 1952.

—. *Endgame*. New York: Grove, 1970.

—. *Ill Seen Ill Said*. London: Calder, 1982.

—. *L'Innommable*. Paris: Minuit, 1953.

—. *The Letters of Samuel Beckett, Volume I: 1929–1940*. Ed. Martha Dow Fehsenfeld and Lois More Overbeck. Cambridge: Cambridge University Press, 2009. *Volume 2: 1941–1956*. Ed. George Craig, Martha Dow Fehsenfeld, Dan Gunn and Lois More Overbeck. Cambridge: Cambridge University Press, 2011. *Volume 3: 1957–1965*. Ed. George Craig, Martha Dow Fehsenfeld, Dan Gunn and Lois More Overbeck. Cambridge: Cambridge University Press, 2015. [Abbreviated as *LSB*.]

—. *Malone meurt*. Paris: Minuit, 1951.

—. *Mercier and Camier*. London: Calder, 1999.

—. *Molloy*. Paris: Minuit, 1951.

—. *More Pricks Than Kicks*. London: Calder, 1966, 1998.

—. *Murphy*. London: Calder, 1993.

—. *Nouvelles et textes pour rien*. Paris: Minuit, 1958.

—. *Proust and Three Dialogues*. London: Calder & Boyars, 1970.

—. *Quad et autres pièces pour la télévision, suivi de 'L'Épuisé' par Gilles Deleuze*. Paris: Minuit, 1992.

—. 'Samuel Beckett's Notes to his Reading of the *Ethics* by Arnold Geulincx.' Geulincx. 311–53.

—. *The Theatrical Notebooks of Samuel Beckett*. Ed. James Knowlson. London: Faber, 1992.

—. *Watt*. London: Calder, 1976.

—. *Worstward Ho*. London: Calder, 1983.

Beckett, Samuel and Alan Schneider. *No Author Better Served: The Correspondence of Samuel Beckett and Alan Schneider*. Ed. Maurice Harmon. Cambridge, MA: Harvard University Press, 1998.

Bennett, J. *A Study of Spinoza's Ethics*. Cambridge: Cambridge University Press, 1984.

Bergson, Henri. *L'Évolution créatrice* [1907]. Paris: Presses Universitaires de France, 1991.

—. *An Introduction to Metaphysics*. Ed. Thomas. A. Goudge. Trans. T. E. Hulme. Indianapolis/Cambridge: Hackett, [1912] 1999.

—. 'Philosophical Intuition.' *The Creative Mind*. New York: Philosophical Library, 1946.

Bersani, Leo and Ulysse Dutoit. 'Beckett's Sociability.' *Raritan* 12.1 (1992): 1–19.

Bixby, Patrick. *Samuel Beckett and the Postcolonial Novel*. Cambridge: Cambridge University Press, 2009.

Blanchot, Maurice. *L'Entretien infini*. Paris: Gallimard, 1969.

—. *L'Espace littéraire*. Paris: Gallimard, 1955.

—. 'Nouvelle Revue Française.' *Samuel Beckett: The Critical Heritage*. Ed. L. Graver and R. Federman. London: Routledge & Kegan Paul, 1979.

—. *Le Pas au-delà*. Paris: Gallimard, 1973.

—. *The Step Not Beyond*. Trans. Lycette Nelson. New York: State University of New York Press, 1992.

Boulter, Jonathan. *Interpreting Narrative in the Novels of Samuel Beckett*. Gainesville: University Press of Florida, 2001.

Bréhier, Émile. *Chrysippe et l'ancien stoïcisme*. Paris: Presses Universitaires de France, 1910, 1951.

—. *La Théorie des incorporels dans l'ancien stoïcisme*. 1908. Paris: Vrin, 1970.

Browne, Sir Thomas. *Pseudodoxia Epidemica*. Ed. Robin Robbins. 2 vols. Oxford: Clarendon, 1981. (Traditional reference, followed by page numbers to this edition.)

—. *The Works of the Learned Sr. Thomas Brown*. London: Printed for Tho. Basset, Ric. Chiswell, Tho. Sawbridge, Charles Mearn and Charles Brome, 1686.

Brunschvicg, Léon. *Spinoza et ses contemporains* [1894]. 3ième édition, révue et augmentée. Paris: Félix Alcan, 1923.

Brunschwig, Jacques. 'Stoic Metaphysics.' *The Cambridge Companion to the Stoics*. Ed. Brad Inwood. Cambridge: Cambridge University Press, 2003.

Bryden, Mary. *Beckett and the Idea of God*. Basingstoke: Macmillan, 1998.

Buning, Marius. 'Samuel Beckett's Negative Way: Intimations of the Via Negativa in His Late Plays.' *European Literature and Theology in the Twentieth Century: Ends of Time*. Ed. David Jasper and Colin Crowder. London: Macmillan, 1990.

Burnet, John. *Greek Philosophy, Part I: Thales to Plato*. London, Macmillan, 1914.

Burton, Robert. *The Anatomy of Melancholy*. Vol. 1. Ed. Thomas C. Faulkner, Nicolas K. Kiessling and Rhonda L. Blair. Intro. J. B. Bamborough. Oxford: Clarendon, 1989.

Caselli, Daniela. *Beckett's Dantes: Intertextuality in the Fiction and Criticism*. Manchester: Manchester University Press, 2005.

—. 'The Promise of Dante in Beckett's Manuscripts.' *Samuel Beckett Today/Aujourd'hui* 16 (2006): 237–57.

—. 'Shadows of Belacqua in *Dream of Fair to Middling Women* and *How It Is*.' *Samuel Beckett Today/Aujourd'hui* 11 (2000): 463–70.

Cassin, Barbara. *L'Effet sophistique*. Paris: Gallimard, 1995.

— (ed.). *Vocabulaire européen des philosophies: Dictionnaire des intraduisibles*. Paris: Seuil, 2004.

Chaucer, Geoffrey. *The Legend of Good Women*. Ed. Rev. Walter W. Skeat. Oxford: Clarendon Press, 1889.

Christodoulou, Kyriaki E. 'Le stoïcisme dans la dialectique apologétique des *Pensées* de Pascal.' *Méthodes chez Pascal*. Ed. Thérèse Goyet. Paris: Presses Universitaires de France, 1979.

Clement of Alexandria. 'Letter to the Corinthians.' *The Apostolic Fathers*. Loeb Classics. Vol. I. London, 1912.

Clément, Bruno. *L'Œuvre sans qualités: rhétorique de Samuel Beckett*. Paris: Seuil, 1994.

Coe, Richard. *Samuel Beckett*. 1964. Rev. ed. New York: Grove, 1968.

Connor, Steven. *Samuel Beckett, Modernism and the Material Imagination*. Cambridge: Cambridge Uuniversity Press, 2014.

—. *Samuel Beckett: Repetition, Theory, Text*. Oxford: Basil Blackwell, 1988.

Cordingley, Anthony. 'Beckett and "l'ordre naturel": The Universal Grammar of *Comment c'est/How It Is*.' *Samuel Beckett Today/Aujourd'hui: annual bilingual review – revue annuelle bilingue* 18 (2007): 185–99.

—. 'Beckett's "Masters": Pedagogical Sadism, Foreign Language Primers, Self-Translation.' *Modern Philology* 109.4 (2012): 510–43.

—. 'Beckett's Pedagogy of Affect and the Algerian War.' *Modernist Emotions*. Société d'Études Modernistes, Université Paris Ouest Nanterre, 22–24 June 2016.

—. 'The Passion of Self-translation: A Masocritical Perspective.' *Self-translation: Brokering Originality in Hybrid Culture*. Ed. In Anthony Cordingley. London: Bloomsbury, 2013.

—. 'Psychoanalytic Refuse in *Comment c'est/How It Is*.' *The Politics and Aesthetics of Refusal*. Ed. Caroline Hamilton et al. Newcastle-upon-Tyne: Cambridge Scholars Publishing, 2007.

—. 'The Reading Eye from Scriptura Continua to Modernism: Orality and Punctuation between Beckett's *L'Image* and *Comment c'est/How It Is*.' *Journal of the Short Story in English* 47 (2006): 49–64.

Cristin, Renato. *Heidegger and Leibniz: Reason and the Path*. Foreword Hans Georg Gadamer. Trans. Gerald Parks. Dordrecht; Boston: Kluwer, 1998.

Critchley, Simon. *On Humour*. London: Routledge, 2002.

Cronin, Anthony. *Samuel Beckett: The Last Modernist*. London: Flamingo, 1997.

Culik, Hugh. 'Raining & Midnight: The Limits of Representation.' *Journal of Beckett Studies* 17.1–2 (2008): 127–52.

Dante Alighieri. *Divina commedia*. Ed. Giorgio Petrocchi. Milan: Mondadori, 1966–7. Florence: Le Lettere, 1994.

—. *Inferno, Purgatorio, Paradiso*. Trans. Robert Hollander and Jean Hollander. New York: Doubleday/Anchor, 2000, 2003, 2007.

Dearlove, Judith. 'The Voice and its Words: *How It Is*.' *On Beckett: Essays and Criticism*. Ed. S. E. Gontarski. New York: Grove, 1986.

Del Moro, Francesca. '"The Divine Florentine": Dante nell'opera di Samuel Beckett.' PhD diss. University of Pisa, 1996.

Deleuze, Gilles. 'Bégaya-t-il. . . .' *Critique et Clinique*. Paris: Éditions de Minuit, 1993. 'He Stuttered.' *Essays Critical and Clinical*. Trans. David W. Smith and Michael A. Greco. Minneapolis: University of Minnesota Press, 1997.

—. *Spinoza, philosophie pratique*. New edition. Paris: Les Éditions de Minuit, 1981. *Spinoza: Practical Philosophy*. Trans. Robert Hurley. San Francisco: City Lights, 1988.

Derrida, Jacques. *Mal d'archive*. Paris: Galilée, 1995.

Di Berardino, Angelo (ed.). *Encyclopedia of the Early Church*. Trans. Adrian Walford. Forew. and biblio. amend. W. H. C. Frend. 2 vols. Cambridge: J. Clarke, 1992.

Diderot, Denis. *Jacques le fataliste et son maître. Œuvres de Diderot*. Ed. A. Billy. Bibliothèque de la Pléiade. Paris: Gallimard, 1951.

—. *Jacques the Fatalist*. Trans. Martin Hall and Michael Henry. Penguin Classics. Harmonsworth: Penguin, 1986.

Diogenes Laërtius. *Vitae Philosophorum* [Lives of the Philosophers]. Ed. H. S. Long. Oxford: Oxford University Press, 1964.

Dobbin (née Burrows), Rachel. Notes to lectures by Samuel Beckett on Gide and Racine at Trinity College Dublin (1931). MIC 60. Manuscripts Department, Library of Trinity College Dublin.

Doherty, Francis. 'Mahaffy's *Whoroscope*.' *Journal of Beckett Studies* 2.1 (1992): 27–46.

Donne, John. *Complete Poetry and Selected Prose*. London: Random, 1946.

Dowd, Garin. *Abstract Machines: Samuel Beckett and Philosophy after Deleuze and Guattari*. Amsterdam: Rodopi, 2007.

Driver, Tom. 'Beckett by the Madeleine.' *Samuel Beckett: The Critical Heritage*. Ed. Lawrence Graver and Raymond Federman. London: Routledge, 1979.

Duffy, Brian. 'The Prisoners in the Cave and the Worm in the Pit: Plato and Beckett on Authority and Truth.' *Journal of Beckett Studies* 8.1 (1998): 51–71.

Eliot, T. S. 'Introduction.' *Pensées*. Trans. W. F. Trotter. 1958. Mineola, NY: Dover, 2003.

*Encyclopaedia Britannica*. Ed. Hugh Chisholm. 11th edn. Cambridge: Cambridge University Press, 1910–11.

Engelberts, Matthijs and others (eds). *Notes diverse holo: Catalogues of Beckett's Reading Notes and Other Manuscripts at Trinity College*

*Dublin, with Supporting Essays*. Amsterdam and New York: Rodopi, 2006.

Epictetus. *A Selection from the Discourses of Epictetus with the Encheiridion*. Trans. George Long. Whitefish: Kessinger, 2007.

Federman, Raymond and Lawrence Graver (eds). *Samuel Beckett: The critical Heritage*. London: Routledge, 1979.

Feldman, Matthew. '"Agnostic Quietism" and Samuel Beckett's Early Development.' *Samuel Beckett: History, Memory, Archive*. Ed. Seán Kennedy and Katherine Weiss. Basingstoke: Palgrave Macmillan, c. 2009, 183–200.

—. *Beckett's Books: A Cultural History of Samuel Beckett's 'Inter-War Notes'*. London: Continuum, 2006.

—. 'Returning to Beckett Returning to the Presocratics, or, "All their balls about being and existing".' *Genetic Joyce Studies* 6 (2006). University of Antwerp. http://www.antwerpjamesjoycecenter.com/GJS/ (accessed 13 November 2007).

Fénelon, François. *Télémaque*. Book 1. Trad into Ancient Greek, Léon Faucher. Paris: M 1830.

Ferguson, Everett (ed.). *Encyclopaedia of Early Christianity*. 2 vols. 2nd edn. New York: Garland, 1997.

Fifield, Peter. *Late Modernist Style in Samuel Beckett and Emmanuel Levinas*. London: Palgrave Macmillan, 2013.

Flaubert, Gustave. *Bouvard et Pécuchet*. Pref. Raymond Queneau. Paris: Livre de poche, 1959.

—. *La Tentation de Saint Antoine*. Introd. Émile Faguet. Paris: Georges Cres, 1913.

Frost, Everett and Jane Maxwell. 'Catalogue of "Notes Diverse Holo".' *Notes Diverse Holo: Catalogues of Beckett's Reading Notes and Other Manuscripts at Trinity College Dublin, with Supporting Essays*. Ed. Matthijs Engelberts and others. Amsterdam and New York: Rodopi, 2006.

Gaukroger, Stephen. *The Collapse of Mechanism and the Rise of Sensibility: Science and the Shaping of Modernity, 1680–1760*. Oxford: Oxford University Press, 2010.

—. *Descartes: An Intellectual Biography*. Oxford: Clarendon; New York: Oxford University Press, 1995.

Genetti, Stefano. 'Molto dopo Chamfort, Beckett.' *Quaderni di Lingue e Letterature* 19 (1994): 163–79. Print.

Geulincx, Arnold. *Ethics, with Samuel Beckett's Notes*. Ed. Han van Ruler et al. Trans. Martin Wilson. Leiden, Boston: Brill, 2006.

—. *Opera philosophica*. Recognovit J. P. N. Land. 3 vols. The Hague: Martinus Nijhoff, 1891–3.

Gibson, Andrew. *Beckett and Badiou: The Pathos of Intermittency.* Oxford: Oxford University Press, 2006.

Gifford, Don with Robert J. Seidman. *Ulysses Annotated.* Berkeley: University of California Press, 1974, 2nd edn 1988.

Gilbert, Stuart. *James Joyce's* Ulysses. New York: Vintage, 1952.

Gontarski, S. E. *Creative Involution: Bergson, Beckett, Deleuze.* Edinburgh: Edinburgh University Press, 2015.

—. 'Creative Involution: Bergson, Beckett, Deleuze.' *Deleuze and Beckett.* Ed. S. E. Wilmer and Audronė Žukauskaitė. London: Palgrave Macmillan, 2015.

—. *The Intent of Undoing in Samuel Beckett's Dramatic Texts.* Bloomington: Indiana University Press, 1985.

Gouhier, Henri. *Blaise Pascal: Conversion et apologétique.* Paris: Vrin, 1986.

Gregory of Nyssa. *Gregory of Nyssa [Against Eunomius. On the Life of Moses].* Ed. Anthony Meredith. London, New York: Routledge, 1999.

—. *Gregory of Nyssa's Treatise on the Inscription of the Psalms.* Ed., trans. and intro. Ronald E. Heine. Oxford: Oxford University Press, 1995.

Griffin, Robert. 'Flaubert: The Transformation of Matter.' *French Studies* 44.1 (1988): 18–33.

Grossman, Evelyne. 'Beckett et la passion mélancolique: une lecture de *Comment c'est.' Samuel Beckett Today/Aujourd'hui* 10 (2000): 39–52.

Hamilton, Alice and Kenneth Hamilton. 'The Guffaw of the Abderite: Samuel Beckett's use of Democritus.' *Mosaic* 9/2. Manitoba: University of Manitoba Press, 1976, 1–13.

—. 'The Process of Imaginative Creation in Samuel Beckett's *How It Is.' Mosaic* 10.4 (1977): 1–12.

Harvey, Lawrence. *Samuel Beckett: Poet and Critic.* Princeton: Princeton University Press, 1970.

Heise, Ursula K. 'Erzahlzeit and Postmodern Narrative: Text as Duration in Beckett's *How It Is.' Style* 26.2 (1992): 245–69.

Hesla, David. *The Shape of Chaos: An Interpretation of the Art of Samuel Beckett.* Minneapolis: University of Minnesota Press, 1971.

Hill, Leslie. *Beckett's Fiction: In Different Words.* Cambridge: Cambridge University Press, 1990.

Horace (Quintus Horatius Flaccus). *The Works of Horace. The Latin Text with Conington's Translation.* London: Bell & Sons, 1905.

Houston Jones, David. '"Que Foutait Dieu Avant la Création?": Disabling Sources in Beckett and Augustine.' *Samuel Beckett Today/Aujourd'hui* 9 (2000): 185–98.

—. *Samuel Beckett and Testimony*. New York: Palgrave Macmillan, 2011.

Humboldt, Wilhelm von. *Über das Studium des Altertums. Werke.* 2 vols. Darmstadt: WBG, 1986.

Hutchings, William. '"Shat into Grace" or a Tale of a Turd: Why it is How it is in Samuel Beckett's *How It Is*.' *Papers on Language and Literature* 21.1 (1985): 64–87.

Inge, William Ralph. *Christian Mysticism*. London: Methuen, 1899, 2nd edn. 1912.

Inoue, Yoshiyuki. 'Beketto to Pasukaru—Beketto no Shobu no Owari ni okeru Kyojin Shisetsu/Rogoku/Fune no Naibu' ('Beckett and Pascal: Asylum, Prison, and the Inside of a Ship in Beckett's Fin de partie'). *Hannan Ronshu: Journal of the Humanities and Natural Sciences* 30 (1995): 99–115.

Jacquart, Emmanuel. *Le Theatre de dérision: Beckett, Ionesco, Adamov*. Paris: Gallimard, 1998.

Jaeger, Werner. *Early Christianity and Greek Paideia*. Cambridge: Belknap Press of Harvard University Press, 1961.

—. *Humanism and Theology*. Milwaukee: Marquette University Press, 1943.

—. *Paideia: The Ideals of Greek Culture*. Trans. Gilbert Highet. 3 vols. New York: Oxford University Press, 1943–4.

—. *Two Rediscovered Works of Ancient Christian Literature: Gregory of Nyssa and Macarius*. [On Gregory of Nyssa's treatise 'De instituto christiano' and the 'Great Letter of Macarius', with the text of the letter]. Ed. and trans. Werner Jaeger. Leiden: Brill, 1954.

Jameson, Frederic. *Postmodernism, or, the Cultural Logic of Late Capitalism*. Durham, NC: Duke University Press, 1991.

Jones, Matthew L. *The Good Life in the Scientific Revolution: Descartes, Pascal, Leibniz, and the Cultivation of Virtue*. Chicago: Chicago University Press, 2006.

Joyce, James. *Ulysses: A Critical and Synoptic Edition*. Ed. Hans Walter Gabler with Wolfhard Steppe and Claus Melchior. 3 vols. New York and London: Garland, 1986.

Juliet, Charles. *Conversations with Samuel Beckett and Bram van Velde*. Trans. Janey Tucker. Leiden: Academic Press Leiden, 1995.

Kahn, Charles H. *The Art and Thought of Heraclitus: An Edition of the Fragments with Translation and Commentary*. Cambridge: Cambridge University Press, 1979.

Kandinsky, Wassily. *Concerning the Spiritual in Art, and Painting in Particular*. New York: Wittenborn, Schultz, 1947.

Katz, Daniel. '*How It Is* Again: Regression as Renewal, Unpleasure as Compensation.' *SBT/A* 29 (2017): 9–21.

—. *Saying I No More: Subjectivity and Consciousness in the Prose of Samuel Beckett*. Avant-garde and modernism studies. Evanston: Northwestern University Press, 1999.

à Kempis, Thomas. *De Imitatione Christi: Libri Quatuor*. Paris: Librairie Tross, 1868.

—. *The Earliest English Translation of De Imitatio Christi, Now First Printed from Ms. in the Library of Trinity College, Dublin, with Various Readings from a Ms. in the University Library, Cambridge*. Ed. John K. Ingram (Early English Text Society). London: Kegan Paul, Trench, Trubner and Co, 1893.

Kenner, Hugh. 'The Cartesian Centaur.' *Perspective* (1959): 132–41.

—. *Flaubert, Joyce, and Beckett: The Stoic Comedians*. London: Allen, 1964.

—. *A Reader's Guide to Samuel Beckett*. London: Thames and Hudson, 1973.

—. *Samuel Beckett: A Critical Study*. London: John Calder, 1961.

Knowlson, James. *Damned to Fame: The Life of Samuel Beckett*. London: Bloomsbury, 1996.

Knowlson, James and John Pilling. *Frescos of the Skull: The Later Prose and Drama of Samuel Beckett*. New York: Grove, 1979.

Krance, Charles. 'Alienation and Form in Beckett's *How It Is*.' *Perspectives on Contemporary Literature* 1.2 (1975): 85–103.

Kristeller, P. O. 'Stoic and Neoplatonic Sources of Spinoza's Ethics.' *History of European Ideas* 5 (1984): 1–15.

Laporte, Jean. *La Doctrine de Port-Royal: les vérités de la grâce*. Paris: Presses Universitaires de France, 1923.

Latta, Robert. 'Introduction.' Leibniz. *The Monadology and Other Philosophical Writings*.

Lees, Heath. '*Watt*: Music Tuning and Tonality.' *Journal of Beckett Studies* 9 (1984): 5–24.

Leibniz, Gottfried Wilhelm. *Discourse on Metaphysics and the Monadology*. Trans. George R. Montgomery. Prometheus Books, 1992 (first published by Open Court, 1902).

—. *Leibniz: Philosophical Essays*. Ed. and trans. R. Ariew and D. Garber. Indianapolis: Hackett, 1989.

—. *The Monadology and Other Philosophical Writings*. Trans., intro. and notes Robert Latta. Oxford: Clarendon, 1898.

—. *Philosophical Papers and Letters*. Ed. and trans. Leroy E. Loemker. 2nd edn. Dordrecht, Holland; Boston: D. Reidel Pub. Co., 1976.

—. *Die philosophischen Schriften*. Ed. C. J. Gerhardt. 7 vols. 1875–90. Olms: Hildensheim, 1965.

—. *Sämtliche Schriften und Briefe*. Vols 1–7. Darmstadt and Berlin: Akademie-Verlag, 1927.

Lennon, T. 'Malebranche and Method.' *The Cambridge Companion to Malebranche*. Ed. S. Nadler. Cambridge: Cambridge University Press, 2000, 8–30.

Levy, Eric. 'The Metaphysics of Ignorance: Time and Personal Identity in *How It Is*.' *Renascence* 28 (1975): 27–38.

Lipsius, Justus. *De constantia*. Lugduni: In officina Hug. à Porta, Apud Fratres de Gabiano, 1596.

—. *On Constancy*. Trans. Sir John Stradling. 1605. Ed. John Sellars. Exeter: Bristol Phoenix, 2006.

—. *Senecae Opera*. Antwerp: Plantin-Moretus, 1605.

Lloyd, David. *Irish Culture and Colonial Modernity 1800–2000: The Transformation of Oral Space*. Cambridge: Cambridge University Press, 2011.

Locatelli, Carla. '"my life natural order more or less in the present more or less": Textual Immanence as the Textual Impossible in Beckett's Works.' *Beckett On and On*. Ed. Lois Oppenheim and Marius Buning. Madison: Fairleigh Dickinson University Press, 1996.

Locke, John. *An Essay Concerning Human Understanding*. Ed. John W. Yolton. London: Everyman, 1965.

Logan, Terence P. 'The Characterization of Ulysses in Homer, Virgil and Dante: A Study in Sources and Analogues.' *Annual Report of the Dante Society* 82 (1964): 19–46.

Luce, John V. 'Samuel Beckett's Undergraduate Course at Trinity College Dublin.' *Hermathena: A Trinity College Dublin Review* (2001): 33–45.

Lucian. *Lucian, with an English Translation*. Trans. A. M. Harmon. Loeb Classical Library. 8 vols. Cambridge, MA: Harvard University Press, 1913.

Machacek, Gregory. 'Allusion.' *PMLA* 122.2 (2007): 522–36.

Magessa O'Reilly, Édouard. 'Ni prose ni vers: *Comment c'est* de Samuel Beckett.' *Dalhousie French Studies* 35 (1996): 45–54.

Mahaffy, John. *Descartes*. Edinburgh and London: Blackwood, 1902.

Maier, Franz Michael. 'Two Versions of *Nacht und Träume*: What Franz Schubert Tells Us About a Favourite Song of Beckett.' *Samuel Beckett Today/Aujourd'hui* 18 (2007): 91–100.

Malebranche, Nicolas. *De la recherche de la vérité*. Ed. Geneviève Rodis-Lewis. 3 vols. Paris: J. Vrin, 1946–65.

—. *The Search After Truth and Elucidations of the The Search After Truth*. Trans. and ed. Thomas M. Lennon and Paul J. Olscamp. Cambridge: Cambridge University Press, 1997.

Mazzoni, Francesco. *Saggio di un nuovo commento alla Divina commedia: Inferno – Canti I–III*. Florence: Sansoni, 1967.

Mercer, Christia. *Leibniz's Metaphysics: Its Origins and Development*. Cambridge: Cambridge University Press, 2002.

Milton, John. *Paradise Lost*. Ed., intro and notes Stephen Orgel and Jonathan Goldberg. Oxford: Oxford University Press, 2004.

Mori, Naoya. '"An Animal Inside": Beckett/Leibniz Stone, Animal, Human and the Unborn.' *Beckett and Animals*. Ed. Mary Bryden. Cambridge: Cambridge University Press, 2013.

—. 'Beckett's Windows and the Windowless Self.' *Samuel Beckett Today/Aujourd'hui* 'After Beckett/D'après Beckett' 14 (2004): 357–70.

—. 'Becoming Stone: A Leibnizian Reading of Beckett's Fiction.' *Samuel Beckett Today/Aujourd'hui* 'Borderless Beckett' 19 (2008): 201–10.

—. 'No Body is at Rest: The Legacy of Leibniz in Samuel Beckett's Oeuvres.' *Beckett at 100: Revolving It All*. Ed. Linda Ben-Zvi and Angela Moorjani. Oxford: Oxford University Press, 2008.

—. '"The Sand Utters its Cry": *Petites perceptions* in the Works of Samuel Beckett.' *Studia Leibnitiana Japonica* 2 (2012): 109–27.

Morin, Emilie. *Beckett's Political Imagination*. Cambridge: Cambridge University Press, 2017.

Morot-Sir, Edouard. 'Samuel Beckett and Cartesian Emblems.' *Samuel Beckett: The Art of Rhetoric*. Ed. Edouard Morot-Sir, Howard Harper and Dougald McMillan. Chapel Hill: University of North Carolina Press, 1976.

Murphy, P. J. *Reconstructing Beckett: Language for Being in Samuel Beckett's Fiction*. Toronto: University of Toronto Press, 1990.

Nadler, Steven. *Spinoza's Ethics: An Introduction*. Cambridge: Cambridge University Press, 2006.

Nelson, Robert J. 'Three Orders in *En attendant Godot* and *Fin de partie*: A Pascalian Interpretation of Beckett.' *French Forum* 1.1 (1976): 79–85.

Niderst, A. 'Le Quiétisme de Télémaque.' *Fénelon: Mystique et Politique*. Ed. F.-X. Cuche and J. Le Brun. Paris: H. Champion, 2004.

Nietzsche. *Beyond Good and Evil*. Trans. R. J. Hollingdale. Baltimore: Penguin Classics, 1973.

Nixon, Mark. *Samuel Beckett's German Diaries: 1936–37*. London: Continuum, 2011.

—. '"Scraps of German": Samuel Beckett Reading German Literature.' In Engelberts. 259–82.

O'Hara, J. D. *Samuel Beckett's Hidden Drives: Structural Uses of Depth Psychology*. Gainesville: University of Florida Press, 1997.

Olney, James. 'Memory and the Narrative Imperative: St. Augustine and Samuel Beckett.' *New Literary History* 24.4 (1993): 857–80.

Overbeck, Lois More. 'General Introduction.' *The Letters of Samuel Beckett. Volume III: 1957–1965.* Ed. George Craig, Martha Dow Fehsenfeld, Dan Gunn and Lois More Overbeck. Cambridge: Cambridge University Press, 2014.

Oxenhandler, Neal. 'Seeing and Believing in Dante and Beckett.' *Writing in a Modern Temper: Essays on French Literature and Thought in Honor of Henri Peyre*. Ed. Mary Ann Caws. Stanford French and Italian Studies 33. Saratoga: Anima Libri, 1984.

Pascal, Blaise. *Œuvres complètes*. Bibliothèque de la Pléiade. 2 vols. Paris: Gallimard. 1954.

—. *Pensées de B. Pascal (Édition de 1670): extraits de quelques lettres à Mlle de Roannez*, avec une notice sur Blaise Pascal, un avant-propos et la préface d'Étienne Perier. Paris: Flammarion, 1905.

—. *Pensées*. Ed. Léon Brunschvieg. Paris: Hachette, 1904.

—. *Pensées*. Trans. H. F. Stewart. London: Routledge and Kegan Paul, 1958.

—. *Pensées*. Trans. Martin Turnell. London: Harvill, 1962.

—. *Pensées*. Trans. A. J. Krailsheimer. Harmondsworth: Penguin, 1966.

—. *Pensées*. Trans. W. F. Trotter. Intro. T. S. Eliot. 1958. Mineola, NY: Dover, 2003.

Piette, Adam. 'Torture, Text, Human Rights: Beckett's *Comment c'est/ How It Is* and the Algerian War.' *Around 1945: Literature, Citizenship, Rights*. Ed. Allan Hepburn. Montreal: McGill-Queen's University Press, 2016.

Pilling, John. *Samuel Beckett*. London and Boston: Routledge and Kegan Paul, 1976.

—. *A Samuel Beckett Chronology*. Basingstoke: Macmillan, 2006.

Pinget, Robert. 'Sur Beckett (extraits de journal).' Bibliothèque littéraire Jacques Doucet, Paris, PNG 354/3 (1958).

Plato. *The Apology, Phaedo and Crito*. Trans. Benjamin Jowett. Cambridge, MA: Harvard Classics, 1909–14.

—. *Cratylus, Theaetetus, Sophist, Statesman. Plato in Twelve Volumes*. Vol. 12. Trans. Harold N. Fowler. Cambridge, MA: Harvard University Press; London: William Heinemann, 1921.

—. *Laws. Plato in Twelve Volumes*. Vols 10 and 11. Trans. R. G. Bury. Cambridge, MA: Harvard University Press; London: William Heinemann, 1967 and 1968.

—. *Republic. Plato in Twelve Volumes*. Vols 5 and 6. Trans. Paul Shorey. Cambridge, MA: Harvard University Press; London: William Heinemann, 1969.

—. *Symposium. Gorgias*. Trans. W. R. M. Lamb. Loeb. London: Heinemann, 1925.

Plutarch. *De virtute morali* [On Moral Virtue]. Ed. W. R. Paton, M. Pohlenz and W. Sieveking. Leipzig: Teubner, 1959.

Pope, Alexander. *Selected Poetry*. Ed. Pat Rogers. Oxford: Oxford University Press, 1994.

Praz, Marioto. *The Romantic Agony*. 2nd edn. London: Oxford University Press, 1951.

Proust, Marcel. *A la recherche du temps perdu*. Paris: Gallimard, 1919–27.

—. *In Search of Lost Time*. Trans. C. K. Scott Moncrieff and Terence Kilmartin. 3 vols. London: Random, 1981.

Quintilian. *Institutio Oratoria*. Trans. Donald A. Russell. Ed. Donald A Russell. 3 vols. Cambridge: Harvard University Press, 2001.

Rabaté, Jean-Michel. 'Entre Lettre et Sens: Badiou traducteur de Beckett (*Cap au pire*).' *Roman 20–50* 60 (2015): 133–46.

—. *Think, Pig!: Beckett at the Limit of the Human*. New York: Fordham University Press, 2016.

Ratcliffe, Sophie. 'Savage Loving: Beckett, Browning and *The Tempest*.' *Samuel Beckett Today/Aujourd'hui* 12 (2002): 147–62.

Reid, Thomas. *The Philosophical Works of Thomas Reid*. Ed. William Hamilton. 2 vols. Edinburgh: James Thin, 1896.

Robinson, Michael. 'From *Purgatory* to *Inferno*: Beckett and Dante Revisited.' *Journal of Beckett Studies* 5 (1979): 69–82.

—. *The Long Sonata of the Dead*. New York: Grove, 1969.

Rodis-Lewis, Geneviève. 'Augustinisme et Cartesianisme à Port-Royal.' *Descartes et le cartésianisme hollandais*. Ed. E. J. Dijksterhauis. Paris: Presses Universitaires de France, 1950.

Rosen, Steven. *Samuel Beckett and the Pessimistic Tradition*. New Brunswick, NJ: Rutgers University Press, 1976.

Rosenmeyer, Thomas G. *Senecan Drama and Stoic Cosmology*. Berkeley and London: University of California Press, 1989.

Ross, Katherine Travers. 'In Other Words: Samuel Beckett's Art of Poetry.' PhD thesis. Columbia University, 1972.

Rousseau, Jean-Jacques. *Émile, ou de l'Éducation*. Paris: Garnier Freres, 1964.

Sadie, Stanley and John Tyrrell. *The New Grove Dictionary of Music and Musicians*. 2nd edn. New York: Grove Music, 2000.

Sainte-Beuve, Charles. *Port-Royal*. 1840–59. 5 vols. Paris: Hachette, 1860.

Schleiermacher, Friedrich. *Hermeneutics and Criticism and Other Writings*. Trans. Andrew Bowie. Cambridge: Cambridge University Press, 1998.

Schofield, Malcolm. 'Stoic Ethics.' *The Cambridge Companion to the Stoics*. Ed. Brad Inwood. Cambridge: Cambridge University Press, 2003.

Schopenhauer, Arthur. *Parerga and Paralipomena: Short Philosophical Essays*. Trans. E. F. J. Payne. 2 vols. Oxford: Clarendon, 1974.

—. *The World as Will and Idea*. Trans. R. B. Haldane and J. Kemp. 3 vols. London: Kegan Paul, Trench, Trübner and Co., 1896.

Seneca, Lucius Annaeus. *Letters From a Stoic and Three Dialogues*. Trans. and notes Robin Campbell and C. D. N. Costa. Intro. C. D. N. Costa. Pref. A. C. Grayling. London: Folio Society, 2003.

—. *Moral Epistles*. Trans. Richard M. Gummere. The Loeb Classical Library. 3 vols. Cambridge, MA: Harvard University Press, 1917–25.

Sextus Empiricus. *Adversus mathematicos* [*Against the Professors*], *Pyrrhoneae hypotyposes* [Outlines of Pyrrhonism]. Ed. H. Mutschmann and J. Mau. Leipzig: Teubner, 1912–54.

Shaw, Joanne. *Impotence and Making in Samuel Beckett's Trilogy – Molloy, Malone Dies and the Unnamable – and How It Is*. Amsterdam and New York: Rodopi, 2010.

Sheehan, Paul. *Modernism, Narrative and Humanism*. Cambridge: Cambridge University Press, 2002.

—. 'Scenes of Writing: Beckett and the Technology of Inscription'. *Samuel Beckett Today/Aujourd'hui* 29 (2017): 138–49.

Shelley, Percy Bysshe. *Shelley's Poetry and Prose*. Ed. D. H. Reiman and S. B. Powers. London: Norton. 1977.

Silverstein, Theodore. 'Did Dante Know the Vision of St. Paul?' *Harvard Studies and Notes in Philology and Literature* 19 (1937): 231–47.

Simon, Roger. 'Empowerment as a Pedagogy of Possibility.' *Language Arts* 64.4 (1987): 370–82.

Sinoimeri, Lea. '"Ill-Told Ill-Heard": Aurality and Reading in *Comment c'est/How It Is*.' *SBT/A* 24 (2012): 321–33.

Smith, Frederik N. 'Beckett and the *Port-Royal Logic*.' *Journal of Modern Literature* 5.1 (1976): 99–108.

—. 'Dating the "*Whoroscope* Notebook".' *Journal of Beckett Studies* 3.1 (1993): 65–70.

—. 'Fiction as Composing Process: *How It Is*.' *Samuel Beckett: Humanistic Perspectives*. Ed. Morris Beja, S. E. Gontarski and Pierre Astier. Ohio: Ohio State University Press, 1983.

Smith, Russell. 'Bearing Witness in *How It Is*.' *Samuel Beckett Today/ Aujourd'hui* 19 (2008): 351–60.

Spinoza, Benedictus de. *Ethics*. Ed. and trans. G. H. R. Parkinson. Oxford: Oxford University Press, 2000.

—, [Baruch]. *Ethics, and 'De Intellectus Emendatione.'* London: J. M. Dent & Sons, n.d.

Stephen, Karin. *Psychoanalysis and Medicine: A Study of the Wish to Fall Ill*. Cambridge: Cambridge University Press, 1933.

Stewart, Paul. *Sex and Aesthetics in Samuel Beckett's Works*. New York: Palgrave Macmillan, 2011.

Taylor, C. C. W. *The Atomists: Leucippus and Democritus. Fragments, A Text and Translation with Commentary*. Trans. and commentary C. C. W. Taylor. Toronto: Toronto University Press, 1999.

Terry, Philip. 'Waiting for God to Go: *How It Is* and *Inferno* VII–VIII.' *Samuel Beckett Today/Aujourd'hui. Beckett Versus Beckett* 7 (1998): 349–60.

Thomas, Yves. 'Traduire l'effacement: Notes sur la traduction de *Comment c'est*.' *Samuel Beckett Today/Aujourd'hui* 2 (1993): 139–46.

Tonning, Erik. *Samuel Beckett's Abstract Drama: Works for Stage and Screen, 1962–1985*. Oxford: Peter Lang, 2007.

*Trésor de la langue française informatisé*. Paris: CNRS, 2004.

Trezise, Thomas. *Into the Breach: Samuel Beckett and the Ends of Literature*. Princeton: Princeton University Press, 1990.

Tucker, David. *Samuel Beckett and Arnold Geulincx: Tracing 'A Literary Fantasia.'* London: Continuum, 2012.

Ueberweg, Friedrich. *A History of Philosophy, from Thales to the Present Time. Vol 1: History of Ancient and Medieval Philosophy*. Trans. George S. Morris. London: Hodder and Stoughton, 1872.

Uhlmann, Anthony. *Beckett and Poststructuralism*. Cambridge: Cambridge University Press, 1999.

—. 'Introduction to Beckett's Notes to the *Ethics*.' In Geulincx. *Ethics*. 301–09.

—. *Samuel Beckett and the Philosophical Image*. Cambridge: Cambridge University Press, 2007.

—. 'Withholding Assent: Beckett in the Light of Stoic Ethics.' *Beckett and Ethics*. Ed. Russell Smith. London: Continuum, 2008.

Updike, John. 'How it is [. . .].' *New Yorker*. 19 December 1964: 165–6.

Van Hulle, Dirk. *Manuscript Genetics: Joyce's Know-How, Beckett's Nohow*. Gainesville: University Press of Florida, 2008.

—. 'Samuel Beckett's *Faust* Notes.' In Engelberts. 2008. 283–98.

Van Ruler, Han. 'Introduction.' In Geulincx. *Ethics*. xv–xlii.

Verhulst, Pim. '"Just howls from time to time": Dating Beckett's *Pochade radiophonique*.' *SBT/A* 27 (2015): 143–58.

Warren, J. I. 'Democritus, the Epicureans, Death, and Dying.' *The Classical Quarterly* 52.1 (2002): 193–217.

Weller, Shane. 'The Anethics of Desire: Beckett, Racine, Sade'. *Beckett and Ethics*. Ed. Russell Smith. London: Continuum, 2008.

—. *Beckett, Literature, and the Ethics of Alterity*. London: Palgrave, 2006.

—. *Literature, Philosophy, Nihilism: The Uncanniest of Guests*. London: Palgrave, 2008.

—. *A Taste for the Negative: Beckett and Nihilism*. Oxford: Legenda, 2005.

White, James. *National Gallery of Ireland*. London: Thames and Hudson, 1968.

Willis, Curt G. '*How It Is*: The Epical Call to Voice at the Limits of Experience.' *Samuel Beckett Today/Aujourd'hui* 14 (2004): 579–93.

Wimbush, Andy. 'Biology, the Buddha and the Beasts: The Influence of Ernst Haeckel and Arthur Schopenhauer on Samuel Beckett's *How It Is*.' *Encountering Buddhism in Twentieth-Century British and American Literature*. Ed. Lawrence Normand and Alison Winch. London: Bloomsbury, 2013, 123–38.

Windelband, Wilhelm. *A History of Philosophy*. Trans. James H. Tufts. London: Macmillan, 1910.

Wolosky, Shira. *Language Mysticism: The Negative Way of Language in Eliot, Beckett, and Celan*. Stanford: Stanford University Press, 1995.

Ziarek, Ewa Plonowska. *The Rhetoric of Failure: Deconstruction of Skepticism, Reinvention of Modernism*. New York: The State University of New York Press, 1995.

# Index